Imagining Rhetoric

Pittsburgh Series in Composition,
Literacy, and Culture

David Bartholomae and Jean Ferguson Carr, Editors

Imagining Rhetoric

Composing Women of the Early United States

Janet Carey Eldred and Peter Mortensen

University of Pittsburgh Press

Published by the University of Pittsburgh Press, Pittsburgh, Pa., 15260

Copyright © 2002, University of Pittsburgh Press
Manufactured in the United States of America
Printed on acid-free paper
10 9 8 7 6 5 4 3 2 1

LIBRARY OF CONGRESS CATALOGING-IN-PUBLICATION-DATA
Eldred, Janet Carey.
    Imagining rhetoric : composing women of the early United States /
Janet Carey Eldred and Peter Mortensen.
        p.   cm. — (Pittsburgh series in composition, literacy, and culture)
    Includes bibliographical references and index.
    ISBN 0-8229-4182-1 (alk. paper)
    1. English language—Rhetoric—Study and teaching—United States—History.
    2. English language—Rhetoric—Study and teaching—Sex differences.
    3. American prose literature—Women authors—History and criticism.
    4. Women—Education—United States—History—19th century.
    5. Women teachers—United States.   6. Forten, Charlotte L. Journal.
    7. Rhetoric—Sex differences.   I. Mortensen, Peter, 1961–   II. Title.   III. Series.
    PE1405.U6 E43 2002
    808'.042'071073–dc21
                                                                2002000267

Contents

Preface

↝ *This book grew out of work on literacy narratives* and civic rhetoric that we began together about a decade ago. While doing background reading on Hannah Webster Foster's *Coquette* (1797), we stumbled onto her *Boarding School* (1798), which, we were surprised to find, not only scripts literacy narratives, but also lays out a full morning's lesson on "Writing and Arithmetic" in the course of advancing its story. At about the same time, we read Patricia Bizzell's provocative article in *Rhetoric Review* urging scholars to look for instances of women's rhetorical theory in places other than the academy.[1]

Given this start, our project diverges somewhat from recent scholarship on women's rhetoric in that it focuses primarily not on oral performance, but on composition pedagogy and practice, and not exclusively on theoretical texts and syllabi, but on fiction, practical writing texts, and anthologies for young writers. It is, of course, difficult to untangle women's writing from women's public speaking; the two phenomena share some common ground when we think of them in terms of purpose and audience. Categorical distinctions along these lines abounded in the early nineteenth century. Women's public address to women's groups signified something different than women's public address to mixed-gender or "promiscuous" audiences; scripted and extemporaneous address signified differently, too, as did standing and seated delivery. Likewise, women's writing out of private need meant something quite apart from writing to reach a mass market, and both motivations were understood to differ from writing with a civic aim. Adding further complication, all of these distinctions played out in both nonfiction treatises and in fiction of varying length. Out of necessity, then, our commentary periodically touches on the aesthetics and politics of oral presentation, even when the gist of our argument has to do with written composition.

Cathy Davidson's *Revolution and the Word* readied us to find discussions of education in early national fiction, but we were unprepared to encounter such explicit pedagogical advice—down to the choreography of particular lessons—often offered under the heading of "rhetoric" or "composition" or even "composition and rhetoric" together. Foster's *Boarding School,* which Davidson discusses briefly, put us on the trail of additional works in the "novel textbook" genre. Early on, Donald Ringe, longtime member of the University of Kentucky's English Department, helped point the way. His kindly instruction, along with Nina Baym's invaluable mapping of the nine-teenth-century novel by women[2] and the Schomburg Library of Nineteenth Century Black Women Writers, edited by Henry Louis Gates, Jr., enabled us to identify a substantial array of texts from which we could chose a manage-able number of exemplars.

With exemplars decided, we proceeded by letting the texts themselves suggest theoretical frames for their interpretation. Debates about domestic-ity and "separate spheres" in our primary sources—as well as in twentieth-century scholarship—led us to hypothesize that women must have been in-volved as speakers and writers in discussing pressing issues of the day, which is to say, involved in speaking and writing about the very issues that preoccupied men. Thus, for example, Judith Sargent Murray's *Gleaner* (1798) invited us to contemplate what she made of Republican Mother-hood, early national language politics, the rise of female academies, and problems defining copyright and authorship. Donald Fraser's textbooks for young women and Foster's *Boarding School* drew us into scrutiny of the de-veloping market for women's instructional texts, and the place of fiction, including epistolary narrative, in those textbooks. And all of these works al-lowed us to glimpse how composition came to be situated in the lives of women in the new nation.

After Murray and Foster published their novel texts, thirty years passed before another cluster of schooling fictions emerged, this time not in the af-terglow of revolution but rather in a moment saturated with anxiety about civic rupture. Against the backdrop of impending civil war, Louisa Tuthill's numerous guides, readers, histories, and novels made commonsense philosophy and Romantic aesthetics salient for us. Almira Phelps's work took us straight to the question of who should teach and how they should be prepared, and to the controversy surrounding home versus public schooling. Finally, Charlotte Forten's journals, though composed of discourses made popular in nineteenth-century fiction, allowed us to compare the imagined world of novels and textbooks with an account of lived experience as a public school student and teacher. The journals prompted us to consider the influence of neoclassical rhetorical forms on abolitionist speech and writing and to gauge the way that educators (female and male alike) adopted belletrism to create space for reading and writing exempt from the worries of abolitionism. Crucially, Forten's journals remind us that the schooling fiction genre was established by white, Protestant, middling-class women, a culturally homogenous group that tried to bracket out the factionalism that so marked U.S. culture at mid-century.

We had originally planned to write about another genre emergent later in the nineteenth century: memoirs of early national and antebellum women's schooling. These texts, such as Catharine Beecher's *Educational Reminiscences and Suggestions* (1874) and Julia Ann Tevis's *Sixty Years in a School-room* (1878), are feasts of sweet detail. Moreover, the very fact of their publication indicates that the profound changes in women's schooling that we take up were of deep interest to the women who lived through those changes. But this, as it turns out, is a project for another day.

It's hard to date the origin of this project, but it's easy to recall when its full shape came into view. Working in the old University of Kentucky library nine years ago, we chanced to meet our senior colleague Don Ringe, who asked us what trouble we were making together. We explained as best we could—an article on gender and writing instruction in early America—and Don pointed us to an enormous set of microcards he thought might be useful. Useful? *Early American Imprints* in microform has proven an indispensable (if eye-straining) resource over the years. More good advice followed, and all the while Don was kind enough not to wonder aloud how we planned to get anywhere, say anything, without the trove of primary texts he helped us amass. And so first thanks go to Don for his sincere interest and uncommon generosity.

Other colleagues at Kentucky also made welcome contributions to our thinking, including Dale Bauer, Virginia Blum, Dana Nelson, John Shawcross, Larry Swingle, and Steven Weisenburger. We thank them all for their frank advice and their friendship.

In the mid-1990s an impressive group of research assistants lent a hand: Jacqueline Brown, Valerie Johnson, Jenny Pitcock, Ron Pitcock, and Jennifer Walls. We're grateful for their support, and to Richard C. Edwards, then dean of the University of Kentucky College of Arts and Sciences, for research assistance funding. (Richard Greissman, the college's long-serving assistant dean, also deserves special recognition here.)

We incurred numerous intellectual debts as pieces of this book appeared as conference presentations and in journal articles. Among those offering invaluable critique and encouragement were Patricia Bizzell, Lillian Bridwell-Bowles, the late Robert Connors, Theresa Enos, Cinthia Gannett, Anne Ruggles Gere, Cheryl Glenn, Patricia Harkin, Deborah Hawhee, Gail Hawisher, Catherine Hobbs, Winifred Horner, Gesa Kirsch, Nan Johnson, Janice Lauer, Andrea Lunsford, Jacqueline Jones Royster, Mariolina Salvatori, Patricia Sullivan, Louise Smith, Kakie Urch, and Rex Veeder. The sense of audience these scholars instilled in us has been sustaining and, when we most needed it, reinvigorating.

Many thanks to David Bartholomae and Jean Ferguson Carr, whose important work on the Pittsburgh Series in Composition, Literacy, and Culture has made a home for this book. They took care to see that the manuscript was reviewed by two anonymous readers, whose fine commentaries significantly strengthened our argument.

Most of the women we write about prized family life above all else. In public, they would have chastised us for completing this book while the mouths to feed under our two dual-career roofs multiplied. In private, they would have shared tips on how to do it as well as they did. We've managed pretty well even without their wise counsel, thanks to the love, understanding, and advice of Richard, Lexy, and Sasha, and Karen, Sarah, and Ellen.

～

A portion of the introductory chapter first appeared as "'Persuasion Dwelt on Her Tongue': Female Civic Rhetoric in Early America," *College English* 60 (1998): 173–88. Copyright © 1998 by the National Council of Teachers of English. Reprinted with permission.

Chapter 1 derives from "Monitoring Columbia's Daughters: Writing as Gendered Conduct," *Rhetoric Society Quarterly* 23, nos. 3–4 (1993): 46–69; and "Gender and Writing Instruction in Early America: Lessons from Didactic Fiction," *Rhetoric Review* 12 (1993): 25–53. Thanks to the editors and publishers of each journal for permission to draw from these articles.

Imagining Rhetoric

1 Introduction

The Tradition of Female Civic Rhetoric

*And, first, by way of exordium, I take leave to congratulate my fair country-
women, on the happy revolution which the few past years has made in their
favour; that in these infant republics, where, within my remembrance, the use
of the needle was the principal attainment which was thought necessary for a
woman, the lovely proficient is now permitted to appropriate a moiety of her
time to studies of a more elevated and elevating nature.*

Judith Sargent Murray, The Gleaner (1798)

⋐ *In the years surrounding* the American Revolution, civic rhetoric
grew rich with opposing images of tyranny and liberation, anarchy
and restraint, lawlessness and justice. This richness, history shows, was
not exclusive to the rhetoric of men. Long before the feminist Declaration of Sentiments and Resolutions was drafted at Seneca Falls in 1848,
civic rhetoric was available to the women of the new republic. True,
full civic membership—legal citizenship—was denied women until
passage of the Nineteenth Amendment in 1920. Yet a form of what we
call liberatory civic rhetoric, written by women and directed toward
their concerns in life, appeared not only in the close privacy of diaries,
letters, and journals, but widely in the public as well, in popular magazines, newspapers, and books. Our aim in this book is to examine the
provenance, authority, and evolution of liberatory civic rhetoric in the
new nation, especially as it shaped women's rhetorical education and
composing practices.

First, some definitions are in order. By civic rhetoric we mean the
kind of discourse common to speeches, printed addresses, essays,
pamphlets, and tracts after the Revolution, a discourse that was preoccupied with matters of government and governance. We are specifically interested in the liberatory strains of civic rhetoric that issued

from a predominately oral, neoclassical tradition. Gregory Clark and S. Michael Halloran observe that rhetoric in American colleges at the turn of the nineteenth century was "strongly neoclassical, which is to say that it was a rhetoric of general citizenship closely tied to the public discourse practiced in pulpit, bar, and senate of the larger society." Rhetors were ethical persons "whose civic duty it was to articulate an established wisdom and focus it on particular issues." Civic rhetoric's announced purpose was to effect political change by revealing public consensus and by enabling appeals to a common sense of what was right. Its goal was not to sway individual opinion, but rather to awaken the collective conscience of a new republic.[1] It was a rhetoric that disdained the popular and sensational rhetor, even as it promoted revolutionary social change. It was a rhetoric that privileged classical form and cadence over the vernacular, even as it argued for an American "federal" language. It was a rhetoric composed for both the platform and the page.

Given the cultural work charged to civic rhetoric, it is our desire to understand how women, through writing instruction, learned to negotiate it.[2] Our inquiry spans the early decades of the republic, beginning with scenes of instruction recorded in the last years of the eighteenth century, a moment when liberatory civic rhetoric was clearly in ascendance. Historians characterize this time as one of legal reform achieved in part by appeals to a classical model of republican government, a model in which consensual, civic rhetoric figures prominently. But as in antiquity, the ruling consensus in the new U.S. government was established exclusively by male voices. The power of these voices is measurable in the time it has taken for women to gain admission to the institutions where the ruling consensus is formed. For example, while Priscilla Mason in 1793 felt "assured that there is nothing in our laws or constitution to prohibit the licensure of female attorneys," it was many years before the federal and state courts agreed with her. In 1869 two women passed bar exams in their home states but were prevented by the courts from practicing. It was 1892 before the U.S. Supreme Court retroactively granted one of the women, Myra Bradwell, a license to practice law. Other examples abound. The first female congressional representative, Jeanette Rankin, took her seat in the U.S. House in 1916. The first woman to sit as a federal judge was Florence E. Allen in 1934. And, of course, a woman has yet to be elected president or vice president of the United States.[3] Yet despite having long been excluded from certain civic institutions, women have never been blind to how discourse sustains and legitimates them. As we will see, women at the turn of the nineteenth century understood quite well the function of men's discourse on civic matters and believed that public expression, conducted according to neoclassical rhetorical principles, held promise for them, too. Not least did they relish, as did men, the prospect of applying a reasoned language of liberation to the task of imagining and enacting fair government.

But what happened thereafter? At the risk of painting in broad strokes, what rhetorical histories tell us is this: as the U.S. grew in the nineteenth century, the cultural influence of neoclassical civic rhetoric waned. Early in the century, neoclassical civic culture had extended outside the academy into a number of consequential realms—the church, for example. But as the century unfolded, transformations in academic, literary, and national culture began to alter and curtail the civic function of public oratory. In the academy, the rhetorical curriculum shifted emphasis from classical to belletristic forms. At Harvard, John Quincy Adams was the last Boylston Chair of Rhetoric whose lectures derived from classical sources. Clark and Halloran observe that "Adams's *Lectures on Rhetoric and Oratory* (1810) were . . . virtually pure Cicero." At the same time at Yale, Timothy Dwight's courses, "influenced by Hugh Blair's *Lectures on Rhetoric and Belles Lettres* (1783)," were "less purely classical than Adams's work," and yet Dwight "still directed his students insistently to use the art of deliberative, forensic, and epideictic discourse to address civic matters." But by "mid-century, the concept of oratorical public discourse and its communitarian ethos as taught and practiced by figures such as [John] Witherspoon [at the College of New Jersey at Princeton], Adams, and Dwight had begun to erode in the United States, both outside the academy and within."[4] Yet, like Dorothy Broaddus, we are reluctant to characterize the move from oratory to belletrism as simply a "transformation." Doing so implies "an evolutionary development that is continuous and concrete," a narrative of linear progress that papers over "jumps, false starts, discontinuities, or resistance" evident in the historical record.[5] While we do argue that women's schooling in composition was transformed in the early nineteenth century—the passage from oratory's influence to belletristic practice is undeniable—we are careful to underscore discontinuities along the way, with special attention to women who resisted both schools of rhetoric and to those who embraced them simultaneously.

In making our case, we naturally draw extensively from the history of rhetoric, but our interest in writing compels us to consult literary and political history as well. In U.S. literary history, the move from oratory to belletrism registers in the diminishing authority of the early national lawyer-writers in the face of an ascendant American Romanticism. Robert Ferguson details the literary prominence of lawyers from 1790–1840: "Lawyers wrote many of the country's first important novels, plays, and poems. No other vocational group, not even the ministry, matched their contribution."[6] But this influence grew less apparent—though not invisible—as elements of what we now call the American Renaissance fell into place.[7] In the political sphere, the advent of Romantic individualism assumed a somewhat different form. Roughly speaking, Jeffersonian republicanism yielded to Jacksonian democracy, seen by some as true popular governance, by others as mob tyranny.[8] Thus, from a variety of perspectives, it is apparent that neoclassical rhetorical practice was under tremendous pressure to change. Granted, neoclassical practice remained relatively stable within the confines of formal legislative and legal activity. Yet as Laura Hanft Korobkin details, even legal discourse in the nineteenth century came to feature belletristic inflections, this by way of sentimental fiction, produced largely by women.[9] But influence is one thing, access another. And access to elective office and the practice of law, as we have noted, is what American women in the eighteenth and nineteenth centuries lacked. Denied access, they could not employ rhetoric to make laws or enforce them; there was no way they could govern in the public sphere. In political theory—and in the world often theorized in women's domestic fiction—women did have access to the public sphere through representation in government. Hypothetically, those at the fringes of the polis could sway legislators with public arguments rooted in civic virtue and aimed at doing collective good. Alternatively, they could seek private encounters with politically powerful men and make their pleas out of the public's view. In political fact, however, the women we recognize as early feminists—for example, women who argued strenuously and publicly for the vote—found no conduit of power linking them with their supposed legislative representatives. This is not surprising, really, given that male legislators were not directly elected by women, were not positioned to hear their concerns, and were in no way obligated to speak out on their behalf. Recognizing this predicament, some women despaired that their rhetoric—in speech or in print—could ever effect change in the culture at large.

Many women, however, initially held out hope that their influence could be felt in the new republic, if only indirectly. Before the constitution was drafted, Abigail Adams learned firsthand the limitations of a politics based solely on private influence. In her famous "Remember the Ladies" letter addressed to her husband in 1776, Adams drew on liberatory rhetoric to lobby her husband in favor of women's right to some independence. She pitted the inherent good of a nation characterized by "independancy" and a "Code of Laws" against the evils of a government characterized by "tyrants" and "unlimited power." While the first kind of government would permit full "Representation," the second would leave many of its citizens with "no voice." She urged her husband to champion truly representative government but acknowledged that, finally, the male "Sex are Naturally Tyrannical." John Adams could only "but laugh" at his wife's proposal. If women were deemed independent, he wondered, who next would make such a claim? Children? Apprentices? Quite a slippery slope! Then, inverting the charge of tyranny, Adams invoked the commonplace that in fact it was men who suffered injustice at the hands of women. Abigail and John Adams's correspondence stands as a poignant reminder of the most serious limitation on female liberatory civic rhetoric: it had always to pass through women's patriarchal "representatives," representatives who were not temperamentally inclined to be cooperative.[10] Given this constraint, it is not surprising that Abigail Adams and others, such as Mercy Otis Warren, became disenchanted, moving, as Joan Hoff puts it, from "prewar optimism to postwar pessimism, not only about female education but also about women's general ability to influence the course of history."[11]

The disaffection of Warren and Adams notwithstanding, other women continued for the duration of the nineteenth century—and beyond—to exercise and promote neoclassical civic rhetoric.[12] Some did so in the context of their struggle for suffrage and some in their struggle against it. The latter case is particularly interesting to us. For a select group of antisuffrage women, it may have been that the achievement of a classical education was its own reward. Another group, opposed to the radical suffragists while favoring gradual, progressive social change, might have been attracted to neoclassical rhetoric's claims that it could reveal clear moral truth, enlighten thought with reason, and enable change by consensus rather than tyranny.

Presumably these women did not need the franchise to feel themselves citizens. So says Nina Baym, who posits that even women who were against suffrage for themselves were not necessarily opposed to formation of a political subjectivity for women: "We have the antisuffrage women's own word that they thought themselves citizens, that they did not think their citizen status depended on the franchise."[13] Still other women, those who reasoned that their disenfranchised status rendered them politically unequal to men, might have found through liberatory civic rhetoric a way to speak and write about men's arrogation and mishandling of power and a way to argue for corrective measures. Arguing for correction, women were not limited to the question of suffrage: temperance, abolition, and education (especially advanced education for women) were also fair subjects. Emerging from public debate on these issues were some of the nineteenth-century's best-known orators—Elizabeth Cady Stanton, Susan B. Anthony, Lucretia Mott, and Sarah and Angelina Grimké—as well as some of the most widely noticed writers favoring domestic economy—Sarah Josepha Hale, Lydia Maria Child, and Catharine Beecher.

Even before the heyday of such speakers and writers, early-nineteenth-century Americans witnessed the emergence of a considerable market for domestic fiction written by women, those "scribbling women" maligned in their day but more recently celebrated for having carved out a rhetorical and aesthetic space for themselves apart from men. It must be said that these women only indirectly engaged liberatory civic rhetoric, while more directly employing other available discourses to compose their authorial identities: the pious discourse of tracts, and the sensational, sentimental, and didactic languages of fiction. Through sheer volume and popularity, domestic fiction, as Cathy Davidson suggests, effected a quiet cultural revolution of its own. As true as this is, we will not be arguing that domestic fiction filled a vacuum left by the retreat of neoclassical civic rhetoric. It is more accurate to say that discursive elements of domestic fiction gradually found their way into civic rhetoric, and vice versa, across the range of women's speeches, essays, and novels that circulated before the Civil War. In this manner, the values of domesticity and individuality had the potential to amalgamate with the notion that a public self could inform (and be informed by) national consciousness.[14]

Even when this potential was not realized, civic rhetors and domestic novelists often drew on the same cultural resources: controversies surrounding women's education, women's place in society, and women's protection under the law. Furthermore, although not the lawyer-writers storied in literary history, women rhetors and novelists frequently engaged the very issues of law, justice, and constitutional governance that preoccupied their male contemporaries in the early national period. Yet studies of early national literature typically mention women only in passing, alluding occasionally to, say, Mercy Otis Warren's dramatic and historical writing. The same holds true for work on political language and the law. Conversely, studies that take domesticity and romance as their subjects routinely focus on women alone. Ironically, the ideology of separate spheres may be even more pronounced in contemporary scholarship than it was in the new nation. In the chapters to come, we strive to get beyond the scholarship of separate spheres to explore women speakers' and writers' affinities with male lawyer-writers and language politicians.[15]

We narrow our exploration somewhat by concentrating on the work of women writers who declared an interest in women's education, who imagined neoclassical civic rhetoric to be an indispensable part of it, and who were aware of neoclassicism's decline in the popular and academic spheres around them. Such writers took a variety of approaches to refashioning neoclassical rhetoric so that it might serve their own ends. Hannah Webster Foster, for example, imagined a place, a boarding school, within which civic rhetoric would discipline the work of young women scholars living and learning together. Letter writing for these scholars became an intellectual activity that framed argumentation as the pursuit of truth, the pursuit of truth as the agency of consensus, and consensus as the foundation of community. Contrast this rational procedure with female oratory, which was viewed by many in Foster's day as radical, unconstrained, and therefore threatening to civil order (that is, if it was not considered simply absurd).[16] So it was that in sheltered spaces such as Foster's fictional boarding school, a decidedly female civic rhetoric tempered radical passion with reason and augmented rhetorical ethics with religious morals. But for some critics, all manner of female expression was inherently radical. Thus Foster advanced another way to safeguard female neoclassical civic culture: when necessary, completely seal it off from whatever audience might object to its seeming radicalism.

We know that the rhetorical education Foster imagined in *The Boarding*

School was pedagogically feasible because something resembling it is found in documentation from Science Hill, a female academy established in the early 1800s near Louisville, Kentucky. Beginning in 1825, Julia Ann Tevis offered young women a boarding school experience that featured a curriculum not unlike that elaborated in Foster's novel. But by 1850, whatever had been considered radical in that curriculum had lost its provocative edge. Letter writing, which the young women of Science Hill continued to practice after graduation, became a "safe," "moderate," and distinctly unintellectual exercise within the confines of individual domestic friendships. Earlier at Science Hill, the carnival specter of the female orator practicing a secular neoclassical civic rhetoric was limited to classroom lessons and commencement exercises. True, these exercises, open to the public, challenged received notions of gender, but only for one day, after which Tevis's orators resumed their roles as daughters and sisters, preparatory to their roles as wives and mothers. And even on that day they had to share the stage with classmates who delivered more appropriately "female" performances: musical pieces and recitations of sentimental and religious poetry.[17]

What Foster imagined and Tevis enacted hardly exhausted the possibilities for realizing female civic rhetoric in the new nation. Judith Sargent Murray opted to mask her gender by adopting the persona of a rational male essayist. As "The Gleaner," she published her polemical writings, occasional essays, and domestic fiction in *The Massachusetts Magazine*. Seeking to cloak revolutionary rhetoric within the garb of moderation, Murray joined Foster in creating conduct fictions that modeled education for women based on neoclassical practice, but in doing so, they subordinated the idea of female civic participation to the rules of proper feminine conduct. Consequently, their vision of neoclassical civic rhetoric, while in many ways novel, was sufficiently infused with the spirit of Christian piety and domestic duty to pose little threat to the established order of family, church, and state.

Yet another strategy for preserving neoclassical civic rhetoric entailed its reminiscence and celebration in biographies, diaries, and autobiographies—unlikely genres in that they center on individual consciousness and experience. A fourth form of reminiscence, history writing, perhaps also allowed women to envision themselves as members of the polis and to contemplate ideal rhetorical practice therein.[18] Indeed, cataloging historical examples of women achieving civic prominence was a common trope in female civic rhetoric. In addition to Murray, Margaret Fuller invoked the trope, and Catharine Beecher roundly criticized Angelina Grimké's use of it. For her part, Murray turned to history to remind readers of an exemplary orator, Hortensia, whose educated words were capable of softening the most tyrannical of rulers: "Persuasion dwelt on her tongue: Her arguments resulting from rectitude, were pointed by reason: And it will be conceived that her rhetorical powers must have been of the first rate, when it is remembered that *the countenances of tyrants betrayed sudden and evident tokens of that remorse which was then first enkindled in their bosoms;* the hue of guilt pervaded their cheeks, and they hastily repealed the injurious decree."[19] Murray most likely gleaned her knowledge of Hortensia from Quintilian. Properly instructed by her father, Hortensia for Quintilian served as an example of the benefits a republic could reap by schooling its young at home, a classical theme that remained just as seductive in the early U.S. as related narratives about the overthrow of unjust rule and the consecration of a new nation blessed in natural abundance.

Educating Citizens of the New Republic

Parental education in the new nation assumed urgency in the absence of public schools that could systematically prepare citizens—and their teachers—to meet the intellectual demands of republican government. Murray worried that the lack of good preceptors in many communities would force families to depend on their own resources. Sometimes this arrangement would suffice: she praised men and women who were genuinely self-educated. But for those who failed to educate themselves, for whatever reason, Murray had little sympathy. The scarcity of schools and preceptors, not to mention the rarity of successful self-education, did not for Murray "diminish the odium so justly affixed upon him, who, inattentive to the means of information with which he has furnished, produces himself upon the world an unlettered blank, waiting the casual impressions of every interested compositor, whom chance may direct to fill up the vacant pages" (499). Murray was not atypical of her generation in holding to this sentiment. In the years just following independence, Americans frequently acknowledged that the task of nation building was largely one of rhetorical education. They were troubled by the inadequacy of educational institutions, envisioning the U.S. as a "nation at risk" if it could not rapidly build a learned, civic-minded citizenry.[20] Thus Murray was unapologetic in her condemnation of those illiterate, "unlettered blank" slates who endangered democracy because the political whims of others could be so easily inscribed upon them.

In Murray's view an enduring republic would have to rely heavily on the obligation each citizen had to be skilled in rhetorical invention and arrangement. She enjoined "persons of all descriptions to seize with avidity every opportunity of accumulating knowledge. He who has neglected to store his mind with ideas, to invigorate the intellectual powers, and to habituate himself to reasoning, comparing, investigating, and concluding, hath not only forgotten to constitute a fund on which he might occasionally draw, but hath also defrauded society of that assistance which mankind had a right to reckon on from his abilities; and thus committed a crime against his species, for which, alas! it is beyond his power to atone" (499). But it was not only fear of the poorly educated that inspired anxiety about a government founded on the power of written laws, it was the nature of republican rhetoric itself: civic rhetoric and written laws could, theoretically, be used to support any cause, virtuous or not. This much was clear to Murray from her study of the classical republics. For her, the chief enemies of a republic were those who could use eloquent arguments to sway unreasoning masses: "Miserable sophist!" she declared, "from whence do you derive this right of rending from innocence the sceptre of reason, and of placing it again in the hands of vice . . . to afflict virtue, to degrade humanity?" (255–56).[21]

To curtail such corruption, governments based on written laws had to depend on both the integrity of language and the character of those who used it. As literary historians have elaborated, the early republic was a historical period in which hotly debated issues of language reform and standardization were tied to equally contentious political controversies. Most of these histories do not mention women's entries into the debates. But as Murray's *Gleaner* reminds us, women of this period included themselves in theorizing the politics of language. Murray, for example, argued for national standards: "National attachment should . . . dictate the studious cultivation of a national language; and it may be worthy the exertions of an enlightened legislature, to erect a standard, to raise, to dignify, to perfect, and to polish a common tongue" (296). Although Murray's use of "polish" could suggest linguistic ornamentation, in fact, we see that overall she was less concerned with eloquence, that favorite tool of the sophists, and more concerned with the Federalist politics of uniformity in linguistic usage. Elaborating upon her advocacy of national standards, she appealed to an authority in antiquity, the Roman republic, which enforced such conformity. Ultimately, though, Murray did not want to reproduce the Roman republic *in toto*—it had failed, after all. Rather, she wanted to build a strong and coherent American nation, one buttressed by a language and literature of unique distinction. An American literature would depend on a society with a unified identity, something she believed language diversity would frustrate. Finally, although Murray drew on classical sources, she advocated a plain vernacular style in legislation and the law. Yet this vernacular, too, would have to rely on standardization for success. She offered in illustration the jury system. How could juries possibly reach just verdicts if they impaneled members who could not understand lawyers' "harangues"? "Justice," she wrote, "frequently hangs upon their forcible, intelligent, and well constructed periods" (296). Justice could not, in Murray's estimation, be translated into the multiple tongues of multiple jurors. Justice had to be written and spoken in a singular way, and the people of the new nation simply had to be trained to this standard.[22]

Of course, it is easy to dismiss Murray's ideas as derivative. She can be written, as happens repeatedly with Abigail Adams, as a footnote to John Adams—the president to whom, incidentally, *The Gleaner* is dedicated. But Murray brought a perspective to early national language debates that no man could. Her interest in political language fused with her concerns about women's roles in the new republic, domestic and otherwise. This fusion is borne out in Murray's condemnation of sophistry, which, as we have seen, begins with her denouncing the sophist's casual regard for reason and truth. As the denunciation continues later in *The Gleaner*, Murray employs unmistakably gendered figures to expose the wages of sophistry: a seduced and fallen Eve and, more generally, a seduced and fallen women who brings illegitimacy into the world. Murray is preoccupied with fighting the dangerous words that make for tragedy in the political and individual seduction stories she tells. For her, the only defense against seductive words are virtuous ones well arranged; thus women need advanced rhetorical training to protect their virtue and to protect the legitimacy of the next generation of Americans.[23]

Murray's concentration on seduction resonates with anxieties expressed by many of her contemporaries.[24] In fact, the subject was so manifest, it was seen as a fit topic for school lessons. For example, seduction gets critical treatment in "An Oration upon Female Education, pronounced by a Member of one of the public Schools in Boston, September, 1791," which circulated widely as a chapter in Caleb Bingham's popular rhetorical reader, *The American Preceptor* (1794). The oration presents a commonly voiced logic: if young men receive schooling in rhetorical skills and young women only in ornamental arts, the stage would be set for seduction, with the final act often revealing illegitimacy, the very antithesis of a government based on written law. As outlined in the Bingham compilation:

> 12. If parents wish to guard their children against an undue attention to external ornaments, against extravagance in dress and gaudy equipage, what better expedient will they find, than to replenish their minds with such a fund of useful knowledge, as shall enable them suitably to contemn all worthless things; to discern where real merit lies, and what constitutes the dignity of their sex?
>
> 13. Then they will not easily be captivated with glittering trappings, trifling toys, and tasteless amusements; but extend their views to more noble objects. What greater barrier against vice of every kind than useful knowledge?
>
> 14. Is it not a melancholy truth, that *man* too often prostitutes his boasted faculties to the destruction of female happiness? How necessary then, to fortify their minds against the attacks of such vile seducers?[25]

These paragraphs arrive at the same conclusion that Murray works out in *The Gleaner*—that seduction and poor education are linked—but do so for a vast audience Murray never reached. In language less eloquent but more accessible than Murray's, the text shades in an oft-drawn picture of the dangers posed by an illogical, unreasoning female population. To secure the legitimacy of the republic, women's minds must be steeled against rhetorical subterfuge. Then, having defended themselves against illicit rhetoric, they would be able to teach their legitimate children, male and female, the importance of civic virtue. They could inculcate these children with the literate values of science and law, a wholly reasonable foundation for succeeding generations.

Murray and other patriots agreed with the oration's author that parents must seize the revolutionary opportunity to school their own children or to have them schooled. As Murray put it, "parents and preceptors" should take responsibility for "the character of the rising generation" because that generation, and not its parents, would ultimately choose "peace or anarchy" for the nation (287). The problem was, as we have said, qualified preceptors were few in number and demand for teaching was great. Men were busy building the institutions of the new nation, and so women, in part because they were already charged with the care of young children, were the logical choice to become teachers. As Murray wrote: "Much, in this momentous department, depends on *female administration;* and the mother, or the woman to whom she may delegate her office, will imprint on the opening mind, characters, ideas and conclusions, which time, in all its variety of vicissitudes, will never be able to erase. Surely then, it is politic to bestow upon the education of girls the most exact attention" (287). Seventy years later, Catharine Beecher would repeat the same argument, lamenting the million or so illiterates whom she perceived as threats to democracy and worrying that their great number would continue to grow unchecked.[26] But Americans just after the Revolution were optimistic. Most believed that women could offer valuable early training for at least those boys who, when grown, would enjoy the benefits and shoulder the responsibilities of citizenship. The spread of this belief led to a tremendous change in American education, a change felt most profoundly by the women who would be readied, then called upon, to instill in America's youth an intelligent respect for written laws and civic virtue.

Educating Women in Early America

The American Revolution dramatically altered women's schooling and the idea of women's place in society, but whether these changes were materially liberating remains subject to debate. Mary Beth Norton, an early feminist historian, has argued that as the Revolutionary War drew men away to combat, civic roles and duties were created for women, and some of these roles carried over into the postrevolutionary period.[27] Those historians who locate a "golden age" for so-called Republican Mothers immediately after the American Revolution offer as evidence such essays as Benjamin Rush's classic "Thoughts upon Female Education." Rush argued that because most

men in the new nation worked, women of middling status had to be educated well enough to act as "the stewards, and guardians of their husbands'
property."[28] However ordinary such an idea may seem now, it was quite unusual when it first circulated. And here is why: under common law, married
women had no legal standing. Rush's proposal had the effect of inventing
for women a quasi-legal status previously unknown.

Yet elevating women's legal status could not be accomplished so simply.
For at least one historian, it remains that the language of the law firmly limited women's claims to citizenship in the new republic. According to Linda
Kerber, "Between 1775 and 1777 statutory language moved from the term
subject to *inhabitant, member,* and, finally, *citizen.* . . . This mode of thinking, this way of relating men to the state, had no room in it for women except as something to be avoided."[29] While single women or widows could be
appointed guardians or stewards of estates, married women (unless their
state of residence provided a refuge in equity courts) found themselves
nonentities, *femmes coverts,* before the law. Entering into marriage, a woman
necessarily relinquished any claim to ownership and management of property.[30] Legal historian Joan Hoff acknowledges that while ideas such as
Rush's were promoted, they were not implemented: "there is no conclusive
evidence that the War of Independence made married women bona-fide citizens of the new Republic or that the legal status of married or single
women improved significantly in other less-tangible areas of civil life in the
first three or four decades following the end of the War of Independence."[31]
In this view, women's access to nontraditional careers was hindered and
their legal status diminished in the wake of the Revolution.

Our own inquiry aligns fully with neither the advance nor the decline
thesis. Within the construct of Republican Motherhood, we see evidence
that the Revolutionary War did indeed create a distinct role for women in
the polity and advanced for a moment their place in the republic. But finally
this new role played out in a liminal way in the public realm. As Kerber observes, "If women were no longer prepolitical, they certainly were not fully
political."[32] Given this ambiguity, the best that can be said is that conditions
were right for a boom in liberatory rhetoric generated by and for women—
surely a major historical development in itself. What that rhetoric wrought
was less, or at least different, than what it promised.

With this in mind, let us return to Rush and read his words not as descriptive of what came to pass in women's schooling but rather as indicative of the effort needed to clear rhetorical space for arguing about reform. In addition to advocating women's stewardship of property, Rush advanced other ideas that were probably more readily accepted and certainly easier to implement. He believed women must be capable of supervising their servants, instructing their children, and instilling in "their sons . . . the principles of liberty and government." In addition, women should demonstrate competence in the ornamental arts of stitching, music, and dancing, as well as a knowledge of "geography . . . history, biography," and even some "astronomy, natural philosophy and chemistry" (although the latter only so that it could be applied to "domestic, and culinary purposes"). Others soon followed Rush in making proposals large and small, novel and derivative. Among them, Emma Willard, founder of the Troy Female Seminary, is remembered for having sat—to have stood would have been to give offense— before the New York State Legislature to appeal for state support for women's schools. Her own school produced graduates who themselves did the often public work of proposing and establishing seminaries for women. Willard believed, as did many of her peers, that the nation could remain strong only if women's "powers of reasoning" were developed and strengthened by schooling in institutions that had to be first imagined, then invented.[33]

Women who attended female seminaries certainly felt as if a new age had opened before them. Take Priscilla Mason, for instance. Oratory is both a "natural talent" and "part of the rights of woman" for her. It is, she grants, a right to be used cautiously, "rest[ing] like the sword in the scabbard, to be used only when occasion requires." The choice and timing of its use should be left to women alone, a stance essential to preserving "the further right of being heard on more proper occasions—of addressing the reason as well as the fears of the other sex." Mason is confident that her audience would someday accept women's entitlement to oratory: "Happily, a more liberal way of thinking begins to prevail. The sources of knowledge are gradually opening to our sex." Church and society, she continues, had already opened doors for women rhetors, doors previously shut by "*Man;* despotic man."[34]

This is all fine and good, but Mason also predicts the welcoming of women into the legal arena. She did not and probably could not foresee that doors opened by the Revolution would be shut once again. In retrospect, though, we can track the arrival of what for Mason must have been a great disappointment. When we look to the texts the new nation composed to educate its young republican women, we find that, despite the potential advanced in liberatory rhetoric, available practice was much more restricted. As textbooks became more distinctly "American," they moved thematically from independence-building lessons that "assisted" young pilgrims to lessons that assisted only young male patriots while they "monitored" young girls of middling status. As textbooks became more conspicuously national, then, they also became more conspicuously gendered, often focusing less on women's rhetorical abilities and reasoning and more on their external conduct and piety. Still, whatever their content, such textbooks improved the chances that women could acquire rhetorical savvy that surpassed what they could accomplish with only basic skills in reading and writing. This change was real and significant, if not revolutionary. But if not revolutionary, could it be liberatory? That is a question we answer in various ways as we work through a range of texts and authors later in this book.

Literacy in the New Republic

To understand the full impact of Republican Motherhood on rhetorical training, and on literacy more generally, it is useful to compare this new literacy with what had been available to generations of men and women before the Revolution. The comparison is necessarily inexact: there was no absolute definition of literacy in colonial America, nor was one fixed in the early U.S. Gender, status, race, religion, and politics all contributed both to how literacy was understood and to what extent it could be attained.[35] Our aim, then, is not to detail language instruction during more than a century of colonial and republican life, but rather to clarify general trends in language education and to comment on the changes brought by independence. These changes, we think, are best revealed by sketching how the instrumental functions of literacy evolved in Britain's North American colonies and then in the fledgling United States of America.

In the mid- to late seventeenth century, a number of colonies enacted statutes that made reading instruction for children compulsory. According to E. Jennifer Monaghan, "From the earliest days of settlement . . . and throughout the colonial period, the colonists expected that all children ought to be able to read, no matter how low their station or how poor their circumstances." The religious motivation for these statutes is clear, she argues: clergy wanted parishioners to be able to read the Bible and be disciplined by that reading. Indeed, texts used in reading instruction at the time reflect the belief that literacy was an essential part of Christian worship. *The New England Primer* (1690), to take a popular example, featured both grammar instruction and a complete catechism and was reprinted often into the eighteenth century. But religion was not the only force determining the uses of literacy in colonial America. Commercial relations with England and among the colonies required various parties to possess an array of literate skills. Texts such as George Fisher's *The Instructor, or Young Man's Best Companion* (revised and published as *The American Instructor* in 1748 by Benjamin Franklin) dispensed with the catechism and added sections on geography, letter writing, reading, and arithmetic. Instructional texts thus reflected the multiple and sometimes competing literacies of the colonial era.[36]

There is ample evidence that *The New England Primer, The American Instructor,* and texts with similar aims—conduct guides, for example—circulated widely in the colonies. But how they were used and by whom is less well understood. The seventeenth-century literacy statutes Monaghan references did not initially specify that towns had to provide for reading instruction. That came somewhat later, and as it did, the gendered nature of colonial reading and writing instruction became more apparent. By the eighteenth century, boys who could read fluently from the primers and Psalters used to school them usually graduated to writing instruction. But most girls did not, even those who had attained high proficiency in reading. Citing Walter Small's study of 200 colonial-era schools where both reading and writing instruction would have taken place, Monaghan reports that "only seven schools . . . definitely admitted girls" and that perhaps another five did as well.[37] But even attending such schools did not guarantee that girls would receive writing instruction. There is some evidence, Monaghan says, that schools that admitted both boys and girls frequently deemed girls' educations to be complete before boys', with writing instruction commencing after girls' departure. And if and when girls were taught writing—in or out of school—the primary focus was usually penmanship, not composition. Exceptions to this pattern were most likely to occur in cities such as Boston, where in at least three cases, "'free' writing schools were open to boys only, although girls could attend as private pupils 'out of hours,' when

the boys were out of school." As a practical matter, then, social status and ge-
ographical location worked in unsurprising ways to mitigate gendered restrictions on writing instruction: "In general," Monaghan finds, "the father
of any Boston girl who wished to learn to write had to pay fees to a public or
private writing master."[38] Restrictions slowly loosened as the colonies moved
toward independence; in 1771 Massachusetts colonial law finally stipulated
that girls should be taught both reading and writing.[39]

Even as young women gained access to writing instruction in the eighteenth century, the teaching of writing beyond grammar and penmanship
remained largely the province of men. Women taught reading to children,
often in household "dame schools," while men, as writing masters, taught
more mature students the elements of composition and rhetoric. Interestingly, this represents the reverse of gendered instruction in the late nineteenth and twentieth centuries: the feminization of reading rather than
writing. Put another way, in early America, reading was perceived to be the
"easy" task, so easy that it could be taught by women to boys and girls together. Writing, difficult and thus best taught by men, was needed only by
boys who would become leaders in their communities.[40]

Still, despite the impediments just enumerated, we know that some colonial women managed to practice composition according to discernible
rhetorical principles. While essays might not have been assigned in town
schools, composition in the form of written meditation was used by Puritan
and Quaker men and women as a devotional aid. The poetry and letters of
Anne Bradstreet, not to mention numerous extant Puritan and Quaker diaries, testify to the probability that certain women were able (and perhaps
even encouraged) to write regularly as part of their devotional duties. But as
clerical authority diminished in the eighteenth century, so did, in some
measure, women's opportunities for devotional writing. By the time of the
American Revolution, secular authority in community life set the stage for
the privileging of secular configurations of literacy, and in this environment
civic rhetoric, invested in the authority of the word, began to flourish.[41] We
must be careful, though, not to overstate the case. It is true that for men,
public life and oratory did become more secular following independence.
But for women, religious traditions of oratory (manifest in speaking for
abolition and temperance), preaching, and written spiritual meditation
continued to shape advanced literacy well into the nineteenth century.

The decades after the Revolution saw a narrowing of the so-called literacy gap between women and men. Historian Richard Brown explains this narrowing in terms of family relations: "Before the Revolution, when Robert Treat Paine married the semi-literate Sally Cobb, social convention had been relatively indifferent if not actually hostile to female learning—John Adams' wife, the learned Abigail Smith, was exceptional—for women's place was understood to be in the home intellectually and psychologically as well as physically. Afterward, in the new republic, it was the Sally Cobbs who became unusual in the North, as a new convention was formulated that required literacy and encouraged schooling for girls. As a result, by 1830 northern women in various ranks closed the literacy gap that had often divided their mothers and fathers in the past."[42] Formal schooling played no small part in closing the literacy gap. After the Revolution, public grammar school education for both male and female children was funded and improved—more so in the North than in the South. According to Kerber, "Middle-class girls began to attend schools for lengthened periods of time. Town academies began to include 'female departments.'" Although attendance fluctuated and retaining teachers was a problem, these changes in young women's education still constituted a significant development.[43] Yet to register this significance does not signal that the education of girls had come to equal that of boys. Even when boys and girls were schooled together, when they were "taught the same subjects, with the same books and methods of instruction," the aims of that instruction were often different, which is to say gendered.[44]

But gendered instruction for women was not always aligned with gendered social conventions in the new republic. This was particularly so in female academies such as Julia Ann Tevis's Science Hill.[45] The rise of such academies was no doubt controversial, as is evident in remarks on the subject by Judith Sargent Murray: "Female academies are every where establishing, and right pleasant is the appellation to my ear. . . . The younger part of the female world have now an inestimable prize put into their hands; and it depends on the rising generation to refute a sentiment, which, still retaining its advocates, grounds its arguments on the incompatibility of the present enlarged plan of female education"(703). As Murray suggests, some may have felt female academies incompatible with predecessor institutions, such as colonial-era adventure schools, because the academies were considerably more substantial, both conceptually and materially. "Located in the homes of the instructors," writes Mary Beth Norton, adventure schools "were short-lived, with no staff other than the owners, and their course of study stressed ornamental accomplishments."[46] In contrast to these local operations, the academies drew pupils from around the new nation and boarded them while school was in session. Having boarding pupils enabled the academies to develop a curriculum with intellectual breadth and depth suited to enabling reflection on the democratic experiment evolving in the culture around them.

As the nineteenth century unfolded, the schooling of young women and men alike became increasingly enmeshed in a self-conscious rhetoric of democracy. The antebellum schooling fictions that we treat in chapters 4–6 brim over with scenes of learning that conspicuously celebrate a democratic mix of social classes, and wonder over the possibility that daughters of rich and humble alike could meet on intellectual common ground within the confines of a well-run female academy or seminary. Even Mrs. A. J. Graves, a writer steadfast in her opposition to female academies, imagined democratic encounters as one point of departure for *Girlhood and Womanhood*, her 1844 fiction about the graduates of Oakwood School: "The characters of the Oakwood scholars were as various and diverse as their situations in life. . . . Each class had also its representatives, from the daughters of the rich planter, the wealthy merchant and the distinguished professional man, to the children of the aspiring shop-keeper and the humble mechanic. Such were the discordant materials and the opposing forces out of which Mrs. Norville produced an agreeable combination, and a harmonious system." Graves advances this position more forcefully in *Woman in America*, wherein she links the young nation's future success to the quality of its mother-teachers: "Under a government like ours, the responsibility of woman becomes ten-fold greater than in the monarchies of Europe. . . . Every mother in our land may have under her forming care its future rulers and statesmen; and in every son she is intrusted with a being who, if he live to manhood, will exercise a voice in the promotion of measures to operate either for his country's weal or woe. . . . Our high places are open to all who strive to reach them; and, therefore, the only classification that our institutions will warrant, is that which is based upon character, and not upon the accidents of rank or fortune."[47] As we suggest in chapter 4, Graves's thesis, striking the familiar chord of Republican Motherhood as it does, means something very different in the 1840s than it would have in the 1790s. What would have seemed optimistic and progressive at the end of the eighteenth century was, fifty years later, antagonistic toward the generations of women who had graduated from academies and founded schools of their own. Yet consider this fundamental point of agreement between Graves and her opponents: regardless of whether women should teach at home or in academies, their attainment of advanced education was nothing less than a patriotic duty.

Admittedly, in Graves's discourse there is dissonance between rhetoric and reality. Contrary to her assertion, rank and fortune did determine who had access to good schooling in the 1840s, especially when we consider how her terms map onto race and gender. As Lucille Schultz notes in her study of "young composers" in the nineteenth century, "it is important to remember that not all nineteenth-century children had access to school. Well into the century, most of the students attending school were European American children, and most often from middle-class families." While the common school movement, which gained ground in the 1830s and 1840s, may have broadened class representation in the early grades, African American and Native American children surely failed to benefit from the movement's supposedly universal reforms.[48]

Even for white women of middling status, what Murray celebrated and Graves lamented took years to achieve. It took almost two decades for the female academies that Murray greeted with such enthusiasm to become widely and numerously established. And once established, it took time to cultivate funding—including from public coffers—that could be used to underwrite tuition and boarding expenses. With respect to Emma Willard's Troy Female Seminary, Baym notes that at most only a tenth of enrolled students were awarded scholarships, meaning that the vast majority of Troy students were young women whose families, while not necessarily wealthy, could afford the seminary's substantial tuition. Generalizing, then, it is fair to say that academy-schooled women in the early national period were probably white, probably Protestant, and probably from the middling and upper classes (with the caveat that class status was as fluid as the national economy).[49]

Certainly this characterization holds for the authors of schooling fic-

tions, all of whom, as far as we can discern, were financially secure (if tenu-
ously so) Anglo American Protestants. Their writing reflects, to a great extent, their circumstances in life. A striking example: they stereotype African
Americans—usually nameless and faceless—as wronged slaves or as devious
or depraved servants, whose narrative function is merely to highlight the
moral superiority of one of the white characters. Native American characters, while rare, were treated as more formidable narrative foils. (In one
novella, Louisa Tuthill has her heroine saved by a Christianized Indian; in
her writing, Almira Phelps boasted that her Maryland academy had been
home to the sisters of tribal chiefs, exemplifying her school's wide democratic base.) Unsaved Catholics make regular appearances, some to be successfully converted, many to remain lost in spiritual darkness.

We should note one important exception to the pattern just elaborated:
the otherwise unrepresentative democracies in schooling fictions often featured at least one daughter of a skilled laborer. It is through these laboring-
class characters that we can begin to glimpse a major ongoing change in education in the new republic. But to what extent real female academies
actually welcomed the daughters of skilled workers remains unclear. The
historical record suggests that population and commercial growth led to increased class diversity in schooling, especially at the elementary level. At the
same time, rural communities, especially in the Northeast, established
school districts—again mostly at the elementary level—that would have ac-
commodated students whose parents were not equally well off. But when it
came to schooling in urban centers, Carl Kaestle argues that "those of
affluent and middling ranks supported an entrepreneurial system of independent tuition schools for their own children and charity schools run by
benevolent societies for the children of the poor."[50]

It was within this tradition of independent schools, and not rural district
schools, that boarding academies and seminaries for young women gained
prominence. And it was within this tradition, as captured in fiction, that
hopes and anxieties about class status could be worked out. Take, for example, the following account from Graves's *Girlhood and Womanhood,* subtitled *Sketches of My Schoolmates.* Sarah Sherman, the "youngest daughter of a
worthy carpenter," possesses an "ardent thirst for knowledge," despite the
fact that her father is unschooled. Though some of her classmates initially
look "down upon her with contempt," Sarah stands as an exemplar of dem-

ocratic success. Sarah's parents are right to educate her because she is book-ish by nature, especially since, upon returning home, she does not shirk her share of domestic duties. She hews, in other words, to the Wordsworthian ideal expressed in the sketch's epigraph: "Plain living and high thinking." Sarah's subsequent marriage to an ambitious lawyer promises that she will rise in station—something she does not seek. But then she and her husband experience a reversal of fortune (a common trope in early national literature and still popular in later fictions such as Graves's). Sarah's intellect and skill-ful domestic economy cannot completely ward off financial crisis, but they steer her family through it and beyond. Despite her humble beginnings, Sarah benefits from her education and learns how to rise properly and how to provide for her husband the spiritual counterweight necessary to offset the ambition and greed of the marketplace.[51]

Graves also sketches Sarah's thematic opposite: a young woman of high birth, Margaret Etherington, who must learn the foolishness of pride in ma-terial wealth. While Sarah experiences a rise in station, Margaret experiences a decline, for a time having to take up work as governess for a newly rich family. Margaret is fortunate to marry out of her reduced circumstances, though she must adjust to the idea that her husband's origins are not so fine as she would like them to be. A worthy man, her husband buys her old fam-ily estate, Etherington Manor. By the end of the sketch, Margaret is "filling the station she once held as the mistress of Etherington Manor, with less pride than she did, as the daughter of Robert Etherington, but with equal el-egance and dignity, as the wife of Henry Bancroft." Margaret and Sarah both come out "right," as it were, but only after Graves puts them through trials that prompt conversion to democratic ideals. Critical to surviving these tri-als are highly developed skills in reading and writing, core subjects in all of the fictional female academies we visit in this book. Although unavailable to women not resembling Sarah and Margaret, "for at least some women"—mostly white, mostly of middling status, mostly Protestant—exposure to the advanced literacy of the academy "served to nurture ambitions and skills" in ways unknown before the Revolution.[52]

Cultivating Female Education

To be sure, this nurturing of young women's ambition and skill created "the first generation of well-to-do American girls who lived away from home and relatives for lengthy periods."[53] And while independence from home enabled greater concentration on studies, it also spawned fears of the "female pedant," of the woman whose learning had masculinized her.[54] To calm these fears, the schooling of young women of status, including rhetorical instruction, was made to look quite different from that of their male counterparts. The curriculum was neither as complex nor as sustained as that available to young men attending college. But to liken female academies to, say, "finishing schools" is to diminish the real learning they encouraged. To be sure, academies in the late eighteenth century represented the end point of a young woman's career at school, and it was well into the next century before that would change. Yet there was little about finishing in the discourse that permeated female academies and much about beginning. Academy graduates were given a sense that their educations had prepared them for a lifetime of learning, the sort of learning needed to apply the principles of female civic rhetoric to the task of mothering the new republic.

Not every mother was so prepared, however. The rising standard of literacy after the Revolution rendered an earlier generation of mothers unprepared to teach their children. Thus, in a trope familiar to eighteenth-century readers, books were figured as surrogate mothers. To this end, European conduct guides, letter-writing manuals, and language primers were all adapted for an American audience that lacked access to literate maternal wisdom. Not every book, though, could substitute for a good mother, for not all books were virtuous. Novels, for example, were thought to inspire "female quixotism," which could result in a woman's moral downfall. Anxieties about women's reading, particularly of romances, appeared centrally in novels such as Tabitha Gilman Tenney's *Female Quixotism* (1801). Ironically, Tenney used the novel form to warn women about the dangers of novel reading and to argue for the sort of advanced rhetorical training that would make women more discerning readers. Her protagonist, Dorcasina, "is educated at home by her father, who allows her to read novels . . . instead of having the benefit of a mother's guidance." As did Tenney and other women writers of her day, female academies discouraged novel reading at the same time they presented certain books as adequate compensation for absent, bad, or ineffectual mothering.[55]

A more pressing question, though, was whether a good teacher, working with good books, could substitute for a good mother's teaching. Proponents of female academies argued that it could be so for at least two reasons. First, academy teaching amounted to instruction at the secondary level, which few mothers had experienced before the Revolution. Second, academy teaching would be done by women specially trained for the job, and, crucially, their efforts would be supervised by women. Such was the claim—and probably the case—in the late eighteenth and early nineteenth centuries, likely the zenith of women's authority over the institutionalized schooling of women. What would follow by the mid-nineteenth century was a decline in that authority, even as women's educational "opportunities increased numerically."[56] And as women's leadership in academy life narrowed, so did the horizons of academy graduates. Academies continued to ready girls to participate in civic affairs, but the opportunities for actual participation grew fewer and more tightly regulated.

Despite these restrictive trends in teaching and learning, female academies did manage to achieve and preserve significant reform in the ideal curriculum for women after the Revolution. This reform is perhaps most visible in the moderation of teaching various "ornamental accomplishments" in favor of fostering "the study of such academic subjects as composition, history, and geography."[57] Arguments for such moderation, and for the advancement of instrumental literacy, were plentiful in the instructional texts that young women would have encountered both at home and school. For example, consider again "An Oration upon Female Education" from Bingham's *The American Preceptor*. In the following excerpt, the concept of ornamentation gradually evolves from that which should be valued to that which should be tolerated and, finally, surpassed:

> 2. The education of youth has ever been considered by all civilized nations as an object of the highest consequence. But, while they have paid flattering attention to the *strength,* they have doubtless too much neglected the *beauty* and *ornament* of creation.
>
> 3. Too long has the pride of man suffered *female* genius, like the unpolished diamond, to lie buried in its native rubbish. . . .
>
> 6. Happy for the fair daughters of America, the thick mists of superstition and bigotry are vanishing away; and the sun of science begins to beam upon our land, and to irradiate the *female* mind.

7. Let infant choirs, composed of male and female voices, join in praise of our political fathers, and all patrons of science. They have, doubtless, reflected on the vast importance of *female* education to a rising country.

8. They have considered how much the sons and daughters of every age, are indebted to their *mothers* for the seeds of virtue and knowledge; that schools and colleges can but cultivate and mature the plants, which owe their origin to the seeds sown in infancy; that from *maternal* lips, our first accents are formed; and, that from *them,* our words, our actions, nay, our every thought proceeds. (48)

This section of *The American Preceptor* acknowledges that women's roles should be in part ornamental. Indeed, with the image of the unpolished diamond, the passage suggests that the female body is inherently so. At the same time, though, it is apparent that women in the new nation must make contributions beyond the ornamental: they must perform the instrumental work of cultivating the next generation of male citizenry. Evident in the "Oration" and elsewhere, the discourse of female education was euphoric in its insistence that the seeds of female learning be sown liberally. The yield, if harvested with care, could prove to other civilized nations the productive value of spreading literacy and rhetorical skill among young women without the usual regard to social rank.

Noticing that women's education is often figured as cultivation begs that we recognize the cultural and material ramifications of that figure. Cultivation functioned metaphorically to organize perception and expression in much the way images of revolution, reason, and governance did. Each image speaks to the need to assert dominion over myriad resources, natural and cultural, that uncontrolled could doom American democracy. In nearly every case, these resources were tied to the land, and so the metaphor of cultivation comes closest of all to illuminating the preoccupation with land and its possession recurrent in writing after independence. Cultivating white women as teachers meant cultivating young white men who would in turn mature to grapple with the two greatest questions that vexed those who saw white America's future in the literal cultivation of its land: how to battle Indian nations for territory on the frontier, and how to reconcile the violence of slavery with the riches to be derived from fields worked by enslaved hands.[58] Addressing these questions, white rhetors avoided appeals to the economic conscience of their brethren: they did not speak directly of opening new lands for settlement by destroying sovereign nations of people native to North America; they did not boast of the fortunes to be made off the backbreaking labor of men and women torn from African roots. Instead, with the same eloquence they applied to promoting women's education, white rhetors spoke of the justice to be had in bringing civility to a hostile frontier, to the national prosperity inherent in fertile land justly domesticated, and to the peaceful order such domestication would inevitably and perpetually engender. To ensure that readers and auditors understood the grounds for these claims, they were reminded that cultivating the land was a Christian imperative. Thus, the reasoning went, white Americans were not educating themselves to usurp or exploit, but to till an Eden in the wilderness, to establish a new promised land. And if biblical authority was not sufficiently persuasive, the discourse of enlightened progress could also be brought to bear. In structural terms, the Illiterate/Savage/Wilderness paradigm of the past had to give way to a Literate/Civilized/Garden paradigm for the future, a solid foundation for a republic that, unlike those realized in antiquity, could not fail.

Consistent with the latter paradigm, *The American Preceptor*'s "Oration" invokes the trope of cultivated land to promote its vision of education for both sexes, a vision that features an unassailable link between female education and American prosperity:

> 19. With such singular advantages, we need but the active mind, the honest heart, and the diligent hand. Thus shall our schools become as pure, enriching streams; our churches flourish as the palm tree, and our land become as the garden of God. . . .
>
> 21. Could the first settlers of this town now stand in the midst of you, how would they lift their hands in admiration! These, would they say, are the blessed fruits of our zeal, our labors and hardships. We traversed the wilderness in want of all things; but these, our children, are enjoying the milk and honey of the land. . . .
>
> 26. Our lot has fallen in a more favored spot. We live in an age and country, where we see children of both sexes acquiring, at school, all the necessary, convenient, and many of the ornamental branches of education.
>
> 27. Spelling, reading, grammar and geography, they acquire at an early age. Writing and arithmetic are taught with great propriety and expedition. . . .
>
> 29. Then shall we see, from year to year, the productions of American

> ingenuity. Our young men will be emulous to exceed the geniuses of the east; our daughters will shine as bright as constellations in the sphere where nature has placed them. (50–51)

Children's minds become so much seed to be tilled carefully unto harvest, a notion resonant with the familiar biblical epigraph that appears on *The American Preceptor*'s title page: "Train Up a Child in the Way He Should Go." To ignore this insight was to risk not simply slippage into an unfortunate past, but to consign women to a status all too familiar to those fighting for the abolition of slavery:

> 24. There was a time, in the infancy of our country, when less attention was paid to the early improvement of the mind. When the advantage of schooling was limited to a few, and those principally of one sex; while the other was devoted to domestic toils.
> 25. And even now, in some parts of united America, as well as among several other nations who can call themselves *civilized*, women are considered but a little better than *slaves* to unfeeling parents, and to idle, lordly husbands. (50–51)

Whether this passage was viewed as inflammatory for joining the failure of schooling with the institution of slavery is difficult to know. There is every indication, of course, that it would have reinforced growing northern sentiment favoring abolition, just as it would have further hardened southern opposition to the question. It is worth noting that the "Oration," as well as at least one other essay in *The American Preceptor,* addressed other controversial subjects as well–gender, education, and literacy among them. Inclusion of these texts perforce meant exclusion of other, more conventional content. From the start, then, American women's rhetorical training was infused with political content that foregrounded the party strife that increasingly dominated public discourse. As we will see in subsequent chapters, arguments for women's schooling persisted over time in sampling dialogically from the discourses of abolition, revolution, nationhood, Indian warfare, and race destiny.

Overview

Drawing on revisionist rhetorical and literary histories, *Imagining Rhetoric: Composing Women of the Early United States* looks at women's rhetorical schooling and composition practices, not only as events contained within separate domestic and educational spheres, but also as activities inseparable from the whole of political life in the early U.S. In doing so, we join others who "seek to show how women's allegedly 'separate sphere' was affected by what men did, and how activities defined by women in their own sphere influenced and even set constraints and limitations on what men might choose to do—how, in short, that sphere was socially constructed both *for* and *by* women."[59]

Chapter 2 examines the emergence of new instructional texts for women, including boarding school novels meant as much to instruct as to entertain. Within the burgeoning market for writing textbooks after the Revolution, we see a modest niche for books intended specifically for a female readership. In 1785 Caleb Bingham published his *Young Lady's Accidence*, which met market demand by offering a condensed version of available British-inflected grammars.[60] In his preface, Bingham defends the text's brevity by arguing that women unfortunately have much less time than men to learn about language. Therefore, he concludes, a textbook should contain fewer pages and fewer rules if designed for women (or for young men whose leisure time is similarly constrained). But condensed grammars were not the only textbooks targeted to women. Chapter 2 reviews a series of books produced by Donald Fraser, one of which, *The Mental Flower-Garden* (1800), was designed explicitly for use by women. Fraser's previous textbooks, written for both boys and girls, focus on reading, grammar, math, and other basic skills, but in his textbook for young women, the focus shifts to monitoring behavior and to investing and protecting women's virtue. There is a similar concern represented in Susanna Rowson's *A Present for Young Ladies* (1811), which counsels that virtuous behavior can be attained through studious attention to books, so long as any writing or speaking prompted by reading is confined to an audience of peers at school.

If textbooks such as Fraser's and Rowson's dismissed the revolutionary language that created a market for them, there was, as Cathy Davidson has established, a shining alternative: fiction. Davidson contends that "the novel inspired education by stressing the sentimental and social value of literacy—as seen in group discussions of reading depicted within the plots of novels and in the formation of similar reading groups in every section of America."[61] Our concern is with a particular kind of fiction, work that takes women's schooling—including rhetorical education—as its primary subject by invoking the discursive conventions of sentimental and sensational novels, as well as those of textbooks, essays, histories, and biographies. The "novel" education advanced in schooling fictions thus straddles two distinct ideological positions: in fairly conservative language, these fictions describe what amounts to a dream of a vastly enlarged sphere of civic authority for women. In this manner, Hannah Webster Foster's *The Boarding School* (1798) leads us to contemplate an ideal scene of rhetorical instruction for young women of the country's first postrevolutionary generation. Written at a time when the U.S. novel was becoming popular and when the idea of women's education was gaining similar popularity, *The Boarding School* promotes learning as a route toward independent identity marked by trained reason and restrained passion. While Foster's preceptress's lectures are didactic, the letters her young students exchange project a rational female ethos, one that credits them with a degree of intellectual authority, if only within their writing circle.

Chapter 3 takes up Judith Sargent Murray's *The Gleaner* (1798), a collection of her work earlier serialized in *The Massachusetts Magazine*. In *The Gleaner* Murray employs a range of genres: the novella, the occasional essay, the formal essay, and the play. Her education novella, which features the brilliant and charming Margaretta, is interspersed throughout *The Gleaner*, where it documents a system of female learning and behavior that derives from the classical practice of copying exemplary models. It is as if Murray extends the idea of commonplace books to all levels of learned and lived experience: if words or behavior are ethically, morally, and aesthetically praiseworthy, then copy them. She fears, however, that this commonplace rhetorical practice might lead to belletristic charges of plagiarism. Defending herself against plagiarism and announcing that the Gleaner—whose voice is male—shall copy whatever "he" finds valuable, young women are urged to search out models worthy of unabashed emulation. (Murray's concerns about emulation and plagiarism are all the more intriguing in light of changes in copyright law at the turn of the nineteenth century, which we discuss at some length.) Although the Margaretta narrative is finally fairly traditional in its advice about proper female conduct, its conservative message is more than offset by its appearance alongside essays that propose, in revolutionary language, new civic roles for women.

Chapter 4 tracks the transition from early national textbooks and schooling fictions to those influenced by antebellum Romantic culture, a period that spans the over thirty years between the publication of *The Boarding School* and *The Gleaner* and the appearance of Mrs. A. J. Graves's *Girlhood and Womanhood*, the latter representative of the second cluster of American fictions to foreground women's schooling. *Girlhood and Womanhood* raises issues engaged by numerous other educator-writers of the 1840s and 1850s: the lifelong efficacy of women's schooling in a domestic economy, teaching as a profession for women, the problems generally of democratic schooling, and instruction in belletristic principles of taste and style.

Chapter 5 looks at several novels and textbooks by Graves's contemporary Louisa Caroline Tuthill, as well as one novel promoted under her name but probably written by her daughter. Like Graves's *Girlhood and Womanhood*, Tuthill's novels reflect a new emphasis on belletristic rhetoric. Tuthill draws on British Romanticism but tempers it with lessons in American domestic economy and, crucially, with lectures on Scottish commonsense philosophy framed as Christian reworkings of classical rhetoric aimed at safeguarding Protestantism in the face of Romantic skepticism. While her novels frequently feature model school settings, Tuthill worries that boarding schools, even those governed by the best preceptresses, instill early prejudices that can only be overcome by adhering to a rigorous and sustained plan of self-education.

Chapter 6 studies Almira Hart Lincoln Phelps's *Ida Norman* (1848, 1854), a work published roughly fifty years after Murray's Margaretta narrative and Foster's *Boarding School*. Phelps's novel illustrates what became of liberatory civic rhetoric under the compounded pressure of American Romanticism, belletristic rhetoric, and Jacksonian democracy. Truly a "usable fiction," the first volume of *Ida Norman*, appearing in 1848, was read to Phelps's students at the Patapsco Female Institute in Maryland. Because it reportedly met with great success in her classroom, Phelps published a continuation of the narrative in 1854. Like the earlier Margaretta narrative and *The Boarding School*, *Ida Norman* stresses the importance of women as educators of statesmen and businessmen. However, Phelps's novel also registers the influence of a Romantic individualism emergent in the U.S., particularly in the narrative's emphasis on self-reliance as a primary virtue in both male and female characters. The good statesmen is a common man who has perfected his individual moral consciousness and is then called by the public to lead through moral example. As for Phelps's women, Republican Motherhood is no longer an adequate goal, though neither, of course, is statesmanship. Instead, women in *Ida Norman* are urged to become democratic teachers who will school young women (and, informally, men) in the rhetorical ethics and religious morals that the new belletristic curricula fail to teach. *Ida Norman* documents the prospect of a new profession for women, teaching, and the creation of a potentially new separate sphere, the female academy.

Finally, our conclusion brings us to the diaries of Charlotte Forten, a free African American woman who pursued an education of the sort imagined by Graves, Tuthill, and Phelps. We focus on entries Forten made as a student and, later, as a teacher in training. While her diaries make use of some of the rhetorical conventions central to schooling fictions—figuring teachers as both mothers and friends, teaching as a fundamentally democratic act, and education as the foundation of self-reliance—the diaries also chronicle her growing sense of melancholy. As she matures, Forten discovers that no amount of education can help her vault the barriers imposed by gender and race. Nor, she finds, does education engage students in the kind of civic liberatory rhetoric that only a generation before had inspired a revolution. Although Forten produces neither textbooks nor schooling fictions, her diaries address the need to teach others to value the equitable treatment of women and people of color. As such, Forten's diaries record the first intervention by an African American into a discursive and educational tradition forged by white Protestants.

∽

In the chapters that follow, we recover what women in the early U.S. imagined instruction and practice in composition should be, and we show how this imagination shaped their awareness of female civic rhetoric—its possibilities and limitations. Concluding our introduction in the spirit of Judith Sargent Murray, we borrow from the text of an essay examination whose author surveys what a good rhetorical education has to offer a young woman like herself. Written roughly 150 years ago by Albana Carson, a student at Julia Ann Tevis's Science Hill Academy, the essay employs liberatory rhetoric to rail against the conditions that lend credence to the charge that women's intellect is inferior to men's. Establishing that cause leads to effect, Carson contends that woman's intellect suffers because her opportunities are so very restricted. To bolster her claim, she draws on a commonplace argument about the danger of ornamentation, echoing the language of *The American Preceptor*'s "Oration upon Female Education," published some fifty years before. "Knowledge is exacting," Carson writes. "She requires all your time and talents. Then, how can one be thoroughly educated, who attempts to grasp knowledge with one hand, and pleasure with the other." What women need, she continues, is the freedom to read widely and deeply. Only then, she concludes, will society "hear less said of her defects, and frivolities, and more of her intellectual capacity, and her companionship with high and noble minds."[62] As the nineteenth century wore on, the influence of neoclassical rhetoric certainly diminished in the male academy and in culture at large. Yet it remained a powerful force abroad in the land, still valued in the corridors of legislative and legal power and on the platforms and pages that sustained the suffrage, temperance, and abolitionist movements. It was no less powerful, though certainly less visible, in the female academies that schooled the likes of Albana Carson and that are remembered for all time in the durable but neglected fictions we recuperate in this book.

*Thrice blessed are we, the happy daughters of this land of liberty, where the
female mind is unshackled by the restraints of tyrannical custom, which in
many other regions confines the exertions of genius to the usurped powers of
lordly man! Here virtue, merit, and abilities are properly estimated under
whatever form they appear. Here the widely extended fields of literature court
attention; and the American fair are invited to cull the flowers, and cultivate
the expanding laurel.*

Hannah Webster Foster, *The Boarding School* (1798)

Schoolmaster Donald Fraser's Columbian Texts

✍ *In 1807 Dr. Benjamin Rush,* the celebrated champion of U.S.
women's education, enthusiastically endorsed the second edition of
Donald Fraser's *The Mental Flower Garden,* recommending its adoption in all women's schools: "ACCEPT my thanks for the valuable
publication which you sent to me. I shall, with great pleasure, endeavour to bring your 'Mental Flower-Garden,' into notice; it is calculated
to do good: if my influence were as extensive as my wishes to promote
its circulation and usefulness, it should be adopted in ALL the *Female
Academies* and Female Schools in the United States."[1] Given Rush's enthusiasm, we expected to find in the recommended textbook a progressive and serious course of study for women. But far from living up
to the promise of Rush's endorsement, or even to the progressive language of Fraser's own prefaces, the New York schoolmaster's work dis-
closes a more limited course of study for women. Fraser adopts revolutionary liberatory rhetoric only in abolitionist discourse. That he
joined Cornelius Davis, "teacher of the African Free School," as an
original member of the Society of Associated Teachers betokens
knowledge of, if not interest in, educational opportunities that extend
beyond the white male population.[2] But outside of these speculations,

we know little of Fraser's attitudes toward those who experienced oppression in the early republic. Certainly not examples of stellar, progressive female education, Fraser's textbooks are interesting for other reasons. Taken as a series, they evince a growing fascination with the creation of a distinctly national curriculum. From 1791 to 1807 his compilations became increasingly identified as "Columbian"; they also became more conspicuously gendered. Fraser's 1791 *Young Gentleman and Lady's Assistant* yields to his 1794 *Columbian Monitor* and finally to his conduct guides, the 1800 and 1807 editions of *The Mental Flower Garden*. Without Rush's endorsement, we might consider Fraser an anomaly, a reactionary figure amidst revolutionary changes in women's rhetorical education. But Rush's endorsement aligns Fraser with the liberatory movement to create educated Republican Mothers and thus prompts us to take a closer look at these examples of the movement's pedagogical products.

We realize that we are researching textbooks just as composition historiographers are advancing compelling arguments against relying solely on textbooks for historical evidence. Textbooks alone cannot provide a complete or accurate picture of the profession as it developed; they cannot assure us of actual classroom practices.[3] Still, for underrepresented groups, basic research into textbooks—and into other forms of educational literature—has not yet been undertaken. These texts can at least provide insight into what educators desired or imagined.

Fraser's Columbian Monitor: *Rhetorical Education in Transition*

In 1794 Fraser set out to create the great American textbook in another work, *The Columbian Monitor*. This aim becomes clearer when the text is compared to its 1791 precursor, *The Young Gentleman and Lady's Assistant*. The *Assistant*, which entered into a second edition the same year the *Monitor* was first published, follows a popular colonial format, one that combines lessons in geography, natural history, elocution, biblical studies, and arithmetic. The very words in the new title—*The Columbian Monitor*—shift attention away from the self-sponsored emphasis of the *Assistant* to a supervised, nationalized pedagogy, one that includes lessons in conduct and etiquette. The *Monitor* consists of five parts—dialogues, catechism, verse grammar, letters, and fragments on deportment and religion—as well as an essay on polite behavior, addressed specifically to women. The foregoing description suggests a coherence that the *Monitor* lacks (as do other Fraser textbooks). But a loss in coherence is a gain in complexity: Fraser's loosely compiled anthologies provide a site for analysis filled with illuminating and contradictory social voices, particularly on topics concerning gender.

The Columbian Monitor, pitched specifically to the children of the new nation, only indirectly markets gendered instruction. Although the *Assistant* advertises a text that could aid both young ladies and gentlemen, its content is relatively gender-neutral: the "Natural History" and "Practical Arithmetic" sections, for example, are not clearly gender coded (*YGLA,* 64–110, 224–64). Oddly enough, the title page of the *Monitor* makes no such overt appeals to "young gentlemen" and "young ladies." But the *Monitor* is heavily gendered, most noticeably in its dialogue and letter sections and in its annexed address on polite behavior. As Fraser's books become more gender-conscious, the very idea of writing and rhetoric gets revised: no longer can literacy skills be acquired independently of teachers, with only the assistance of a book. Writing—now conspicuously gendered—becomes a form of conduct that must be carefully monitored.

Fraser's entry into the particulars of gendered conduct and the political construction of Republican Motherhood is illustrated in his dialogue section. Even a cursory summary of the *The Columbian Monitor*'s twelve dialogues points to the evolving nature of Fraser's texts. Five dialogues addressed to women are rooted in colonial notions of religious literacy. These dialogues script women's voices and issues in a style that shifts from parabolic to didactic. In these, there is no talk of becoming great through literacy. Instead, the dialogues address *"Detraction"* (looking at fine clothes instead of listening to a sermon), self-pride, and proper conduct toward inferiors (*CM,* 18–25). The last few encourage women to read specific Scriptures and—lest they arrogate interpretive authority—to study approved scriptural commentaries (*CM,* 25–30). Six dialogues addressed to men, on the other hand, are more closely related to the ideal of literate citizenship. The dialogues cover such topics as "Shewing how a boy may become a great man" and "Shewing how a boy may make every one love him" (*CM,* 1–2, 3–4). A third dialogue reinforces the previous two and, important to our purposes here, advocates literacy or "diligent application to . . . books" as the means through which a boy can "become a great man," "make every one love him," and receive "honor and applause" (*CM,* 4). One of the twelve dialogues is addressed to neither a specifically male nor female audience and features a conversation with an archetypal Republican Mother. This dialogue features an important change: we see the beginning of a national script featuring women who promote literacy.

The *Monitor*'s letter section (complete with model complimentary or "calling" cards) shows us another feature of this period: the rise of the sensational novel and the centrality of a female-centered romantic discourse (*CM*, 87–114). Although this section includes male voices, it devotes more time to secular literacy for women. Indeed, the letters in this book prove an interesting choice: many revolve around courtship, making use of the discourse of romance, a discourse that many feared would lead young women astray. But again, this section begins with advice to young men and only slowly evolves into lessons explicitly addressed to women. The letter section opens with remarks that elaborate on a passage from Locke. Here, young men are advised to think about their subject from "every point of view" before beginning to lay out a plan (*CM*, 88). While there are no constraints on content, they are advised that "the greater variety your letter contains, the more acceptable," but that a "letter should wear an honest, cheerful countenance, . . . not like a vain *fop* admiring his own dress" (*CM*, 88). The plain style is preferred, though this style should clearly reflect the "good breeding and humanity" by which "a gentleman ought to be distinguished" (*CM*, 89). The letters that follow this male-centered advice locate women's discursive strengths in the epistolary form. The first letter aligns polished letter writing with female accomplishment, suggesting that the guidelines established for good correspondence lend themselves more to women's behavior than to men's: "To write *letters* well is a very desirable excellence in a woman. . . . Your sex, in general, much excels our own, in the *ease* and graces of epistolary correspondence" (*CM*, 89). Specifically, women's lack of education and training in social graces prepares them to be more honest and engaging conversationalists and, thus, better writers. The compliment, however, is somewhat backhanded. Women, the letter continues, are not "cramped with the shackles and formality of rules, their thoughts are expressed *spontaneously*, as they flow and become, more immediately, what a letter should be, a lively, amusing, *written conversation*. A *man* attends to the niceties of grammar, or well turned periods; a *woman* gives us the effusions of her soul" (*CM*, 90). Although earlier associated with ornament, women here are seen as plain, natural, at ease. Men "often labor only to be dull" because they try too often in writing for "distant ornaments" and, in doing so, "chill the natural fervor of the soul" (*CM,* 90).

Perhaps most interesting here is a gendered configuration that has been common in rhetorical education for the better part of two centuries: the tension between pedagogy that stresses expressive, "authentic" writing and that which fosters proficiency in transactional, specifically "academic" forms of discourse. Indeed, this debate seems to be revitalized whenever rhetorical education is enhanced and extended to previously excluded groups. This tension is grounded in a cluster of dichotomies important to myths of progress and development in Western culture. Not surprisingly, it was particularly salient as the American identity shifted from colonized to colonizer. Here we find opposed the "natural" and the "cultivated" (out of which grows nostalgia for a lost "primitivism" in the midst of decadent, urban culture, and, paradoxically, the condemnation of "savagery" as a threat to the promise of cultivation, of polite society).[4] Structurally, these same narrative binaries are repeated when it comes to gendered literacy instruction. The *Monitor,* like other texts of the period, suggests that women can produce more "natural" personal prose of the kind found in letters. This opens a space for women's writing, and indeed, women in this period did excel at letter writing and were publicly recognized for this talent. Of course, such recognition brings almost immediate devaluation (as was the case with the novel, another genre in which women excelled). Still, to say that women made use of letter writing is not to say that they were participating only in the expressive tradition. As the increase in published novels, letters, and essays attests, women did become substantially more literate as colonial instruction gave way to a new national purpose. But to overstate this case misses an important point: women, though they might be highly fluent writers in some forms of discourse (letters, for example), rarely had the opportunity to practice the rhetorical conventions that would have given them access to the discourses of power. For example, as we shall see, women could imagine using and perhaps did use the letter form to explore different voices and to promote their own learning. This valuing of women's letter writing, however, obscures their exclusion from a different kind of space: the academy, for instance, or legislatures. The voice women could not assume in public, at least not without the risk of ridicule, was an academic voice. They had to remain in the more "natural" realm of intimate letter writing because more public circles were made unnatural places for them to be.

The *Monitor* draws on the female epistolary romance genre, incorporating three lively letters of coquetry and courtship. The first of these offers a model of how *"To break off a rash Contract in Love Affairs,"* outlining an argument that stresses false pretenses (*CM*, 105–6). The second two are related: *"From a Lover to reproach a scornful Mistress"* and *"The Lady's answer"* (*CM*, 108–10). The "lady" who answers the scorned lover clearly gets the better in this sequence, offering for young women a surprising model, a voice that is strong, reasoned, and boldly sexual. Although the letter is long, we quote it in its entirety so that all the logical turns are represented:

> Poor angry Harry,
>
>   I am somewhat sorry to find you so much vexed, as I am not conscious of having given you any just reason for it: If you complain that I have rejected your love, I candidly own it; and you yourself admit, that I am at liberty to smile on whom I please, and place my affection where I like best, and since I only have taken that liberty you have given me, what just reason have you, sir, to be so very angry? O! but it seems you have frequently neglected *your most urgent business* to serve me! Have you truly? I can assure you, I like you none the better for that; nor did I ever desire it: Your services to me were all free and voluntary, I supposed; and I as such received them, and thanked you for them; and that was, in my opinion, sir, as much as they merited: But the principal crime you charge me with is, my deceiving you with false promises, when in truth I never made you any: I confess I told you once that you might hope—and so you may do still, if you think fit, but this is no more than a word of course, for I have said as much, perhaps, to several others, but never was taxed yet, with breach of promise, by any but yourself. Upon the whole, sir, with all your boasted accomplishments, I perceive you are entirely unacquainted with the modern manner of *courtship:* You must know, that we women take a pride in having many lovers, and give them all good words, that, when we please, we may take which we please; and it sometimes so happens, that when one urges us hard, we are compelled then to declare ourselves, and acquaint him we have made another choice, merely to get rid of his impertinence, and this is all the crime that I am chargeable with towards you; for which, if you are so squeamish as to hate all women, with all my heart; for I truly believe that our sex will not lose much by your disaffection. As I perceive, sir, that you are a little whimsically inclined, and may, perhaps, hereafter change your present resolution, with regard to our sex,

I thought fit to drop the foregoing hints, to enable you to manage matters better with your new mistress; for my own part, I shall never be

Yours,

J. F—— (*CM*, 109–10)

J. F—— reverses gendered rhetorical stereotypes, speaking through an earlier eighteenth-century persona that is reasoned and framing "poor angry Harry" as whimsical, passionate, and irrational. She also draws on available secular and national discourses (rather than religious or even moral ones). She speaks a legal discourse of contracts, breaches, and crimes, a discourse closely related to a litigious culture and to rhetorical concerns about the specious quality of words.

The idea of using such models to teach writing might seem somewhat curious, but Fraser was not alone in trying such methods. Though many writers, including Dr. Rush, were crusading against romances and novels, many were simultaneously using novels at their most sensational to instruct women.[5] The three letters in the *Monitor* thus reflect a trend and a fear in educating women: novels could educate women, yet they could also lead them astray. Just as he did in the *Monitor,* in his next text, *The Mental Flower-Garden,* Fraser would continue to include public discourse on gender and to illustrate the culture's preoccupation with making women literate.

First Flowers: Rhetoric as Gendered Conduct

The title *The Mental Flower-Garden,* with its emphasis on delicate beauty, indicates that this text will move in a direction even more focused on rhetorical etiquette than *The Columbian Monitor.* To supplement this ornamental component, the *Flower-Garden* continues to make use of the dialogues, catechism, verse grammar, letters, and lessons on deportment that comprise the *Monitor.* Added to this material are many more short verse selections, lessons in elocution, and short biographies. In 1807 *The Mental Flower Garden* was republished, although in a significantly different version. These revisions—that is, both the revision of the materials from the *Monitor* into *The Mental Flower-Garden,* and the revision from the first (1800) to the second (1807) edition of the latter text—document a restrictive translation of the discourse of Republican Motherhood into rhetorical pedagogy.

For the 1800 edition of the *Flower-Garden,* for example, the dialogues and letters have been revised in telling ways. Some of the dialogues in the

Monitor were, as we have pointed out, already pitched to women. But in the first edition of the *Flower-Garden,* the material aimed at young men is entirely dropped. In just one case a gender substitution is made: now one dialogue discusses literacy as the means by which a child—male in the *Monitor,* female in the *Flower-Garden*—can earn love. Yet what follows this advice is not further encouragement for young women to advance their rhetorical training, but dialogues carried forward from the *Monitor* that warn against false pride and urge reflection upon Scriptures. Conspicuously absent from the *Flower-Garden* are the *Monitor*'s dialogues about becoming "great" or earning "honor and applause" for "diligent application to . . . books" (*CM,* 4).

Likewise, the letter section has grown increasingly moralistic. The *Flower-Garden* does not make use of the *Monitor*'s courtship letters or any other form of women's secular discourse. ("Poor angry Harry" and his scornful mistress have no place here.) Instead, the *Flower-Garden* contains a series of letters between a mother, Portia, and her daughter, Sophia, who is enrolled in Mrs. Bromley's boarding school. This move to fictional representation of women's education is, as we indicate in the introduction, part of a rising subgenre of boarding school fiction that imagines in detail ideal curricula for women. Because Portia is separated from her daughter, she "will endeavour to supply by letters" what she "cannot perform in person": that is, she aims to provide Sophia with good advice, to educate her (*MF-G,* 93). Yet what becomes clear is that Portia's evaluation of her daughter's reading and writing is based solely on proper content. Sophia earns her mother's praise because her "expressions of duty and obedience are extremely agreeable" (*MF-G,* 103). Indeed, almost all of the letters convey restrictive advice about behavior, choosing friends, hygiene, proper dress, and the like. The focus of this section, then, is not on advancing female learning but on curbing female pedantry.

Overall, *The Mental Flower-Garden* includes very few pieces enthusiastic about female learning. The presence of three biographical sketches of female scholars might seem to offer examples of extraordinary women to be emulated. Indeed, these brief pieces are apparently included to show "how forcibly" these "*authentic* sketches . . . confute the sneering sophistry of *Chesterfield* . . . and other invidious detractors of *Female Genius!*" (*MF-G,* 143). Yet these shining examples of female scholarship are undercut in several ways. None of the women resides in the U.S., thus rendering their achievements remote. And, in each case, the narration emphasizes that these women do not neglect their domestic duties and that they continue to display "taste" and other important social accomplishments (*MF-G*, 139). The text makes plain that these women are included only because they display ornamental as well as scholarly talent: "A woman, who has no other merit than that of being learned, is certainly wanting in her duty to society" (*MF-G*, 143).

In addition to the biographical sketches and Rush's abridged "Thoughts upon Female Education," one other extract is included, and this, surprisingly, defies the tone and content of the rest of the *Flower-Garden*. The passage builds on an architectural metaphor, arguing that the strength of the country depends upon women's learning: "Those principles of freedom, those maxims of education, which embrace only half mankind, are only half systems, and will no more support the burden of humanity, than the perpendicular section of an arch will support a column" (*MF-G*, 67). Although it owns that women are placed by nature in a separate sphere than men, it also argues that daughters should have the "same relations" to parents (and country) as sons (*MF-G*, 68). Given training in science, women could be "equally competent" (*MF-G*, 68). This passage reiterates the ideal of Republican Motherhood, the view that "the first moulding of the human mind, falls so naturally" upon women: "How shall our children learn fortitude from mothers who scream at the appearance of a spider? How shall they learn that they are formed for their country and mankind, from mothers who know nothing of the history of either? How shall they learn that 'the mind is the standard of the man,' from teachers who are forever directing their attention to their persons?" (*MF-G*, 68). It would be a national failure, the passage argues, to continue with such a focus on the ornamental. Common sense should teach the new republic that women must be allowed to learn and to move beyond mere ornamentation. But even if common sense were to fail, the writer contends, there are numerous examples of "women breaking down the barriers of the tyrant man, and storming the temple of fame"; these women should convince leaders that all should be educated (*MF-G*, 68). Ironically, this essay on "breaking down the barriers of the tyrant man" appears in a book that subordinates all rhetorical training to conduct, to decorum.

Still More Flowers

In 1807 a new edition of Fraser's *The Mental Flower Garden* appears, this one complete with the recommendation from Dr. Rush as well as various endorsements, including one by *"some of the most respectable Teachers in the City of New-York,"* and *"some respectable Female Teachers in the City of New-York"* (*MFG*, v). The changes between the 1800 and 1807 editions are not merely cosmetic—the text is restructured, the material rearranged and refocused. First consider the title page from the 1800 edition:

THE

MENTAL FLOWER-GARDEN

OR

INSTRUCTIVE AND ENTERTAINING

COMPANION

FOR THE

FAIR-SEX.

CONTAINING,

A VARIETY of elegant poetical pieces—Pleasing and Admonitory Letters

—Cards of Compliment—Devotional Poems—Dialogues—Writing-pieces

—English Grammar in Verse; and some Sketches of Female Biography:

To which is added, a short but Sure Guide to an accurate Pronunciation

(which may save some young Ladies a *blush* in company.)

The 1807 edition's title page makes the changes immediately apparent:

THE

MENTAL FLOWER GARDEN:

OR,

AN INSTRUCTIVE AND ENTERTAINING

COMPANION FOR THE FAIR SEX.

IN TWO PARTS.

CONTAINING:

1. A variety of entertaining and moral Dialogues, partly *original*, calculated

for Misses from Eight to Twelve Years. A collection of useful Rules relative to genteel behaviour, and a polite address. Poetic pieces, Devotional Poems, Writing

Pieces, &c.

2. Miscellaneous Essays, worthy the perusal of *Women*, at any period of Life. To

which are added, interesting sketches of FEMALE BIOGRAPHY.

While the first edition stresses elegance in conduct and speech, the second stresses continued female learning, the idea that women's education should be sustained into adulthood. Not only the title page is revised for the second edition. The greatest differences come in the second half of the book, which now appeals to older (that is, postadolescent) women. The letter section condenses the Portia-Sophia series of letters (leaving out, for example, a substantial sequence on choosing proper friends) and returns, instead, to the essay praising women's letter-writing talents, originally published in the *Monitor*. Perhaps most significantly, more essays appear that engage debates about female education.

One essay, with the vaguely suggestive title "Of Pleasures," not only encourages women to read, but to read "more estimable" works by women (*MFG*, 168, 172). The essay goes so far as to assert that a "Lady might even form a library of the books written by women only" and includes a list of possible authors, a few U.S. writers (Ann Eliza Bleecker and her daughter, Margaretta Bleecker Faugeres) among them (*MFG*, 172). It also encourages women to look for partners, male partners presumably, who can converse on their level: "It cannot be too much recommended to women to prefer the conversation of such persons to the babbling of these empty coxcombs: there is every thing to gain on one side, and every thing to be lost on the other" (*MFG*, 173).

Such changes in the second edition seem to promise a new, progressive textbook. Yet however promising these changes might look at first glance, they do not finally result in a textbook more encouraging of women's learning. The essays selected do not all unequivocally advance education for women, and some even trivialize women's scholarship. The very first essay readers encounter in the second section sends mixed signals about the worth of women's education. "Candid Remarks Relative to the Female Sex" opens with a discussion about the unfairness of men's mischaracterizations of women. However, instead of a revised picture of their worth, we discover a reaffirmation of prevailing views: women's minds are adequate, their hearts superior, their bodies "master-piece[s] of nature" (*MFG*, 145, 148). The passage finally argues not for the education of women, but for the education of men. If women are to be perfected, men need to learn to praise women in a balanced fashion, so as not to foster vanity.

Another noteworthy essay, "Of the Studies Suitable to Women," begins more positively; it argues that the soul can only be developed by exercising the mind (*MFG*, 153). Supportive of the project of educating women, it even exposes the specter of the (pedantic) female quixote: "The ridicule thrown upon a pedantic knowledge had so much discredited all knowledge, that many women prided themselves in clipping the words of their language. But there have always been found women, who, freeing themselves from the prejudices of fashion, have dared to think and speak reasonably; and we see, in the present day, many who do not blush at being better informed"(*MFG*, 158). The agenda this writer sets, however, is as restrictive as those in the other pieces collected. While the essay advances the case for women's learning, it articulates as its main purpose the project of making women better conversationalists for men. Given this purpose, the studies appropriate for women become very limited, as does the kind of knowledge women might most appropriately acquire: "It is necessary for women to possess a less dazzling knowledge, which will be more in unison with their disposition" (*MFG*, 155). To cultivate this disposition, the essay gives women permission to enter learned realms traditionally occupied by men. But women's intellectual journeys in such places are to be temporary: they may visit these realms only to acquire a little "useful" knowledge that might "give assistance to their imaginations" (*MFG*, 155).

Throughout, "Of the Studies Suitable to Women" is characterized by two competing discourses, one of liberation and one of restraint. Thus the essay promotes "physic and history" as subjects worthy of women's attention (*MFG*, 155). But we learn that instruction in physic simply means practice in observing and understanding some divine order in the physical world. History at first seems to offer much more. Some late-eighteenth-century women believed that the study of history had the potential to hone their sense of judgment. "Of the Studies Suitable to Women" avers that from history one can learn that "women, in all ages, have had a great share in events"; by reading history, women can "reclaim their rights" as agents in the world (*MFG*, 156). Nina Baym points out that between the 1790s and 1820s, women studying history "would discover that the need for educated women was itself a historical phenomenon, since it had not existed in earlier times." Because male authorities encouraged women's study of history—just as they denounced women's reading of novels—it seems plausible that "the study of history may be theorized as an attempt by the establishment to secure the allegiance of this marginalized population." But Baym argues that it is wrong to conclude from this theorizing that reading and writing history disempowered women, partly by denying them the subversive power that novel reading and writing might confer. She notes that women who came of age during the American Enlightenment perceived the "logocentrism" of history reading and writing "as what in some sense it assuredly was: the key to their literary empowerment." In Baym's view, this "logocentric key" allowed "homebound" women to enter an ungendered public sphere of print. In this sphere, "out of their bodies," women could "participate in . . . woman-centered and general political discourses." Indeed, they "wrote confidently as women but, like men, consistent with their beliefs that neither mind nor language (by which mind makes itself known and effective) were sexed."[6]

If "Of the Studies Suitable to Women" starts out by proposing history reading and writing as ungendered and liberatory activities, it concludes by reversing field. According to the essay, women should engage in historical study in order to "drain from history useful lessons for their conduct in life" (*MFG*, 156). Good conduct for women, as we have already seen, does not entail having agency in important social situations, but instead involves bearing and raising the male citizens who can deliver persuasive oratories and perform significant political acts. At the end of the essay, we learn that "the most necessary and most natural" study for women is "the study of men" (*MFG*, 158). Knowledge of men will make women better, more powerful mothers, for it is through the study of men that women "make us do whatever they wish, and that the strongest is in fact governed by the weakest" (*MFG*, 159). The result of this study is knowledge that supposedly secures for women a governing authority over men that transcends the boundaries of domesticity, a kind of authority that frequently did not materially exist.

"Of the Studies Suitable to Women" is not the only essay that initially promises advocacy of women's education, only to fall short in its exposition of the subject. For example, "Remarks on Female Education,—by the Celebrated Fenelon" promises a discussion of schooling but in fact delivers only a diatribe, warning women against paying excessive attention to dress (*MFG*, 268–69).[7] Despite all assurances, then, the second edition of the *Flower Garden* seems discouraging of women's advanced rhetorical training. Tellingly, the second edition, like the first, includes no dialogues on being great or on receiving honor and applause for scholarship. Granted, the condensed version of Rush's "Thoughts [up]on Female Education" is carried into the second edition (*MFG*, 214–20). But omitted is the untitled extract that advances a platform for women's training in history and science, that argues most strenuously against ornamental learning, and that invokes the revolutionary image of "women breaking down the barriers of the tyrant man" (*MF-G*, 68).

Lynne Templeton Brickley suggests that as female academies grew in number, young college men would have assumed teaching posts in them.[8] An outcome of this male instruction, she argues, may have been a more challenging curriculum, one that included (alongside the ornamental arts) the kind of schooling Rush recommends. But we see the reverse tendency in the textbooks by Fraser that were designed for use in female academies and endorsed by progressives such as Rush. The *Assistant*, with its colonial roots, balances basic instruction in rhetoric, arithmetic, natural sciences, and religion, and actually provides more substantial learning for women. The *Monitor* lays the groundwork for restrictive education of women by promoting learning as conduct, the propriety of which is determined by gender. Finally, the *Flower Garden*, attending entirely to U.S. women's schooling, advocates a course of study not of the rigorous sort Rush recommends, but of a simpler, moral nature. It seems odd that Rush would endorse the *Flower Garden*, as it appears that Fraser adopted only half of the good doctor's advice. He seizes the idea that education and national purpose must be closely linked but ignores Rush's suggestions for an advanced curriculum.

Fraser's textbooks show how liberatory rhetoric can be used to advocate women's education without that education being, in fact, very liberating. What Fraser and textbook authors like him aimed to produce were not intellectual stars that would shine brightly like the women in Fraser's histories, but rather tidy little plots where the passive beauty of mental flowers might give pleasure to passersby. The garden metaphor obviously has its limits, as did the pedagogy Fraser sponsored. Fortunately for the new nation's rising generation, other authors could imagine women's education in terms that recognized more promise than peril in the liberatory rhetoric of the day.

Schooling Fictions: Hannah Webster Foster's Boarding School

In 1798, two years before the first edition of Fraser's *Mental Flower-Garden*, Hannah Webster Foster published her educational text for women, a novel entitled *The Boarding School; or, Lessons of a Preceptress to Her Pupils: consisting of Information, Instruction, and Advice, Calculated to improve the Manners, and form the Character of Young Ladies. To which is added, A Collection of LETTERS, written by the Pupils, to their Instructor, their Friends, and each other.* Brought out by, among others, Caleb Bingham, who himself had opened a girls' school in Boston and had compiled and published other late-eighteenth-century instructional texts, *The Boarding School* tells the story of an ideal institution and is dedicated to an audience no smaller than "the YOUNG LADIES of AMERICA," with the stated purpose of "improving" on the "many advantages of a good education."[9] Its publishing history, particularly when shown in relief to *The Coquette*'s, suggests to us that it was not as popular. Published first in Boston in 1798, it was reprinted again in 1829, the year after *The Coquette* saw its eleventh edition. Referred to by historians and literary historians as either a novel or a textbook, it refuses both categories. Sarah Emily Newton suggests a different category—conduct fiction—for *The Boarding School* and other similar works that blend "behavioral advice with fiction." Rather than any sustained narrative action, in conduct fiction "didactic anecdotes or tales satisfy narrative interest and at the same time hit home some precept of conduct so that the writers can deny writing the much maligned 'novel.'"[10] Not nearly as engaging as *The Coquette, The Boarding School,* when read as a novel, is of only slight interest to literary historians. Read as a textbook, what emerges is its great difference from grammars and readers used in formal institutions; it is this very difference that has much to teach rhetoricians.

The Boarding School contains two sections: the first detailing instruction, the second providing a collection of letters. *The Boarding School* opens with the preceptress, Mrs. Williams, delivering a series of lectures during the last week of the school year. Her lectures, which are labeled not as chapters but as blocks of school time (for example, Monday, P.M., Tuesday, A.M.), follow a rhetorical pattern resonant with the eighteenth-century periodical essay.

They contain statements of position and advice, followed by instructive anecdotes on subjects ranging from friendship, to arithmetic, to religion. Germane to our inquiry, one of the lectures is on reading, and another on writing. The instructional sequence comprises about one-third of the book. The rest contains letters written after the students have completed their term at Mrs. Williams's school, letters both to their preceptress and to each other.

Mrs. Williams's curriculum balances healthy physical exercise with instruction in manners, morals, and academic subjects: all are inseparable. Lessons on writing are inextricably bound with decorum and ethics. The many anecdotes about young girls raised by merchant fathers suggest that Mrs. Williams's pupils (and Foster's imagined audience) are largely from merchant families committed to making themselves virtuous citizens of the new republic. Raised in "the metropolis" of Boston, they have been removed to the rural retreat of Harmony-Grove, where they can learn the virtues of the simple, rural life (BS, 6). Education, the text suggests, is the only fixed point on the new horizon, a horizon shimmering in the variable light of religious, revolutionary, and legal rhetorics. In the world beyond that horizon, the ignorant and illiterate, no matter how virtuous, cannot hope to survive. At least one letter from Maria, Mrs. Williams's daughter, bears witness to the danger of illiterate females. Maria reports the case of an unnamed seventeen-year-old girl, a poor, single, illiterate mother who can find no work. She is taken into Harmony-Grove as a servant, but Maria plans to help her further by teaching her to read. This young woman, Maria writes her friend, provides an important lesson: "Her fate impresses, more forcibly than ever, on my mind, the importance of a good education, and the obligations it confers. Had you or I been subjected to the same ignorance, and the same temptations, who can say that we should have conducted better?" (BS, 230). Mrs. Williams's students must have the kind of education that can combat such verbal traps to preserve their reputations. Not that education always works, the text warns. Still, it is the only chance women really have.

Moreover, the message of personal responsibility is strong: women without educations can be excused if they fall from grace; those who know better cannot. As Maria puts it, "Contrasting our situation with her's, how much have *we* to account for, and how inexcusable shall *we* be, if we violate our duty, and forfeit our dignity, as reasonable creatures!" (BS, 230–31). Maria here echoes the sentiments of her friend Julia Greenfield, who has earlier taken the same stance: "I am generally an advocate for my own sex; but when they suffer themselves to fall a prey to seducers, their pusillanimity admits no excuse" (*BS*, 184). Julia's rhetoric is harsher than her actions, as we see when she relates the story of the well-educated "Clarinda," seduced by promises of marriage by Florimel. Julia, who has learned discretion at Harmony-Grove, writes of the situation but keeps the secret by using a pseudonym. Clarinda has discreetly retired to give birth at a house in the country (a tavern bought for just this purpose). Julia discovers Clarinda with babe in arms, listens to her tale, and hears her pain: "To-morrow my dear babe is to be taken from me! It is to be put to nurse, I know not where! All I am told is, that it shall be well taken care of! Constantly will its moans haunt my imagination, while I am deprived even of the hope of ministering to its wants; but must leave it to execrate the hour which gave it birth, and deprived it of a parent's attention and kindness" (*BS*, 191).

Clarinda's story represents just one of the sensational instructional narratives that constitute *The Boarding School*. To compensate for sensationalism, Foster frames the story with a moral purpose: thus sensationalism, in this typical eighteenth-century rhetorical turn, serves its opposite—morality. When Maria receives Julia's letter, she shows it to her mother. Mrs. Williams, always in search of new stories, decides to use the letter to instruct her new group of pupils, and when she does, we learn still more about the connection between composition, seduction, illiteracy, and illegitimacy. One of the students reacts to the story by bursting into tears, later revealing that she herself is the "illegitimate offspring of parents, whom I am told are people of fortune and fashion" (*BS*, 194). The child is left with people who want only the money, which they soon spend. Her support now comes from servitude; she receives no schooling and is the object of ridicule. Fortunately this illegitimate child encounters a happy family—a conspicuously literate one at that—on one of her errands selling herbs:

> In this manner [in servitude and disgrace] I lingered away my existence, till I was twelve years old; when going, one day, to the house of a gentleman in the neighbourhood, to which I was often sent to sell herbs, and other trifles, I was directed into the parlour, where the most beautiful sight in nature opened to my view; while the contrast between my own situation, and that of children blessed with affectionate parents, gave me the most painful sensations. The lady of the house was surrounded by her four sons, the eldest of whom was reading lessons, which she most pa-

thetically inculcated upon all. As the door was open, I stood some min-
utes unobserved; and was so delighted with the tender accents in which
her instructions were imparted, and the cheerful obedience with which
they were received, that I had no disposition to interrupt them. (*BS*,
195–96)

This story concludes happily, with the herb-selling child firmly ensconced in
the literate household. She has been "snatched . . . from obscurity and misery, and given . . . so many advantages for improvement" (*BS*, 197). Her wish
is that *her* story be relayed back to Clarinda, so that "she may be induced to
have compassion upon her defenceless offspring" (*BS*, 197).

These anecdotes, which we would characterize as "literacy narratives,"
offer several insights.[11] In them, we find an emerging middle-class ideal of
literacy: literate behavior can overcome disadvantaged birth and connect
one with prosperity and upward mobility. Literacy is a more than simply
something that promotes spiritual and moral growth: it is a means of advancement. We learn also that helping less-fortunate individuals to become
literate is a proper act of charity. But the ramifications of literacy go far
beyond the personal. The anecdotes also teach us about the relationship between civic responsibility and literacy, a relationship underwritten by gender. What the female child witnesses is the ideal of Republican Motherhood—that is, a mother instructing her sons. The female child has a place in
this scene, not with the sons as a student, but as a Republican-Mother-to-be.
To her will pass the task of instilling virtue in the next generation of men.
While the construct of Republican Motherhood (powerfully articulated by
essayist Judith Sargent Murray, whom we take up in chapter 3) might seem
to modern audiences to be restrictive, it did allow eighteenth-century U.S.
women to critique the educational system for women. By invoking the trope
of Republican Motherhood in her fiction, Foster is able to advocate reform,
reform dependent in part on women's composition practices. What education is available, she suggests, is simply insufficient to endow young women
with the dual powers of reason and virtue (feminine moral virtue, not male
civic virtue). It cannot fortify them against verbal seduction, against putting
stock in the wrong words. Moreover, left to negotiate the expanding world of
print without further training, women were apt to read the wrong sort of
texts, the result being, as Cathy Davidson posits, a different "kind of seduction."[12]

Published as it was in 1798, *The Boarding School* offers a glimpse of how writing instruction for women was imagined during the time when a new national purpose had set into motion the transformation of adventure schools into female academies. The schooling in literacy offered to the herb vendor-cum-adoptee by her new Republican Mother, ideal as it is, is not enough. The girl is sent to Mrs. Williams's Harmony-Grove, one of the new female academies, for further instruction.

Imagining Writing Instruction

Although *The Boarding School* reads in part like a novel, it also reads like a teacher training manual, covering pedagogical issues ranging from constructing a whole curriculum to handling daily lessons. It functions, perhaps, much as we expect teaching memoirs to function today.[13] The beginning of *The Boarding School* lays out the schedule at Harmony-Grove, one that Mrs. Williams will depart from only when she lectures in the last week. Mrs. Williams's curriculum, as we have pointed out, consists of an ideal balance of physical exercise, productive free time, moral lessons, and academic instruction. We quote at length to emphasize that reading and writing formed part of a tightly integrated unit in this imagined curriculum. We also believe readers might find interesting Mrs. Williams's authority and the fair and just use she makes of suspending it:

> The young ladies arose at five; from which they had two hours at their own disposal, till the bell summoned them at seven, to the hall, where, the ceremonies of the morning salutation over, they breakfasted together; their repast being seasoned with the unrestrained effusions of good humour and sociability. On these occasions, Mrs. Williams suspended the authority of the matron, that, by accustoming her pupils to familiarity in her presence, they might be free from restraint; and, feeling perfectly easy and unawed, appear in their genuine characters. By this means she had an opportunity of observing any indecorum of behaviour, or wrong bias; which she kept in mind, till a proper time to mention, and remonstrate against it; a method, the salutary effects of which were visible in the daily improvement of her pupils.
>
> The breakfast table removed, each took her needle-work, except one, who read some amusing and instructive book, for the benefit and entertainment of the rest. The subject was selected by Mrs. Williams, who conferred the reading upon them in rotation.

At twelve o'clock, they were dismissed till one, when dinner called them together, which was conducted in the same manner as the morning repast.

Having resumed their occupations, the reader of the day produced some piece of her own composition, either in prose, or verse, according to her inclination, as a specimen of her genius and improvement. This being submitted to Mrs. Williams's inspection, and the candid perusal and criticism of her companions; and the subject canvassed with great freedom of opinion, they withdrew from the talks of the day to seek that relaxation and amusement, which each preferred. No innocent gratification was denied them. The sprightly dance, the sentimental song, and indeed every species of pastime, consistent with the decorum of the sex, was encouraged, as tending to health, cheerfulness, and alacrity. (*BS*, 8–10)

Although education for women is much improved, the passage underscores a point worth repeating: advanced writing instruction for women is imagined as an activity thoroughly different from that which young men are to engage in.

But the fact that needlework, sprightly dancing, and physical exercise are part of the curriculum does not mean that writing instruction in *The Boarding School* is devoid of intellectual challenge. In addition to a concern for the "formation of the characters"—reminiscent of the colonial preoccupation with penmanship—we notice in Mrs. Williams's lecture on writing evidence of a growing sense that rules of propriety govern the production of prose and oratory. Even the most casual correspondence, it seems, must "be written with propriety and accuracy. The formation of the characters, the spelling, the punctuation, as well as the style and sense, must be attended to" (*BS*, 32). The starting point for writing is reading, where reading is a form of invention based on classical strategies. "The mind," she notes, "is obliged to exertion for materials to supply the pen. Hence it collects new stores of knowledge, and is enriched by its own labours. It imperceptibly treasures up the ideas, which the hand impresses" (*BS*, 30). Reading is thus defined as the process of accumulating intellectual treasures, with writing being the best mode for taking inventory of what one has stored away.

But her next section explains that this is not exactly the case. It turns out that arrangement is not merely a way to present stored-away ideas; it can also improve them. Further, revision is necessary to exercise and sharpen thought: "by repeatedly arranging and revising your expressions and opinions, you may daily improve them, and learn to think and reason properly on every occasion" (*BS*, 30). Mrs. Williams's major pedagogical tool is the commonplace book, where ideas can be noted and commented upon. Later, both ideas and commentary can be called up, rearranged, revised, in short, classically exercised. All of this rhetorical activity is meant to strengthen the power of thought and to provide "use" (*BS*, 30). Perhaps most important, instruction in writing occurs as a group activity, not an individual one. At Harmony-Grove, revision of compositions takes place within the circle of students, with each member benefiting from the oral critiques offered by others (a practice continued today in most creative writing workshops).

While the treasuring of useful knowledge provides the pedagogical basis for writing instruction at Harmony-Grove, Mrs. Williams shows that constructing ethos in writing is also important. In written prose, a woman must be careful to author the person she wants to be read. To write a letter is to offer "in some measure the picture of your hearts"; it is also to write "your futurity": "Your characters during life, and even when you shall sleep in the dust, may rest on the efforts of your pens. Beware then how you employ them. . . . Suffer not the expectation of secrecy to induce you to indulge your pens upon subjects, which you would blush to have exposed. In this way your characters may be injured, and your happiness destroyed" (*BS*, 33). A virtuous character is everything: behavior, speech, and writing—all must conform. The point is important enough to Mrs. Williams (and Foster) to warrant an instructive anecdote about two indiscreet female letter writers who correspond about a beau, Silvander. Although the situation is light— two young women writing frivolously about a suitor—the end of the anecdote reaches dramatic extremes. Silvander, mortified to find that "his name was used with so much freedom," sabotages them by passing their "letters among his acquaintance" (he, of course, first removes all references to himself) (*BS*, 35). His action, "fixed the stamp of ignominy on the correspondents; and their names and characters were rendered as ridiculous as scandal and malicious wit could desire" (*BS*, 34, 35). The consequences of poor composition are thus heightened. Writing for women is not about attaining high marks or economic success, but rather a matter of virtue and character. It can improve their possibilities for a good life or can ruin them. In this case, one of the young women "died in melancholy, regret, and obscurity" (*BS*, 35). And lest it seem that Mrs. Williams sympathizes with the unfairness of such a heavy tax on women's character, the last line of her *writing* lesson discourages such an interpretation: "However censurable the unjust and ungenerous conduct of Silvander may be deemed, yet no adequate excuse can be offered for the young ladies, who dishonored their pens and their talents by a most improper and unbecoming use of both" (*BS*, 35).

Given such an outcome, why would women in the late-eighteenth-century U.S. willingly risk writing? It is clear from Mrs. Williams's lecture that Foster felt a sense of possibility in writing as well as a fear of public reprisal. The paragraph on possibility is comparatively short—but it is also uncharacteristically ebullient. Wrapped in revolutionary rhetoric, the passage offers us a sense of the promise that women in the early nation felt: "Thrice blessed are we, the happy daughters of this land of liberty, where the female mind is unshackled by the restraints of tyrannical custom, which in many other regions confines the exertions of genius to the usurped powers of lordly man! Here virtue, merit, and abilities are properly estimated under whatever form they appear. Here the widely extended fields of literature court attention; and the American fair are invited to cull the flowers, and cultivate the expanding laurel" (*BS*, 31). Women could "cultivate the expanding laurel," not perhaps through writing the much disparaged novel (which, nonetheless, many did, often anonymously, and which Foster herself had done just a year before). According to Newton, although writers of novels themselves denounced the genre, "writers of conduct books are among the most vehement in attacking fiction for its heightening of female sensibility, its celebration of romantic passion, and its apparent encouragement of women to revolt against the constraints of traditional roles. . . . Some writers who might otherwise have been writing in the straight conduct mode turned to fiction because people were reading it and the writing of it was good business. But it is more than this. Novelists and conduct writers were to some degree in the same business—the constructing of a version of reality which dramatized the possibilities, limits, and consequences of female behavior. Conduct books supplied the typology upon which engaging fiction could be hung."[14] Women could gain respect and attention by writing poetry, essays, and, most important, letters. In the late eighteenth century, letters were an art that women could perfect, and did.

In letters (and in epistolary novels that decried the worthlessness of novels), women could speak in voices sophisticated, contradictory, and varied.

The Boarding School exemplifies the possibilities of the form. In the advice section of *The Boarding School,* Foster makes no complaints about women's place in the culture: she simply advises young women how to survive the dangers posed by drawing on their resources of reason and virtue. However, in the letters that follow, we see the critique. Written by both the preceptress and her students, the letters offer more examples of Mrs. Williams's intertwined advice about composition skills and morality. Although the monologic voice of the preceptress still is the weightiest, in the literary critiques that are scattered through the letters, we hear analysis and criticism of contemporary gender roles. With its "multiple female narrators," *The Boarding School* creates "a spectrum of the eighteenth-century woman's point of view effectively and dramatically."[15] That it is a spectrum necessarily limited in scope does not narrow the accomplishment. If we are to understand writing instruction for women in the late-eighteenth-century U.S., we must understand the important place of the letter as a central object of composition pedagogy.

Gender, Writing Instruction, and the Epistolary Form

The proliferation of letter-writing manuals after the mid-eighteenth century provides evidence of rhetorical education (in some cases advanced) conducted outside the sphere of formal education. Some of these manuals merely present letters calculated for a variety of likely occasions and "concerns of life" (and several unlikely, such as "*From the Lord of Strafford to his son, just before his Lordship's execution*"). More than a few of these manuals included an extensive apparatus describing how to compose original missives. Among these, *The Complete Letter-Writer* offers its readers advice on how to match audience to style, how to plan a letter (have things arranged "in your head" before writing), and how and when to revise ("a blot is by no means so bad as a blunder"). Competing texts present similar advice. A curious feature of some manuals is a rather obvious conflict in the gender of their implied readerships. For example, *The Complete Letter-Writer* advertises in its preface that it contains a sufficient number of letters "as to answer the purpose almost of every individual, from the boy at school to the secretary of state." Yet while this and other passages define the manual's readership as exclusively male, the model letters tell another story. A majority of letters in *The Complete Letter-Writer* are written by or addressed to women in a variety of stations: for example, *"From a young lady to her mamma, re-questing a favour," "From a young woman, just gone to service, to her mother at home,"* and *"To a young lady, cautioning her against keeping company with a gentleman of bad character."* The Complete Letter-Writer promises a functional experience rather than a literary one. The preface warns that although it contains letters "by eminent authors," readers will also "meet with many epistles of the lower class. These could not be omitted without deviating from the grand point in view, namely, General Utility." Still, even with the privileging of utility, instruction in style remains a substantial part of the lessons. The book counsels its readers to achieve a style that conveys ease; it eschews "all pomp of words."[16]

These letter-writing guides prove to be just one kind of composition text in the epistolary mode. *The Boarding School* makes reference to a very popular work by Mrs. Chapone, *Letters on the Improvement of the Mind*, first published in London but well received in the states as well. Mrs. Chapone's book is constituted almost exclusively of moral instruction presented in the form of letters to her niece. The last fifth, however, departs from moral instruction and describes an academic course of study for women, a course based on recommended readings in geography and history. Works such as *The Boarding School* or Rowson's *Mentoria* participate in this tradition but add to it a "novel" dimension, blurring generic distinctions between fiction and nonfiction.

Following Mrs. Williams's initial lectures, *The Boarding School* shifts into epistolary mode. The letters the women write serve double duty, dispensing advice of the kind that Mrs. Chapone offers and acting as models, much like we would see in *The Complete Letter-Writer* and similar texts. When the students leave Harmony-Grove, letters supplant commonplace books as the primary pedagogical tool. The young women continue their lessons in writing, sending poems or brief compositions along with or as part of their correspondence. These letters are not simple in form and are not merely utilitarian, at least not in any immediate commercial sense. They embed essays, poems (both copied and written for the occasion), and reviews of books. The women study the form of published letters, compose their own letters, and include in them critiques of those penned by others. Some critiques center on the desired form of letter writing—treating it as an art judged on its style and substance. Others address the struggle between the sexes in the epistolary form. They often include attempts to persuade men that women are capable of intellectual pursuits.

Letters, then, are not just an exercise or duty, but a crucial, conversational link to others: female friends, male friends, and parents. They are an engaging means of "enjoying intercourse with those from whom you are far removed, which is a happy substitute for personal conversation" (*BS*, 32). As conversation, care must be taken to keep up correspondence: "Never omit noticing the receipt of letters, unless you mean to affront the writers. Not to answer a letter without being able to align some special reason for the neglect, is equally unpardonable as to keep silence when conversation is addressed to you in person" (*BS*, 32). Tone is an important consideration: not only "formality" and "bombast," but "all affectation . . . should be laid aside" (*BS*, 32). Just as advised in *The Complete Letter-Writer, The Boarding School* suggests that the proper tone balances "ease, frankness, simplicity, and sincerity." Letters are a public, social form of discourse, with no quarter for a private or personal voice.

Indeed, to engage in too private a conversation—that is, to see letters only as an engagement of everyday and local information—is judged a compositional defect. Letters are meant to be conversational in tone, but that conversation is meant to be overheard. In a letter to one of her classmates, Caroline Littleton critiques the published letters of the marchioness de Sévigné: "They are replete with local circumstance, which, to indifferent readers, are neither amusing nor interesting. True, the style is easy and sprightly; but they are chiefly composed of family matters, such as relate to her own movements and those of her daughter; many of which are too trifling a nature to be ranked in the class of elegant writing" (*BS*, 125). Here audience and subject matter outweigh style as rhetorical concerns. In the end, however, Caroline suspends her judgment of the marchioness, because she admits she has only read the first two volumes of her work. (This reference to quantity of reading is not unusual. The language of treasuring and storing knowledge necessarily leads Mrs. Williams's students to read through enormous amounts of material in order to locate the few pearls that would reward them for sustained, advanced learning.)

With all this forward-looking advice, Harmony-Grove is hardly a "finishing" school for Mrs. Williams's students. Instead, their lessons are a point of departure for lifelong learning, but learning that must take place without the discipline imposed by school. Letters, it seems, may prove an adequate substitute for that discipline. Ideally, women's reading after their school years was to be guided by recommendations from a network of friends, linked informally by their letter writing. In such a network, Julia Greenfield recommends Mrs. Chapone's *Letters on the Improvement of the Mind,* the last fifth of which prescribes such classics as Virgil and Homer (in translation). Sophia Manchester recommends that Caroline Littleton read *Bennet's Letters,* passing along advice from her mother: they "will richly reward your labour. You have, indeed, completed your school education; but you have much yet to learn. Improvements in knowledge are necessarily progressive. The human mind is naturally active and eager in pursuit of information; which we have various and continual means of accumulating" (*BS,* 178). In what becomes a common refrain in fictions about women's schooling, Foster argues that it is only before marriage that women are "free from those domestic cares and avocation," that they have all the time needed to lay in an ample store of knowledge. After marriage, study time would be curtailed, though not entirely eliminated: "The duties and avocations of our sex will not often admit a close and connected course of reading. Yet a general knowledge of the most necessary subjects may undoubtedly be gained, even in our leisure hours" (*BS,* 202–3). To make the most of such leisure, then, works should be read, reread, critiqued, and recommended (or not) in letters, thereby ensuring that others in one's epistolary network will not read the wrong books.

The epistolary genre provides for women a writing space in which they could practice and expand their rhetorical talents, where they could develop confidence as writers. Foster imagines young women self-assured enough to critique even such an accomplished master as Pope. While one student, Caroline Littleton, acknowledges Pope's reputation and concedes, "there are good sentiments and judicious observations, interspersed in his letters," she finally faults him for being all style and no substance: "the greater part" of his letters "have little other merit than what arises from the style" (*BS,* 126). Realizing the boldness of her stance, she does not apologize, but instead invites her friend to create a like one:

> Perhaps you will charge me with arrogance, for presuming to criticize, much more to condemn, publications which have so long been sanctioned by general approbation. Independent in opinion, I write without

reserve, and censure not any one who thinks differently. Give me your sentiments with the same freedom upon the books which you honor with a perusal, and you will oblige your affectionate

CAROLINE LITTLETON. (*BS*, 125–26)

Caroline's move might seem less intrepid (and less "independent in opinion") when read in conjunction with *The Complete Letter-Writer*, in which Pope's work is called "too elaborate and ornamental." One of the sample letters in this text quips: "let me tell Mr. Pope, that letters, like beauties, may be overdrest."[17] Still, what passes as "independent" response is marked by Foster with positive value. Not seasoned critics, Caroline—and Foster's readers—are young women who explore existing ideas that, if not new, are at least new to them and so still worth debating.

Caroline's friend Cleora Partridge takes her critical self-assurance a step further, formulating a defense of a woman's right to have an opinion about what she reads and learns. Cleora's father, it seems, reads Caroline's critique of Pope and the marchioness and finds the young woman's confident voice amusing. Cleora recounts: "He took it [the letter] out of my hand, and read it; then returning it with the smile of approbation; I think, said he, that your correspondent has played the critic very well. Has she played it justly, Sir? said I. Why, it is a long time, said he, since I read the Marchioness de Sevignè's letters. I am not, therefore, a judge of their merit. But, with regard to Pope, I blame not the sex for retaliating upon him; for he always treated them satirically. I believe revenge was no part of my friend's plan, said I. She is far superior to so malignant a passion; though, were she capable of seeking it, it would be in behalf of her sex" (*BS*, 127). Cleora thus assumes the guise of the reasonable critic, one who is beyond such a base motive as retaliation. Even in the face of acknowledged misogyny, the critic can remain dispassionate. This is only one of several places in the letters that women respond to a prevalent judgment of them, namely, that they are passionate, not reasonable, and that their tastes are inclined toward the trivial.

In letters, Mrs. Williams's students practice their defense by constructing rhetorical arguments that refute the stereotype. In one example, Anna Williams writes to her sister Maria after returning from commencement ceremonies at Cambridge, where she has heard a young (male) graduate discourse at length on the subject of "female garb" (*BS*, 142). In response to this speech, Anna employs irony to rhetorical effect, a device that many critics (those predating revisionist literary histories, anyway) believe the didactic and sensational novelists incapable of. To her sister, Anna remarks that she "never knew before that dress was a classical study; which I now conclude it must be, or it would not have exercised the genius of some of the principal speakers on this public occasion!" (*BS*, 142). The rest of the letter posits that one can find fault with both male *and* female dress. Finally, she concludes on a conservative note, an ideological shift not unusual in Foster's works (or Chapone's). Women, Anna concedes, must be particularly careful about conventions of dress, so that they will not conform to male stereotypes.

Likewise, *The Boarding School* takes issue with the popular logic that women's trivial conversations and tendency to gossip reflect their naturally defective and inferior intellects. Matilda Fielding rebuts this assertion by drawing on a familiar counterargument that posits that women are idle and vacuous only because men make them so by restricting their access to knowledge: "Our sex have been taxed as defamers. I am convinced, however, that they are not exclusively guilty; yet, for want of more substantial matter of conversation, I fear they too often give occasion for the accusation!" (*BS*, 151). Part of the responsibility for women's behavior thus rests with the society at large, a patriarchal society that has failed to educate them properly. And part remains with women themselves. Matilda's stance surely reflects an argument familiar in Foster's day, wedged as it is between traditional and progressive positions on women's conduct.

In yet another anecdote from *The Boarding School,* Sophia Manchester tells of having to educate the brother of a friend, Sylvia Star. The two young women encounter Sylvia's "studious" brother, Amintor, in his library (*BS*, 204). It seems a positive gesture that he welcomes their visit and offers to loan them books—until he selects from his shelf those titles he believes the women will enjoy. The taste acquired at Harmony-Grove now comes into play. Amintor first offers Sterne's *Sentimental Journey.* "You have indeed mistaken my taste," Sophia tells Amintor, offering the critique, "Wit, blended with indelicacy, never meets my approbation" (*BS*, 204). Amintor smiles in reply and, judging her "serious," hands her a volume of sermons—actually ironic sermons, presumably also by Sterne, which she also declines (*BS*, 205). After turning away Swift as well, she takes up a volume of *American Biography,* in which she finds an agreeable passage on Christopher Columbus (*BS*, 206). Mrs. Williams's students are influenced, after all, by

Mrs. Chapone's recommendation that history has the most wisdom to afford. The reference to the Columbus passage indicates that they have not adopted Mrs. Chapone's attitudes toward colonization: "you will find the accounts of the discovery and conquest of America very entertaining, though you will be shocked at the injustice and cruelty of its conquerors. But with which of the glorious conquerors of mankind must not humanity be shocked!" Furthermore, "In America, the first European conquerors found nature in great simplicity—society still in its infancy—and consequently the arts and sciences yet unknown: so that the faculty, with which they overpowered these poor innocent people, was entirely owing to their superior knowledge in the arts of destroying."[18] (French colonization, as all things French, she views favorably.)

True, Mrs. Williams's students might appear overly cautious, even prudish, in their reading tastes. But we learn constantly in *The Boarding School* that more than taste is involved in decisions about what to read. In order to convince men of women's seriousness, women had to remain serious in the face of men's doubt and ridicule. Thus Matilda Fielding will recommend "Millot's Elements of Ancient and Modern History" and suggest that her friend Harriot Henly reread it (*BS*, 201). Though it may be tedious, she suggests (sounding very much like Mrs. Chapone), it is important reading, especially for women who must overcome their aversion to particulars, a feat accomplished in part by using writing as an aid to memory and comprehension.

The Harmony-Grove graduates are serious students, but they are not to their own minds scholars, nor would Mrs. Chapone or the fictional Mrs. Williams want them to be so. Sophia Manchester writes to her classmate Caroline Littleton: "I do not wish to pursue study as a profession, nor to become a learned lady; but I would pay so much attention to it, as to taste the delights of literature, and be qualified to bear a part in rational and improving conversation" (*BS*, 182). The aim of a woman's education is twofold: to be an interesting conversant, even in the company of men, and to be a teacher of young children. The strongest proponents of women's education feared what might happen if women became not merely students, not merely domestic pedagogues, but more. Here, for example, are Mrs. Chapone's ideas on the subject, the very Mrs. Chapone whose London *Letters* recommends a rigorous course in ancient and modern history. Such a course is safe for women, it turns out, so long as it is grounded in translations, not in the original Greek or Latin. Though the passage begins with praise for those few ladies who know "the learned languages," it soon evolves into a complaint against the female pedant. Such a fear is common as well in the early U.S., even as the nation seeks to turn its "diamonds in the rough" into polished, educated jewels:

> As to the learned languages, though I respect the abilities and application of those ladies, who have attained them, and who make a modest and proper use of them, yet I would not advise you—or any woman who is not strongly impelled by a particular genius—to engage in such studies. The labour and time which they require are generally incompatible with our nature and proper employments: the real knowledge which they supply is not essential, since the English, French, or Italian tongues afford tolerable translations of all the most valuable productions of antiquity, besides the multitude of original authors which they furnish—and these are much more than sufficient to store your mind with as many ideas as you will know how to manage. The danger of pedantry and presumption in a woman, of her exciting envy in one sex and jealousy in the other—of her exchanging the graces of imagination for the severity and preciseness of a scholar, would be, I own, sufficient to frighten me from the ambition of seeing my girl remarkable for learning.[19]

Women of the period—in the U.S. particularly—labored mightily to attain higher levels of learning, to tap into the spirit of revolution that pervaded government and the law. But they did so carefully, mindful of the need to convince critics that their hard-won intellect would not imperil postrevolutionary culture.

Much more so than Fraser, Foster presents this vision of women's achievement in a fresh form that is neither purely expository nor purely novelistic. This hybridity may give some readers pause. Let us stress, then, that our main concern is not whether Foster accurately portrays the new female academies of her day, although we are interested in their histories and believe them important. Instead we ask of Foster more general questions. Would letters have been an essential part of any curriculum? Did young women diligently read their recommended course of studies, record entries in commonplace books, and forward their observations, queries, critiques, and compositions to friends? Probably so, but not in the way idealized by Foster. That is why we turn to sources such as *The Complete Letter-Writer,* which help us read something closer to actual practice into Foster's narrative. To take one example, the *Letter-Writer* contains numerous models for composing letters that apologize for correspondence that is late, absent, or trivial. The very first letter is *"From a brother at home to a sister, abroad on a visit, complaining of her not writing."* And others follow: *"From a daughter to her mother, by way of excuse, for having neglected to write to her," "A letter of excuse for silence, and assurance it was not out of disrespect," "Miss J——, in answer to Mrs. L——, making an apology for not answering her letter sooner."*[20] Mrs. Williams's fictional students may have been perfect correspondents, but those who turned to *The Complete Letter-Writer* obviously were not.

What Mrs. Williams's curriculum allows us to consider that *The Complete Letter-Writer* does not are questions that often escape us when we study only "factual" primary source material. As Jacqueline Jones Royster theorizes in her study of nineteenth-century African American women, historical reconstruction of women's composition practices—or the practices of any group whose efforts have been loosely archived or erased—can be enriched by "keep[ing] the eyes and the mind open for the imaginable, that is, for opportunities to make connections and draw out likely possibilities."[21] Such an "imaginative" narrative methodology proves instructive for composition scholars teasing out the possibilities of a limited archive. But this method is equally instructive when applied to fiction by authors describing what they envision as possible, or to forms of nonfiction such as conduct books, which, as Nicole Tonkovich reminds us, might better represent what was desired than what was.[22] The fictive, the imaginary, understood in this light, is as powerful an artifact of history as traditional "fact"; the imaginary elaborates the bare outlines of truth. Our illusions and dreams, a twentieth-century author reminds us, are as much a part of us as our *"bones and flesh and memory."* The substantial and the insubstantial both influence our actions. And just as the realm of fact, traditionally understood, is not removed from politics, neither is the realm of the imaginary. As Henry Giroux articulates, our aspirations and dreams "are neither ideologically neutral nor politically innocent."[23]

Such twentieth-century views hold just as much credence for the postrevolutionary period, a time in which a new group of leaders and those they governed were preoccupied with erasing a dual history of colonization (erasing roles both as colonists and colonizers) and dreaming a new republic. Although they did not hold legislative, judicial, or executive posts, women writers were deeply involved in the project of imagining what the United States might become. The liberatory rhetoric surrounding the Revolution prompted women of this newly declared nation to imagine how they could best fit themselves to a new national purpose. Their fictions might just as easily be understood to point to what was *not* happening in women's schooling. Each representation of the possible also implies what was absent; each suggests, "See what we could be—as a sex, as a nation." Perhaps it is coincidental that the boarding school genre emerges at the same time that teachers such as New York schoolmaster Donald Fraser were compiling textbooks that increasingly restricted the scope of women's learning. And then again, perhaps not.

3 A Commonplace Rhetoric
Judith Sargent Murray's Margaretta Narrative

It is not possible to educate children in a manner which will render them too beneficial to society.

Judith Sargent Murray, The Gleaner (1798)

⤳ *Writing with an earnestness* born of the American Revolution, Judith Sargent Murray, essayist and playwright, shared her compatriots' faith in the power of rhetoric and felt strongly that this power could and should be claimed by women. Indeed, Murray suggested that the Revolution provided the impetus for her ideas about gender equality.[1] But as we discussed in the introduction, Murray also shared her compatriots' fear of sophistry, their fear that rhetoric misused might turn an illiterate populace against republican virtue. To ensure its effectiveness, republican rhetoric had to be safeguarded. For Murray the political essayist, a national language standard, a common polished tongue, could provide this necessary safeguard, could mitigate the ills of sophistry, and could ensure the success of the Columbian experiment. Yet for Murray the fiction writer and playwright, the need to hew to a language with formal standards is not so evident. *The Gleaner: A Miscellaneous Production* (1798) mixes speech registers and extant literary genres so much that the finished three-volume book contradicts the very language policies she articulates in the political essays contained therein. In the style of *The Spectator, The Female Spectator,* and *The Rambler, The Gleaner* includes Murray's serialized work from *The Massachusetts Magazine* (familiar essays, historical and political essays, reviews, and brief fictional letters) as well as two complete plays, *Virtue Triumphant* and *The Traveller Returned.*[2]

To get a sense of Murray's "miscellaneous production," one need only glance at *The Gleaner*'s opening chapters. While the first chapter introduces a *Spectator*-like male author of familiar essays, the second self-reflexively incorporates a didactic narrative typical of contemporary productions by and for women. Chapters 3 and 4 return to essays, familiar and ironic, on contemporary issues. Chapters 5 and 6 shift course again, returning to the self-reflexive strategy that links the essays with the didactic narrative in progress. And so *The Gleaner* rambles fitfully across the fertile loam of late-eighteenth-century topics and genre.[3]

Today Murray is likely to be read (if she is read at all) as an early American dramatist or, more likely still, as a novelist, the author of what has come to be known as the "Margaretta narrative," a didactic fiction Murray interspersed among her serialized essays. The narrative focuses on the life of a young woman, Margaretta Melworth, who is introduced in the second installment as a reader of the very magazine in which her life story will appear. That story is penned by her adoptive father, Mr. Vigillius, who has just begun publishing serial installments under the name "the Gleaner." He provides a brief sketch of Margaretta's early life: she is presumed to be orphaned, is raised by an aunt in South Carolina, and upon the aunt's death is taken into the Vigillius family. Several installments later, a number of fictional characters voice complaints in letters about the subjects and style of the Gleaner's essays, and all clamor for more information about Margaretta. Two of the male readers play into Murray's satire of the early national marriage market; they seem concerned with Margaretta only as a possible mate. Bellamour, writing from Dissipation Hall, is convinced that Margaretta (and a few of the acres that go with her) would help him *"reform, live within bounds,"* that with her help he would "make . . . a very good sort of a husband."[4] Timothy Plodder, on the other hand, has all the acres he needs but, at age fifty, has been too busy to have children to furnish heirs for his estate. He is, consequently, in search of an *"industrious,* and *uniformly economical,* but also extremely *docile"* wife, and wonders if Margaretta might suit him (56).

As one might expect, marriage is a central topic for writers interested in revolutionary possibilities for young women. But it is typical of Murray's interests, and the interests of others in the early national period, that another topic takes precedence—education. Thus, three other letters inquire not about whether Margaretta is marriageable, but rather about whether her successful education could provide a model for other young women. Again, though presented as caricatures, these inquirers represent the middling classes of people who Murray thought posed possibilities for and threats to the new republic. George and Deborah Seafort, though not "fond of an uncertain navigation" of the Gleaner's essays, are impressed with the job he has done with the "little yawl belayed along side [his] anchorage," and they look to him for a plan to anchor their own child's education (50, 52). Monimia Castalio, a motherless semiliterate who has been forbidden by her father from reading novels or attending plays, hopes to find some "pretty *historiettes*" that might provide the instruction she is lacking at home (53). Finally, Rebecca Aimwell, writing from the "Saloon of Solitude," tells of being orphaned herself and of an education "much neglected" (54). Her husband now dead, she asks the Gleaner for more news of Margaretta so that she might have a plan of education for her daughter, the only thing that still "attaches me to humanity" (54). *The Gleaner* uses language variation and dialect to illustrate the range of the eager, energetic populace that needed educating, that needed the knowledge necessary for a successful republic.

Prompted by imagined voices of republican readers, Murray has the Gleaner willingly agree to talk about education, both of boys and girls, a topic recurrent throughout the volume. In a later chapter the Gleaner argues that education for boys retains a skewed focus in a new economy not anchored to a landed aristocracy: too many boys expect "opulence and respectability" (134). But, the Gleaner observes, someone must still do the work of building the new nation. While many feel disdain for printers and trunk makers, the Gleaner suggests that these are respectable professions (135, 137). He holds up Benjamin Franklin as the example of a man destined to be great, rising from his humble beginnings as a printer to become an important statesman. For these reasons Murray opposes instruction in classical languages, which she sees as "ornamental," particularly if those languages receive more attention than English, which she views as "useful," the language "in which they are destined to *converse, transact business,* and *adjust their pleasurable pursuits*" (294). Murray presents English not as the best political choice, but as the "natural" choice of the new nation (295). As a child Murray apparently appealed unsuccessfully to her parents to be allowed to study Latin; by the time she formulates her *Gleaner* essays, she has come to agree with her parents that Latin would be of little use to girls in the new republic or, as she extends their reasoning, to boys.[5] So that she not appear parochial, Murray argues against instruction in classical languages by, ironically, appealing to classical authority: "Neither the Greeks nor the Romans incumbered themselves with a variety of tongues; their own language always obtained a just *pre-eminence*" (295). Murray thus qualifies her principle that there is no such thing as too much education. There is no such thing as too much education, provided that education is rendered through English: "I should not be satisfied, if my sons and daughters did not speak, read, and write English, *grammatically, critically,* and even *elegantly*" (294–95). All educated citizens of the new republic should be able to "readily decline a noun," easily identify "cases nominative, possessive, and objective," and effortlessly "follow the verb through number, person, mood, and tense" (294). To make clear this point, Murray sketches the story of the well-born Leontius, educated by the best, most erudite preceptors in Latin from the age of six. Such schooling unfits him for any productive role in the new republic:

> If he assayed the, to him, arduous talk of entertaining his friends with an English book, false pronunciation, emphasis, and accent, were visible in every paragraph; comma's assumed the distinction of full stops, while the finely turned period lost all its beauty: Colons, semicolons, notes of interrogation and administration, these were all promiscuously huddled together; and while by one continued monotony of sound, ideas were jumbled, and the auditory nerve disgusted, it was in vain that his hearers fatigued themselves by an expectation of the sentiment of an author. Harmonious accents, delicate inflexions of voice, and that animation, or energetic propriety, which is the vehicle of intelligence—of these he had no idea; he seemed in effect the determined foe of good reading, and he ought to have been arraigned as the murderer of sense. (297–98)

Leontius, we learn, is unqualified even to teach his own children. His potential has been wasted by a faulty education.

But if there are problems with the education of young boys—namely, that they are being schooled on Old World models—they pale in comparison to the problems of educating girls. Both problems, according to Murray, are part of the same tendency: too much attention to the ornamental, insufficient attention to the useful. Of course, in the case of young women, problems are further compounded by the narrow scope of what is considered adequate female knowledge. Murray later in *The Gleaner* develops her ideas in four installments that function as a coda to her 1790 "On the Equality of the Sexes" and to Mary Wollstonecraft's 1792 *A Vindication of the*

Rights of Woman. In these later chapters, the narrow strictures of female education are much more forcefully addressed, even supported with testimony, as if being presented to a jury, as if the crime of narrowing female education and underestimating female accomplishments has been brought to bar. Specifically, she lists and elaborates ten premises:

> *First,* Alike capable of enduring hardships.
> *Secondly,* Equally ingenious, and fruitful in resources.
> *Thirdly,* Their fortitude and heroism cannot be surpassed.
> *Fourthly,* They are equally brave.
> *Fifthly,* They are as patriotic.
> *Sixthly,* As influential.
> *Seventhly,* As energetic, and as eloquent.
> *Eighthly,* As faithful, and as persevering in their attachments.
> *Ninthly,* As capable of supporting, with honour, the toils of government. And
> *Tenthly,* and *Lastly,* They are equally susceptible of every literary acquirement. (711)

Underlying these ideas is her thesis. Given women's history, a history of extreme containment, it is not surprising that "they evince so little stability of character" (709). In the new postrevolutionary era, the Gleaner predicts, women will enjoy equality and will experience a broader range of opportunity, with the satisfying result of composing a nation of women who have cultivated reason.

Murray has her masculine Gleaner willingly provide information for what is "rather an extensive plan of education" (58). But having introduced the subject, he shifts responsibility and authority for Margaretta's education to Mary, his model republican wife. The proper spokesperson for women's education, Murray implies by this narrative strategy, is not a man such as Benjamin Rush, but a woman, a Republican Mother. Like Foster's curriculum at Harmony Hall, Mary Vigillius's plan is meant to construct a foundation for ongoing learning. The familiar cultivation metaphor establishes the principle: in early education the "seeds of knowledge might be implanted in the tender mind" so that later in life there is a strong predilection for continued self-instruction (58). Such instruction is particularly valuable in a climate of economic instability, for "unless the faculties of the mind are deranged," acquired knowledge cannot "be lost" (59). But in the Margaretta narrative, female scholarship, valuable as it is, is curbed, taking its place in the hierarchy of Christian principles (for Murray, Universalist Christian principles) and of social custom (including woman's most traditional role as companion for man).[6] In the concrete construction of Margaretta, the narrative penned by the author of the "On the Equality of the Sexes" resembles surprisingly the work of Donald Fraser, complete with cultivation metaphors of "mental flower gardens" so relished by the latter: "But while we have been assiduously employed in cultivating the mind of Margaretta, we have been endeavouring to eradicate the seeds of that over-weening self conceit, which, while it would induce an ostentatious exhibition of those talents, natural, or adventitious, which she may possess—like a rampant weed would impede and overshadow the growth of every virtue" (63). Finally, the Vigilliuses' plan is for Margaretta to be a pleasing companion for some worthy future husband, a wife and mother capable of using persuasion for uplifting purposes.

Elsewhere the Gleaner diverts attention from such a single-minded focus on educating wives and mothers. He argues that this focus plays into fears that intelligent young women will become "*old maid*[s]" if they do not work hard to avoid remaining single (138). While this fear results in the obvious social problems—women married to insolvent, deserting, or abusive men—it also perverts women's education, redirecting the emphasis from civic virtue and use to, for lack of a better term, "man-getting" (excessive attention to ornament, to scheming, to flirtation). While the Gleaner would like to see girls taught every proper accomplishment, he would also have them taught independence, industry, and order. Above all, the Gleaner stresses, women must "*reverence themselves,*" must be willing to remain single and find their own social use rather than marry badly and risk debasement (139). He offers as an illustration the story of two sisters, Misses Penelope and Helen Airy. The older of the two, Helen, declares herself "a mortal enemy to reflection" and leads a life of dissipation (142). She is idle, does not wake until late in the morning, occasionally plays the pianoforte, is obsessed with clothing, and spends time with bad suitors. We know this about Helen because she confides it in a letter to her younger sister, Penelope. By contrast, Penelope is studious and invests her money wisely. She has inherited some of this money, but the rest she earns steadily from her own industry, sewing—enough so that she can supply her own needs and offer what is extra to charity. Penelope does not fear becoming an old maid. She instead looks to her Aunt

Dorothy, a wonderful model of the single life. We learn that, in the long run, Penelope ends up happily married, and the dissipated Helen ends up the old maid, dependent on her sister. Single women, this parable illustrates, can make for a better citizenry, particularly if they are skilled money managers who understand the importance of quietly practiced charity.

The Gleaner stresses this point as he tells of the experiment he conducted to test Margaretta's ability to manage a modest purse of her own. He is pleased to learn, by way of his wife, that Margaretta has in essence invested the small sum he gives her to improve the lot of a poor family she comes to know. Having noticed on a visit to an intemperate, impoverished household a small girl intently studying a spelling book, Margaretta makes it her responsibility to improve their lives and foster the girl's budding literacy. In order to make the drunken mother a more productive member of her family and nation, Margaretta buys her a spinning wheel; for the girl's father, she provides business supplies. The girl herself, Margaretta sends to school. All of this charity is performed quietly; rumors, rather than Margaretta's letters, bring the story back to the Vigilliuses.

Murray's conception of Republican Motherhood is elastic enough to refer to any woman—single or married, with children or childless—who assumes maternal roles or helps others do so. The Gleaner offers as the "perfect model of the maternal character" a childless woman who, over the forty years of her childless marriage, took in no fewer than twenty orphaned girls (203). Indeed, Murray places the burden for this republican maternal charity on younger women who are typically better educated and have more opportunities to act effectively in their families and communities (703–5). She is especially anxious that women of previous generations, denied the "aids" of education, should not be faulted for their marginal literacy (718). She raises to near heroic status women of advanced age who seek out literacy instruction. In one of the later essays that extend Murray's "On the Equality of the Sexes" argument, the Gleaner offers a nonfictional account of a Massachusetts woman who "grew up almost wholly uneducated" but who worked "diligently to remedy the evil, and soon made great proficiency in writing, and in arithmetic" (728). As a result of her learning, she becomes "a complete *husbandwoman*," possessed of "a vast stock of general knowledge" (729). She is self-sustaining in her pursuits. But more than this, she contributes in important ways to the well-being of her community: she con-

tributes herbs for medicinal purposes and has developed expertise in cultivating fruit trees "from which, gentlemen, solicitous to enrich their fruitgar-
dens, or ornament their parterres, are in the habit of supplying themselves"
(729).

Finally, the Gleaner recommends a course of study for women that, by
early national standards, is ambitious in scope and in aim—to make
women independent in the event they should be confronted with the choice
of a bad partner or no choice at all, or become widowed. The Gleaner underscores the need for women to be capable of achieving financial independence: "the term, *helpless widow*, might be rendered as unfrequent and
inapplicable as that of *helpless widower*" (727–28). Some of the "branch[es]
of improvement" fall clearly under our images of finishing schools: needlework, French, reading in a charming fashion, neat and easy penmanship,
simple clothing design, music (preferably pianoforte), poetry, and sketching
(drawing) (59). But much of the suggested course of study moves beyond
the ornamental: a young woman should study to be "a good accomptant";
she should know geography, narrative history, and chronology (60). Indeed,
the largest blocks of time should be devoted to these endeavors. History requires systematic study, at least one hour a day, and this just for reading. After reading, another hour should be spent conversing and still another writing, presumably about the subjects taken up in the course of reading. As in
The Boarding School, epistolary writing (to figures real or imagined) assumes
a crucial role in the narrative as a whole and in the imagined curriculum.

In *The Gleaner*, Margaretta practices for the day she will be separated
from her mother.[7] Mother and daughter both retire to their respective
rooms and begin an epistolary correspondence. There are rules to the exercises: nothing in the letters can be discussed face-to-face, the letters are delivered between mother and daughter by a servant, and the letters cannot be
so private that they cannot be shared with others. When her friend Miss
Hayden pokes fun at the mother-daughter correspondence, Margaretta reacts by refusing to show the letter to her friend, a decision she is sure her
mother will support, especially since Miss Hayden presumably is deficient in
language skills (she cannot spell, reads poorly, and displays faulty elocution). But far from winning her mother's endorsement, Margaretta receives
a severe upbraiding: letters should openly circulate, at the very least, among
female friends. The epistolary exercises also establish the relationship be-

tween ethical criticism of fictional characters, which is permissible, even desirable, and criticism of actual acquaintances. Mary writes back, remonstrating Margaretta for the indiscretion of criticizing Miss Hayden. She tells Margaretta that she has no "right, either to arraign or condemn" Miss Hayden—nor anyone else, for that matter (339). Fearful of losing her mother's approval, Margaretta apologizes to Miss Hayden. Now the letter functions as it should: she shows Miss Hayden the missive, who in turns shows it to her mother, who in turn comments on it in a way that is instructive for both young women.

Still the letter episode has not been played to its fullest. The breach between Mary and her mother is narrated as a breach between lovers, complete with the effusiveness of a lover's discourse. After Margaretta reconciles with the Haydens, she writes again to her mother, begging forgiveness. Promptly, Mary writes back, restoring her approval and her physical affection:

> Come to me, my angel child—come to me immediately. . . . Upon an occasion so every way answerable to my fondest hopes, we will dispense with forms—we need not recur by words to an affair, the termination of which has filled my bosom with unutterable joy—words will not be necessary; and if they were, I should not have it in my power to command them. But my eyes, so lately darting the chilling glances of reserve, are now humid with the gush of tenderness, and they shall speak every thing my Margaretta wishes—every thing she so richly merits. Come to me, my best girl, and let me imprint upon that lovely cheek, the fondest kiss I have ever yet bestowed—we will mingle some delicious tears, and I will clasp to my bosom, with augmented complacency, as the richest boon with Heaven can bestow, my sweet tempered, my virtuous child! (347)

Interestingly, Mary has directed this whole romance of Republican Motherhood and has created this emotional pitch in Margaretta *intentionally,* for the purpose of educating her daughter. Such manipulation, which is finally effective, stands in contrast to the strong words Murray reserves for the "spare the rod" school of childrearing. The Gleaner argues strenuously against punishing children as criminals for words mispronounced, sentences forgotten, or falsehoods told. Using that favorite cultivation metaphor, the Gleaner decries not just the ethics of using physical punishment or overly critical words, but also the effectiveness: "Severity will always operate upon the opening mind, like chilling blasts of winter upon the tender plant; it

droops its blighted head, its powers are rendered torpid, its strength is pros-
trated" (289). It is impossible, the Gleaner suggests, to train up a plant by
such methods.

While the kind of manipulation Mary uses may have temporarily
"blighted" Margaretta, the maternal training pays off when the young, vulnerable daughter is away from home and encounters the smooth-talking
Sinisterus Courtland. Margaretta is "saved" because she has been trained by
her mother to "unbosom" herself without reservation, such that her letters
tell all (67). From New-Haven, Margaretta writes detailed letters to her
mother about the landscape, about the gardens, but also about the eager en-
treaties of Mr. Courtland. This clears the way for Mary to write back in a
manner that exerts parental influence. Letters can be so instructive that
Mary recommends fictional letter writing, of the kind represented by the
Seaforts or Bellamor, as yet another tool for educating young women. We
learn that fictional letters, epistolary fictions, and even straight-up fiction
can all be more useful than essays, familiar or scholarly. "The voice of the
narrator," the Gleaner writes, "will still be heard, when, perhaps, the most
elaborate essays, not thus embellished, which ever issued from the closet of
the studious, will pass the torpid ear without leaving the slightest impression" (49).

In fact, the Gleaner suggests, there are situations in which a novel is the
only ethical choice of genre for the writer. When, for example, Margaretta
seems destined to succumb to the flattering words of a villain, the Gleaner
and his wife are tempted to employ "the whole force of [their] artillery" to
save their daughter, body and soul (74). Upon reflection, however, they pursue a gentler course and defend it on ethical grounds: "we regarded persuasion, considering the tender and conceding mildness of that heart which
was almost in our hands, as no better than a specious kind of tyranny" (74).
That is, persuasion has the potential to be no better than the sophistry practiced by the villain who tries to seduce their daughter with specious rhetoric. Instead, an instructive story—call it a novel if one wishes—seems the
better choice; like a parable, its appeal is staked in high moral ground.

Two hundred years after its initial publication, the Margaretta narrative
is valued less for its instructive and moral strengths and more for its self-
reflexive gendered play. Lifting Margaretta's story from its original contexts,
as does Sharon Harris in the *Selected Writings of Judith Sargent Murray*

(1995), enables contemporary readers to glimpse the remarkable gender doubling performed by Murray through her male narrator, who, writing as the Gleaner, reveals himself to readers as Margaretta's adoptive father.[8] And its merits will certainly be enjoyed by more readers because of its publication in shorter paperback form. But this separate publication has the unfortunate effect of divorcing the Margaretta narrative from most of the essays (ironic, political, passionate, imaginative) that surrounded it in its original serial magazine and collected book forms—that is, from its structural, intellectual, and generic contexts. Here we look at just one context, debates surrounding literary borrowing, that is established by the essays and thereby structures the Margaretta narrative. This context, it turns out, is central to Murray's project, as is evidenced by her choice to unify her miscellaneous production under one title: *The Gleaner*. Most important, this "literary borrowing" forms the core of Murray's rhetorical instruction for young women, instruction that she felt, as did many of her peers, was crucial to the success of the new republic.

The Villainy of Plagiarism

Full well I knew Sinisterus Courtland. I knew him much better . . . than he was apprized of; I knew him to be base, designing.

Judith Sargent Murray, *The Gleaner*

So says the Gleaner, Margaretta's father, as he introduces the villain of the story. And Sinisterus *is* base and designing, winning the virtuous (but young) Margaretta's attention by paying her a "compliment in a style so new, so elevated, and so strikingly pleasing" that her heart instantly favors him (67). With three children born out of wedlock and a record of debt to motivate him, Sinisterus represents just one of many threats in a new society of "fashionable dispositions," witty conversations, and, most dangerously, silver-tongued seducers. Numerous early American novels sketch seduced and fallen women such as those Sinisterus leaves behind; Susanna Rowson's *Charlotte Temple* and Hannah Webster Foster's *The Coquette* are but two better-known examples. As Sarah Emily Newton suggests, "there is not much distinction made in this regard between seduction itself and erroneous marriage, which is assumed to have begun with the fatal conjunction of a woman's weakness and a seducer's rhetoric."[9] Over and over in early U.S. literature, we find anecdotes about imaginary, fallen women who believe in untrustworthy words. Asks Caroll Smith-Rosenberg, "Can we hear behind fantastical plots about virtue endangered and independence abused echoes of another quite different discourse, that of republican political theory?" She continues, "The vocabulary found in both genres is remarkably similar. In both corruption undermines 'independence'; the vicious, nonproductive elegance of the aristocracy threatens 'virtue'; reason and restraint serve the common good while passion promotes self-interest and civic disorder."[10] According to one tally, seventy-six narratives and "almost as many more moral essays" in *The Massachusetts Magazine* take as their subject "seduction and resultant misery."[11] Thus it is not unusual that Courtland should be figured a vile seducer.

But one feature makes Courtland stand out from the gallery of fictional villains: he is also a wanton plagiarist, or, more accurately, a person who pirates others' texts.[12] In his pursuit of Margaretta, he is caught submitting as his own a poem written by the better match, Edward Hamilton. The poem had "its admirers; and Courtland either saw, or thought he saw, an advantage in adopting this fugitive relation of the Parnassian lasses. . . . Courtland was repeatedly complimented upon his poetical abilities, and he hesitated not to wear the bays" (84). The fraud is discovered when a friend of Edward recognizes the poem and puts this charge to Courtland: "Is it not enough that you have stepped between him and that hoard of felicity which he fondly fancied was treasured up for him? but must you also *poorly steal* that pittance of fame, which justice reserved for him?" (85). That Courtland's plagiarism should be figured as an evil on par with his seductions and debt is somewhat odd because Murray defends and practices a kind of literary borrowing that she fears her contemporaries would call plagiarism: this at a time when notions of authorship and creativity are being refigured restrictively; when American copyright law is becoming increasingly protective of individual, private intellectual property; and when charges of plagiarism are appearing more frequently and with greater intensity. It is in this context that Murray fashions what we call a *commonplace rhetoric* for women of the new republic, a system of selecting, arranging, and delivering commentaries on familiar topics aimed at producing an "original version" and—crucially—an instructive effect.

To understand how Murray's commonplace rhetoric operates in *The Gleaner*, we must examine the related but ultimately separate histories of copyright and plagiarism. We look first (and briefly) at early American copyright law because it helps us recognize, from our late-twentieth-century perspective, some of the powerful institutional forces that situated Murray as an author—that is, as a public figure with an income from writing, aspiring to a reputation worth protecting. Then we turn to a somewhat more detailed discussion of how plagiarism was constructed in the late eighteenth century, for it is from this construction that we may come to know Murray's particular concerns about authoring grounded in a commonplace aesthetic.

At the time Murray was writing, copyright debates centered on whether individual works of literary art contributed to the public good and therefore belonged to that public, or whether such works were individual property, the use of which the author—and printers and booksellers—could circumscribe. In addressing this dilemma, the framers of early American copyright law surely benefited from a century of English struggle to define the legal status of "literary property." That struggle had its defining moment in 1710 with the passage of the Statute of Anne, generally agreed to be the first modern law of copyright. The law charted a middle course between two parties in dispute: the monopolistic booksellers of London's Stationers' Company and booksellers elsewhere in England and Scotland who desired to break that monopoly. By establishing a copyright that protected published works for a period of fourteen years, the statute ended the Stationers' perpetual monopoly, and individual publishers were empowered to hold short-term monopolies over individual titles.

Yet as Mark Rose points out, the Statute of Anne failed to resolve certain crucial questions. Did authors possess a natural right to their literary property before assigning it to publishers? And did that right revert to authors once a publisher's copyright expired? Legal challenges to the statute during the eighteenth century largely answered these questions.[13] But complicating the answers is the fact that, according to Rose, while the original statute established the author "as a legally empowered figure in the marketplace," it did so "well before professional authorship was realized in practice."[14] Thus *Pope* v. *Curll* (1741), which affirmed that unpublished writing belongs to its creator in perpetuity, was "one of the first cases in which a major English author went to court in his own name to defend his literary interests."[15] After *Pope,* booksellers theorized that authors could assign their perpetual rights to them. But *Millar* v. *Taylor* (1769) upheld the booksellers' interest in published texts—limited by statute—as separate from an author's interest—un-limited by natural right under common law. This decision would not become governing. Five years later, in *Donaldson v. Beckett* (1774), the House of Lords determined that the statute's time limits supplanted—and did not augment—an author's perpetual copyright in common law. In other words, *Millar* had established copyright as an author's right, but *Donaldson* ensured that this right would be controlled by the pecuniary interests of publishers. Most significant, *Donaldson* had the effect of establishing that "copyrights are governed by statute" rather than common law, under which authors are construed to possess rights to their work in perpetuity.[16]

It was not long after the *Donaldson* decision in 1774 that, across the Atlantic, authors and publishers in the new United States began agitating for legal protection of literary work. During the 1780s "literary gentlemen"—Noah Webster chief among them—lobbied the states for protective statutes. Twelve of the thirteen original states obliged with laws that borrowed heavily from the Statute of Anne. Some states, such as Murray's native Massachusetts, "gave the author 'the sole property' of his works if the name of the author were printed in the published work." Overall, copyright as written in these states' statutes favored authors over printers. Finally, however, such a distinction did not matter, as these formulations did not hold and "the copyright they provided for apparently never came into existence." But the statutes were useful nonetheless, as their ineffectiveness underscored the need for federal protection. (James Madison argued as much in the Federalist Papers.[17]) So it was that the United States Constitution, drafted in 1787 and ratified a year later, came to establish congressional authority "to promote the Progress of Science and useful Arts, by securing for limited Times to Authors and Inventors the exclusive Right to their respective Writings and Discoveries." Congressional legislation, passed in 1790, specified the actual process by which copyrights and patents could be secured. (It should be noted that the 1790 law, as well as a major revision of it undertaken in 1870, allowed free publication of foreign titles.[18])

Murray was possibly aware of these developments, most notably as they affected the ability of periodicals such as *The Massachusetts Magazine* to republish the work of others. But her concerns about authorship, especially as expressed in the Margaretta narrative, have more to do with that part of the intellectual property debate *not* touched by the evolution of American copyright law. For there is nothing in the Constitution, nothing in statutes of Murray's day, that makes commonplace plagiarism an actionable offense. Or rather, the only form of plagiarism relevant under copyright law is that which involves the theft of an entire work. In Rose's terms, what is at issue by the end of the eighteenth century—and certainly for Murray—is "propriety" as much as "property."[19] Early American copyright law established a legal context for Murray's authorship, but cultural definitions of plagiarism framed her own understanding of that authorship. And what most complicates that understanding are the conflicts she recognizes between her sources of authority—classical rhetorics that valued imitation—and the emerging Romantic authorities who scorned imitation as plagiarism and instead prized original composition.

Plagiarism

In *Plagiarism and Imitation during the English Renaissance,* Harold Ogden White lays out the basic principles of classical aesthetics as they relate to plagiarism and imitation during the English Renaissance. At least four of these principles remain evident in the late eighteenth century: (1) "imitation is essential"; (2) "fabrication is dangerous"; (3) "subject-matter is common property"; and (4) indebtedness to others should be proudly "avowed." But this avowal, in Murray's day, was only beginning to take the form we are most familiar with today: quotation marks. According to Margreta de Grazia, "Not until the end of the eighteenth century, was the use of quotation marks made mandatory. . . . They were not standardized until near the close of the century. Only then did they assume their routine modern function of guaranteeing that the passage within quotes has been accurately reproduced and correctly ascribed. Before this period, grammar books prescribed no rules on the use of quotation marks. Nor was it customary in printing houses to bracket statements with quotes in order to indicate that they belonged to a given speaker or writer." In fact, de Grazia goes on to point out, quotation marks before the end of the eighteenth century served an entirely different function: "A single or double quotation mark, generally in the margin . . . pointed to or indicated an authoritative saying like a proverb, commonplace, or statement of consensual truth. . . . Rather than cordoning off a passage as property of another, quotation marks flagged the passage as property belonging to all—'commonplaces' to be freely appropriated (and not necessarily verbatim and with correct authorial ascription)."[20]

That schemes of attribution shifted radically in the late eighteenth century suggests that there was ongoing a broader revision of what could and should count as original composition. Originality, while certainly valued in classical and neoclassical aesthetics, was achieved by selecting "only the best features of the best writers" to imitate. A good writer would "reexpress an old idea in the spirit of one's day," says White, shaping it through individual perception into something that seems natural, not artificial. Neoclassical writers recognized degrees of imitation, ranging from mere copying (plagiarism) to complete transformation (original composition). The final element of a classical aesthetics, the complete transformation—the "improvement on all that have preceded"—is extraordinarily difficult to achieve and is manageable, perhaps, only by *men* of genius.[21]

The trouble arises precisely here: to follow these last two tenets—acknowledging indebtedness and improving on sources—was to invite charges of imitation and possibly plagiarism. Thus plagiarism became a much-used and much-feared critical rebuke, even in an era, such as Murray's, when imitation was still essential to the creative process. Take, for example, the alleged plagiarisms in Laurence Sterne's *Tristram Shandy,* which became controversial in the late 1790s. Sterne is said to have kept a "commonplace book into which he copied passages from his reading." Whether he made fair use of his copying is a judgment that depends very much on whether a classical aesthetic is in ascendance or decline.[22] Consider, too, Thomas De Quincey, himself a liberal borrower, who several decades after the Sterne affair excoriated Samuel Taylor Coleridge for lifting long sections of the *Biographia Literaria* from an array of German philosophers. Critic against author, author against author, as Thomas Mallon quips, "one can barely conduct a study of plagiarism amid the deafening sound of literary pots roaring at literary kettles."[23] As the eighteenth century became the nineteenth, everyone, it seems, was accusing someone of plagiarism or at least dismissing writers, many of them women, as mere imitators.[24]

Plagiarism controversies percolated on both sides of the Atlantic at the time Murray assembled *The Gleaner.* But again, such controversies—and, not surprisingly, Murray's stance toward them—were not altogether new.[25] Samuel Johnson's *Rambler* "No. 143" from 1751 argues that plagiarism charges are not merely annoying, but dangerous and malicious. It is the criticism of last resort: "When the excellence of a new composition can no longer be contested, and malice is compelled to give way to the unanimity of applause, there is yet this one expedient [a charge of plagiarism] to be tried, by which the author may be degraded, though his work be reverenced."[26]

Murray strikes a similar pose in *The Gleaner*, focusing on the unjustly accused: "It is, perhaps, true, that the heaviest charge preferred against literary adventurers, is that of plagiarism: After an original thought, a hue and cry is raised—it is traced from author to author—the cheek of innocence is tinged with the indignant blush, excited by suspicions of fraud; and a group of respectable characters are supposed to stand convicted of the high crime of *knowingly* and *wittingly purloining their neighbours' goods*" (464). Such criticism is more galling given Johnson's premise that even in the most original books, "there is little new beyond the disposition of materials already provided."[27] This is a point upon which Murray elaborates: "Originality is undoubtedly rare, and it is probable it will become still more so. A writer finds many subjects touched, and retouched, if not wholly exhausted. . . . What, I would ask, constitutes originality? or, in other words, cannot an original thought be twice conceived?" (464–65).

Further, Murray illuminates the absence of legal recourse in cases of copyright infringement and plagiarism. But she is most compelling when she argues the need for relief from libelous reviews that level accusations of plagiarism. By the time *The Gleaner* was copyrighted in 1798, Americans had spent over a decade defining copyright infringement, yet little effort had been spent to make unfounded accusations of plagiarism an actionable offense, perhaps because on their face such accusations generally appeared accurate and just: a charge of plagiarism brought with it the presumption of guilt. If libelous plagiarism charges could be challenged, Murray theorizes, it would be in state courts of equity, whose powers were waning by the 1790s: "To condemn, upon presumptive evidence, is both treacherous and cruel, and it is a procedure which finds no place in the decisions of equity. I do not contend that plagiarism is never practised—far from it; I believe it constitutes the essence of many a volume, and that it is a kind of depredation, which is too often the *dernier resort* of the scribbler; but I *insist,* and I can produce proof positive of my assertion, that the charge of plagiarism is frequently *unfounded,* and consequently *unjust*" (464).

Murray's position is precarious. Yes, she could prove false accusations if there were a court to hear them. And yes, she grants, as does Johnson, that imitation as a principle has been abused, and that plagiarism of the sort Courtland commits is rampant. But for Murray, the easiest solution—simply to avoid imitation—is impossible. Instead, at issue must be the nature and quality of the imitation that all writers necessarily practice, whether they admit it or not. Johnson speaks to the distinction between good and poor imitation that Murray highlights: if persons of inferior genius show good judgment in their copying, this is sufficient to earn them the status of author, but as authors they must not then lay claim to genius.[28] At this point, however, Murray departs from Johnson. Rather than restating the classical principle that the best imitation improves the *object* imitated, Murray stresses that remaking something old for a new age furnishes individuals with some stability in economically unsettled times. A storehouse of knowledge, literary acquisition, was a good investment for men and women of the new nation: "Learning . . . renders the possessor not only more valuable, but also more amiable, and more generally useful. . . . And while the goods of fortune may be whelmed beneath the contingencies of revolving time, intellectual property still remains, and the mental funds can never be exhausted" (59).

While such economic stability would itself prove valuable to the new republic, Murray makes still larger claims for the value of composition, no matter how derivative: the act of composing educates a citizenry. Imitation done well does not produce a select few men of genius, but rather many men and women of good judgment, the latter essential to a strong democracy. In other words, Murray equates "mental funds" with "intellectual property." For Murray, intellectual property in a democracy consists of anything stored in the mind; what is learned belongs to the learner, both as an individual and as a part of the democratic collective. Far from being a threat to real genius, a "mental *Commonwealth*" would promote it (126). Value would be placed on the acquisition of intellectual property and on collective wisdom, and "the road to literary honours" could, theoretically, be traveled by anyone (126). This of course contrasts greatly with what we recognize as intellectual property before postmodernism, with its emphasis on individual, "original," artistic authorship. Murray's ideas here thus coincide with those represented in Edward Young's *Conjectures on Original Composition* (1759). Young's *Conjectures* is often cited as one of the earliest and most influential works equating literary value or worth with originality, mentioned "most frequently as a showcase for emerging ideas, a mileage-marker on the road from Neoclassicism to Romanticism."[29] And indeed, to some extent, Young's work does investigate and praise the "genius" of "original" writers. But Young also set out to discuss composition as a useful, moral art, particularly to those growing older and closer to the end of life. Young contends:

> Some are of Opinion, that its [Composition's] Growth, at present, is too luxuriant; and that the Press is overcharged. Overcharged, I think, it could never be, if none were admitted, but such as brought their Imprimatur from *sound Understanding,* and the *Public Good.* Wit, indeed, however brilliant, should not be permitted to gaze self-enamour'd on its useless Charms, in that Fountain of Fame (if so I may call the Press,) if Beauty is all that it has to boast; but, like the first *Brutus,* it should sacrifice its most darling Offspring to the sacred interests of Virtue, and real Service of mankind.
> This Restriction allowed, the more Composition the better.[30]

Having recognized the civic value of literary endeavors, Young still wants to carve a space for genius of the kind that transcends the ages. The ancients, according to Young, fell into genius by default: with no models before them, they had no option but to produce "original" imitations of nature.[31] Writers since antiquity, however, have had to live and write in the shadows of the ancients. For Young, the trick becomes how to pay the homage the ancients deserve without surrendering to their influence, without falling into weak imitation: "for nothing *Original* can rise, nothing Immortal can ripen, in any other Sun." Young's solution, ironically, advises imitation: "Imitate; but imitate not the *Composition,* but the *Man,*" a course of action Murray at least in part recommends.[32] For example, Murray believes that parents who possess "minds capacious and extensively cultivated" are clearly worthy of imitation: "From such parents we expect a result happy for the individuals immediately under their tuition, and auspicious to society at large" (251). But Murray cannot accept the insistent linking of composition with the character of the living author. She cannot accept, as Foster warns in her writing lesson, that writing necessarily entails exposure of self and subsequent judgment of that self by readers. Therein lies the problem with the "imitate the man" theory: it makes the body too visible, thus inviting body politics. Theoretically, pseudonyms work to disengage author and composition. Yet if pseudonyms provide a mask for the author, it is a mask, Murray discovers, that readers seem determined to peer behind. Murray imagines that "a considerable majority" of the Gleaner's "engaged" readers "seemed more occupied in detecting the *real author,* than in essaying to investigate the merits of his productions!" (104). The point is important enough for the Gleaner to offer a passionate rebuke: "I cannot help regarding this *hunting after names,* as descriptive of the frivolity of the human mind: No sooner does an anonymous piece make its appearance, than curiosity invests itself in the stole of sagacity, conjecture is upon the rack—Who is he? Where does he live? What is his *real name,* and occupation?" (105). In still another section, the Gleaner laments the situation of writers aspiring to literary recognition: "But alas! how are their steps environed with peril! their family, their education, their persons, their characters—these all become standing subjects of [presumably unflattering] conversation!"(463–64).

For Murray, this rooting out of character is more irritating because readers in a mental commonwealth have more important things to do, namely, to discover what is of value and store it in memory, to accumulate that intellectual property so essential to the Columbian experiment: "The business of the reader is to scan the *intrinsic value* and *general tendency* of the composition; if that is considerable, if that is laudable, he ought to leave the author to announce himself under what auspices he shall judge proper" (105). Imitate, Murray advises, but imitate the composition, not the man.

Refiguring the Plagiarist

Both writers and readers in Murray's idealized mental commonwealth are gleaners who select intellectual property based on schooled values. Writers are not to promote their work as models; rather, readers are to go in search of imitable prose. The Gleaner, for example, although he advocates modeling throughout his essays, refuses the role: *"I have no where proposed myself as a model: It may be, that I am experimentally qualified to descant upon the disadvantages attendant upon early inattention"* (295). Of course, when the Gleaner is unmasked, *he* is revealed to be Murray, a woman whose early education was incomplete and was subsequently composed of what she learned from her brother's formal schooling and what she picked up by spending time with the learned company her clergyman husband encountered as he was called to preach throughout the Northeast. Murray likely felt vulnerable to criticism that could damage her reputation as an author and thus compromise her ability to earn money and sustain her family on her writing income. But more than an economic imperative was at stake: Murray had aspirations to produce work of literary merit and understood that as a woman such work would be undervalued, or, if valued, judged as mere imitation or, worse still, literary theft. The preface to *The Gleaner,* written in the voice of Constantia, worries about such charges. Finally, however, Murray is willing to write, to be "laid open to all the severity of criticism" and "arraigned, tried and condemned." She is "preparing for . . . the severest pangs" (14).

Just how does Murray prepare to endure these pangs? In the book's first chapter, Constantia gives way to the Gleaner, the consummate imitator, a male persona more ironic and defensive than Constantia in tone, bolder in aspiration and wit, who can navigate inconspicuously through public space. Murray imagines her worst critics and scripts the Gleaner's confrontation with them. In a scene reminiscent of Cervantes's *Don Quixote,* Murray imagines her Gleaner overhearing his (her?) critics in the coffeehouse. The Gleaner is "regarded as free plunder, serving as a mark at which to point their keenest shafts of satire" (47–48). They guess the Gleaner to be a parson of sorts, "a student in Harvard College" who *"needs instruction"* (48). He is judged humorless: there is not "a single sentence of sheer wit." Their most stinging critique concerns plagiarism—there is no "hope of originality." The Margaretta character has *some* potential, it is asserted, but the author "just popt her upon us, and very soon running himself out there, whip, in a moment, she was gone." The observer continues: "Take my word for it, Gentlemen, (and he shook his head with great sagacity) the Gleaner is not worth our attention; he is poor, despicably poor—low, pitifully low; and I hesitate not to pronounce him a mere trite, common-place observer" (48). Murray treats such imagined criticism characteristically: first by confronting it, then by embracing it, making it central to both the mental commonwealth and her writer-self. Commonplace observers, men and women who observe everyday people and events and store such things in their minds, are just what the republic needs for survival.

Murray thus makes an expressive move similar to what James Kinneavy describes in his analysis of her contemporaries—the authors of the Declaration of Independence.[33] She declares, in this case, her *dependence* on her predecessors and creates a literary self, a person who can write and survive the "pangs" of authorship. Rather than choosing to face the pangs of oblivion, she opts to reinscribe the task:

> Upon mature deliberation I have thought best to adopt, and I do hereby adopt, the name, character, and avocation of a GLEANER. . . .
> Here pride suggests a question, What is any modern scribbler better than a Gleaner? But I very sagaciously reply, Let my brethren and sisters of the quill characterize themselves. . . .
> The truth is, I am very fond of my title: I conceive that I shall find it in many respects abundantly convenient; more especially, should an accusation of plagiarism be lodged against me, my very *title* will plead my apology; for it would be indeed pitiful if the opulent reaper, whose granaries are confessedly large, and variously supplied, should grudge the poor Gleaner what little he industriously collects, and what, from the richness and plenty of his ample harvest, he can never want. (17)

It is as a trickster that Murray finds a veil for her ego and a shield against the critical eyes of "the Grammarian, the Rhetorician, [and] the Poet," all of whom look to find her "an unpardonable offender against the rules of language, and the elegance and graces of style" (14). Rather than flee the charge of plagiarism, Murray revels in it, defining a genius of both status and abundance, yoking the rural images of Wordsworthian Romanticism to her status as a commonplace observer, a wanderer in the rich field of words. Moreover, rather than the image of a passive author vulnerable to critics, she cuts the figure of a writer who aggressively orders the critical landscape around him: "I shall ransack the fields, the meadows, and the groves; each secret haunt, however sequestered, with avidity I shall explore; deeming myself privileged to crop with impunity a hint from one, an idea from another, and to aim at improvement upon a sentence from a third. I shall give to my materials whatever texture my fancy directs; and, as I said, feeling myself entitled to toleration as a Gleaner, in this expressive name I shall take shelter, standing entirely regardless of every charge relative to property, originality, and every thing of this nature, which may be preferred against me" (17).

To escape the charge of plagiarism, Murray declares herself not a thief, but a borrower and, in the Margaretta narrative, spells out the difference between the two. The villain, Sinisterus Courtland, is a plagiarist; the heroine, the Gleaner's daughter, is a judicious borrower, well instructed by her Re-

publican Mother. The Gleaner, with "his" commonplace observations, dis-
perses the intellectual estate he has inherited into the commonwealth. For
Murray, the hope for America lies not in creating the new, the original, the
great American author, but in gleaning lessons and words from the past in
order to forge the supports of a new, strong nation. It is a woman's job to
teach children—hers and others'—the art of commonplace observation. It
falls to Republican Mothers to instruct the new nation in the art of plagiarism.

4 Sketching Rhetorical Change
Mrs. A. J. Graves on Girlhood and Womanhood

"The Rights of Woman" are almost as warmly and wildly contested as "The Rights of Man;" and there is a revolution going on in the female mind at the present day, out of which glorious results may arise.

Mrs. A. J. Graves, *Woman in America* (1841)

↬ *The fictions* in Hannah Webster Foster's *The Boarding School* and Judith Sargent Murray's *The Gleaner* certainly evince an interest, perhaps even a preoccupation, with imagining how young women in the early years of nation making might best acquire and use an advanced rhetorical education. It is possible, however, that neither *The Boarding School* nor *The Gleaner* circulated widely in the new republic. And so, while the impetus to create these schooling fictions was strong, their influence was no doubt limited. It would be some time, decades in fact, before such imaginings, penned by a new generation of U.S. women, would reach a widespread audience. Although, as Cathy Davidson outlines in *Revolution and the Word*, women's education continues to figure as subtext in novels written in the teens, twenties, and thirties, not until the 1840s does there reappear a flurry of schooling fictions generically similar to *The Boarding School*. Yet there is clearly something different about this second generation of schooling fictions, a difference that reflects the changes in national and local economy, in sectional politics, in schooling, in rhetorical practice, in modes of authorship and readership, and in the production and dissemination of a widening variety of print material. In her 1841 political treatise, *Woman in America*, Mrs. A. J. Graves seizes on liberatory civic rhetoric to claim this moment as revolutionary for U.S. women. Still, although Graves's forward-looking treatise advocates a U.S. democracy that centers on rhetorically astute and politically virtuous women, her revolution is not Murray's, but rather one "in the female mind" itself. Graves was the first of several authors to attempt a comprehensive assessment of women's situation in the United States under the title *Woman in America*. She was followed in 1850 by Maria Jane McIntosh *(Woman in America: Her Work and Her Reward)* and 1857 by M. Farley Emerson *(Woman in America: Her Character and Position as Indicated by Newspaper Editorials, and Sustained by American Social Life)*. And surely Graves's title (if not her sentiments) resonates with Margaret Fuller's better-known and better-remembered *Woman in the Nineteenth Century,* published in 1845, an expansion of a *Dial* essay that appeared two years earlier and the precursor of formal demands articulated at the Seneca Falls convention in 1848.

Three years after the appearance of her *Woman in America,* Graves publishes a retrospective narrative, *Girlhood and Womanhood* (1844), a book we will refer to by its more descriptive subtitle, *Sketches of My Schoolmates.* Nina Baym describes *Sketches* as "one of the most technically accomplished of the morality fictions so common in the late thirties and early forties," and as a "fine example of the merging of a progressive view of woman's abilities and a stress on the need for education, self-respect, and self-dependence, with the conviction that woman could most effectively fulfill herself and realize her mission, in the home."[1] *Sketches* imagines not the promise of women's schooling, but its limitations, and does so by using the very genre—schooling fiction—that Hannah Webster Foster used to promote her vision for ideal female education, her Harmony-Grove. As did Foster's *Boarding School, Sketches* builds the strongest case for institutionalized schooling: the novel begins in the ideal imagined space of the Oakwood School, run by the exemplary Mrs. Norville, and insists throughout on the high quality of education this "instructress" makes possible for her students. But unlike Foster's narrative, *Sketches* comes around to critique its opening scene. Ultimately, Graves maintains that the legacy of home life is indelible and can never be rewritten by even the best schooling. That legacy, Graves insists, takes root in infancy. And, Graves implies, if infant training determines adult behavior, then efforts to reform adult society should be directed to that fundamental place of learning, the home.

While it had become, by the 1840s, commonplace to argue that girls' boarding schools had been vastly improved by the introduction of science courses, Graves felt such arguments were misdirected. Yes, science—domestic science—could improve girls' education, but domestic science was best learned early, under the tutelage of one's mother. Though resonant with the principles of Republican Motherhood Foster once advanced, Graves's position is hardly nostalgic for the early national fervor that conditioned Foster's prose. Instead, Graves is alive to the ways in which motherhood has been dramatically reshaped by the social impulses associated with domestic economy. Among these impulses, education outside the boundaries of formal schooling—self-education—figures prominently, linked as it is with the burgeoning rhetoric of self-reliance and commercial individualism.[2] And whereas self-education for women had previously been imagined as a "finishing" that should commence after formal schooling and be completed before marriage, theories of human development popular by the 1830s suggested—consonant with Graves—that the important habits of life were set very early in life, before school. Attempts to *begin* self-education in late adolescence would thus prove futile. Such theory notwithstanding, Graves faced practical opposition from a growing class of professional female teachers, a phenomenon only vaguely forecast in early national literature. These teachers (with whom we will become better acquainted in chapter 6) compete for the educational duties heretofore inherent in motherhood. And mothers, or more accurately their advocates, resist the professionals' efforts, striving to update and thereby strengthen the early national preference for situating the education of youth in the home. In this resistance, specific emphasis is placed on perpetuating a generational cycle of home education for girls that would address the moral and material complexity of housekeeping while obviating the need for ever crossing out of the domestic realm into public schooling. (After early lessons at home, boys could be properly schooled in the public realm, where, as men, they would live out their useful lives.)

What seems to be working out in this period, then, in rhetoric and in deed, is a remarkable transition: from republican-Enlightenment thought, in which some patriots could imagine (as did Foster) a boarding school as the proper place to prepare women for motherhood as a civic duty, to liberal-individualist thought, in which some patriots chastised the surrender of girls to a boarding school as an act of civic neglect. Antebellum schooling fictions thus turn on the polemic of instruction at home versus instruction in academies.

It may be tempting to view the controversy over girls' boarding schools as a political—and rhetorical—litmus test. But it would be wrong to suggest that those who favored domestic instruction were, by the 1820s or 1830s, necessarily "conservative" defenders of moribund republican ideology and its neoclassical rhetorical principles. Boydston, Kelley, and Margolis argue that it would be incorrect to assume that proponents of domestic economy saw no civic role for women outside the home. Using the Beecher sisters as their case study, they hypothesize that many "nineteenth-century women . . . organized to reform American society. Convinced that the values they upheld in the home uniquely qualified them to become both the conservators and the final arbiters of morality in society generally, large numbers of antebellum women began to move into organized benevolent work, establishing maternal associations and tract societies; founding orphanages and homes for the aged and widowed and unwanted; and raising money for direct relief—food, fuel, and clothing—for the urban poor."[3] It would be equally wrong to claim that boarding school and academy partisans were somehow purely "liberal" advocates of a new democratic reality undergirded by a rhetoric that celebrated Romantic genius and individualism. Rather, as our overview of Graves and her contemporaries suggests, republican ideology did not die away: in some ways, the writing of Graves, along with that of boarding school opponents Susan Ridley Sedgwick (Catharine Maria Sedgwick's beloved sister-in-law) and Sarah Josepha Hale, evidences Republican Motherhood with a vengeance, a rhetorical stance we explore at some length later in this chapter. Even Catharine Beecher, an advocate of girls' boarding schools, assumes a stance toward Republican Motherhood that does not distance her so very much from Graves, Sedgwick, Hale, and other contemporaries. Like Graves, Sedgwick, and Hale, Catharine Beecher was concerned about the education of young women—she headed the Hartford Female Seminary from 1823 to 1831—and explored in surviving publications the implications of such schooling for the conduct of domestic life. But unlike the others, Beecher made no fictional forays into the world of schooling, so our treatment of her here must be brief.[4]

In the 1830s Beecher fixed on the moral education of young women as an enterprise quite apart from training in domestic arts and sciences. She imagined that the best venue for such an education would be a seminary with its own residence hall. Indeed, early in the school's history she tried twice to persuade the people of Hartford to finance the residence hall, but to no avail. Instead, students boarded with those local families that Beecher felt certain would exert proper moral influence.[5] What sets Beecher apart from other domestic economists is her investment in a version of commonsense philosophy that, according to Kathryn Kish Sklar, bypassed "Enlightenment thought" and "drew instead on the issues central to the Calvinist tradition: the importance of the social community, and the nature of the relationship between internal piety and external morality."[6] Hence Beecher could justify a learned and learning place for girls outside or alongside the home that would, like ideal family life, foster and protect girls' rectitude. As sites that could collect and magnify individual morality, boarding schools and academies held the potential to be much more powerful in guiding moral development than individual families. In fact, Hale and Beecher themselves finally settle on a commonsensical, communitarian approach to the domestic arts (including the arts of persuasion) as a defense against both the reactionary elitism that lingered in the decline of Federalist republican thought around 1800 and the perceived radical excess of democracy that followed.

Curiously, for reasons we will examine, Graves does not appeal openly to commonsense philosophy, as Beecher does. Their differences concerning home and institutional schooling are an artifact of the ideological unrest that prevailed as the new nation matured. Steven Watts observes that this "fundamental" unrest, "though broad and far-reaching, did not appear as stormy or even dramatic. To the contrary, a complex subtlety defined its nature and often befuddled participants. While republican society and liberal society represented different stages in the historical development of the postfeudal West, they did not stand diametrically opposed in America, as some scholars would have it, with defenders of civic virtue angrily arrayed against the minions of self-regarding individualism."[7] And so as we turn to Graves to document the complexity and befuddlement entailed in struggles to imagine how the new democracy should shape schooling, how in that schooling aesthetic taste ought to be addressed, how the limits of such schooling might be recognized and regarded, and whether, finally, the story of education for young women should unfold in or away from public view. Of Graves's two books, it is the narrative *Sketches of My Schoolmates* that provides the most useful touchstone for our historical argument. It begins with three chapters describing the breakup of Mrs. Norville's Oakwood School and the personalities of the young women who must return to their families. Subsequent chapters, composed almost as parables, recount the worldly paths followed by the narrator's supposed classmates. Each class-mate's journey tells us something about Graves's perspective on the present and future of rhetorical education for U.S. women. And each journey pre-pares us to understand better the teachers and writers who imagined rhetor-ical education for the generation of girls who would grow to womanhood on the eve of a second revolution—the Civil War.

Taste and the Rise of a Belletristic Aesthetic

Whether it be that the rich in our country, or those aiming to be thought so, are sel-dom persons of real refinement, we know not; but certain it is, that though we find in many mansions a cumbrous and gaudy excess of ornament, there are very few in which is exhibited anything like correct taste.

— Mrs. A. J. Graves, *Woman in America*

The introduction of belletristic rhetorics, such as Blair's, Newman's, and Jamieson's, shifted the focus of instruction from scripted oratory to tasteful prose, which is to say, more attention was now paid in schools to reading lit-erature as a way to foster the writing of original compositions. Halloran at-tributes this shift in emphasis from neoclassicism to belletrism to a number of causes, one being the rise of a middle class, and within that class, a body of professional men whose family ties and upbringing did not alone fit them for their new stations in life. Rhetorical training in aesthetic appreciation was required to complete the job.[8] What is lost in this transition, according to Halloran, is the means by which men of middling station could be pre-pared to contribute to a common civic life. Instead, by the early nineteenth century, such men prepared to make lives for themselves and their families and to participate effectively in building professions that were an end in themselves.[9] Implicit in Halloran's assessment is the idea that ethical instruc-tion waned when rhetoric became an aesthetic affair. Not so, argues Sharon Crowley. While cultivation of the *vir bonus dicendi peritus* (the good man speaking well) may have disappeared from the college curriculum, the ideal of the "genteel man of taste" still entailed a deep interest in the moral charac-ter of a new generation of college men.[10] Ethical instruction changed, but perhaps only subtly, when belletristic rhetorics were made more salient than earlier neoclassicism. Neoclassical models were also challenged, as Jane Tompkins and other feminist critics remind us, by the oratorical power of the revival movement and its later extension into print via the American Tract Society and women's sentimental fiction. In the mid-nineteenth century, sentimental and political rhetorics relied on "a single representative [narrative] case, strikingly presented" to provide the "most effective form of evidence."[11]

As Murray's *Gleaner* suggests, this slow introduction of belletristic aesthetics was not without gendered inflection. Women's schooling fictions from the early national and antebellum periods struggled in different ways to theorize and contest this belletristic aesthetics and to modify its practice in the curricula of female academies. Primarily they do so by appealing to patriotism, a strategy Graves employs in her sketch on "fashionable ambition."[12] On one level, the sketch of Amanda Malvina Burton seems narrated only to arrive at the clichéd conclusion, "Be it ever so humble, there's no place like home." Amanda Burton begins life as a shopkeeper's daughter, experiences a precipitous rise in fortune, and, as an heiress, marries a suitor whose main appeal is his title. Such a rise in station, however, in the fluctuating republic, was frequently impermanent. Shortly after her marriage, Amanda learns that her father's wealth was gained illegally ("sins of the father" manifest frequently in these texts); his possessions are seized by creditors. Amanda thus discovers herself no longer an heiress. Nor has she a title. Her husband too has proven duplicitous: he has invented his title to win her hand and fortune. Typically in such a narrative, Amanda would discover her husband to be a lascivious, intemperate brute who leaves her, burdened with children, to toil incessantly for earnings that he squanders. But Graves's parable is cheerier. Amanda has the good fortune to marry a husband penitent, sober, and industrious. He loves his wife and supports his family in a way befitting Amanda—he keeps shop. Only occasional bouts of pride, the narrative reveals, mar Amanda's fortunate return to her rightful, humble station.

Still, like the other sketches of which this forms a part, Amanda's serves to underscore some point about female schooling, some thesis about school's efficacy, in this case, a point concerning taste. "A mother should sedulously cultivate the intellectual tastes of her children," Graves writes prescriptively in *Woman in America*.[13] But just what Graves means by "taste" is suggested rather than precisely defined. On the one hand, taste clearly refers to a consumer culture in which humble people like the Burtons dream the wrong dreams. At every turn in the narrative, the democratic Mrs. Graves makes this point. Mr. Burton is described as "a shrewd, sensible little man and the very prince of shopkeepers," as a man not content with his modest station, a man "whose highest ambition was to see his daughter become a fine lady and prospectively a rich heiress" (20). He sacrifices his integrity to effect this. His wife, on the other hand, supplies social manners attendant to the new title, and here is where "taste" comes more definitively into play. Mrs. Burton has drawn her "high notions of gentility" from English novels not appropriate to a democratic society (21). Her daughter shows the limitations of such notions in her "excessive admiration" of all things foreign (90).[14] This leads Graves to a long discussion of "indigenous" taste, by which she means taste more suitable to the democratic United States, one which, interestingly, despises imitation: "Rich and independent as we really are, or ought to be in our native resources, yet the propensity to borrow and to imitate seems to be a national idiosyncrasy. We not only draw upon foreign fashions, foreign talent, and foreign capital to contribute to our supposed improvement, but we also feel the necessity of sending agents to an absolute monarchy in Europe, to procure a system of popular instruction for the children of a republic" (90). Taste, as here explicated, encompasses the virtues of wise consumerism as well as proper rhetorical action: rather than slavishly imitate, one should consult her own taste. Moreover, the principle of indigenous taste, as Amanda demonstrates, extends to *speech:* Amanda "could not describe any thing without an hyperbole, and with her the most common objects became invested with beauty or grandeur—a grass plat was styled a lawn and a lawn became a park; her father's two story house was a mansion and the little room opening into the shop by a glass door was dignified by the name of a drawing-room" (22). Graves's notion of taste thus both borrows from the new belletrism (it eschews imitation) and alters it, rejecting British-inflected poetic language in favor of more American, democratic prose.

The Burtons, with their hyperbolic foreign taste, certainly represent democratic anxieties about the upwardly mobile. Yet the sketch of Amelia Dorrington allows us to see that for Graves the problem of excessive taste is a result of excessive wealth. The story is simple: Amelia Dorrington, a "self-willed girl," marries Charles Sefton, a "spoiled child of fortune," and they in turn have children (147, 148). Charles squanders his fortune and, when

Amelia's father dies, squanders hers as well. But here Graves breaks the cycle. As reprehensible as Charles is, his excesses are merely financial. Amelia's, it turns out, have infused her entire being, including her sexuality: "She received the attentions and admirations of other men" and soon descends into the "lowest state of vice and wretchedness . . . too revolting to repeat" (149). Still, the narrative does recount enough for us to get the picture: she becomes the "inmate" of the "lowest negro hovels," is frequently brought into night court for "disturbing the peace in midnight brawls," and serves two stints in prison for theft (149). Long before these degradations, her husband casts her off and takes custody of the children, who remain "happily ignorant that they have a mother living" (149). Nor is Amelia allowed to live much longer in her intemperate, howling state. She dies a particularly gruesome death in an almshouse.

While the moral of this story might seem (more than) evident, as with all the sketches, Graves's narrator articulates the lesson for us—and it comes as a bit of a surprise. It seems that neither Charles nor Amelia is to blame for her fate; that blame rests squarely with her parents, with the pampering they began "from earliest infancy" (29). Finally, this story of "the lost one" is a parable explicating "that most fearful of all responsibilities, parental power—parental influence!" (151). Amelia's parents have failed in their most important task—"to implant into the minds of their children the strictest principles of virtue and purity." For daughters such "implanting" takes on a specific rhetorical direction; parents must "instill into their daughters the most refined ideas of feminine propriety in all their words and actions" (151). Indigenous, proper, refined: taste determines all. And such taste, in Graves's democracy, is best rooted in humble, prosaic domesticity.

In *Woman in America* Graves reflects still further on what she sees as the problem of "erratic" excess, and this reflection shows how lessons on taste infuse the sentiment growing against female orators who leave behind the prosaic space of the home and venture out to speak publicly to "promiscuous" audiences: "We lament the erratic course of many of our female reformers, believing that they have inflicted deep injury where they intended good, by drawing woman away from her true and allotted sphere—domestic life. Nor are our female lecturers and female politicians alone at fault; for it is to be feared that even some Christian ministers . . . have, by their impassioned appeals, sent woman abroad into the highways and by-ways of life."[15]

In the 1830s it was not uncommon to hear, or at least hear reports at second- or thirdhand, of women's rhetorical performance on the public stage. The Grimké sisters, Sarah and Angelina, and Lucretia Mott spoke out with vehemence against slavery. Frances Wright, Elizabeth Cady Stanton, Elizabeth Oakes Smith, and others lectured to promiscuous audiences on a variety of subjects, including the rights of women.[16] The moral opprobrium heaped upon these women was great and came from many quarters. Not the least "vocal" of these critics were the editors and contributors of the new popular ladies' magazines, part of whose mission was to circulate this civic, indigenous taste.

Much fell into place by the 1830s that allowed interest in magazine reading to spread as it did. The circulation of general interest periodicals expanded rapidly, and, to sustain wide interest, editors sought topics they believed would be of national interest, including issues surrounding women's changing roles. Between 1800 and 1850, no fewer than twenty magazines bearing some form of the word *lady* in their title debuted. Most lasted but a year or two, if that long. Three lasted almost ten years, and three more endured the test of decades, among them *The Lady's Book,* later known as *Godey's Lady's Book,* which appeared for nearly seventy years, from 1830 to 1898, promoting what was referred to even then as domestic economy. For most of its run, *Godey's* was edited by Sarah Josepha Hale, whose interest in women's education, like that of other women editors—Caroline Kirkland, Harriet Beecher Stowe, Caroline Augusta White Soule, and Lucy Stone, for example—may have been stoked by her prior years as a teacher.[17] As Patricia Okker points out in her study of Hale, less than three years after assuming editorship of the *Ladies' Magazine,* Hale shifted from espousing Enlightenment rhetoric to embracing Victorian morality. Yet even when in full Victorian mode, Hale recommended that women engage in the rational study of "mathematics, philosophy, and rhetoric," a seeming contradiction that marks much of the antebellum movement that scientized women's duties in the home.[18] Indeed, domestic economy shows marks of three potentially contradictory movements: Republican Motherhood, with its investment in American revolutionary rhetoric and its emphasis on the hearth as the center of the nation; British Romanticism, with its emphasis on alternate mental and emotional states; and Scottish commonsense realism, with its interest in governance of mental, physical, and spiritual behavior. Domestic economy, as it gets promulgated through the conduct and advice literature of ladies' magazines such as *Godey's,* was promoted as the way that women could rationally and morally hold together a nation threatening to split under the political pressures of immigration, popular democracy, and, of course, slavery.

Writing in Hale's *Ladies' Magazine* in 1836, Almira Hart Lincoln Phelps defends women's involvement in this literary mission: "Why should not all educated women be literary? Why should they not sometimes impart the results of their experience, or communicate their sentiments through the medium of a Ladies' Magazine?"[19] Why not, indeed. For, as Phelps puts it, "exhortations to duty from female pens, though the sentences be not constructed with the strength of Johnson, or the periods rounded with Addisonian elegance, may affect the hearts of other females." What Phelps imagines spreading by way of ladies' magazines is finally not so much literariness per se, but an outlook on domestic life that could be shaped according to tasteful belletristic principles. Phelps contends that "the aspiring mind of man . . . strike[s] deep into the paths of science and philosophy," leaving room in print for "the tender, the affectionate, and humble offerings from female hearts." Ladies' periodicals were, as Phelps further articulates, a "common medium of communication, through which female talent may diffuse and expand itself," exerting influence "upon each other, and society at large."[20] Delivered discretely by mail and read within the privacy of the home, periodicals could teach women how best to conduct domestic life. But—as we will see in future chapters—this instruction could only work if women were schooled to understand prevailing belletristic ways with words. Rather than writing leisure material, Hale and other women magazinists wrote prose with the purpose of augmenting labor. As the purveyors of a domestic, middle-class, print-centered taste, ladies' periodicals disciplined Romantic sensibility with a commonsense philosophy adapted to suit the kind of life these women imagined—life in a Protestant democracy where reputations were created and recreated within each generation.

The Limits of Belletrism

Her sensibilities were naturally keen and had become morbidly so, under the unlimited indulgence of a widowed mother. . . . The sight of pain or anguish was more than she could bear, and I have seen her turn, shuddering, from a wounded bird or

a crushed insect, while her countenance vividly expressed the keenness of her sympathy. Oh how much need was there of a guiding hand to strengthen and prepare her for the pilgrimage of life!—She was unfitted for the world and for earth's alloyed happiness. Ever vacillating between the extremes of joy or sorrow, one moment she would be almost wild in the exuberance of her spirits and the next she would be convulsed with grief, from some cause which in one of a different temperament would scarcely have given rise to a tear. Mrs. Norville would often say to me "my dear Ellen this sensitive child needs much of our care, . . . and we must both endeavor to fortify her mind and bring her sensibilities into healthful action."
—Mrs. A. J. Graves, *Sketches of My Schoolmates*

With these brief words of concern, Graves's narrator, Ellen Maitland, introduces us to Anna Percival, her best friend during their years together at the Oakwood School. When Ellen hurries her narrative ahead to sketch another Oakwood acquaintance, she leaves us to wonder whether she and Mrs. Norville—whether the Oakwood curriculum—successfully fortified Anna's mind. Did Anna, in other words, grow healthfully from motherhood into womanhood? Were her lessons at school enough to instill what another friend, Emily Howard, seemed naturally to possess: a "similar" kindhearted character marked by "feelings . . . less keen" and, crucially, "better regulated" (19)? As we learn somewhat later in *Sketches,* Anna Percival does not become like Emily, but instead succumbs most tragically (though not permanently) to sensibility: she becomes, in Graves's words, "the Maniac Mother" (50). And so Graves alerts us to a profound shortcoming of belletristic education at Oakwood, and presumably elsewhere. It cannot protect mind and body from ill health.

Not the least of belletrism's failings was its attractiveness. In this sketch, the excessively romantic Anna Percival marries Frederick Elton, her "imaginary standard of perfection" (51). That Anna fantasizes his perfection is only part of the problem: that Elton embodies taste foreign rather than indigenous forms the other. Having just returned from Europe, he cuts a refined, elegant, fluent figure—one the commonsensical Ellen Maitland does not trust. But Anna Percival, with her excessive, unrestrained sensibility, falls under the spell of *his* romantic sensibilities, his "rapturous admiration of the beautiful or sublime in nature or art," "his eloquent declamations on the glowing inspirations of genius" (52). Elton's sensibilities are seductively, distinctively male; they lack a countervailing female sentiment. His polished sensibility is, as Ellen notices, too superficial, too "scientific": "his feelings seemed to be untouched" by it all (52). Despite Ellen's warnings, Anna marries. And there begins the downward trajectory of her plot. Her husband insists on taking her to Europe, where for some time after the marriage, Anna continues to idolize her husband. But Italy changes all this. There Elton makes "a jest of domestic happiness," leaving "her society for that of other females," revealing himself to be a "heartless libertine" and drunkard (58). He cuts his wife off from her family and friends, so that she when she gives birth to their son, she is alone and weak.

As a result of such treatment Anna devolves into a "maniac" mother who murders her child in a moment of confusion and displaced rage (62). (She sees in the child her husband—"the demon that haunts me"—and flings the boy out an open window [63].) Interestingly, her infanticide is rather easily forgiven in the narrative. Anna suffers a period of amnesia, and then comes to terms with her actions after Ellen is finally able to fortify her overwrought sensibility with the power of the Gospel. Anna and her mother, who is also now converted, spend the rest of their lives performing "errands of love and mercy" (65). By doing so, Anna "lost the sense of her own misfortunes, and found a rich reward in the approval of God and the testimony of a good conscience" (66). Graves makes plain here that Anna's mental derangement is caused by a force external as well as internal: her Byronic husband. Anna herself is at root good; her untempered sensibility, when played upon by her husband, drives her to become momentarily the sort of "invalid" (62) that, according to Diane Price Herndl, populated much nineteenth-century woman's fiction. In such fiction, invalid women fall ill, Herndl argues, not because of "'natural' weakness" but rather as "the result of men's behavior and a system that leaves no other practical alternative." But Anna's invalidism is brief and acute, brief enough to conclude that Graves is not holding up chronic invalidism as justification for ongoing domestic oppression. If invalidism can *"work"* for Anna (to use Herndl's term), it is simply as a strategic move that extricates her from an untenable marriage and unbearable motherhood. Death is the usual endpoint of a woman's domestic invalidism, Herndl observes.[21] But in Anna's case, Christian salvation brings an end to illness; her fate is not, after all, governed by the melancholy aesthetic that her Oakwood years could not prepare her to reject.

Yet this is not always the case in *Sketches*. Graves also offers us a case that is not so cleanly resolved as Anna's, primarily because the illness in question envelops both mind and body. Whereas Anna's invalidism is primarily mental and stems from the influence of a bad marriage partner, the fate of Matilda Harwood begins with maternal indulgence, develops into poor physical fitness, and evolves, finally, into permanent disability of both mind and body. When Ellen seeks out Matilda, she is distressed to find her "very much indisposed" (153). Matilda complains to Ellen that she has "had so much sickness" that she can tell the extent of her "own indisposition even better than any physician" (153). Matilda has grown so desperate, in fact, that she has resorted to homeopathy, here equally as suspicious as some conventional medicine. In this condition, Matilda can think of the past only in terms of its freedom from pain and sickness (154). She is able to think little of her present or future—her twelve children, seven of whom have survived infancy. (Matilda's husband, Mr. Granville, ascribes the five babies' deaths to the carelessness of nurses in his employ.) Reflecting on her tragic life, Matilda exclaims, "Oh, you know not, my dear Ellen, how much you have escaped by remaining unmarried" (154).

At this point we may be inclined to understand Matilda's plight as similar to Anna's: that is, either a bad husband or unreasonable domestic demands (twelve children!) accounts for her retreat into invalidism. But Graves's narrative takes us in an unexpected direction when Ellen expresses not sympathy but scorn: she lets readers know that she believes Matilda to be the worst kind of hypochondriac. True, Matilda complains bitterly of digestive trouble and makes much of her need to eat small amounts of food at intervals all through the day. Yet to Ellen it seems that Matilda takes excessive amounts of food at these intervals and, what is more, by covering this food with cayenne pepper virtually guarantees herself "heart-burn" (155). Disabled by peptic upset, among other ailments, Matilda demands to be waited on constantly, and in so doing shifts her domestic burdens to her young stepdaughter (Mr. Granville's only child from a previous marriage). Assessing the whole situation, Ellen proclaims Matilda "selfish" and "indolent" (156–57) and wonders, "What can it be, that could thus cause a wife, a mother, and the mistress of a family to become so dead to the affections and duties of married life" (158).

No one, it seems, can persuade Matilda that her invalid state results from poor diet and hygiene—not her friends, nor her legitimate physicians, nor the unsavory doctors who profit from her imaginary illness—and so she seems doomed to the fate Anna escaped. Yet this is not the real tragedy of Matilda's story. It is, rather, the very real decline of her stepdaughter, Sophia. Ellen learns some time after visiting Matilda that the much-abused Sophia is dying; she visits again, only to find Matilda vying for attention and sympathy, essentially stealing it from the deserving girl. Sophia dies, and Graves once again emphasizes that she was worn to exhaustion by assuming the domestic duties that Matilda should have discharged. Mr. Granville grieves: Sophia "was all that was left to me by my angel wife, and she too is taken from me, but I have deserved it all—wretched, cruel father, my remorse is now my punishment" (170–71). Soon thereafter, Mr. Granville dies, and Matilda puts all of her remaining children in "boarding-schools" (172). Ellen muses that the tragedy of Matilda Harwood Granville began in her youth, when her own mother coddled her during illness rather than urging her to restore her strength by such measures as taking fresh air during outdoor exercise. The narrator offers this sage advice for women who become ill: "So far from expecting attention to every little ailment she may experience, she must not dwell on them, but must rouse herself from the disabling effects of indisposition, by strenuous, persevering exertion in the path of duty. Her husband will look to her as the head of his household, as the one who is responsible for the care and management of all that he entrusts to her. The numerous and pressing duties of domestic life, must be attended to, though her strength may fail under her constant and fatiguing exertions" (173). "Self-inflicted monomania" is not to be a refuge from the fatigue (175). That, Graves seems to say, would be tantamount to living in the foreign fictional world of the novels that certain girls smuggled onto the Oakwood campus against Mrs. Norville's wishes. Instead, Graves has Ellen argue that an active life is the solution. One meets the demands of domestic life by becoming physically able to do so. On this count Ellen recalls a conversation between Matilda's mother and a wise family physician: "'Your daughter, my dear madam,' said he, 'has no disease that requires medical attendance. All that now ails her, is the consequence of sedentary confinement, and want of exercise. Let her rise early, and attend to those domestic duties which . . . you should now resign to her. Let her eat plain and simple food, instead of those dainties with which you indulge her capricious fancies'" (160). Once again, we see that the culpability for women's failings lies in their upbringing. Sophia's demise is traced to her stepmother, Matilda's in turn to her mother.

So it is that Matilda—and her innocent family—might have been spared their awful fate, not by knowledge learned in school, not by knowledge gained from a sedentary belletristic curriculum, but by leaving poetry about nature behind and venturing out into the world rendered ineffable in poems.

Indeed, domestic economists encouraged a healthful mix of soul (faith), mind (intellect), and body (labor). One theory of health that circulated widely in the late 1830s was that of Sylvester Graham, who proposed that the body was more of a republic than a monarchy—which is to say that all of its parts (mind, spirit, and body, and individual organs within the body) needed attention so that they might exist in "sympathy" with one another.[22] Other writers, Elisha Bartlett for example, argued that there must be a union of intellect and body if the health of both is to be maintained. Catharine Beecher incorporated these theories into her own writing on domestic health, warning that there was "a terrible decay of female health all over the land . . . that was increasing in a most alarming ratio"—though she did not sound her alarm until 1855, when such ideas were already familiar.[23] A decade before Beecher, Graves appears to have tapped into this thought as a way to ensure efficient, economic homes run by women who took affirmative steps beyond a life of the mind to safeguard their health. She supports the notion of "able-bodied womanhood" as a defense against the perception that women were worse off in the nineteenth century than in the eighteenth—a perception that was in all likelihood empirically false, but nonetheless was argued with persuasive force in both domestic fiction and in the discourse of professional medicine at mid-century. Verbrugge reports the mortality and life expectancy statistics gathered for early-nineteenth-century Boston by Lemeul Shattuck, which show that men's and women's health, on balance, did not decline during the antebellum period. Life expectancy hovered around thirty-eight years throughout that period; when broken down by gender, women outlived men on average by a few years. What did change during this period was the nature of illness and death. As Boston grew in population and density, more adults died of epidemic diseases—cholera and typhus, for example. At the same time, though, fewer persons died of vaguely described ailments such as nervous disorders. Perhaps the most striking figure Shattuck compiled points to the sizeable number of deaths ascribed to tuberculosis—between one-seventh and one-quarter of all deaths in a given year. As Verbrugge points out, conditions were

thought to be worse in other northern cities, and, both in Boston and elsewhere, illness and death reached near-catastrophic levels among recent
(mostly Irish) immigrants.[24]

Ellen's advice to the fashionably ill does not address other causes of
women's poor health (immigration for instance). And there were numerous
other causes cited in the literature of the day. One argument against
women's public oratory, for example, was that it threatens the speaker's
health, a point manifest in Hale's work as well as Graves's. Hale's *The Lecturess* (1839) features Marian Gaylord, who destroys her marriage by insisting that she continue her public lecturing, despite her husband's disap-
proval. Her husband leaves her and, subsequently, she wastes and dies. To
what extent the husband is culpable in Marian's death is left unclear—perhaps he failed to enforce his wishes with sufficient vigor. But it is clear that
Marian's choice, if not the freedom to make that choice, leads rather directly
to her doom. As the case of Graves's Anna Percival shows us, men were perceived as greatly accountable for declines in women's health. In *The Boarding School,* remember, Hannah Webster Foster figured knowledge of rhetoric as prerequisite to fending off the seductive advances of unworthy suitors.
A failed defense, a successful seduction, could lead to illegitimacy and dire
consequences for mother and child, and for the new republic that depended
on legitimate unions to establish property and political entitlements. But
the rhetorical world of Foster and Murray was one dominated by an Enlightenment calculus in which mind and body could be figured as separate
entities, with the logical mind ultimately ruling the body. Not so in Graves's
day. The rhetorical norms in which she was steeped suggested a much more
complex relationship between utterances and mental disposition and, indeed, between mind and body. The body, with its capacity to be touched by
the aesthetics of its surroundings, could influence the logical operations of
the mind. The mind, in turn, needed conditioning to control these valuable
sympathies. Graves's assertion that a belletristic education lacked sufficient
power to exert such control plays out two ways in *Sketches.* There is Anna
Percival's case, in which an unfortified mind lets sympathies rule, nearly to
the point of Anna's ruination. And there is Matilda Harwood's, in which
failure to care for the body ultimately erodes a perfectly sound mind. Both
cases, we argue, have ramifications for more than just the women described,
for in Graves's period it was not uncommon to view the body as a synec-

dochic republic, with the story of a body's tribulations, then, an allegory for republican life.

For Graves, women had to be prepared to intervene during those times when rhetorical, belletristic instruction—no matter how good—failed to shield "a sister" from harm, a point explored in the sketch of the Grosvenor sisters. While Anna's downfall stems from her mother's poor early influence—too much Byron, not enough Bible—romantic sensibility remains a problem even under the guidance of the best of mothers. Mary and Ellen Grosvenor are model students at Mrs. Norville's school: "They had been educated at home in much seclusion and had mingled very little with girls of their own age. Though this had made them reserved when with strangers, yet it had preserved them from many evils resulting from the association of numbers ... which the most careful instructress cannot always guard against.... Their principles had become strengthened by a home education, before they entered upon the ordeal of a boarding-school" (25). Despite such a strong domestic beginning, Ellen Grosvenor falls prey to her imagination: she "viewed every one through the medium of her own fancy, and too often invested them with virtues not their own" (119–20)—shades of Anna Percival's downfall. Ellen Grosvenor's fancy leads her to marry Edmund Bolton, a man who "knew how to accommodate himself to every taste, and to appear to every one all that they wish," a man interested in her beauty and her fortune. What the new Mrs. Bolton soon realizes after her marriage is that her husband frequently exercises a "violent temper," and that "she was now irrevocably his own" to exercise it on (120). Like Anna Percival's husband, Edmund Bolton is flagrantly unfaithful, carrying on "freely" with women in her presence, "sneeringly smiling at the effects they produced in disturbing her peace" (121). His wife soon feels little but contempt for her husband, little, that is, except for duty. Mary tries to persuade her sister that wifely duties "are cancelled by his conduct," but Ellen Bolton feels differently: "My Bible dear Mary does not tell me this. . . . I am his wife, and my course is prescribed both by reason and religion" (127). And so, in spite of her poor health, which declines steadily under the stresses of living with her husband, Ellen Bolton continues to perform her wifely duties, including giving birth to twin daughters. Fortunately, Edmund's lifestyle catches up with him, and he dies of a fever, expressing a few words of remorse, which his wife "treasured in her heart, to the exclusion of all his neglect and unkindness" (130). She "mourned his loss as if he had realized her dearest expectations, and fulfilled all her brightest dreams" (130). Still, however much Mrs. Bolton can revise the facts of her marriage, she cannot as easily revise economic reality: she is now widowed, in ill health, with two children to support. She is fortunate to have a sister who has never married and is willing to undertake the care of her family. Sisterly love alone heals: Mary sets things aright by becoming the husband that Edmund wasn't, devoting herself to her sister's twins (also named Mary and Ellen) and providing a version of a healthy family with two mothers held together in sisterly love. As Okker notes, women's periodical editors and writers such as Ann Stephens transformed "a hierarchical structure of moral women influencing corrupt and powerful men into a sisterly structure of women speaking to each other."[25] In her sketch of the Grosvenors, Graves literalizes the metaphor of sisterhood.

Like many of the antebellum writers, Graves was interested in defining women as more than wives and mothers. Consider, for example, Hale's advice. "The End and Aim of the Present System of Female Education" (1835) posits that women should be "prepared for *any* lot which might befall them."[26] Mary supports her family in a way familiar in schooling fictions— she opens "a school" in their "former happy home," one that will provide for them "with ample means" (130). Education functions in this sketch only as the way that she can support this revised female family. Her students are invisible; we hear nothing about her as a teacher. The school is simply the family business.[27] Female seminaries thus prove valuable for Graves insofar as they provide economic opportunities for women, but they are not "considered all-sufficient" for "finishing" young women, and certainly not for "starting" them (10). Finally, it is the home instruction that the Grosvenors received that allowed at least one of them to excel in the arts of domestic economy and to engage the failsafe of sisterhood. It was the home that provided the bonds of sisterly love so necessary for the maintenance of two generations of women.

Domestic Instruction versus Boarding Schools

The great responsibility of making man or woman what they should be, rests not upon teachers, upon whom God has not laid it, but upon parents, and upon them alone.

—Mrs. A. J. Graves, *Sketches of My Schoolmates*

Mrs. A. J. Graves admits that female seminaries bear investigation if only because they make it "easier to find the requisite varieties, and to study human nature as it usually presents itself unchecked in its tendencies in youth" (vi); such a study, according to her, can yield only one thesis: "As the girl is, the woman will be, unless some powerful counteraction has intervened" (vi). Throughout *Sketches* Graves makes clear that female seminaries and boarding schools cannot supply that "powerful counteraction," indeed, that they cannot—even when run well—effectively remediate the long-range effects of poor early training in the home. Each sketch in her serial narrative reinforces the point first introduced by the novel's narrator, Ellen Maitland:

> The school at Oakwood united as far as it was possible the advantages of home and school education—and the system pursued by Mrs. Norville was more like that of a mother than a mere instructress, yet even with all the faithful guardianship and constant solicitude with which she hovered around us, even in our hours of unrestrained amusement, there were one or two who evaded her watchful care by bringing among us immoral works, poisonous to the unsuspecting credulity of childhood. And if such abuses could creep stealthily in, under a preceptress such as she was, what must be the case in a crowded boarding-school, where external discipline is entirely depended on, and where little or no care is taken in the cultivation of moral principles—and where the opportunities for successful deception are so frequent, as even to discourage those who endeavor to unite both modes in training the young committed to their care. (25–26)

Only the most extraordinary girls—such as the Grosvenor sisters, who came to Mrs. Norville's Oakwood uncorrupted by schooling outside the home—exhibit moral fiber strong enough to resist schoolgirl temptations. As evidence of this, Ellen Maitland recalls that "if a book were offered to the sisters with a caution not to let Mrs. Norville see it, they would instantly decline taking it and appear surprised that any one could wish to read what their instructress disapproved" (26). Only such girls of "gifted . . . minds and tastes" could be trusted to read what they as young women of "love, peace and intellectual refinement" should (27). Implicit in Ellen's praise for the Grosvenor sisters is the notion that rhetorical training, at its best, *might* be able to shield women, especially impressionable young ones, from the "contaminating influence" of dangerous words, but its shielding powers, as the sketch of Ellen Grosvenor Bolton attests, cannot be relied on (25). Rhetorical training, for Graves, has its limits, namely, that no amount of "right training," presumably in rhetoric and all other proper subjects, can *instill* the moral good that, finally, needs be inborn and cultivated in infancy (v).[28] Thus for Graves, rhetorical training ideally nurtures and protects goodness, but it cannot be its source or its guarantor. Such goodness must be tended by a structure of sisterly care and watchfulness and, just as important, must begin in the nursery under proper parental (mostly maternal) instruction. Graves's aphorism might better have been, "As is the girl, so is her mother." As her many sketches of fashionable, inattentive mothers and profligate husbands suggest, Graves's hope for skilled maternal instruction does not mean that she was sanguine about the realities of home life for many women. Mothering, particularly of female babies, needed reforming: "We begin wrong with the female even while an infant in the cradle."[29]

Graves's stance resonates in many ways with Susan Ridley Sedgwick and Hale, both of whom admit some complexity to the question of whether young women should be taught at home or in boarding schools. Both women conclude that domestic instruction is strongly preferable, but each is less emphatic than Graves that boarding schools are too loosely supervised, too worldly, too *public* to be of much countervailing value. They incline, instead, to label such schools inferior because a teacher cannot scrutinize a girl so well—and for so long—as a mother can. Nearly a decade before Graves took on boarding schools, Sedgwick, whose stories and novels were popular beginning in the 1830s, argued in an essay appearing in the New York *Knickerbocker* that "the fact is, that school education is *too much* relied on,— social and domestic education *too little*. The best schools in the world, can never supply the want of nursery culture,—of early moral and intellectual training. And if this be true of the best, what shall we say of those which, though more eagerly sought and prized, for young ladies, and more resorted to than any other, are above all others to be deprecated—viz: what are termed *Fashionable Boarding Schools?*"

Like many women writing in the 1820s and 1830s, Sedgwick also insists that girls "are to be educated for private not for public life,—for the fireside, not for the forum."[30] Graves, too, argues for private rather than public education for young women: "Whatever may be urged in favor of a public education for boys there can be no doubt that a private one is preferable for girls" (25). Boarding schools, whose very survival depends on their reputation—on public opinion—are necessarily tainted by their associations and subject to all of the speciousness of the marketplace or politics against which domestic writers align themselves. Writes Sedgwick, "Is it true, that when public examinations of some of these schools take place, the most dishonorable means are resorted to on the part of teachers, to create a good reputation for the school?" She goes on to explain: "What can be a more open countenancing of deceitful practices, and downright falsehood, than to let the scholars know beforehand, precisely the questions that will be put to them, in each branch, so that they may carefully commit the answers, which are to serve as the test of their general acquaintance with the study?" Put simply, sustaining the reputation—the value—of a boarding school leads to practices that are lamentable in the public realm, but unforgivable in what ought to be a domestic reserve. If public exams lead to their corruption, what more—what worse—might happen should girls be forced to follow their male peers through more of the "trials and temptations which they must sooner or later encounter"?[31] Still, for Sedgwick the problem is not integral to the boarding experience, but rather to its pedagogy, specifically, to the use of public examinations.

Sedgwick implies that there is affirmative value to such study if certain principles are followed. First, schooling should be viewed as "merely for discipline," as an occasion "to train and fit the mind for future action and improvement." Given this principle, then, Sedgwick maintains that "studies should not be so multiplied as to occupy the whole time of young persons, leaving them no leisure for reading,—no chance to acquire a taste for general knowledge." It is this reading, presumably guided by rhetorical principles, that will serve young women well, long after they have concluded formal schooling, a premise familiar from literature of earlier times. Yet again, the context for Sedgwick's comments is strikingly different: in the end, for Sedgwick, the difference between boarding school and domestic instruction maps onto a distinction between mind and body. Domestic instruction permits attention to the "jewel" that is the mind, while boarding school education indulges only the "perishable casket" that is the body.[32] That the mind could be separated from the physical manifestations of femaleness *and* still remain gendered female marks the ideological distance traveled away from the Enlightenment possibility of a sexless mind and toward the enduring sexing of mental processes that followed thereafter.

Some years before Sedgwick weighed in on boarding schools, Sarah Josepha Hale had also surveyed the problem—like Sedgwick, in the blunt prose of an essay. But to understand this prose, it is helpful to know, as Hale's readers would have from her 1827 novel, *Northwood*, that she put supreme value on young women's education. Without it, *Northwood* makes plain, women stand at considerable disadvantage in marriage.[33] Graves, of course, worried about this disadvantage to the extent that she finds hardly anything to recommend marriage, a refrain surprisingly common among the domestic economists. Yet Hale entertains a vision of marital bonds in which women can claim authority, if not equality, by possessing the humanistic and scientific knowledge useful to domestic work—where that work, and its sphere, is defined with more elasticity than Graves and Sedgwick imagined. So consistent with the suggestion that education might improve the married state, Hale stresses the need for young women to be well schooled—at home, preferably, but in a boarding or academy situation if necessary. Indeed, Hale represents an interesting compromise on the question. In an essay leading the April 1831 issue of *Ladies' Magazine* (which she edited), she appears at first to strike a stance as unequivocal as Graves's and Sedgwick's: "We think, then, the *mother* of a family should always consider herself the responsible instructress of her daughters, and no boarding school education should *finish* the young lady. Till the idea of this *finishing* is exploded, education will be something apart from domestic life, as incompatible with our common duties as religion has been falsely represented to be with our innocent pleasures." But three pages later, after laying out a scheme of education that has girls attending district schools for basic studies, then returning home for more schooling, Hale abruptly offers that schools such as Emma Willard's Troy Female Seminary "are necessary as auxiliaries in instruction, and we rejoice to see the efforts constantly making to improve and extend them." In this we witness a departure from the defense of Republican Motherhood implicit in Graves and Sedgwick. Sedgwick objected to boarding schools in part because they permitted "no leisure for reading" of the sort of novels that Sedgwick and her better-known sister-in-law wrote.[34] Hale might have expressed a similar sentiment had she continued to write novels herself. But she did not. Instead, she turned her pen and the journal she edited toward the production of a different kind of reading material: moral in tone like novels could be, but more practical in orientation, invested in the application of scientific knowledge to the efficient management of the home.

One long-standing objection to boarding schools, of course, was that they removed children from the environment—the home—that was naturally most conducive to their moral upbringing. As the nineteenth century unfolded and the values of individualism, specialization, and Protestantism ascended, motherhood began to be seen as a particular kind of virtue (Protestant evangelism) and as a particular kind of science (domestic) to be performed in a particular place (the home). This yoking of the public with the domestic, the religious with the secular, was not without its tensions, threatening, as did the union itself, to fly apart under the slightest pressure. The argument for boarding schools had always been that, under good circumstances, the education young women could receive at a boarding school surpassed what most mothers could manage at home. As women of the middling classes became more highly educated, it was less easy to see boarding schools as simply an extended family in which learning could take place effectively and efficiently under more accomplished tutelage. Changes in rhetorical climate figure in here as well. The agonistic rhetoric that was once thought to serve the republic was increasingly seen as an instrument of disunion, while the turn toward belletrism in rhetoric, with its emphasis on the reception rather than production of texts, suited the needs of those who valued language instruction but who loathed putting it in service of party strife. The belletristic turn also served those who desired to defend girls' schooling in the face of a new scientized domesticity: rhetorical knowledge cultivated taste, and taste—indigenous and civic—guided the decisions that would make for harmony at home and harmony in the nation. It took some time, until roughly the 1840s, for a vocabulary to evolve that could reconcile changes in home life and rhetorical instruction with the continued desire for the advanced schooling of girls. That commonsense philosophy had evolved into a distinct rhetorical tradition meant that there was a ready blueprint for reading and writing activities that tempered Romantic excess with mental discipline. This approach characterizes rhetorical instruction as imagined in the textbooks and novels written in the 1840s and 1850s by writers such as Louisa Caroline Tuthill and Almira Hart Lincoln Phelps, the quite different subjects of our next two chapters.

The Commonsense Romanticism of
Louisa Caroline Tuthill

A labored defense of woman's rights might do for the meridian of Constantino-
ple. All the rights which she ought to claim, are allowed in this blessed country.
The only danger now is, that she may overstep the bounds which modesty and
delicacy prescribe, and come forward upon that arena of strife which ought to
belong exclusively to man. . . . The paths that are open to us are many, but they
lie along "the cool sequestered vale." Such are the vicissitudes of life, that we need
all the resources which can be accumulated. Few of you, my friends, probably
either expect or wish to become authoresses; but you all wish to enjoy the pleas-
ures of literature, and will not deny the utility of being able to write a perspicu-
ous and pleasing style.

Louisa Caroline Tuthill, *The Young Lady's Home* (1839)

Favoring feminine delicacy and ardently opposed to woman suffrage, Louisa Caroline Tuthill might seem an unusual subject for a
study of women's civic liberatory rhetoric. A prolific writer of juvenile
fiction, Tuthill occupies a minor place in the history of women's fiction—and that perhaps only because the influential Sarah Josepha
Hale found occasion to mention her in *Woman's Record.*[1] Tuthill's
standing is further diminished by discussions of her deficiencies as a
novelist: namely, that her narratives are hopelessly didactic. "Many
woman's fictions," Nina Baym reminds us, "are long, complex, densely
plotted novels containing numerous characters, experimenting with
dialogue and dialect, developing set pieces of lush nature description."[2] It would be a stretch to describe Tuthill's fiction as either
"densely plotted" or "lush."

Yet there is a dimension to nineteenth-century women's fiction beyond the aesthetic, one that has been largely screened out by twenti-

eth-century critical preferences: according to Baym, women writers can often be seen "deploying rhetorical and oratorical strategies whose terminology we have forgotten and which we no longer have the skill to recognize."[3] Tuthill does indeed experiment with "rhetorical and oratorical strategies" (including dialect), discursive moves perhaps unfamiliar to contemporary literary critics but not to rhetoricians. There is, then, another way to view Tuthill's didacticism. Given her professed allegiance to the ideas of Dugald Stewart, George Campbell, and Hugh Blair, Tuthill is better studied not as a failed novelist but as a schooled "new" rhetorician. Her work is consistent with a tradition that "survived well into the twentieth century": one characterized by "a strong sense of nationalism coupled with a strong moral flavor" and marked by the idea that "in teaching literature they were teaching a vision of the good."[4] Put simply, Tuthill works from a tradition in which narrative—in fact, all belletristic modes—are subordinate to the force of a rhetorical ethics.

Tuthill published articles and books anonymously for over a decade before her name appeared on two volumes of rhetorical instruction for women: *The Young Lady's Home* in 1839 and a companion anthology, *The Young Lady's Reader; arranged for Examples in Rhetoric: for the Higher Classes in Seminaries.* J. P. Brace, principal of the Hartford Female Seminary, judged the latter to be "entirely unlike any of the reading books now in use," a book "well calculated for the object in view,—to teach and illustrate rhetoric; and the principles of style, by examples." Lydia Sigourney likewise found the *Reader* a "varied, and tasteful selection of prose and poetry, arranged on rhetorical principles . . . admirably calculated to supply a deficiency which has long been felt to exist, in the higher departments of education."[5]

We know little of Tuthill's life other than what can be inferred from her published writings—and publish she did.[6] Considering the length of her career, her frequency of publication, and her association with major presses in Boston, Philadelphia, and New York, we can conclude that Tuthill must have been widely known among a popular readership. Scholars note Tuthill's *History of Architecture from the Earliest Times* (1848) as her most significant contribution to American letters, followed by her edited volumes of Ruskin's work (for Wiley and Sons, several completed in the last years of her life). In between, Tuthill published a slew of conduct-of-life guides and fictions, mostly for young people, as well as moralistic fictions for mature audiences.

Around mid-century, when a new Tuthill title was appearing nearly every year, she penned a series of books for Putnam on occupations for men—merchant, lawyer, mechanic, sailor, and so on. Through all of this work runs the commonsense rhetorical and philosophical principles Tuthill laid out for a female audience in her *Home* and *Reader*. Whereas the influence and popularity of someone like Almira Phelps (see chapter 6) is indicated by the frequent reprinting of key titles, we would argue that Tuthill's influence and popularity are better gauged by assessing the sheer number of titles she produced in the course of a lifetime.

Throughout this lifetime, Tuthill's emphasis on literary taste registers a shift in American rhetorical history wrought by the pressures of Romanticism—but a Romanticism different from that presented in conventional literary histories. In the late 1980s, feminist critics began documenting the role of a "dissenting"—perhaps competing—Romanticism, an alternative to that established by "the 'Big Six' (Blake, Wordsworth, Coleridge, Byron, Shelley, Keats)." Underscored in such feminist scholarship is the "wealth and significance of the literary production that occurred outside of the limited corpus of these particular male poets" who "endorsed a concept of the self as a power that gains control over and gives significance to nature."[7] In the alternative tradition,

> the language of the common man and woman is found not in the poems of Wordsworth but in the tracts, ballads, broadsides, and penny-dreadfuls of the street, a vernacular discourse that literary critics of the Romantic period have until very recently ignored. . . .
>
> We must read with renewed attention and appreciation the hundreds of female and male writers working in the early nineteenth century, all those novelists, essayists, journalists, diarists, and letter-writers who had narratives to tell other than those plotted as . . . "the romantic sublime" or "romantic irony." In these forgotten or wrongly dismissed writings, we may find stories of equal or greater significance than those told by Blake, Wordsworth, Coleridge, Byron, Percy Shelley, and Keats, . . . tales of *shared* rather than solitary experience.[8]

This alternative Romanticism is what Tuthill adapts for presentation to U.S. audiences. While she excerpts in the *Reader* several passages from her favorite British Romantics, Wordsworth and Coleridge, she notes in the introduction that many of her examples are drawn from American authors, a decision she defends as needing "no apology" (*YLR,* iv). Indeed, she remarks that "it is a pleasure to find that they [Americans] have already contributed so largely to English Classic Literature," an observation that highlights Tuthill's commitment to producing literature that addresses distinctly American concerns (*YLR*, iv).

It is not the emphasis on solitary experience that attracts Tuthill to British Romanticism. Rather it is the prospect of rendering emotion and other heightened psychological states in language. But whereas some Romantics idealize such rendering as a process unconstrained, Tuthill seeks to govern it by application of common sense. Her textbooks draw heavily on the Scottish commonsense school's tremendous influence on rhetoric in American colleges: she professes a new Christian belletristic rhetoric, one opposed to the kind of "extreme" liberatory civic rhetoric that authorizes the campaign for women's suffrage. Consequently, Tuthill's rhetorical practice differs markedly from, say, that of Elizabeth Cady Stanton or Lucretia Mott. Stanton and Mott are committed to oratorical presence and public visibility; Tuthill and those like her cleave to the emerging, quieter tradition of belles lettres. Put another way, if Stanton and Mott as early feminists stand for an older tradition of public oratory, Tuthill as a domestic economist represents the gendered outcome of print's encroachment on oratory, a move arguably complicit in the curtailment of women's full enfranchisement.

Given her preference for print, Tuthill cannot be seen as emulating all that the commonsense ecclesiastics have to offer. For example, while adopting their temperament, she adapts their oratorical technique to "reading," by which she means reading aloud, a skill she believes women should acquire along with talents in music and art:

> A fine reader may contribute as much pleasure to the domestic circle, during the course of life, as a skillful performer on the harp or pianoforte. The instrument for reading is ever at hand, and seldom out of tune. Every body has an ear for it. It amuses childhood, instructs youth, soothes manhood, and cheers old age.
>
> When a young lady has acquired this accomplishment, why should she not entertain a circle of friends by reading, as readily as she would sing or play for them? Custom sanctions the one, why should it not the other?
>
> The following rules are universally acknowledged to be requisite to good reading, namely:

Full and distinct enunciation of syllables, and correct and elegant pronunciation.

The voice should be pitched in the natural key; raised so loud as to be
heard without effort, and not so loud as to fatigue the auditor and reader.

Reading should not be so rapid as to be unintelligible, nor so deliberate as to be wearisome.

A monotonous tone,—"the drone-pipe of the humble-bee,"—should
be avoided.

A graceful attitude and pleasant expression of countenance, should
not be considered beneath the reader's notice.

Above all, it is requisite to read *intelligently*—to enter into the meaning
and spirit of the author. Without this, all other rules are in vain. Much assistance about the modulation of the voice, may be given by teachers of
elocution, but nature and good taste, are the best teachers of *emphasis* and
expression. (YLR, iii)

Tuthill scorns her countrywomen who exceed the limits she inscribes here
but praises those willing to accept advanced instruction in a new kind of
rhetoric, useful both in female academies and at home. In doing so she joins
those who wish to teach domestic rhetoric: rigorous in attention to logic, argument, and style but limited to literacy.

In articulating a rhetoric of domestic economy, Tuthill illuminates for us
a period of upheaval in U.S. rhetorical history, a period distinguished by the
rise of coeducational common schooling and, later, women's achievement of
suffrage and their movement into the professions. Despite Tuthill's invisibil-
ity in accounts of rhetoric during this era, she and other domestic economists set in motion practices that remain powerful as we move into the
twenty-first century. We can, for example, recognize something like the
rhetoric and ideology of domestic economy in the "coincidental" rise of
multiculturalism and argument textbooks: namely, a hope that the "neutral"
tools of logic will "neutralize"—will domesticate—the contentious political
discussions that permeate everyday American life. Then, as now, Americans
look to home and family as the stabilizing center of democracy. Then, as
now, rhetoric could be imagined as a way of containing strident public
voices that challenge deeply held values.

To say that Tuthill espouses a rhetoric of domestic economy runs the risk
of diminishing her intellectual standing. Case in point: The recent rediscov-
ery of Tuthill as a key figure in the early history of U.S. architecture centers

on her effort to become an "arbiter of taste."[9] She may have had such aspirations, but it is necessary to remember that Tuthill would have understood taste as a concept with deep philosophical implications, not a superficial inclination toward one fashion or another. So it is that Tuthill's *History of Architecture from the Earliest Times* reminds us of Tuthill's lifetime fascination with the private interiors—mind and family—that are sheltered by and formative of the complicated facade that is public life in a democracy. Her work, as we shall see, is all about linking taste to its commonsense philosophical underpinnings in ways that readers of her forty books (thirty-three authored, seven edited) would find not only appealing, not only persuasive, but life altering and life affirming.

Common Sense in Tuthill's Young Lady's Home *and* Reader

The "new rhetoric" emerged in Scotland and England (and subsequently North America) under the guiding influence of the commonsense ecclesiastics, the best known of whom are, of course, Campbell, Blair, and later Whately. Although the new rhetoricians continued to promote some aspects of classical traditions in rhetoric and literature, they also advanced the Renaissance preoccupation with style. And they departed from ancient wisdom in two other ways. First, the Scottish ecclesiastics found classical models of argument insufficient support for a *Christian* democracy, and so the rhetoric they articulated was distinctly Christian—and particularly Protestant—in its aims. Second, they contended that classical thinkers attended far too little to human nature and, specifically, to the nature of the human mind. Thus they judged classical and neoclassical rhetorics inadequate (although hardly without merit) because the ancient rhetoricians did not study what the Christian rhetorician most needed to know: how to convict and convert.[10] Consequently, the new rhetoricians, grounded in emerging studies of "mental science," were heavily invested in the prospects of scientific method and rational thought and saw no inherent conflict in using science and logic to further the highest aim of their religion: to inspire faithfulness.

Much of Tuthill's work on the philosophy of mental science comes not from rhetoricians Blair and Campbell, but rather more directly from the popular work of Dugald Stewart, a commonsense philosopher widely read in American universities.[11] In *Elements of the Philosophy of the Human Mind*

(1792), Stewart articulates the task of philosophy and education as, in part, being one of overcoming biases or prejudices formed by early impressions and linked not logically, but merely by temporal accident. Ideally, children ought to be taught properly from the start: instead of allowing them to commit sense impressions to memory *seriatim*, by rote memorization, they should learn a systematic way of recording observations. Indeed, Stewart believes that a science of rules and models—algebra is his example—might someday evolve into a philosophy that would account reliably for human morals and politics. But this does not mean that the arts of morality and politics would be thoroughly subordinate to scientific disciplines. Rather, Stewart recognizes the value of distinct disciplinary perspectives and argues that scientific findings can inform the arts, just as knowledge in the arts can improve the pursuit of scientific inquiry. He also maintains that across all disciplinary horizons and at all levels, formal education should emphasize the effective organizing of knowledge, not simply its acquisition. That way, education can lay a foundation for the inquiry that should persist under self-sponsorship throughout a person's lifetime.[12]

In the *Home,* Tuthill selects an epigraph from Stewart to forecast her project's main objective, self-education: "There are few individuals whose education has been conducted, in every respect, with attention and judgment. Almost every man of reflection is conscious, when he arrives at maturity, of many defects in his mental powers, and of many inconvenient habits, which might have been prevented or remedied in his infancy or youth. Such a consciousness is the first step towards improvement; and the person who feels it, if he is possessed with resolution and steadiness, will not scruple to begin a new course of education for himself. *It is never too late to think of the improvement of our faculties*" (*YLH,* 6). In their original context, Stewart's words tout not so much the importance of self-education—for him, necessary only because of faulty early training—but rather the importance of beginning the logical arrangement of knowledge in earliest childhood. Tuthill inverts Stewart's argument: it is essential to cultivate the will to self-education later in life because, at least for women, foundational knowledge gained in formal schooling will never be enough. Her concern, like that of other writers such as Hannah Webster Foster, is for the graduates of female academies.

Tuthill takes on the problem of faulty early learning most extensively in a chapter of the *Home* entitled "Prejudice." In addition to "selfish prejudices," she details two related forms: prejudices learned from parents and teachers and those learned from books (*YLH,* 220). It is a given, she implies in this chapter and elsewhere, that such prejudice undermines educational efforts throughout the new nation, especially for women. Poor teachers in weak institutions guarantee it. They prize rules and precepts rather than lauding the prejudice-crushing principles one needs to become an "accountable moral agent" (*YLH,* 222). (Tuthill explores the distinction between shallow precept and deep principle in her preceding chapter, "Acting from General Principles.") Of course, female seminaries are often exactly the places where young girls acquire silly prejudices, and Tuthill twice makes use of Joanna Baillie's *Orra* to reinforce this point. She includes it in its entirety in the *Reader,* and in the *Home* she offers a synopsis of the play, holding up for ridicule a "listening circle of staring school-girls spell-bound" by ghost stories that "made the heart thrill with mingled fear and delight" (*YLH,* 223). While such diversions might at first seem innocent—the nineteenth-century equivalent of horror movies—Tuthill fears that their damage to the mind's rational capacity could be significant and sustained. She declares: "How hard it is for cool sober reason to overcome . . . phantoms of prejudice; it grapples with them and they are overthrown, but not vanquished until after long and severe struggles" (*YLH,* 224).

Youth is not alone in succumbing to prejudice. Teachers—specifically, writing instructors—are susceptible, especially in times of high "*party strife*." According to Tuthill, writing assignments are particularly vulnerable to this sort of early national corruption. She reports that one writing master assigned this line for students' copybooks: "Deist, Atheist, Democrat, Devil" (*YLH,* 224). Other writing prompts, such as the following, might reinforce prejudices against certain religious denominations:

> Episcopalians, are mere formalists.
> Presbyterians, are all sanctimonious.
> Methodists, are a set of wild fanatics.
> Quakers are sly rogues with grave faces, &c., &c.
> (*YLH,* 225)

Even studies in history and poetry, two pursuits Tuthill advocates, can lead to prejudicial thinking, especially in the glorification of warfare and elevation of heroic (or demonic) figures.

Because all minds are prone to prejudice—with girls' more prone than boys'—they must be consciously and conscientiously strengthened. Just as did Hannah Webster Foster and Donald Fraser, Tuthill promotes the years after graduation from the academy as the best time for women to improve their minds: "Hitherto, your time has been mostly under the control of others; now, you have more freedom, more leisure, and the one, five, or ten talents, which the all-wise Dispenser has bestowed, must be doubled by your earnest zeal, and untiring perseverance. The work of self-education must go on" (*YLH,* 206). It is for this reason that Tuthill composes the *Home.* Its introduction, which follows the Stewart epigraph cited above, begins with a brief dialogue about three young women who are graduating from a female academy. There is an obvious protagonist (Clara, an ideal American patriot committed to self-study and reflection) who spars with traditional foils (Geraldine and Isabella, women who disparage their country and who believe that a trip to the Continent will finish their educations). Tuthill ends her sketch with a brief dedication that succinctly states her aim: to compose a textbook that women can use for home study: "To aid my young countrywomen, who have arrived at this interesting and important era of life, *in estimating the value of knowledge already acquired,* and *to assist them in that most momentous part of all education,* namely, *self-education,* this little work is offered with much diffidence, and earnest prayer for its success" (*YLH,* 11).

Recognition of human prejudice and a commitment to lifelong education provide the arduous beginnings of Tuthill's curriculum, which builds to include advanced subjects that are calculated to exercise all facets of the mind. This strengthening of the intellect or "mental culture" itself is a momentous task, made all the more difficult by the nature of the mind, a point Tuthill draws from Stewart (*YLH,* 17–23). In chapter 2 of the *Elements,* for example, Stewart posits that not everything that is perceived is necessarily attended to. Reading, he observes, entails a process of perceiving first letters, then syllables, then words, then the meaning of sentences, and it is entirely possible that this "process . . . passes through the mind, without leaving any trace in the memory."[13] In fact, perception without attention is all too common in reading and is likely the result of poor education: "Nothing, in truth, has such a tendency to weaken, not only the powers of invention, but the intellectual powers in general, as a habit of extensive and various reading, without reflexion."[14] Yet even if perception is coupled with attention, as it must be when one reads with the intention of writing, things can go awry: "Suppose that a man of letters were to record, in a common-place book, without any method, all the various ideas and facts which occurred to him in the course of his studies; what difficulties would he perpetually experience in applying his acquisitions to use? . . . A common-place book, conducted without any method, is an exact picture of the memory of a man whose inquiries are not directed by philosophy. And the advantages of order in treasuring up our ideas in the mind, are perfectly analogous to its effects when they are recorded in writing."[15]

What for Judith Sargent Murray promised a mental commonwealth—observation and wide reading—for Stewart foreshadows chaos. In Stewart (and Tuthill) we find no celebration of a gleaner ransacking fields. Instead of random gleaning, Stewart suggests less reading and more attention to ordering what one draws from reading. He offers five strategies that imprint impressions into usable, retrievable memory. First, he suggests that disciplines must provide particular methods for arranging the knowledge in their purview; ideally, then, one would learn from the mathematician or the historian not only content but method. Second, readers are responsible for exercising curiosity: they must learn how to find in a dull presentation something interesting and thus memorable. It becomes the reader's burden to fashion the impressive from the boring; it is not primarily an author's responsibility, nor should impressiveness be imagined as a quality necessarily inherent in a useful work of prose. Third, readers must patiently endeavor to discern useful and connected truths from details that are seemingly irrelevant, understanding that a sustained effort to make connections leads to the formation of a context within which what is learned can be ordered. Fourth, readers should practice the process of association. A text or idea should be linked with like ones; nothing should be stored in the mind as a singular impression. Finally, Stewart deems the fifth strategy the most important of all: arrangement and classification. All learning derived from reading should be categorized hierarchically.[16]

For Stewart—as for Tuthill—education would be more effective if young scholars were to read with greater selectivity and then organize the knowledge they glean with extreme care. Consistent with this advice, Tuthill recommends for women a foundational course of study in classical languages (at least Latin, if not Greek) and modern languages (Italian, German, and

French—though not, she warns, for the purpose of reading French literature). She also recommends natural science, mathematics, philosophy, political economy, and history (biblical, ancient, European, and American) and includes such reading in mental science as Stewart's *Philosophy of the Action and Moral Powers of Man* and Watts's *The Improvement of the Mind*. Most important, to organize all this information, Tuthill prescribes rigorous methods for observation, acquisition, and recall. She gives lectures on how to integrate new knowledge into old and how to correct the error of biased interpretation: "Recall some book that you may have studied; analyze it; compare it with whatever else you have read on the same subject. Or take some subject of practical moment—contentment, for example; arrange in order all the reasons you have for it, count over the rich blessings that cluster around you, until your heart overflows with gratitude. . . . Read first the index of a book, and know what are the subjects of most practical value; what knowledge it contains, of which you are ignorant; what, that you ought to be most anxious to fix in memory. Mark such subjects with your pencil, and in the course of reading, rivet your attention upon them" (*YLH*, 21–22).

The third chapter of the *Home* concerns the function of memory and lays out instructions for a detailed "Common-Place Book" or "Mnemonica" (*YLH*, 27, 28). Tuthill seeks to free her readers from the "rote-system" and to immerse them in critical thinking and methodical observation (*YLH*, 25). Instead of being memorized and recited, bits of knowledge need to be "classified," made meaningful through their assignment to scientifically defined categorical relations: "*cause and effect,—premises and conclusion,—genus and species, &c.*" (*YLH*, 27). To aid in classification, Tuthill suggests that girls keep a notebook with pages divided into thirds as follows:

I.—FACTS.

Allow two or three pages under this division, for
each of the following subdivisions; namely,—

    1. RELIGIOUS,
    2. POLITICAL,
    3. LITERARY,
    4. SCIENTIFIC,
    5. PRACTICAL,
    6. MILITARY.

These may be extended much farther.

II.—PRINCIPLES.
    1. AXIOMS,
    2. GENERAL TRUTHS,
    3. CAUSE, OR ORIGIN,
    4. ELEMENTS, OR CONSTITUTENT PARTS.

III.—SENTIMENTS.
    1. RELIGIOUS,
    2. MORAL,
    3. POETICAL.

(*YLH*, 28)

Finally, however, Tuthill stresses that such a notebook, as well as other mnemonic devices, are only tools to build memory: "Memory is like a true friend,—the more you confide in her the better she serves you" (*YLH*, 28).

In the second part of the chapter on memory, the extended biographies of two extraordinary minds, Maria Galtana Agnesi and an unnamed American woman, point to another influential feature of commonsense philosophy: its connection to Protestantism and its sworn opposition to Catholicism. Tuthill praises both women's genius—their mastery of languages, mathematics, and literature, and the expansive reach of their minds and memories. But she laments the tragedy of Agnesi, an Italian Catholic, whose genius leads only to cloistered gloominess and misery—to radical skepticism—while celebrating the American Protestant's ability to keep her prodigious talent in perspective, never losing sight of God's greater purpose for her. In offering such an anecdote, and similar ones elsewhere in the *Home*, Tuthill underscores the very concern about philosophical skepticism that Stewart raises in *Elements*. For Tuthill, the problem is especially gendered and denominational: if wise men are susceptible to skepticism, then it is all the more important that women, man's moral anchor, be sustained by proper faith.

Thus Tuthill highlights what attracts her most to the commonsense school: its reformed Christianity. Blair and Campbell were ordained clergy who had advanced their perspectives on rhetorical theory and practice in part out of dissatisfaction with the state of homiletics at a time when they felt the reformed tradition needed an effective defense against its antagonists. For Stewart, like Blair and Campbell, it is crucial that faithful philosophers, educators, and Protestants generally combine to combat the simple and unquestioning mindset, "the implicit credulity," that leads many to submit to corrupt religious or secular authority. Such an effort has to be undertaken carefully, for it turns out not to be easy, even for the faithful, to distinguish between unhealthy skepticism and "vigour of intellect" as they appear in others. And for Tuthill, as for Stewart, battling skepticism is particularly difficult in the case of Roman Catholics: "The Roman catholic system is shaken off with much greater difficulty, than those which are taught in the reformed churches; but when it loses its hold of the mind, it much more frequently prepares the way for unlimited skepticism." Also difficult is the case of students of history, in whom skepticism might arise should they believe that human progress and enlightenment are the result of chance temporal associations or, worse, purely human design. Educated skeptics may fancy themselves above "the multitude," Stewart warns, but they share the "very same weakness" of the multitude—the absence of reason. The challenge of education, then, is to teach people to maintain a "steady course of inquiry" that will enable them to navigate between implicit credulity and unlimited skepticism.[17]

Tuthill and Romanticism

Tuthill, in her *Reader*, is careful to anthologize Romantic poets who are critical of philosophical skepticism rather than those who revel in it. In a section on metaphor, she includes Felicia Hemans's "The Sceptic," which imagines a "cold sceptic" who builds his home not on sturdy rock but "on quicksand's base" and "rejects the promise of a brighter state" (*YLR*, 40). That Tuthill keenly feels the influence of the emerging female Romantics is demonstrated by her admiration for and use of the work of Hemans (1793–1835) and Joanna Baillie (1762–1851), the latter a prolific playwright who manages to merge the Scottish commonsense tradition with British Romanticism.[18] Baillie's *Series of Plays*, rechristened *Plays on the Passions*, began appearing anonymously the same year that *Lyrical Ballads* was published. According to Marlon Ross, "Whereas Wordsworth and Coleridge's literary offering received little and ambivalent notice, this volume of plays created a sensation within the literary circles in London and Edinburgh."[19] Baillie's popularity with Tuthill registers in the number and prominence of passages excerpted in the *Home* and *Reader*. In fact, in the *Reader*, Baillie's *Orra*, the exemplar of tragedy, enjoys pride of place next to Shakespeare's *As You Like It*, the exemplar of comedy. Further, in the *Home*, Tuthill frequently employs quotations from Baillie as chapter epigraphs. The composition chapter, for instance, features lines culled from Baillie's poetry:

> Books, paper, pencil, pen, and slate,
> And column'd scrolls of ancient date,
> Before her lie, on which she looks
> With searching glance, and gladly brooks
> An irksome task.
> (*YLH*, 72)

That Tuthill should rely on Baillie so heavily is not surprising given Baillie's reputation. Stuart Curran notes that prior to "Wordsworth's celebrated preface, [Baillie] had published her own seventy-two-page argument for naturalness of language and situation across all the literary genres."[20] Baillie's treatise prefaced her three-volume *Series of Plays,* which "was hailed in comparison to Shakespeare and, of all contemporary influences, exerted the most direct practical and theoretical force on serious drama written in the Romantic period."[21] Baillie, as did Tuthill, shows an interest in psychological theories of the mind and writing. Most important, Baillie and Tuthill share the sentiment that rationality must come to govern human passion, and that writing is the best means of achieving this governance: "Despite her interest in near-Gothic emotional stimulation," writes Ross, "Baillie's project is ironically classical and rationalist, stressing the fatefulness of passion and emphasizing how reason and self-knowledge can help us to control our deepest desires." Baillie thus creates "a didactic literary theory that relates psychological behavior to moral decision-making, a theory which advocates exploiting poetry as a way of regulating the passions in order to foster moral habits."[22] For Tuthill it is not so much writing poetry, but writing in prose genres that effects this regulation.

Although there are references to writing as regulation throughout the *Home*, it is in chapter 9, entitled "Composition," that Tuthill takes up the subject most fully (see appendix 4 for text of the chapter). Therein she offers composition as, among other things, an alternative to strident female oratory. As in other early national texts such as Foster's *Boarding School*, the epistolary tradition is strong: composition of letters remains an agreeable way to maintain the bond between separated friends. Handwriting and neatness count, as well as folding and sealing. Self-expression and style, however, now also have value: Tuthill recommends memoirs as aids to writing because they exhibit the "concise and spirited style" she prizes. Still, while modern memoirs may "furnish many excellent examples," imitation of the sort Murray promoted is finally recast as bad practice: "a letter, to be agreeable, should be individual; that is it should show exactly the author" (*YLH*, 74).

Tuthill also encourages another kind of writing, the "exercises in prose composition" learned in schools: "Exercises in prose composition, that are often much disliked at school, are of acknowledged utility, and should not now be discontinued" (*YLH*, 75). But given her emphasis on individualism, style, and literary taste, it is somewhat surprising that Tuthill disdains another practice—school exercises in writing poetry. Poetry exercises seem to create only "sentimental scribblers, puffed up with self-conceit" (*YLH*, 75). Without God-given talent, the composing of poetry amounts to self-aggrandizement, and, in the long run, true poetic genius cannot be daunted by "repressing the early exhibition of poetical talent" (*YLH*, 75). Curiously, Tuthill discourages students from poetry writing even as she accepts Romantic definitions of genius and argues for the importance of imagination for individuals and society. She links creative imagination with sensibility, but she also links it just as strongly with sympathy. It is for this reason that imagination is *"a powerful incentive to virtue,"* and that it can lead *"to trustfulness of disposition* and *warmth of friendship"* (*YLH*, 41, 42). If one can imagine sympathy with others, then the value of imagination is indisputable, as is the place of any literature, including poetry, that cultivates imagination. If one is lacking in imagination, she needs to read more in order "to soar a little in fancy-land" (*YLH*, 45). Toward this end, Tuthill recommends works such as *The Merchant of Venice:* "It is very far from being one of Shakespeare's most imaginative plays, and is on that very account better to begin with" (*YLH*, 46). Imagination, it seems, like any other skill, must be acquired incrementally.

But Tuthill also accepts critiques of imagination—its potential to foster "morbid sensibility"—particularly as such critiques are directed toward women (*YLH*, 43). She is "compelled to acknowledge, that the noble power of imagination is often uncontrolled by reason" (*YLH,* 42). Characteristically she offers a stepwise solution:

> 1. Enquire earnestly what are the object and end of your existence. You will find they are too serious and momentous to allow you to dream away any part of life. A brief probation, involving the interests of eternity, demands all your energies.
>
> 2. Learn your true condition in life, and enter actively into its duties. Regular employment will give you a healthy tone of mind, as well as invigorate the body. Early rising, and laborious occupation, are admirable correctives to a disordered fancy.
>
> 3. Endeavor to relieve or to alleviate the sufferings that come within your reach. Instead of wasting your feelings upon fictitious sorrow, seek out that which is real, and be zealous in the ministry of consolation.
>
> 4. Read books of sound reasoning, or sober fact; abjure novels, and deny yourself, for a time, the luxury of poetry of a sentimental character.
>
> 5. Cultivate and learn to value, the society of people of practical plain sense; they will teach you the folly of romantic expectations; by contrasting their cheerful contentment with a humble lot, with your own wild reachings after ideal happiness, you may learn to extract comfort from your condition. (*YLH,* 44–45)

As this passage makes abundantly clear, Tuthill is drawn to the psychological promise of Romanticism but she fears its excesses—skepticism, morbidity, solipsism, and a love of beauty for beauty's sake. If for Tuthill the excesses of Romanticism are the moral equivalent of disease, then common sense is the source of lifesaving immunity.

Of Boarding Schools and Backwoods Girls

Tuthill's fiction makes concrete many of the abstractions she expresses in her nonfiction prose. Among her favorite fictional subjects are boarding schools and academies, subjects she takes up with an eye toward critiquing their ability to train away prejudices and instill common sense. One such fiction, *The Boarding-School Girl* (1848; 5th ed., 1852), running a slim 139 pages, was doubtless written for a juvenile market. The book chronicles the boarding school years of Frances Jerome, a modest young woman from a good family who must learn self-reliance, which in Tuthill's moral universe means learning not to trade on one's family's good name and, instead, to develop one's own intellect and morality. Frances's classmates at Sorora, as Mrs. MacOver's boarding school is known, have also acquired preju-dices—some to be corrected in the course of the novel, and some too in-grained to be changed. Two young women in particular are incapable of change: the hopelessly romantic schoolgirl poet, Marion Telfair, and the il-literate southerner, Arethusa Slam. Yet insofar as prejudices can be over-come, or at least controlled, it turns out that for Marion and Arethusa writ-ing can play a melioristic role. In fact, throughout *The Boarding-School Girl*, scenes of proper writing and reading play out as correctives to faulty early schooling.

In chapter 4, for instance, the plain style of student Meta Sevane, illus-trated in a letter to her mother, renders ridiculous the sentimentality of Marion Telfair's "missile" to a classmate (*BSG*, 20). Marion's letter is written while she ought to be preparing for the next day's algebra class. Meta's letter, on the other hand, is presumably written on her own time; its purpose is to request in the most polite terms that Meta be allowed to invite Frances home over school vacation. Not only is Meta's letter polite, it also freely dis-closes that Frances is her intellectual and moral better, and that she has cheerfully submitted to Frances's efforts "to improve" her (*BSG*, 24). Thus Tuthill, like earlier writers we have seen, establishes letter writing as a crucial part of the boarding school experience. Good letter writing preserves the bond between mother and child, a bond that for Tuthill can protect a daughter against corrupting influences at school.

But Tuthill worries about the dangers of writing, particularly the kind that inspires action. She fears, in short, just the sort of revolutionary rheto-ric in ascendance when Murray and Foster were writing. In 1852 such rheto-ric assumes new significance given the impending threat of disunion. Fic-tional classrooms become for Tuthill venues wherein national politics are writ small. Take, for example, the case of Miss Dracy, Miss MacOver's assis-tant. The students of Sorora sign a petition to have Miss Dracy dismissed; the chief agitator turns out to be Isabel Rowe, a young woman usually ac-knowledged for her "sweet compositions." While Isabel circulates the peti-tion late at night, it is only Frances Jerome who recognizes the petition as an instance of writing put to ill use. She refuses to add her signature, even un-der the pressure of her peers. Then, when Frances is unjustly accused by the preceptress of instigating the affair and is sentenced to a week's confinement with a diet of bread and water, the opportunity to witness a more appropriate use of writing emerges. Despite the fact that she has been wrongly accused, Frances uses the time alone to correspond with her mother and to keep a daily journal in which she reflects on Scripture and her own moral failings: "What a mercy it is that I have been shut up here for a quiet, calm consideration of my own character and conduct!" (*BSG*, 51). Finally, the episode ends happily when Frances is pronounced innocent and the offending petition torn "to atoms" as Miss MacOver gives the scholars a lecture on "obedience to authority" (*BSG*, 45).

If rhetoric that stresses action is problematic, language that excites the passions is all the more so. Here, Marion Telfair once again proves the negative model. She composes a note to an apothecary's boy whom she wishes to meet off campus. Frances gets wind of the plan and promises Marion she will report it to Mrs. MacOver. This prompts Marion to wrap the note around a stone and pitch it out her window for the boy to find. But the note is intercepted by the vigilant preceptress, and the next morning she reads it aloud to her assembled scholars. It is deemed a "detestable morsel of prose," with poetic passages that are "a medley of morbid sentiment, incorrect measure, and bad grammar" (*BSG*, 61). Mrs. MacOver concludes her lesson in humiliation by attributing Marion's infelicities to the "moral poison" of sentimental novels, known to have been circulated at Sorora by Miss Arethusa Slam (*BSG*, 65).

Arethusa's influence (or rather the influence of the novels she steadily reads) is so dangerous that Mrs. MacOver eventually orders the novels collected and shipped back to her father. In addition, the preceptress institutes a policy forbidding the scholars "to borrow books of any kind to read in their own rooms" (*BSG*, 65). As we find out later, Marion is so warped by her reading of sentimental poetry and romances that Mrs. MacOver's lesson does not affect her. The quixotic Marion tries to publish her poetry and shares with Frances her astonishment when the local newspaper editor rejects it as weak. Indeed, Marion cannot even earn publication within the school. While other students' work is copied and recopied in commonplace books, Marion's finds no favor among her peers.

These illustrations of bad writing are, in turn, countered with representations of good composing. Isabel, who must have learned her lesson from the ill-fated petition drive, uses writing to preserve authority and maintain order at the school when Arethusa foments trouble. And Arethusa is trouble from the start: from the time she is introduced in chapter 5, with her "queer name," "coarse voice," "affected manner," and trunks full of novels (which immediately affect the quality of recitations at the school), she is at odds with life at Sorora (*BSG*, 28, 29). Suffering from homesickness and from fatigue brought on by cramming for her examination, Arethusa announces that she is done with her studies and has come only as a parlor boarder to be "finished": "Yes; geography and grammar I *done* up long ago, and pappy said I need not be pestered with all those silly *ologies* that girls now learn, just to be laughed at as blue-stockin's" (*BSG*, 29–30). She proudly announces that she has never studied "a word" of rhetoric, astronomy, or mental philosophy (*BSG*, 30). Moreover, Arethusa takes every opportunity to boast of her father's wealth and reveals at every turn her ignorance:

> "Are you a native of this country?" asked Kate Murray.
> "Awfulsuz! No; I hate the *abrogoins*."
> "What do you hate, Miss Slam?" inquired Marion.
> "The *abrogoins*, the natives, the Indians; you know who I mean!" (*BSG*, 30)

Forced to study yet unable to, Arethusa decides that the students "ought to have a rebellion"—an illustration of revolutionary, liberatory rhetoric run amuck (*BSG*, 67). This is when Isabel, the one-time rebel turned prizewinning student, steps in. She wants to preempt disorder and thus sets a trap for Arethusa: Isabel agrees to write notes to her schoolmates arranging for a "butter rebellion" at the evening meal (*BSG*, 67–68). But what Arethusa does not know is that Isabel crafts a note that will leave the young southerner the only rebel. In so doing, Isabel delivers Arethusa to Mrs. MacOver. As Isabel explains: "Since she [Arethusa] planned it, I was determined that she alone should execute it. For this purpose, I wrote notes to all the girls, which they can show you, that they need not to interfere with this butter rebellion. Miss Slam is the heroine, alone in her glory" (*BSG*, 70). Although Isabel is lightly reprimanded for the deception, the preceptress acknowledges her motive to be good and her method necessary to prevent a disruptive affair. Isabel is thus "pardoned" (*BSG*, 70).

Seven years later, in *Edith, the Backwoods Girl* (1859), Tuthill narrates a similar conflict, this time featuring juvenile party strife and secret societies. When Edith's father marries an old friend, Edith must relocate with her family from rural Wisconsin to the thriving metropolis of Cincinnati. There she meets a hostile stepmother and stepsister, Josephine, and attends the academy of the virtuous Mrs. Seabury. But despite Mrs. Seabury's talents as a teacher—which are considerable, we learn—she cannot forestall the rift that occurs as a result of Edith's fragmented family. The overly sensitive Ida Hamilton, Mrs. Seabury's niece, is distraught to discover that Josephine has organized a party of girls against Edith. Ida cannot bear the slight and so arranges with seven girls to wear silver dove ornaments, to show their alliance with Edith, whose beloved pet is a white dove. When Josephine sees the silver doves, she determines that her allies "must have a badge, too," even if it means that she has to pay for them herself (*EBG*, 121). She commissions eight swans from a jeweler—the eighth in the hopes that she can persuade Ada, the one girl who has not yet affiliated, to join her party. Ada, though her sister Ida is the Doves' leader, is a girl with "common sense," who finds the whole affair beneath her (*EBG*, 129). Her simple response is to rechristen the parties the "geese" and the "chickens" (*EBG*, 126).

Over the course of several days, Mrs. Seabury notices the parties rising, but "wise woman that she was, she made no inquiries," even when the recitation proves "a very poor one," even when she realizes that her "pupils had evidently been thinking more of their badges than their lessons," and even when "the Swans were vultures in spirit, and the Doves like daws" (*EBG*, 124, 127). When Mrs. Seabury does intervene, she acts by giving a particularly apt composition lesson. She assigns "Politeness" as the topic, later reads the girls' work aloud to them, and then concludes by remarking on the "great want of politeness, and of kindness among the members of this class" (*EBG*, 131, 132). Edith steps forward and accepts blame as the "cause of the division," and Ida accepts responsibility for buying the silver doves (*EBG*, 131). The Swans, however, act dishonorably. Josephine refuses to stand up, and finally her friends turn on her: "'Traitor! traitor!' whispered Josephine, followed by a loud hiss, which was joined in by two or three others" until it sounds "through the room as though the swans had been suddenly turned, indeed, to living, hissing geese" (*EBG*, 133).

The party strife scene in *Edith* illustrates what we have argued is Tuthill's favorite theme in the foundational *Home* and *Reader:* the danger of prejudicial thinking and the necessity for acting with common sense. As we have seen, *Edith* situates the problem in early education—more or less predictably. But elsewhere the novel also asks, What would happen if a girl were raised away from society, away from party politics and other bad influences? Further, what if she were intentionally kept illiterate so that she could not acquire prejudices through reading? Such questions are answered as we learn about Edith's life before moving to Cincinnati. Her father is a poet who has become disillusioned with society after his work has received a succession of unfavorable reviews. A skeptic given to bouts of melancholy, he is emotionally unequipped to cope with the death of his wife. Determined to keep his daughter safe from the literary and social ills he has experienced, he builds a rustic cottage in the backwoods of Wisconsin and takes as a servant the deaf and dumb Dorothy. Although he teaches Edith to speak properly, he purposely keeps her ignorant of the written word. Edith grows up as "brown as an Indian," who "had it not been for the rich, brown curls, instead of straight black hair, . . . might have passed for an Indian girl" (*EBG*, 7, 35).

The experiment works admirably well in some ways. Edith is at harmony with nature. She places little value on material riches: "*Old family plate* and *old family china*, idols . . . of thousands of intelligent people, were to her simple mind just nothing more than useful articles for the table" (*EBG*, 50). She has an independent mind that "has not been perverted by books" (*EBG*, 29). Indeed, Edith has "escaped much foolish trash, by not knowing how to read" and has never come to rely on rote "memorization" for learning (*EBG*, 104, 128). Rather, her father has taught her to classify and arrange what she observes in the world. The result is that when Edith eventually arrives at Mrs. Seabury's school, she is a quick study. With her proper speech, Edith is clearly superior to the girls who have received their education in the city. She finds the "most fashionable dances" to be graceless, a judgment for which she is corrected by her "quondam school-mate" Maria Mills: "Don't say so, if you do not wish to be *oystercized*" (*EBG*, 159). Mills continues by giving the history of the word she has just mispronounced: "Once upon a time there was a man in Rome, or Greece, or some of those old countries, who was very unpopular in society, and so the people wrote his name on oyster shells. . . . So, ever since, when a person is not genteel, or rich, they are *oystercized* from the best society" (*EBG*, 160). Edith knows a version of the story with considerably more cultural clout: "I have heard of the banishment of Aristides the Just, but never before of this application of his sentence" (*EBG*, 160).

But in some ways the Edith experiment fails. While she has good personal hygiene—always close in the background of discussions of illiteracy—she has no housekeeping skills. When Edith boards with Mrs. Seabury, her room and dress are frequently untidy, because, as she says, "I had no mother to set me an example of the beautiful order in which I am so deficient" (*EBG*, 129). Most important, Edith resembles the noble savage in one too many ways: she is a heathen. But Tuthill does not leave her long in the dark. Edith is saved by two unlikely prospects: a barely literate peddler who leaves her a New Testament and a young Indian woman, Malula, who has been schooled (and converted) at a missionary school in Green Bay. Because Edith's mind is "entirely unshackled by prejudice," it is extraordinarily receptive to "religious truths" (*EBG*, 166). Malula, whose social manners we discover "were sooner forgotten" than the moral truths instilled at Green Bay—she gnaws a mutton bone "like a dog"—is surprised by Edith's appearance, stunned by her illiteracy, and shocked by her heathen state (*EBG*, 40). Tuthill's rendition of the scene, especially the dialogue, foreshadows all the characteristics of bad Hollywood westerns: "Me thought all white girls can read," she said; "you most Indian—most brown like me. . . . You not know what Testament is; you no Christian then? . . . Poor heathen! That what they call poor Malula, when she first went to mission school. Where your farder? where your mudder? Why they no teach you be Christian, pray to the great God, read Testament?" (*EBG*, 41). Malula's training at the Indian school makes conflicts between her family and Edith's easier to settle than those between Edith and her steprelations. When the Indians with Malula steal some silver, she sneaks off in the night—her tribal family, sleepy with rum, is unaware of her movements—to retrieve the stolen goods and to apologize to Edith. As her use of dialect shows, Tuthill's appreciation of Native American literacy is not deep, though it is deep enough to prompt some discussion on the distinction between "civilized" and "primitive" behavior. Edith recognizes irony in the fact that the "primitive" Malula has learned to do good as the result of mediocre religious training, while Josephine, Edith's eminently "civilized" stepsister, routinely performs acts of savage cruelty, including slowly killing Edith's pet dove.

The Belle, The Blue, The Bigot

Tuthill is not, as are the writers discussed in previous chapters, overly worried about female pedantry. As long as the aim of knowledge remains clearly and rightly Christian, advanced learning cannot cause problems, no matter how detailed or complex. *The Belle, The Blue and the Bigot* (1844) illustrates numerous instances in which well-schooled women end up lacking true conviction, biblical knowledge, or the ethos that forms so crucial a component of Christian rhetoric. (The book, actually written by Tuthill's eldest daughter, Cornelia Louisa [1820–1870], was widely attributed to Tuthill on the basis of advertisements that suggested mother, not daughter, was the author. Our presumption is that most of the book's readers, especially those who found it in the decade following its publication, would have understood it to be a production of Louisa Tuthill's prolific pen. In any event, the thematic preferences and prose style of the daughter are indistinguishable from those of the mother.[23]) Subtitled *Three Fields for Woman's Influence, The Belle, the Blue and the Bigot* comprises three sketches, each one exemplifying in Baillie-like fashion some extreme passion—for self, for learning, for hate.

The Bigot

In the last of the sketches, "The Bigot," Tuthill explores woman's influence on religion by offering both positive and negative examples: Joanna Melville is quietly faithful, while Gabriella Bradon is pious and rigid. The distinction is made particularly stark in Tuthill's characterization of how these young women handle their servants, both of whom are Irish Catholic and profoundly illiterate. The characterization is one that Tuthill's readers would likely have recognized. Consider, for example, this observation by Catharine Maria Sedgwick, Tuthill's contemporary and a novelist popular in her day: "Providence has sent the starving hewers of wood and drawers of water from other lands to us to be taught in our kitchens, and to [be] borne on by the mighty wave of progress that is steadily tending onward and upward here. It is not left to our choice. Providence makes of our homes Irish school-houses! of our mother and daughters involuntary missionaries."[24] Consistent with Sedgwick's perspective, Tuthill suggests that the servants' illiteracy is not merely incidental: it is, rather, fostered by the "Romish" church and the attitudes of its believers (*BBB*, 250). Both Gabriella and Joanna clearly see it as their task to convert their servants to "true" Christianity—literate Protestantism. But while Gabriella lectures to her servant about the wrongs of Catholicism and evil generally, Joanna helps her servant to read letters from home, thus decreasing the servant's dependence on her Catholic priest. Joanna's persuasion is more effective than Gabriella's because she does not use invective and does not decry denominational factionalism. Rather, she locates the servant's concern for her family and capitalizes on her desire to learn how to communicate with them at a distance. It is, finally, Joanna's schooled "judicious treatment" of her servant that enables her to first teach the servant to read and write, and then to effect her conversion to the Episcopalian faith. In contrast, Gabriella's conspicuous piety achieves nothing at all (*BBB*, 264).

Why does Joanna do so well and Gabriella so poorly in applying the lessons of persuasion learned at school? In answer, Tuthill gives us a glimpse of their school at the beginning of "The Bigot," an occasion Tuthill uses to take up the subject of female academies. Although Gabriella does not acquire what she should at Miss Vinton's Seminary for Young Ladies, the school is actually a model of propriety, a point underscored as one of Miss Vinton's former pupils, Fanny, reflects on her schooling in preparation for future life in marriage. As Fanny anticipates moving into her new household, she looks through her trunks, including those that contain her school journals, sermons, prophecies, and other papers. Fanny thinks she is ready to be rid of such things; if her future husband were to see these "girlish" works, he would be "mortified" (*BBB*, 242). But Tuthill thinks otherwise and takes the time to elucidate the value of female scholarship. Such papers are instructive and useful references, we are told; often they serve as the only record of important words spoken by a person who has died unpublished.[25] Yet Tuthill realizes that in advocating continuing education for women, she faces two possible problems: limited civic prospects for the use of that knowledge and a conflict with woman's "divine purpose." Indeed, for boarding school graduates, life assumes a reality in which schooled knowledge might not seem properly applicable. But as Tuthill argues in the *Home,* the solution to this problem is simply a matter of adjusting one's perspective on the value of knowledge (*YLH,* 14–15). If one, like Gabriella Bradon, expects the value to be expressed in terms of public recognition, disappointment is inevitable. But if one is able, like Joanna Melville, to avoid flaunting knowledge without also hiding it, there will be ample opportunity for learning to come into play "naturally."

The Belle

If Joanna Melville represents the benefits of female scholarship to family and society, then Wilhelmina Buchanon represents its potential for harm. The sketch "The Belle," or "Woman's Influence in Society," begins with the death of Horace Buchanon, a poet who realizes on his deathbed that "his genius had been wasted" (*BBB*, 9, 10). What is more, he is troubled by the knowledge that he has failed in the education of his "motherless" daughter, as he has not schooled her to confine herself to women's proper sphere (*BBB*, 10). Mr. Buchanon fears, and rightly so we discover, that his daughter will not follow the example set by her "sweet" cousin Ellen, who has cultivated "the gentler virtues" (*BBB*, 12). With her father's death, Wilhelmina Buchanon, at eighteen years of age, becomes "mistress of herself and of a large fortune" (*BBB*, 13). A "weak-minded" aunt, one who "exerted but little influence upon others," is installed as the nominal head of the household (*BBB*, 13). Under these circumstances, Wilhelmina, though intellectually gifted, cannot help but put her mind to ill use: she trades on her beauty and intellect to capture the attention of men—as many as possible.

Wilhelmina begins her conquests with the easy pursuit of the Reverend Dallas. She places herself at the center of a church sewing circle—with no intention of sewing—and succeeds in gaining the attention of the easily distracted minister. Flattery gets her everywhere: "'Will you have the kindness to explain to me one passage in your last sermon,'" she invites, and then repeats "the finest passage, almost word for word" (*BBB*, 23–24). Reverend Dallas falls—as hard as any unsuspecting heroine. "'Indeed,' said the young pastor, blushing with delighted surprise, 'I did not know that I had so attentive an auditor'" (*BBB*, 24). Although attentive, Wilhelmina it seems needs tutoring, and so when Reverend Dallas "can spare an hour" he visits her with the announced purpose of reading "the morning's discourse" (*BBB*, 24). The roles of auditor and author, however, become dangerously confused as Wilhelmina memorizes and critiques Reverend Dallas's sermons, until he begins to write them as Wilhelmina would, lacking a spiritual dimension and becoming "mere essays," empty of the "pure spirit of piety" necessary to lead a congregation (*BBB*, 41). Score one for the belle.

When not in pursuit of the minister, Wilhelmina works on the sculptor, Mr. Aulden, a man of acute romantic sensibility. Once again, flattery works. Wilhelmina "stood gazing" upon his sculpture of Queen Esther, "apparently absorbed in admiration" (*BBB*, 25). "As if unconsciously," Wilhelmina assumes the posture of the statue and becomes his model, his muse, assured of further invitations to the studio (*BBB*, 26). Aulden then begins to squire his muse to social outings, something that becomes awkward because Aulden, who has a mother and sister dependent on him, has little money. As Aulden's relationship with Wilhelmina grows, so does his debt, and so does the gap between him and his poor honest mother. At his lowest point, he snubs his mother, ashamed to recognize her in her poverty.

Despite her involvement with the minister and the sculptor, Wilhelmina ends each day with spare time on her hands. After her cousin Ellen charges her with corrupting men too young for her, Wilhelmina invites and wins the marriage proposal of the sixty-year-old Judge Whittingham, a man "as old as [her] father would have been"—and a man she has no intention of marrying (*BBB*, 95). Although he is wise enough to recognize flattery, Wilhelmina offers the counter he wants to hear: "'Truth spoken to Judge Whittingham, would be flattery to any other man'" (*BBB*, 36). Judge Whittingham's grown son, indignant "to see his honorable and dignified father the slave of such a syren," confronts his father, which results in a rift in their relationship (*BBB*, 73). After the confrontation the judge "left the library angered at his son's opposition," determined to propose (*BBB*, 74). Wilhelmina's refusal of the proposal moves the judge to apoplexy, from which he subsequently dies.

Still, Wilhelmina has not extended her evil influence to all possible fields. To win the heart of the young lawyer Ravenscroft, she reads and discusses works of philosophical skepticism, "German metaphysics," and "French morals," reinforcing the "infidel" thinking made possible by life in the city (*BBB*, 67, 127). Ravenscroft begins the decline already experienced by her other suitors when, fortuitously, his romance with the belle is punctuated by sudden news of his sister's illness. Ravenscroft rushes to his sister's bedside, and Wilhelmina's influence diminishes once the lawyer is able to breathe fresh country air in the wholesome presence of kin.

While the title "The Belle" suggests a woman known for her beauty, this is the least dangerous of Wilhelmina's attributes. She also has impressive genius. But finally it is not her genius that makes her character problematic. Wilhelmina's problem, as we know, is that her father has educated her at the expense of practical and religious instruction. Thus she uses her intelligence for troubling purposes: she finds it most useful in attracting an abundance of suitors, which allows her to avoid the convention of spending all her "stupid days with one stupid man" (*BBB*, 133). Because she lacks spiritual grounding, she can even claim, blasphemously, that such behavior is "most Christian-like" (*BBB*, 19). Sadly, Wilhelmina feels nothing but contempt for the men she can so easily manipulate. As she explains to her cousin Ellen, it is her suitors who are to blame: "What taste men have. Here are a learned sage, a pious parson, and a philosophic lawyer, all declaring that I am perfection, the sine qua non of Justice, Religion and Philosophy. How dare a simple girl like yourself, question the judgment of such wiseacres. When I am on the bench, I shall sentence you to severe punishment for such contumelious conduct. No one will dare accuse me then of leading young men into folly" (*BBB*, 95). Through this combination of audacity, intellect, and beauty, Wilhelmina destroys or nearly ruins a series of men, young and old. Fortunately, most of the fallen are eventually rescued by truly pious women. For example, the plain Miss Sanford uses "Christian sincerity" and "bluntness" to lead Reverend Dallas back to his fold (*BBB*, 118). And under the influence of a sister deathly ill, Ravenscroft's "unbelief," which had been reinforced by Wilhelmina, "tottered and fell" (*BBB*, 130).

The Blue

The sketch situated between "The Belle" and "The Bigot" examines another field for influence: "woman's influence in literature" (*BBB*, 143). If Wilhelmina shows the dangerous potential of learned women, the heroine of "The Blue," Caroline Knox—who resembles Joanna Melville, particularly in the subordination of her learning to Christian and domestic aims—shows how such talent might rightly be put to use. And while "The Bigot" only suggests the benefits of advanced female literacy, "The Blue" makes the case explicitly for women's scholarship and women's writing in a climate prejudiced against bluestockings. Caroline's future husband is warned against marrying her because her "literary taste and finished education, will unfit her for the drudgery of domestic life" (*BBB*, 144). But her future husband, Mr. Lyndsey, is more progressive than his friends. A clergyman, he sees Caroline's femininity and education as assets to his ministry, for he believes that "a woman is much quicker in detecting the avenues to the heart . . . and can instruct the ignorant more easily, without alarming their pride" (*BBB*, 144).

Mr. Lyndsey's words fairly describe Tuthill's position on women's place in the sphere of commonsense philosophy. To the extent that women can cultivate sympathy, they can change the hearts of others in ways more effective than men. In rhetorical terms, women are endowed with a superior talent for making ethical appeals, reminding us of the ascendance of *ethos* (to rival *logos*) in the new rhetorical tradition.[26] In order to have even a chance at successfully converting, the "presentation of an attractive character" is paramount: "Blair and Campbell reiterate traditional wisdom regarding the necessity for an orator to convey sincerity, goodwill, and authority as well as to assess (and appeal to) the particular nature of the hearer's habit of mind," but they did so in order to defend and bring people to Christianity.[27] Because the final goal for rhetoric is conversion, women have a role to play. As long as their education takes the form of quiet influence through, among other things, effective writing, their learning is not considered threatening. Thus for Tuthill, the higher education of women can be easily reconciled to women's Christian domestic duties—hence her willingness to challenge any prejudice against female authorship of the appropriate kind.

The case of Caroline Knox Lyndsey demonstrates quite forcefully how female authors can improve literacy and morals in their communities. The Goodhue children—neighbors to Mrs. Lyndsey—are the typical spectacle of illiteracy, poverty, and degeneracy: they seem destined to immoral and unsuccessful lives. But after many lessons with Mrs. Lyndsey, the Goodhue children, brightened by literacy, are fast on their way to being more productive members of society. But Tuthill does not let the point stand. The Goodhue children are made to rethink and express their assumptions about authorship generally and women writers specifically when their teacher presents them with a book, an anonymous publication that John Goodhue suspects was written by their very own teacher. When John suggests to his sister, Sue, that Mrs. Lyndsey wrote their work, she is astonished: "Wrote this book! Why what are you thinking of, John? It is printed, not written like a copy-book. Women can't print. Books are made by men that lived hundreds of years of ago. . . . She might write a paper book, covered with a paste-board, but not a printed one, with a cover like this" (*BBB,* 172). Although John and Sue finally agree that they could benefit from a book Mrs. Lyndsey would write, they cannot quite conceive of women as authors. Indeed, there was a time not long before when Caroline Lyndsey could not imagine her-self an author. Caroline's younger brother, Frank, in aspiring to be a pub-lisher, seeks to overcome the very disbelief that the Goodhue children voice. Frank laments how publishers have ignored men of genius in the current generation in favor of authors long dead. And he invites his sister to con-tribute her writing to the press, but she declines, thinking her work inade-quate. Later, employed by a reputable publishing firm, Frank again invites a submission from his sister. This time Caroline is ready, with a manuscript composed of stories she has told her own children. Part of Caroline's com-pliance has to do with timing: her husband is ill, putting her household fi-nances in disarray. But her husband's financial setback is temporary, and once he again supports the family, Caroline, in order not to flaunt her inde-pendence, agrees that her income should go to the family charity pot—a gesture that preserves both her marriage and the influence of her words.

Others in the community respond to Caroline's authorship with the sur-prise of the Goodhue children. They spread rumors that Caroline "spends half her time and a great deal of paper in writing nonsense, while her hus-band has great holes in his stockings and her children are crying for supper" (*BBB,* 187). Tuthill clearly wants us to see that these rumors have no basis in truth. The book has worked good in the community, so much so that liter-ary critics eventually call her work part of "a new era in literature" that is "effecting a radical reformation." They conclude, "This author cannot fail to be popular and useful" (*BBB,* 202). Of course, the book is most useful be-cause it lifts children out of illiteracy. The Goodhue children, unlike their coarse parents, will finally, thanks to Mrs. Lyndsey's instructions and books, see literacy as a prized possession, more valuable than mere wealth:

> "Do you know," said John . . . "that I have found out why we are so much happier than Bill Hansen and his sisters, though they can have meat three times a week?"
>
> "No," said Sue, all attention, for she entertained a proper respect for wisdom of the other sex, that of her brother John in particular.
>
> "It is because we know how to read . . . and I have been thinking that

people that write books must be still happier than we are, for they can make a new one as soon as they have read the old one through." (*BBB*, 173)

Happy, indeed. Because Caroline's heart and aims are true, her husband can trust that "her fondness for scribbling" will not interfere with her domestic duties, that it will actually add to the pleasures of their household (*BBB*, 144). Caroline proves him right, both supporting the family with her author's income when needed and turning that income toward charity when it is not. She is many things—wife, mother, author, and volunteer teacher—but she is not an activist. In fact, at one point she uses her authorial success to influence an aspiring sentimental poet to abandon writing in favor of a life in domestic service.

Belletrism, Common Sense, and a New Civic Liberatory Rhetoric

Tuthill is never at a loss for commentary on the influence women should have in shaping national culture. Consider this passage from the *Home:* "Every American woman should be familiarly acquainted with the history of her own country, its constitution and form of government. She should know that the stability and permanency of a republic depends upon the intellectual, moral, and religious character of the people; upon this broad principle she must act, and endeavor to induce every body to act, over whom she exercises influence" (*YLH*, 299). It is tempting to understand this argument, divorced from context, as a brief for what we today call Republican Motherhood. But the works we have surveyed in this chapter suggest quite another reading. True, Tuthill knows well the narrative of Republican Motherhood, the historical proposition that republics are made stronger when the mothers of citizens and statesmen are educated. Yet for Tuthill, something about the centrality of women to the historical processes of democracy rings false in this story. Sounding much like Dugald Stewart, Tuthill argues that historical events are properly organized around conventional topics, such as "The influence of *women*," "The progress of the *fine arts*," "The influence of *Christianity* upon national prosperity," and "The causes that have advanced *religious* liberty" (*YLH*, 55–56). History should not, in other words, center on radical and unproven propositions, such as the claim that women's active presence in society enables or even causes democracy to rise and be sustained. For Tuthill, women *are* central to traditions of faith and morality, even if that places them on the periphery of democratic activity. In support of her stance, she contends that accounts of women patriots during the time of the American Revolution are distorted. The progress women experienced during the Revolution should not be measured in terms of the spread of female academies or of women's successes in commerce, but rather according to the depth of personal sacrifice women made: "They, like their husbands, had that unity of purpose, intent upon the attainment of a great object, which produces strength and true greatness of character. They remained at home, discharging their duty, while their husbands were engaged in the senate, or in the field of battle" (*YLH*, 105). In other words, a Christian republic has hope of succeeding precisely because it does not place women in the public eye as the Roman republic did. Tuthill's history traces the demise of the classical republics: "The folly and extravagance of Roman women, were only equaled by Cleopatra herself. Their time was spent at the theaters, baths, and other places of public amusement, and the moral influence of home was no longer felt among a degenerate, corrupt people, hastening to their downfall" (*YLH*, 101). So it is not the creation of an American republic per se, but the elevation of Christian principles that leads to the American republic's success, and the happy place for women in America and "all countries where its benign, holy influence" is felt (*YLH*, 102). Tuthill's liberatory rhetoric is a distinctly Christian one: national fervor and religious fervor together, but neither alone, are responsible for the republic's good fortunes.

Tuthill both argues for religious authority and draws authority from her religion. Such authority stipulates that women who speak publicly transgress a gendered boundary. Across that line lies agonistic rhetoric and, crucially, the agonistic behavior it induces. By this logic, Tuthill is able to add historical fuel to the argument against women as orators: classical republics fell because women became ambitious—because they impersonated men— just as she believes suffragists in the 1830s are doing:

> What shall we say of those bold and daring innovations which of late have given startling proof that some, at least, are not contented with that humble sphere. Has any female demagogue, though condemned by all sober well-wishers to their country and to the interests of the human race, exerted a baleful influence? Has Miss Martineau aided in persuading American women that they are not allowed the rights of free citizens?

Alas! are we to be persuaded out of our best and truest interests by these masculine marauders? . . .

Can any one deny, that there is a desire to mingle in public affairs, a wrangling in controversy, and a hankering for public applause, unbecoming the dignity and delicacy of woman? If any doubt this, look at the societies formed of both sexes, where *the ladies* take an active part in debate and management. Listen to their voices, from various parts of our land, loudly claiming the right of suffrage, the right to have endowed colleges of their own; in short, the right to be free, independent Americans. . . . Where will these bold innovators stop? Not if they love power as well as these maneuvers indicate, till they snatch the reigns of government itself into their own grasping hands. (*YLH,* 107–8)

If everyone engages in the masculine art of agonistic debate, the feminine element of culture is diminished, the republic degraded, its fate classic. So goes the history Tuthill narrates.

In Tuthill's liberatory civic rhetoric, then, good citizenship is a byproduct of true faith. In that faith, to which citizenship is subordinate, Christian self-denial, self-government, and "feminine nature" demand that women's speech should remain neutral, that it not be agonistic, that it feature instead forbearance, delicately stated advice, parables, and even silence. Voice and expression are thus best saved for writing, a practice Tuthill recommends without reservation to her constituency of wives, mothers, and teachers. Her attention to rhetorical theory and composition pedagogy on behalf of her constituents earns Tuthill a berth in rhetorical and literary histories. And, in the context of our study, she is important for another reason: she illustrates what women lost—the prospect of ungendered, unmonitored rhetorical agency—in the transition from oratorical to belletristic culture.

6 Independent Studies
Almira Hart Lincoln Phelps and the Composition of Democratic Teachers

The time has gone by, when it was necessary for a female to seem ignorant or childish in order to be interesting. Women are now looked upon as rational beings, endowed with faculties capable of improvement, and bound in duty to assume a high rank in the scale of intelligence.

Almira Hart Lincoln Phelps, *Lectures to Young Ladies* (1833)

⮌ *Over a half century* after the Revolutionary War, liberatory civic rhetoric fueled a growing women's suffrage movement, just as it remained a feature of prose that imagined or prescribed the conditions of women's schooling.[1] But by this time, as we saw in the case of Louisa Tuthill, there had come to be a sharp divide between those who spoke out directly for political rights and those who, as educators, wrote and promoted writing as a way to inscribe women's power through domestic influence. Almira Phelps, like Tuthill, provides an example of the latter stance. The success of Phelps's many books and several schools signals the popularity of her stance—for the recognition of women's intellect but not the validity of their ballots—and places her among the most progressive educators of the antebellum period.

Phelps, born in 1793, just as Judith Sargent Murray was beginning to publish in periodicals, came of age at a moment when the neoclassical sentiments Murray espoused were falling out of favor. Living through the better part of the nineteenth century—she died at ninety-one in 1884—Phelps was affiliated with four major female institutes in her day, including the pathbreaking Troy Female Seminary, founded in 1821 by her sister, Emma Hart Willard.[2] After the death of her first husband in 1823, Phelps joined her sister's faculty at Troy. The institution was thriving then with one hundred thirty-eight pupils, seven teachers, and three assistant teachers. Because of good relations with the nearby Rensselaer School, Troy was able to offer its young women a substantial program of applied science courses.[3] When Willard took leave for an extended trip to Europe during the 1831–1832 academic year, Phelps became Troy's acting principal. Shortly thereafter, with the encouragement of Catharine Beecher, Phelps published her Troy "Saturday lectures" under the title *Lectures to Young Ladies* (1833) and subsequently had the book reissued under various titles. Soon Phelps built on the administrative experience she had gained at Troy, serving as principal of schools for young women in West Chester, Pennsylvania, and Rahway, New Jersey, before settling into a long-term position as head of the Patapsco Female Institute in Ellicott's Mills, Maryland. This last school, under her capable administration, would become widely known for providing an education on northern principles for young women of the South. At Patapsco, Phelps collected her addresses from weekly convocations and yearly commencements, arranging them in a volume first titled *Hours with My Pupils* (1859). In addition to her administrative accomplishments, her frequent contributions to ladies' magazines, and her publication of lectures and addresses, Phelps authored several highly successful introductory botany and chemistry texts and three novels for young women: the brief *Caroline Westerley* (1833), the much lengthier *Ida Norman* (1848, with an expanded edition in 1854), and *The Blue Ribbon Society* (published serially in 1869 and as a novel in 1879).

These accomplishments notwithstanding, it would be a mistake to see Phelps as an early feminist, like Elizabeth Cady Stanton, who studied at Troy during Phelps's time there.[4] Indeed, as did Tuthill, Phelps saved some of her most heated language for radical proponents of women's rights. Writing in *Lectures,* she distances her progressive aims from theirs:

> if a Mary Wolstoncraft [*sic*], or a Frances Wright, have thrown aside that delicacy which is the crowning ornament of the female character, if they have urged the rights of their sex to share in public offices and in the command of armies;—if they have demanded that they shall be permitted to leave the sacred hearth, the domestic altar, and all the delights and duties of home, to mingle in political commotions or the din of arms, they have but expressed the overflowings of their own restless spirits, their own unnatural and depraved ambition. *They* are not to be considered as the deputed representatives of our sex; they have thrown off the female charac-

ter, and deserve no longer to be recognized as women; they are monsters, a kind of *lusus naturae,* who have amused the world to the great injury of that sex whom they have pretended to defend.[5]

Phelps hardened this position as she aged, so much so that in her late seventies she circulated a petition *"protesting against an Extension of Suffrage to Women"* for the Woman's Anti-Suffrage Association and wrote antisuffrage articles for various women's magazines.[6]

Why would such a strong advocate of women's education—not to mention a proponent of female self-reliance and a supporter of independent teachers—oppose rights and suffrage for women? Presumably she felt for her own success it was necessary to separate their controversial project from hers: she aimed to establish "public" female academies, whose facilities were built and maintained at public expense, whose teachers were qualified to instruct in academic areas as well as in Christian faith, whose tuition was affordable to "daughter[s] of the most humble mechanics and farmers," and whose curriculum was calculated to satisfy "the wealthiest and most powerful" of citizens (*LYL,* 96). While these aims distanced her from suffrage activism, they did not require her to give up using activist discourse. In fact, when it came to advanced study for women and the professionalization of teachers, Phelps *was* willing to put civic liberatory rhetoric in service of an activist end. Indeed, she did so as early as 1850, when she argued for the inclusion of women in professional teacher associations. In the *Patapsco Young Ladies' Magazine,* Phelps quotes at length from the constitution of the Maryland College of Teachers, first citing criteria for college membership and then launching into this critique of the organization's discriminatory practices: "though a woman may possess all these claims, she is not eligible to be admitted to membership in the Maryland College of Teachers; while any ignorant young man in his teens, who is employed in teaching children, can become a member. Among the many inconsistencies in human society this is one, not confined to the Maryland College of Teachers, but existing throughout our enlightened, *liberal* country, far more than in European society, where women are made queens and permitted to govern empires." Clearly, Phelps abhorred rules that denied female teachers access to the same professional resources available to less-qualified male teachers, and not just because the denial hurt women. Phelps warns that without women, the Maryland College of Teachers will experience "worse confusion . . . than now prevails in that august body, the House of Congressional Representatives at Washington." Yet because woman is "an enigma," a "mystery," Phelps suggests that women should aspire only to membership, not leadership, in professional teachers' groups.[7] Ideally, then, Phelps hoped that women and men together could promote sound models of public schooling, if not through the Maryland College of Teachers, then perhaps under the auspices of emerging national organizations such as the American Institute of Instruction. Still, Phelps recognized limits to what women and men could and should accomplish together. While she argued that women must remain activists on an ungendered pedagogical front, she thought they should also immerse themselves in the highly gendered literature of another profession: domestic economy. Thus in the culture at large, Phelps felt gender separation was appropriate and necessary; at the same time, she called on all teachers, regardless of gender, to participate in state and national professional organizations.

As the sister of Emma Willard, Phelps knew well that resistance to female education went beyond opposition to proposals for women's advanced and professional schooling at public expense. She was, of course, intimately familiar with Willard's now-famous 1818 address to the New York State Legislature, with its restrained appeal for public support of young women's education.[8] Even as the address employs female civic liberatory rhetoric to urge, in Phelps's estimation, "the claims of the daughters of the republic" by insisting that young women "share, in some small degree, with the sons, in those privileges for mental improvement," it promises that such schooling will not move women out of their appropriate sphere (*LYL*, 38). Quoting from her sister's address, Phelps underscores the novelty of the project and strives to link it to early national aims for a virtuous, long-lived republic, free from tyranny. Willard claims that no country in history had ever invested decently in women's education, but that now history "points to a nation, which, having thrown off the shackles of authority and precedent, shrinks not from schemes of improvement" (*LYL*, 38). Despite the encouragement of New York's governor, who supported the plan, the "novelty" of Willard's petition "caused considerable sensation" (*LYL*, 39). And while "the more enlightened members seemed, generally, in favor of considering females as the legitimate children of the state, and making some provision for their intellectual improvement," ultimately Willard could not persuade the legislature before which she modestly presented her address (*LYL*, 39). Tellingly, in an action symbolic of the shift from an oratorical to a belletristic rhetoric, Willard did not "deliver" her address, but read it sitting down. Following this example, Phelps, in her teaching and antisuffrage activities, always upheld the distinction between the impropriety of delivering oral addresses to male or promiscuous audiences and the propriety of reading written addresses—or having them read—before men and mixed company.

Naturally, Phelps laments the legislature's rejection of her sister's plan to endow a female seminary with state funds. Assessing the cause of the defeat, she names the opposition she would face throughout her career: influential men who worried about the potential "evils which might result, from enlightening" women, men who believed that women should occupy a "subordinate sphere" (*LYL*, 39). Yet the story of Willard's school does not end with her defeat before the New York State Legislature. Willard was able, through her "devoted zeal," to appeal to the "liberality of the city of Troy" such that the city did what the state "refused to do": advance "funds for the purchase of the extensive grounds . . . appropriated to the use of the Seminary, and for the erection of the spacious and commodious building" (*LYL*, 44). Troy's substantial physical plant and the significant preparation of its teachers would forever distinguish it from schools conducted in private homes. At Troy students could "retire to [their] own rooms for study, and at all suitable times, have access to teachers, who, devoted to their particular departments of learning have the opportunity of preparing themselves for their duties" (*LYL*, 43).

Troy Female Seminary became Phelps's blueprint for future endeavors. It featured "recitation rooms, where each particular branch of knowledge receives undivided attention" (*LYL*, 43). Thus in the all-important study of "chemistry, mineralogy and botany, the objects of investigation" were always readily at hand (*LYL*, 43). As for the humanities, "the very atmosphere" at Troy was "redolent of literature; not that which is exhaled from the muddy waters of abridgments and compendiums," such as the type Donald Fraser and Louisa Tuthill produced, "but from the copious and unadulterated fountains of knowledge" to be found in a well-provisioned library (*LYL*, 43–44). Troy Seminary thereby gloried in the qualities so important to earlier Columbian educators and so unattainable at home: it created the ideal space in which "the youthful mind is in a measure to be formed, and . . . fortified against the seductions of the world" (*LYL*, 48).

Though a blueprint, Troy Female Seminary was finally Willard's school, not Phelps's, and she chose to move on after her sister returned from Europe. Phelps then passed several years writing for various periodicals, revising her science texts and lectures, and trying to realize the best of what she had seen in her sister's school. Her immediate problem, as Willard's had been, was to convince some public entity that funding women's education was neither wasteful nor dangerous. She attempted to do so by publishing work on public education that combined the older civic liberatory rhetoric and the rising rhetoric of domestic economy. This enabled Phelps (as well as other female educators, including Emma Willard) to advance potentially incendiary arguments favoring women's learning while promising that such learning posed little threat to tradition. As a practical matter, Phelps and her compatriots often began by addressing misconceptions about educated women, suggesting, for example, that advanced education would actually slow women's assault on gendered prerogatives such as the right to vote. Then they would enumerate the many benefits—practical, moral, religious, societal—that would result from women's proper schooling: "What would be the state of society, if females were generally taught the laws of the material and mental world, the nature of right and obligation, their own duties, and their high responsibilities as moral and intellectual beings? Would such knowledge be likely to cause them to forsake the path of duty, and to seek a sphere of action, which, from knowing the constitution of society, and especially the nature of their own obligations, they perceive does not belong to them? There is an absurdity in such suppositions" (*LYL*, 40). Phelps not only devoted her own life to overturning this proposition, she made it her students' responsibility to show the world that they were useful servants of society: "My dear pupils, may the whole tenor of your own lives be a constant refutation of the degrading assertion, that '*woman must be ignorant in order to be useful*'" (*LYL*, 41). The public, Phelps believed, was watching her graduates; their high profile demanded vigilance and demanded particularly that they abjure the promiscuous stage of public speaking (a lesson that young Troy student Elizabeth Cady apparently failed to heed): "On you the attention of many is fixed, and your future conduct, will be hereafter referred to as proving or disproving the problem, *'Is it for the good of society that women shall receive a liberal and enlarged course of education?'"* (*LYL*, 41). The question could be answered in the affirmative, Phelps would contend throughout her career, so long as her graduates upheld the obligations of marriage and domesticity. Failure to do so, however, could have grave consequences for the union. Did women take this advice seriously? Many did, but it is obvious that the middle way counseled by Phelps, Tuthill, and others was ultimately not the path of reform that led most directly to property and voting rights for women decades down the line.

Republican Mothers, Democratic Teachers

Tagged conservative in the end, Phelps began her public career striking a conspicuously activist stance. Arguing for public support of women's schooling meant arguing against extant forms of education, sometimes vehemently. As we have remarked, female schools conducted in homes were one target. Still popular were schools run by women of fashion with "superficial accomplishments," against whom such writers as Murray and Foster had earlier railed (*LYL*, 41). More formidable, however, was the underlying idea of Republican Motherhood itself. By the early 1830s, the efficacy of mothers instructing their own children or opening their homes to instruct others'—that staple image in Columbian educational prose—had yet to be fully challenged. In her Troy *Lectures,* Phelps initiates that challenge by identifying the premise of Republican Motherhood, "that of all others, a mother was the most proper person to superintend the education of a young female," and then setting out to dismantle it (*LYL*, 33). This seemingly natural claim, Phelps maintains, is a fiction put forth by novelists, perhaps even Judith Sargent Murray and Hannah Webster Foster, though she is not specific. In truth, Phelps counters, educational progress is hindered by maternal emotions that are too strong and thus "not favorable to a steady and even course of education" (*LYL*, 33). Moreover, young girls must have experience in the world if they are to become valuable members of society, a condition that cannot be satisfied by schooling at home: "a young girl always kept at home, is awkward and constrained in her manners, often selfish and unamiable in her disposition, and ignorant of the customs of society" (*LYL*, 34). Phelps returned to this argument as late as 1869, when she disparaged homeschooling in *The Blue Ribbon Society.*

Continuing, Phelps acknowledges that attacking the worst of home-schooling may not be her strongest argument, and so she subjects the best Republican Mother she can imagine to scrutiny: one well-schooled in the ways of the world, well-educated in formal subjects, virtuous, and even-tempered—that is, not given to excessive maternal displays. Even such a mother, Phelps argues, cannot teach her daughters with any degree of success: "We will suppose the mother herself to be entirely competent to instruct in all necessary branches of female education. Is it certain that she will have the requisite time for superintending her daughter's education, and conducting it on those systematic principles which will ensure a suitable attention to each department of knowledge? The mother, however competent she may be to the task, however anxious to devote herself to her daughter's improvement, has many other claims upon her than those of maternal duty" (*LYL*, 34).

While instructing children is laudable, the task done well is all-consuming and thus detracts from other concerns of critical importance, namely wifely duty to husband, family, and society (including social calls and charitable work). It is impossible, Phelps believes, for women to meet all of these obligations and to teach at home as well. Any attempt will fail; all obligations will be only partially met. Inevitably, at home, "interruptions break in upon the regularity of the prescribed systematic division of time, and the pupil feeling it very uncertain that her lesson will, if learned, be heard, relaxes her diligence" (*LYL*, 34–35). In this way, not only is learning curbed, its effects are reversed. Constant interruptions breed inattentiveness that at some later point must be unlearned. Home instruction, then, can only result in lapses of duty and dangerously miseducated children.

Phelps's argument works cumulatively: she has yet to complete the catalog of "the claims that younger children may have upon the mother's care" (*LYL*, 35). She does so by telling the story of a well-intentioned friend, "an energetic and judicious woman" who, because of money concerns and negative suspicions about boarding schools, tries to educate her own daughter (*LYL*, 35). The result is disastrous: her sixteen-year-old daughter possesses the knowledge of a ten year old; she is also awkward and thoroughly entrenched in bad habits—a hopeless case. Building on this damning sketch, Phelps continues her critique of home instruction. She proceeds to summarize a case she does not wish to elaborate: that many mothers are "inadequate to the task of instructing" because of their own "defective education" or poor health (*LYL*, 37). Stepping back to review the totality of her argument, Phelps concludes that what sounds simple and elegant in novels and poems is hardly so in practice: "We, see then, that however beautiful in theory it may be to educate girls at home, it is not easy in practice" (*LYL*, 36).

All this leads Phelps to what becomes one of her major contributions to female education: her unstinting advocacy of the normal schools that would train women for lives as single professionals. Phelps recognized that normal schools would construct a professional identity for women, whether they needed one because of a reversal of fortune or simply because they were fortunate enough to remain unmarried. In any event, having professional prospects meant having options in life. As Phelps would later write in an address to her Patapsco students, if a woman enters "into the marriage state," as might be her duty, "she multiplies her chances of unhappiness" (*HMP*, 137). A young woman might be better off if she "does not consider marriage as necessary to her happiness and respectability in life" (*HMP*, 115). That happiness and respectability could come not from immersion in "domestic cares," but from following another "high calling": "a noble profession fitted to bring forth the very best faculties of the soul" (*HMP*, 132, 151).

For Phelps, single women are the best teachers because "an instructor has, or ought to have, her mind free from other cares than those connected with her profession" (*LYL*, 36). She should be interested in her students, but not excessively, not maternally so. Lest her readers doubt this, Phelps provides a vivid account of what married life can bring: "Pain and sickness;— and, what is more trying to the mind than personal suffering, . . . the anguish of watching over the distresses of others; of witnessing death in its triumph over the objects nearest to our affections. . . . Some of you will mourn over dying children, some will experience the sorrow and desolation of widowhood" (*LYL*, 16).[9] Not that single teachers are exempt from trials. She reminds young women that whether or not they marry, their lives will be a sequence of trials that they should welcome as evidence of God's love for them ("whom He loveth He chasteneth" [*HMP*, 115]). Still, teachers will experience a particular kind of chastening, less severe than those who marry but more visible: "While so many of our sex live for their own enjoyment, or confine their efforts to the little domestic circle which bounds their sympathies, we live for the public; to us are allotted trials and difficulties peculiar to our profession" (*HMP*, 131). These trials, as Phelps details, have to do with losing students to death or to circumstances in which the good work of schooling might be undone by unfit parenting, bad marriages, or fashionable society. Single teachers must also deal with issues still resonant today: low salaries and lack of community respect, especially for teachers of younger children.

Phelps was willing to grant that some teachers—both women and men—were undeserving of respect because they were unqualified for their jobs. She was also concerned about "how miserably defective" many schools were "as respects the qualifications of teachers and their facilities for giving instruction" (*LYL*, 41). To address these problems, at least as they affected women, Phelps proposed reform in three areas: women needed advanced study in subject areas ranging from science to literature to classical languages; they needed instruction in pedagogical methods; and school trustees needed to assume responsibility for creating ideal physical spaces for learning.

Phelps hoped her reforms would produce teachers and schools vastly superior to those she experienced in childhood, when a "single teacher often had the charge of forty or fifty pupils, assembled in one apartment, where writing, embroidery, rhetoric, philosophy, arithmetic, chemistry and spelling, were all mingled together, in a chaotic confusion" (*LYL*, 43). Problems in setting were compounded by teachers who had little mastery of the subjects they taught:

> In the former and less improved state of education, a pupil commencing the study of grammar, was required to commit to memory page after page of principles, rules and exceptions; these he was required to repeat before commencing the important process of *parsing*. In some cases, teachers continued to keep their pupils to the recitation of grammar lessons, concealing their own want of knowledge of the science, by pretending that it was necessary to understand every word of their book before they could begin to make an application of its principles and rules. Other teachers there were, who really believed that this repeating by rote constituted the whole mystery of the science, and doubted not but in hearing their pupils recite, they were teaching grammar in the most profitable manner. (*LYL*, 90–91)[10]

Phelps believed much had improved since "those days of grammatical darkness and error" (*LYL*, 91). There were now better materials and methods:

"books have been prepared on new principles of teaching, and the *inductive* method has been generally adopted" (*LYL*, 91). Sound pedagogy had indeed been developed, though Phelps knew that women were excluded from the professional associations that disseminated it.[11] An optimist, she predicted that the associations would eventually admit women, and that female graduates of normal schools would prove themselves excellent teachers in seminaries and academies. Teaching would then be generally respected as the "noble" profession for women Phelps believed it to be.

Ida Norman, *or Phelps's "Novel" Lectures*

> She spoke . . . of the importance of education to females, as a profession.
> —Almira Hart Lincoln Phelps, Ida Norman

Although such a line might have come from Phelps's Troy lectures or Patapsco addresses, it actually appears in *Ida Norman,* a novel she began in 1846 and read chapter by chapter to her Patapsco students during a weekly lecture period. (Following her usual pattern, Phelps expanded the book, first published in 1848, and had it reissued in 1854.) Subtitled *Trials and Their Uses, Ida Norman* chronicles the life of a daughter of a well-heeled politician of national renown, James Livingston Norman. When Mr. Norman accepts an ambassadorship in Europe, Ida is sent away to a reputable female academy, Science Hall. There, she finds her course of life altered by tragic news: her fashionable mother has died, and her father has lost his diplomatic post as a result of embezzlement and leads a debauched life on the European continent. As she endures this personal trial, Ida is fortunate to be under the tutelage of the well-schooled and virtuous Mrs. Amelia Newton, who introduces her pupil to the noble profession of teaching.

Although Phelps chooses with her subtitle to emphasize the book's Christian theme, she might just as well have chosen "self-reliance" to underscore the secular concerns that pervade the narrative. Ida, her brother Louis, and the other major characters—Mrs. Newton, Julia Selby, and William and Laura Landon—all provide models of self-reliant citizens who, together, contribute to a strong nation of independent yet interrelated individuals. Self-reliance for Phelps is a quality unbounded by social status, as the novel's characters demonstrate. Phelps includes in *Ida Norman* examples of working women who earn a degree of financial independence through sewing or baking and who, importantly, instill the value of self-sufficiency in their children, who in turn rise socially. The simple Mrs. Goodwin, a widow with ten children, runs a bakery shop, "chiefly frequented by the poor" (*IN*, 129). The values of faith and industry she passes on to her eldest son, Tom, result in his precipitous rise. He begins as an honest delivery boy and newspaper vendor and soon becomes, in his mother's uneducated words, "the iditur of one of the very papers he used to sell" (*IN*, 130–31). Yet even with his success and his "good salary . . . he works jist as hard as ever" (*IN*, 131). Because of this, people predict that Tom may someday win political office, perhaps even the presidency. Phelps likes Tom's story well enough to tell it twice—once in volume 1 and again in volume 2, where she underscores that trials early in life prepared him for professional achievement (*IN*, 130–31, 375–77). Tom Goodwin stands in marked contrast to the Selby children, both born to affluence and ease. Frank Selby in particular is overly dependent on the family fortune; he sports a carefree attitude that renders him hopelessly unfit for life in a democratic nation where industry is central. Frank is lucky; his father's fortune holds, and although Ida Norman will not have him, he is able to marry a Science Hall graduate from a respectable old family, a woman who makes a stable home for him and humors his attraction to New York's high life. But something rings hollow in their marriage. The novel leaves Frank in a state of perpetual adolescence, attended to by a wife who subsequently neglects their children, leaving them frequently, even when they are ill, in the care of domestics. More telling still, Frank's life stands still as young men of humbler means rise to superior positions of affluence and influence.

Finally, Phelps provides numerous examples of middle-class women who learn to expect and value self-sufficiency, which translates in most cases directly into teaching. Mrs. Newton, the preceptress of Science Hall, both lives and preaches this message, echoing many of Phelps's sentiments from the Troy lectures and Patapsco addresses. Science Hall offers a valuable alternative to the kind of French school Ida's flighty mother wants to send her to. At Science Hall, Ida starts with many bad habits to break and much to learn about thrift, independence, domestic economy, democracy, and self-governance. Like other boarding school belles, Ida wants to attend Science Hall as a parlor boarder, but Mrs. Newton instantly clarifies that she makes "no distinctions" among her pupils, that all students, no matter their background, will labor to keep their rooms tidy and the school running efficiently (*IN*,

51). Although not a public institution of the sort Phelps promoted, Science Hall, which overlooks Long Island Sound, is unusually spacious and comes complete with a revolutionary legacy. An Englishman built the "baronial mansion" and established its "extensive pleasure grounds," "grottoes, artificial lakes, and rustic temples," before the war (*IN,* 44). After the war, the mansion is owned by Judge Walsingham, who bequeaths it to his daughter, Amelia. Amelia marries a certain Mr. Newton, bears several "beloved children," all of whom are "consigned to the grave," and soon loses her husband as well (*IN,* 45). A childless widow, Mrs. Newton is a perfect Phelps character who learns Christian humility from her trials. After her initial grief passes, she comes to accept that "she had loved" her family "too well," that "it was, 'Good for her that she was afflicted,'" and that, in the words of that favorite Phelps biblical verse, "'Whom the Lord loveth, he chasteneth'" (*IN,* 45). When Mrs. Newton accepts this spiritual truth, she receives a vision of a new useful life, one in which she is surrounded by children, and in which a private legacy that predates the Revolution is transformed into a postrevolutionary democratic institution. She stuns the community by opening a school: "Great was the surprise expressed by many, that so elegant and accomplished a lady as Mrs. Newton should descend to be a teacher. . . . 'Who would have thought that the lofty Amelia Walsingham would ever have come down to be a school teacher!'" (*IN,* 47–48). By the time Ida enrolls, Mrs. Newton's school is flourishing and comes highly recommended.

Although it is the wealthy Mrs. Selby who recommends Science Hall, it is Mr. Norman who insists that Ida attend Mrs. Newton's school, for reasons that shape the narrative's plot. We learn that Mr. Norman, "naturally noble and ingenious," has been corrupted by his political aspirations and practices: "Endowed with talents of a high order, and gifted with the power of eloquence, he had exercised those talents, and wielded this power for the advancement of his own private interests, rather than for the good of his country" (*IN,* 13). His patriotism had "gradually sunk . . . in the baser aspiration of the partizan and politician" (*IN,* 13). Still, at the beginning of his career, he held promise, and it is then that he first met and wooed Amelia Walsingham. When Mr. Norman begins to wander from the path of financial rectitude (he forges a banknote off his father's account), the virtuous Amelia parts ways with him. Many years and two children later, on the cusp of more financial misconduct, Mr. Norman recognizes that Amelia's virtue might be all that stands between his daughter and ruin: "Ida may be left an orphan without fortune; and I know that in this noble, generous women she will find a mother and friend; aye, more and better than either father or mother have been to her; a guardian who will teach her that she has a soul, who will awaken the dormant powers of her mind . . . and render active, her moral powers and intellectual energies which have hitherto slumbered" (*IN*, 52). Former schoolmates of Amelia wrongly judge her foolish for giving up "the elegant Mr. Norman" (*IN*, 48). Had their match taken place, they whisper, Amelia might now be living in Europe "as the wife of the American minister" (*IN*, 48). Still, both she and Mr. Norman know differently. As the plot will have it, Mr. Norman has gotten the silly, shallow wife he deserves. While her husband muses aloud about Mrs. Newton's virtues and ponders silently the potential economic ruin ahead, Mrs. Norman continues to spend extravagantly and worry only about her daughter's clothes and amusements. Phelps might have allowed readers to revel in such ironic justice but for this: the pairing of corrupt politician and fashionable wife threatens not just the Norman family but the nation at large. This is a cultural pattern that Phelps's novel sets out to undo and correct. Thus the plot of *Ida Norman* turns on matching promising, educated, virtuous politicians with promising, educated, virtuous young wives. Where Republican Mothers have failed to produce good mates, democratic teachers will succeed in producing solid, influential wives.

One such future wife is Laura Landon, who very early in the novel is introduced as a Science Hall student. It is Laura who gives Ida those all important first lessons in self-governance. And it is Laura whom Mrs. Newton holds up as an example of self-sufficiency when she is trying to prepare Ida to hear the news about her reversal of fortune. Laura benefits from what Phelps views as an excellent Republican Mother, one wise enough to send her daughter off to be schooled. Her mother is exemplary in other ways, too. Although "descended from one of the oldest Dutch families in New York," she marries a clergyman against the wishes of her socially prominent father. She marries, in other words, virtue rather than wealth (*IN*, 33). When her supposedly wealthy father dies insolvent, Mrs. Landon's choice of virtue is confirmed. Later, upon being widowed, her levelheadedness surfaces again; she takes in sewing to maintain some independence. Her treatment of household help is so fine that one of her domestics, Serena (who will func-

tion symbolically later in the novel), elects to stay with her even under reduced circumstances. Despite the family's plummeting fortunes, Mrs. Landon continues to instruct her children in virtue and in faith. When Mrs.
Newton finds a clerkship for son William and offers to school daughter
Laura at Science Hall, Mrs. Landon gratefully accepts, even though it will
mean the loss of her children's contribution to the home economy.

With such a solid foundation, Laura Landon quickly becomes Mrs. Newton's prize student, training to become a self-sufficient teacher. When other
students tease her about needing charitable support, Laura rises above the
taunts, explaining to her closest friend, the wealthy Julia Selby, that she has
"enjoyed one advantage" that paying students have not, the advantage of
poverty (*IN*, 62). But she does not stop with this surprising statement; she
compounds it for effect: poverty affords "not one advantage, but many," including the opportunity to experience gratitude (*IN*, 62). Like the humble
Tom Goodwin, the Landon children represent a class girded up by education. Despite financial uncertainty, Laura and her brother, William, have a
solid foundation upon which to build toward new social and economic
heights. That Laura reaches these heights by marrying rather than teaching
does not diminish the significance of her proper schooling: Laura *prepares*
to be independent but *accepts* that her destiny is marriage.

In contrast, Ida Norman is a study in miseducation and remediation.
Born to wealth and influence, her early education is faulty, with no sustained
course of study, no lessons in domestic economy, and no moral grounding in
Christian faith. When she enters Science Hall at age thirteen, Ida is dependent and willful. Phelps makes it plain that Ida inherits these faults from a
mother whose education is similarly lacking. The stylish Mrs. Norman is full
of bad advice for her daughter. She urges her to stay away from Mrs. Newton's star pupil: "Laura Landon is to be educated for a teacher; you to shine
on the grand theatre of life" (*IN*, 34). She reassures Ida that she need not labor at school, no matter Mrs. Newton's policies: "You have plenty of money,
and can hire the servants to do for you what the rules may require that is dis-
agreeable" (*IN*, 54). Above all, if Science Hall fails to please, Mrs. Norman assures Ida that she may come home, even if that home is in Europe (where,
Phelps's narrator avers, Ida would suffer for lack of needed social and language skills, and where the European education she would receive would
completely unfit her for a life in the democratic United States).

All of this maternal ill advice puts Ida in conflict with Mrs. Newton and her school from the start. When the Normans' carriage rolls away, Ida throws a fit, allowing her passions to run wild, behavior definitely frowned upon at Science Hall. In response, Mrs. Newton has this "sad example of an ungoverned child" locked in her room (*IN*, 56). "Do you not despair," one of the assistant teachers asks Mrs. Newton, "of being able to do any thing with one so headstrong and unmanageable?" (*IN*, 56). Mrs. Newton does not despair: "does the physician abandon his sick patients, and say there is no use in trying remedies for bad cases? The educator is, in some respects, a physician, though the maladies he is to cure are those of the mind rather than of the body. There would be little merit in succeeding only with pupils who are already amiable and obedient" (*IN*, 56).[12] In Mrs. Newton, Ida has met her match, and Laura Landon helps her to see it. After reading a psalm that brings Ida to her knees, Laura advises her classmate to write Mrs. Newton an apology. Ida agrees, and with this resignation of will, she begins her peculiarly nineteenth-century journey toward self-governance and independence.

That Ida quickly learns self-governance is providential, Phelps has us believe, preparing the new student as it does to face trials of a more substantial nature. Three years after entering Science Hall, after unlearning and relearning lessons in economy, basic English, and other simple subjects, Ida receives news of her mother's death. This news, however, is not nearly so devastating as the gossip, idle but true, of the novel's bad girls, Sally Pry and Maria Crump, who gather intelligence by eavesdropping on teachers conversing behind closed doors. From their malicious chatter, Ida discovers the sins of her father, namely that he has lost his ministry appointment, has "fallen into bad habits," and has, worse still, "married a foreign woman of doubtful character" (*IN*, 77). Ida's prospects go from bad to worse, or do they? She is left to ponder ways not only to sustain herself, but to compensate Mrs. Newton, who for some time, in the absence of payment from the Normans, has silently supplied Ida's needs and wants. As does Laura Landon, Ida will find the means to repay Mrs. Norman's gratitude, but not, as other novels might have it, by sitting "in the back-room of a shop, with twenty poor girls, like herself, about her, ashamed to look up" (*IN*, 95). With this shift in plot, Phelps fictionalizes the educational plan she first adopts at Troy: prepare all women both to be good domestic economists and single, independent teachers; prepare them, in other words, for whatever their providential fate—dependent wife or independent teacher. Ida thus plans to become a teacher at Science Hall, and, the novel insists in short order, she becomes a good one. The new, independent Ida Norman in her capacity as teacher is "lofty and commanding," a sympathetic friend, and a "judicious adviser" (*IN*, 155). By her pupils she is loved and demonstrates love in return, "but when her duty obliged her to command," she is a model of self-governance, "decided and inflexible" (*IN*, 155). The transformed Ida Norman resembles nothing of the wild young woman who entered Science Hall. As Mrs. Newton exults, "think what she might have been without trials" (*IN*, 189).

In good Phelps fashion, Ida professes to accept her destiny as a single, independent woman, even as she continues to envision marriage, in this case to Laura Landon's brother, William. On one page of the novel, we hear Ida doubting that she will ever be married. Instead, she dreams of having her old family back—her father, her brother, and maybe even her mother (who is, conveniently, dead). On the next page, however, we find Mrs. Newton noticing "with much anxiety" that "William Landon was often in Ida's thoughts" (*IN*, 191). Mrs. Newton's anxiety stems from Ida's station: Julia Selby, now a young woman of means and the world, seems interested in Landon as well. A young woman in Ida's situation had best keep her mind on pedagogy.

It is perhaps one of the strengths of Phelps's romance that Ida realizes all her fantasies, at least by the end of the second volume, which Phelps finished eight years after publishing the first. Volume 1 ends with Ida out of the Science Hall classroom and back in her family home. Her father has been found (by none other than William Landon), their grand home has been repurchased, and Ida has been ensconced as mistress of the Norman household, helping her father in the effort to put his affairs back in order. Ida works hard examining "huge masses of account books, and immense piles of papers" to prepare for a lawsuit to restore her father's good name (the embezzlement, it turns out, can be explained) (*IN*, 300). Phelps understands that her juvenile audience might not grasp this particular familial fantasy and uses Ida's father to help them read the scene: "remember that in fulfilling your domestic duties, you are acting that part which by divine wisdom is allotted to woman; and though, 'To tread the same dull circle, round, and round,' may be wearisome and distasteful, yet considered in the light of

duty, things in themselves trifling, become invested with dignity and importance" (*IN*, 298). Still, Ida's life is not all domestic drudgery. She has accomplished in this time what "few women have the intellectual ability to do":
"grasp abstruse legal points, and enter into long and complicated business
accounts" (*IN*, 338).

Moreover, as we learn further in volume 2, Ida has not completely given
up teaching. She has in her spare time—all Phelps's good characters are very
industrious—founded an orphan school, which thrives, helping young orphan women achieve independence and "usefulness in various conditions of
life," chiefly in the teaching field (*IN*, 335–36). For this work, Ida receives
high praise from her mentor, Mrs. Newton: "How many teachers in your orphan-school have you assisted to educate, who are now supporting widowed
mothers or younger brothers and sisters by their labors, or who are elevated
in society through your benefactions" (*IN*, 336). Once her father clears his
name in the courts, Ida decides to throw her energies—"as Providence
seemed to destine her for single life"—into "planning improvements for her
orphan-school" in order to better instruct "a class of young teachers, to fit
them for future duties" (*IN*, 339). The plan involves moving the orphan
school to the Norman mansion, where she could "make of her little school
another 'Science Hall'" (*IN*, 339).

Ida is full of plans for a rewarding single life when the obstacles separat-
ing her from William Landon are removed, a process that occupies most of
the brief second volume. Although Phelps does marry Ida off to William,
the end of *Ida Norman* does not focus exclusively on their marriage, nor
does it celebrate the details of their domestic bliss. Instead, the novel shifts
focus back to minor characters, particularly to Julia Selby, the wealthy so-
cialite William chooses not to marry. By this time in the narrative, Julia has
long since been reformed from debutante schoolgirl, but not in ways one
might expect.

Julia begins life in *Ida Norman* as the daughter of wealthy parents and, although she has not enjoyed the "advantage" of poverty, she is still one of the
good girls, at least while at Science Hall. Julia is "generous and lofty in dispositions and principle"; however, once out of Science Hall, her fatal flaw is revealed: she is motivated by "an inordinate love of praise, worldly ambition,
and the desire for admiration" (*IN*, 161). Science Hall's system of discipline
draws out the best in the beautiful and imaginative Julia, but she is not so fa-

vorably disciplined by the brilliant world of New York's "gay saloons," nor by the promise of fame offered by authorship (*IN*, 161). Unfortunately, then, she leaves school and the influence of Mrs. Newton to become "the reigning belle of New York," a dizzying height from which she seems doomed to tumble (*IN*, 160). Although Julia always listened attentively to her teachers at Science Hall, Mrs. Newton fears "the effect of the world, and its allurements upon the heart of Julia," as well she might, given the glimpse we have of her at her "*soiree*": "lustrous with rich jewels, and radiant with smiles and animation" (*IN*, 166, 169). A little later, Ida hears Julia utter words even more ominous: "'I do not depend so much on Mrs. Newton's oracular wisdom, as formerly,' said Julia, 'she was never much conversant with the *beau monde*, and her notions are now, of course, very antiquated; the truth is, we must all learn the world for ourselves'" (*IN*, 267).

Julia shortly learns a great deal, not about the *beau monde*, but about its trials. And like Ida Norman's, Julia's trials stem from the immoderate actions of a father whom she adores. The widowed Mr. Selby surprises his daughter by bringing home a new bride, "the accomplished Miss Blossom, her former school companion," a woman young enough, as the expression goes, to be his own daughter (*IN*, 304). Julia now has a strong desire to be independent, rather than submit to a stepmother her own age. It is this trial that drives her back to the wise counsel of Mrs. Newton, who welcomes her ("Come back to me, Julia") and sets her on the only course of independence the novel can articulate: Julia Selby the belle will become Julia Selby the teacher, who—in a new wrinkle—is also a professional writer, "not of vitiating novels or vapid poetry, but of useful and instructive books," of the kind that Almira Lincoln Phelps herself published (*IN*, 304–5).

Phelps's Conjectures on Original Composition

> Write as if you had something to say, not as if you attempted to say something because you must write.
>
> —Almira Hart Lincoln Phelps, *Lectures to Young Ladies*

In her roles as both teacher and writer, Julia's accomplishments are recognized as rare, especially for a young woman who inherits a fortune from her mother and still collects an income from her father: "No ordinary character was the learned and intellectual Miss Selby, who with fortune at her disposal, chose to devote herself to literary pursuits, an inmate of an educational establishment" (*IN*, 327). The figure of the beautiful woman of means, with access to high society and prospects of a good marriage, works against the prevailing notion that women become authors or teachers because they must. Julia *chooses* her single life and her professions. And she succeeds in them: "When she was known as an author, it became fashionable to praise her writings, and newer aspirants for literary celebrity sought the prestige of her name and patronage. Publishers of Magazines and Annuals, solicited her name to grace the list of their contributors; and those who delighted in exhibiting celebrities at their literary re-unions, urged her attendance upon their receptions" (*IN*, 327).

Phelps clearly means for readers to admire Julia's accomplishments, for Julia plays out the narrative possibilities foreclosed by Ida's marriage to William. Julia's ideas about art and teaching as professions occupy a good portion of one of the novel's concluding chapters. Julia is unapologetically Romantic in her inclinations, accepting even the notion that she has that elusive (and dangerous) quality of "genius." More so than Louisa Tuthill, Phelps seems quite willing in the characterization of Julia to tap into Romantic definitions of literature, including, surprisingly, the value of pleasure and the idea of the artist as a creator with godlike powers: "The creative powers of genius, so far as I possess genius, in a small degree, is, to me, a precious gift. I can call around me the creatures of fancy, and endow them with what gifts I please; my power over them is unbounded; they are never rebellious to me, however they may treat each other and the rest of mankind; they are never ungrateful. The play of thought, the rainbow hues of the imagination[,] delight me" (*IN*, 410–11). In a similar vein, Julia styles herself the Romantic rebel, the artist who stands at the edge of society, a deity unto herself. She writes to Ida, "You see that I am married . . . to my own spirit, and with this I hold communion which is to me the best part of my life" (*IN*, 411). As a teacher, she is similarly committed to Romanticism. She leaves instruction in "care, arrangements, &c." to other faculty, reserving for herself a task she loves, that of leading "young minds away from the beaten track of scholastic teaching" into "unexplored regions" (*IN*, 412). Julia also follows the convention of the Romantic artist driven by the inner workings of her own mind. In this sense, she is acting with, rather than against, what seems to be her destiny. "She is not," as Ida's future husband proclaims, "formed for domestic life,—with her, the intellectual absorbs the emotional" (*IN*, 399). Or as Julia herself puts it, "I write because I have a mind that must work; because I *think,* and with pen in hand, new thoughts enter into my mind, and they ask to be expressed in words" (*IN,* 411).

More often than not, however, Julia uses not the Romantic language of being "driven," but rather the language of choice and self-reliance, veering close to the words of women's rights activists: "I thank you, but beg you to believe I am satisfied with my lot, and never intend to change it. I am following my own choice in the life I lead" (*IN,* 412). To explain her single status, she sends to the newly wedded Ida a long critique of bourgeois married life:

> I might have bestowed my fortune and my hand upon one of them, and become the slave of his humor and caprice, sacrificed my own tastes and independence, and future improvement; and the world would have thought it all well. . . . I might have lived in a large house with marble front, and had elegant parlors, with card-baskets of silver or Dresden china, filled with cards and invitations from my hundred and one particular friends; and my time might have passed in a round of vapid calls or tiresome parties, where the intellect is abased, and the external appearance alone considered. Thus might my life have passed;—or, robbed of property and peace of mind, I might have shrunk back into obscurity, a broken-hearted wife!
>
> Yes, I might have married;—I might have been Mrs. Dick Snobbs, or Mrs. Mortimer de Courtney; the *"shadow of a name"* might have rescued Julia Selby from the opprobrium of old maidism. (*IN,* 412–13)

In defense of single professional life, then, Julia works out what Phelps has expounded in her lectures and dramatized in *Ida Norman.* Yet lest some readers think Julia an advocate of women's rights, Phelps has her character deride the movement: Julia declares flatly that she is "no advocate for the 'rights of women,' according to ridiculous modern pretensions" (*IN,* 413). Her platform, she argues, is simple and unpretentious; she is merely "assert[ing] the right of every woman to marry, or not to marry" (*IN,* 413). Moreover, she wants to impress upon people that a single woman is not "a victim to be commiserated"; instead, people should turn their sympathy to the married woman, "the suffering ill-treated wife, who, in her servitude, loses all power to feel, much less to assert that she has any rights" (*IN,* 413). Through Julia, Phelps identifies a cause she feels is worthy of civic liberatory rhetoric, the defense of ill-treated wives, and she takes a stand on their behalf by discrediting the liberatory claims of abolitionists:

Let those who are expending their sympathies upon southern slaves, think of the households where an unhappy wife is concealing in her heart's core wrongs known only to her Maker, and to him who inflicts them. Let the pretended philanthropist who would benefit his country by throwing into her midst the torch of disunion, step aside from the log cabins of the negro, where resound the sounds of merriment coming from light hearts that feel no cares; let this philanthropist learn the secrets of domestic unhappiness in many a home, and then decide that the institution of marriage ought not to exist because it is abused by bad husbands, and we must confess, too, by wives neglectful of their duties, or by their vices rendering home accursed. (*IN*, 413–14)[13]

We know that Phelps disliked abolitionist activism, though probably not for the reason offered here. While she would doubtless grant that abolitionist speech revealed genuine abuses, she also felt strongly that such speech threatened the union.[14]

Julia's Romanticism and her insistence that she is married "to her own spirit" are not of themselves problematic for Phelps. However, like Tuthill, Phelps worries about Romantic excess, especially insofar as such excess might impair a woman's physical health and conflict with her Christian duty. As part of her Troy lecture on composition, Phelps warns that if there is danger in writing, it is the potential for "excess of sensibility" (*LYL*, 256). To emphasize this point, Phelps narrates the story of Lucretia Davidson, a student at the seminary "whose precocious powers" were once admired by faculty and students alike: "On her entering the Seminary, she at once surprised us by the brilliancy and pathos of her compositions" (*LYL*, 256). Her work reflected "the power of her genius," but unfortunately, Phelps relates, her intellect and imagination were not disciplined: "from studies which required calm and steady investigation, efforts of memory, judgment and consecutive thinking, her mind seemed to shrink" (*LYL*, 257). Lucretia fell "victim to an extreme and morbid sensibility" and tragically died at the age of seventeen (*LYL*, 256). Her poetry was published in a posthumous volume to great acclaim. If genius of this kind were necessary for successful authorship, Phelps continues, she would not recommend composition for women: "If one could not be a fine writer, without becoming unfit for the duties of life; if talents were necessarily connected with eccentricities, I would at once warn all my sex from attempting to acquire these dangerous gifts" (*LYL*,

258). But, Phelps assures, this is not the case. Many successful women writers balance their creative enterprise with their Christian domestic duties.

How to strike this balance is a lesson Julia must learn the hard way. Early on in her authorial career, she develops habits that threaten her health and sensibility. As Serena (the Landon's faithful domestic) reports, "she is always writing, and sits up very late, because she says she can write better at night, when no one disturbs her" (*IN*, 424).[15] For a time, Julia also becomes "so fascinated with authorship" that she neglects her social obligations (*IN*, 323). "This *cacaethes scribendi*, is a serious disease when it takes possession of one," and Mrs. Newton candidly admits she has experienced it but overcame it with "reason and judgment" (*IN*, 323). Eventually, too, Julia Selby achieves the balance in life necessary for a woman writer. When Ida travels to Europe with Mrs. Newton and her sister-in-law, Laura, Julia frequents the orphan school and so is drawn back into the world. By keeping her intellect and imagination under "subjugation" thereafter, Julia succeeds both as a useful Christian woman and as one of the "first literary women of her age," "desiring to consecrate her talents to useful purposes" (*IN*, 327, 399).

One other factor makes it possible for Julia to recover from her "disease": the expanding market for prose. Julia achieves balance as a writer because she need not be a poet. She instead brings "useful" material to the public: books for juveniles, religious tracts, and educational material, all of which, Phelps noted twenty years earlier in her Troy lectures, provide "proper employment for the exertion of female talents" (*LYL*, 250). That women could publish was welcome news, Phelps believed, both because it expanded their range of employment and because it could aid them in discharging their social and religious duties. Even a person of limited education, Phelps suggests humorously in the concluding pages of *Ida Norman*, might aspire to authorship: "It has been hinted that Serena has even commenced a volume to be entitled, *"Summer's First Flowers,"* [presumably a recipe book] but from the length of time required to compose her letters, it is not likely the volume will soon, if ever, be completed. Yet if the employment serve to amuse good Serena Summers, let her be encouraged to go on" (*IN*, 431). Serena's aspiration to publish, however harmless, is also somewhat absurd, because, as Phelps explains in her *Lectures,* publishers and reviewers are demanding in ways Serena's meager productivity could never satisfy. Too, Phelps suggests that as a result of more women publishing their work, the idea of a professional woman writer is no longer a specter, which puts much-needed pressure on women to compose better products: "The time has gone by, when a publication meets with indulgence, because its author is a *woman;* we must now expect to be judged by our real merits" (*LYL*, 250–51). Phelps contends that in reviews of works in print, gender is no longer an issue, an odd notion when one considers that Phelps frequently emphasized her gender by advocating and publishing in ladies' magazines, by capitalizing on her name ("*Mrs. Lincoln's Botany*"), and by composing texts destined for a female audience (chemistry for the kitchen, botany courses for female seminaries, and instructional novels for young women finished with school).

Phelps considers education the richest market for women's work—literally, as she herself earned an estimated 200,000 dollars from her publishing and teaching.[16] But such riches are figurative as well. Writing educational texts offers women a chance for broader intellectual fulfillment because it often requires them to do advanced research on the subjects they treat: "Education is . . . desirable for woman herself, promoting her happiness, her dignity, and her usefulness."[17] For example, in order for Phelps to write her most popular textbook, *Familiar Lectures on Botany* (twenty-eight editions from 1829 to 1872), she likely pursued an intense course of study under Amos Eaton of the Rensselaer School, perhaps even attending the lectures alongside young men there.[18]

Yet Phelps is not willing to see her advanced learning as pathbreaking or extraordinary. In what is perhaps some wishful thinking, by 1833 when she published her Troy lectures, Phelps believes the female quixote to have been vanquished. She argues that too many women had completed courses in advanced education for a learned woman still to be a spectacle: "as there are now so many educated females . . . there is little temptation for any one to be vain of her learning; the effect which Hannah More anticipated as the result of more enlarged systems of education is now realized. A female possessing a cultivated mind, is no longer regarded as a prodigy, and we have far less of *les bas bleus* than formerly" (*LYL*, 277). But as *The Belle, the Blue and the Bigot* (1844) shows—not to mention the attention Julia Selby commands when she dedicates herself to scholarship and writing—"blue" at mid-century was an appellation to be feared. (Typically, Julia is less feared because she continues to present herself as a beauty: "Stately and queen-like was Miss Selby; though she had become somewhat of a *'blue,'* she neglected none of the cares of the toilette" [*IN*, 328].) In 1841, when Phelps offered students at Patapsco advanced courses in mathematics and the sciences, it took eight annual five-day public examinations, in addition to the usual musical recitals and recitations of original compositions, to convince the community that women were capable of mastering complex, theoretical subjects. After eight years these public examinations finally became tedious, and Patapsco moved to the more standard practice of open private oral examinations coupled with year-end commencements, at which student compositions and musical recitals were showcased. Reviews in the *American and Commercial Advertiser* in 1844 and the *Howard Gazette* in 1853 praise Patapsco students' abilities. In 1853 a writer for the *Gazette* remarks on both the moral and intellectual attainments of Patapsco students, demonstrating that Phelps had been successful in making her learned young women not appear as threatening *"lusus naturae"*: "Those compositions were certainly of a high character in tone and sentiment,—such as could only have been produced by cultivated minds and pure and chastened hearts. Indeed these original compositions in most cases also exhibited a high order of intellect in the writers, and the rich fruits of the culture bestowed upon their minds."[19]

How much of Julia Selby's philosophy of composition informs Phelps's? Surprisingly little, judging by her Troy lectures, which contain only passing comment on the pleasures of imagination and a brief warning, already noted, about excessive sensibility. The composition lecture itself is highly practical: it specifies recommended texts as well as approaches to studying them. For instruction in the fundamental qualities of taste—"refinement, delicacy and correctness"—Phelps recommends Newman's *Rhetoric* (*LYL*, 250). Blair's *Lectures on Rhetoric* makes the list as well, but she judges it too voluminous for use as a course text. On the other hand, an abridgment, supposedly fit for classroom use, she judges a "mere skeleton" (*LYL*, 251).[20] Later, at Patapsco, Phelps required Boyd's *Rhetoric* as well as Newman's for the junior year. The following year, students undertook Campbell's *Philosophy of Rhetoric* and Kames's *Elements of Criticism*.[21]

Given its historical moment, it is not surprising that Phelps's Troy lecture on composition pays considerable attention to style, a common element in all of the texts she recommends. Still, the study of style and the acquisition of broad curricular knowledge are finally subordinated to the project of original composition: "the different branches of knowledge we have already considered [including reading, grammar, languages, geography, history, astronomy, chemistry, zoology, botany, mineralogy, natural philosophy, and mathematics], are all conducive to one great end, that of enabling a person to compose with elegance and facility" (*LYL*, 250). This observation, she stresses, applies to all writers, whether male or female: women, she counsels "are permitted to use the pen as [their] tastes, genius, or mental acquirements may direct" (*LYL*, 250). Phelps continues in her lecture to explain that rhetorical theory and literary criticism are likewise subordinate to the writing of original compositions: "The study of Belles Lettres, or of rhetoric and criticism is introduced into education, principally for the purpose of improving the young in the art of composition" (*LYL*, 254). Criticism, too, is an "agreeable" exercise: "but it is still more desirable, still more delightful to be able of ourselves to *execute*, to be able to catch the ideal train, as they glide through our minds, and paint them in all their freshness and originality for our future examination, or for the inspection of others" (*LYL*, 255).

Education in multiple subject areas provides the "courage and skill" needed to compose, particularly those very difficult original compositions, the kind that would later be read at year-end public examinations or commencements (*LYL*, 255). Original composition might include an occasional exercise in fiction, but too much fiction writing, Phelps warns, overindulges the imagination. For all but the most exceptional student, poetry is off-limits, because it might lead to excessive sensibility and to Lucretia Davidson's ugly fate. (Like Tuthill, Phelps—who herself composed and published in the genre—believed that poetry was best left to those few whose true genius was regulated by reason and faith.) Even given generic restrictions to make it safer to engage in, original composition is difficult enough to challenge minds both prosaic and imaginative. The difficulty rests in the demand that expression be clear, simple, and tailored to a specific topic. Phelps cautions against broad subjects like "gratitude," "such as would require a philosopher to investigate," and counsels students to confine themselves to subjects they know well: "be careful of going out of your own depth . . . and occupy yourselves with subjects you most readily and fully comprehend" (*LYL*, 259, 262). But this advice should not be read as resonant with the rhetorical expressivism that would become popular in America over a century later. Phelps's students are constantly to be broadening their comprehension by way of schooled observation of natural and social phenomena, not by deepening their capacity for introspection in the absence of academic study. Original composition, the proper "end" of her curriculum, thus depends on the "stock of intellectual wealth" that results from reflectively applying scientific, moral, and philosophical principles—learned from lectures or print—to experience in the world (*LYL*, 250, 259). Indeed, original composition is only for students who can demonstrate mastery of scientific and philosophical subjects. For students who are new to serious study (or who have been inattentive or unreflective), Phelps recommends "translation" as a starting point (*LYL*, 259). Original composition, then, ought to be positioned late rather than early in the curriculum.

In her Troy lectures, Phelps is fairly concrete about what shape original composition should take; inquiry into the curriculum at Patapsco sheds further light on her thinking. The Troy lecture on composition suggests that a student might describe something very familiar, like her home, beginning first with technical detail (length, width, construction materials) and then, with "a little reflection" and "some previous learning," tie such a description to general ideas about architecture (*LYL*, 260). Originality is thus produced when personal experience and observations combine with received ideas. The titles of Patapsco examinations in 1842 and 1844 are consistent with this idea. Students apparently wrote on familiar themes from life and contemporary literature: idealized rustic scenes ("The Ambitious Shepherd," "An Indian Tale"), amplifications of moral aphorisms ("The Fairest Flowers soonest fade," "Happiness not Attendant upon Greatness"), or issues in the lives of schoolgirls ("The School Girl's Trials," "Recollections of My School and Teachers"). Curiously, compositions for the 1853 commencement were notably more abstract and reflective of Romantic preoccupations ("Love of Truth," "Pleasures of Memory").[22]

During the 1849–1850 school year Patapsco students and teachers joined to produce a school literary magazine, the content of which adds to our understanding of composition practices at the school. Phelps's son suggests that the magazine's outlines were drawn from a literary magazine he brought home from a visit to Princeton. Whatever the inspiration, from its title (the *Patapsco Young Ladies' Magazine*) to its content, the publication was self-consciously female. The introduction to the volume explains that the editorial staff rejected the idea of opening with a letter from the "Editors'

Office": "The idea of masculine employments is immediately suggested by the sound of the word 'office,' and remote allusions to cigars, political articles, stump speeches, and other unfeminine possessions, are awakened." Phelps's Patapsco students would not be fingered as "masculine marauders." They choose instead to address their missive from the "Editors' Boudoir." The young women also explain that such a linguistic turn makes it possible for them to venture into authorship: "we have often longed to allow our un-fledged genius to try its wings beyond the precincts of our literary home. And yet we were too timid to venture into the broad fields of literature, lest some hawk-like critic should put a period to our author-existence." In a somewhat strange mix of metaphors, a boudoir, they explain, is a place where "young ladies might be allowed this little flight of fancy."[23] Essays in the magazine, written by Patapsco students and teachers alike, tend to grapple with serious, abstract subjects. As biographer Emma Bolzau notes, "Death furnished the sad theme for many of the articles," an indication that Phelps might have been losing the battle against Romanticism's excessive morbid sensibility.[24]

There are, of course, limits to what can be inferred from essay titles and descriptions, and so we return to Phelps's lecture on composition to further tease out her sense of original writing. While the lecture certainly encourages young women to "glean" the wisdom of authorities, there is clearly a difference between her advice to writers and that of Judith Sargent Murray, a difference that signals the distance between the belletristic and oratorical curricula we have described in preceding chapters. While both writers condemn the wholesale pirating of another's work, Murray defends and celebrates selective plagiarism, that is, building a commonplace rhetoric on the practices of gleaning and modeling. Phelps, on the other hand, declares plagiarism to be unlawful and immoral. She instructs her students:

> do not allow yourselves to borrow from others. On reading a very spirited or profound composition from a young lady of limited talents and opportunities, a teacher immediately believes that it is borrowed, even should it chance that she has not before seen the same thing. This is not only stealing, but defrauding yourselves. If you begin with compositions, above your own capacities, you must continue them, or the deception will at once appear to your companions, as well as teachers. But I should very unwillingly believe that any pupil can be so lost to honorable sentiments as to wish to gain reputation for talents she does not possess, or so unjust

to herself as to prevent her own improvement in the attempt to seem to be, what she is not. (*LYL,* 261)

As with Hannah Webster Foster and Louisa Tuthill, writing for Phelps is an extension of character rather than a construction of multiple and rhetorically useful personae à la Murray. In the Troy lecture on composition, expression is monologic: a good composition reveals the author's true identity. Plagiarism is a misrepresentation of one's self, nothing less than an attempt to steal somebody else's identity. Oddly missing from the lecture is the more complex vision of written self-expression that figures so prominently in *Ida Norman.*[25] In the novel, Phelps retains something of Murray's notion of self-fashioning; the link between writing and essential character is repeatedly dramatized in ways that complicate an easy correspondence between expression and identity.

Writing in *Ida Norman*—other than that represented by Julia Selby, the writer-teacher—is used largely for purposes that are expressive, in the sense James Kinneavy uses the term in *A Theory of Discourse.*[26] That is, expressive discourse aims to compose or recompose identity, and through that identity to establish or reestablish relationships with others. While plagiarism does not figure into *Ida Norman,* a related "writing crime" disruptive of identity and relationships does. Forgery wreaks havoc in the novel not only because an individual is maliciously misrepresented, but because genuine relationships are preempted when false ones are established. As with the Tom Goodwin rags-to-riches tale, Phelps likes forgery as a plot device well enough to employ it twice: in the first volume to interrupt for a short time the union between Laura Landon and Louis Norman, and in the second, to suspend for a long period the engagement of Ida Norman and William Landon. In each case the novel's bad girl, Maria Crump, has—in collusion with her sister and Sally Pry—committed the forgery. (Maria is, in fact, so irredeemable that she is one of the few "patients" even so good a "physician" as Mrs. Newton cannot heal; she must be expelled from Science Hall.) Maria's forgeries work because the lovers involved have not learned to scrutinize letters for the character underlying them. Louis, Mrs. Newton scolds, should have intuited that Laura Landon, a paragon of Science Hall virtue, would never have written anything so "course and low" as a letter with a line reading: "you permit your sister to be a teacher, which shows you to be mean-spirited" (*IN,* 176).

He should also have noted that the paper was very thin, and thus the signature on it easily traced. In the case of William and Ida, Maria's skill at forgery has improved with age. The content of the letter is more plausible: the forged document has Ida simply thanking William for his attention and making clear her resolve to remain a teacher, devoted to her father. Such fraud, the novel suggests, is less easily detected. Even those so sharply trained as William and Ida cannot identify it.

Yet even here, William and Ida share responsibility for their miscommunication. Both are hesitant to express feelings in person because their emotions have been schooled to the extent that they rely too much on writing as a form of emotional expression. This is made nowhere more obvious than in Ida's diary, which begins the second volume of the novel. And if fraud and delusion between parties is possible in written declarations of love, self-delusion is also a danger in private written self-expression. In her diary, Ida reinscribes her misperceptions about William: she is convinced, for example, that William and Julia Selby are more than "literary friends" (*IN*, 315). Further, she wonders why her "ideal of manly perfection" has been so "strangely inconsistent [in] his conduct" (*IN*, 315). The result of this writing is that Ida builds up resentment and defenses against William Landon—and Julia Selby—that need not be there. In speaking with Julia, Ida adopts a "tone of voice . . . somewhat of asperity, noticed by Mrs. Newton with a degree of pain" (*IN*, 329).

Ida's reformation, her remarkable change in character, also reflects Phelps's concern with self-expression. The reformation is focalized through the device of a written document: a conversion letter Mrs. Newton reads to the pupils of Science Hall. While semiprivate letters and diaries in *Ida Norman* are unreliable forms of self-expression, conversion narratives written for public consumption are the ideal. For example, Ida's great reversal of fortune is seen as an opportunity to recompose herself, but not privately. Mrs. Newton calls an assembly at which she first thanks God for the "providence" of Ida's reversal and then takes to task the gossips, Maria Crump and Sally Pry (*IN*, 93). The Science Hall students are permitted "to give vent to their various emotions," which range from surprise (Ida "would never be a teacher"), to malice, to admiration (*IN*, 94, 96). All this sets the stage for Mrs. Newton's reading of Ida's letter. In it, Ida communicates her purpose: to "unburden" herself and to state her new resolutions (*IN*, 96). She lists her faults, chief among them her pride, and then declares herself to be an "orphan" and a humble normal student—a teacher in training not unlike others receiving charitable support (*IN*, 98). She asks her classmates to help her to keep her "good resolutions," "to help the proud Ida to be meek and gentle" (*IN*, 97–98).[27]

In an even more dramatic (and implausible) narrative event, Ida's father, upon his return from profligacy, composes a long "arraignment" of himself, concluding with a resolution to reform (*IN*, 231). Presented in the novel as "Mr. Norman's auto-biography," this exercise in "self-examination," "self-accusation," and "self-justification" is penned while he lives a new life as the Hermit of Valambrosa (*IN*, 233). As does Ida, he refers to his old self in the third person. The Hermit resolves to look at Mr. Norman's past, a task, he explains, that the third-person perspective helps him perform honestly and impartially. The Hermit indicts Mr. Norman for his early crime of forging a note on his father's account. And in a move that underscores Phelps's idea that the principles of domestic economy apply to men as well as women, the Hermit chastises Mr. Norman for his poor choice of spouse and his bad parenting: "How dare a man, neglecting domestic ties and duties, call himself a patriot; talk eloquently, and with pathos, of his country's welfare, while his home is made miserable by his alienation from its claims and interests!" (*IN*, 237). It is at this point that the autobiography makes its first move toward self-justification: "The Hermit of Valambrosa has promised to be just to the character of Livingston Norman; and justice pronounces that his path was a difficult one" (*IN*, 237). The roots of Mr. Norman's difficulties apparently can be traced back to his wife, his bad conduct stemming from her "superficial and worldly education" (*IN*, 237). Phelps urges readers to accept this justification, despite its obvious logical inconsistency: while the justification certainly supports Phelps's thesis—that virtuous wives can make virtuous politicians, and vice versa—it does little to explain the crime of juvenile forgery the young Livingston commits before he meets the wife responsible for making his life so difficult.

The Hermit also confesses to Mr. Norman's embezzlement, though here again justification is offered. Mr. Norman was apparently under financial pressure from two sources: his wife's extravagant failure to practice domestic economy and his need to pay the costs of political office, which he calls "the expense of his political honors" (*IN*, 237). He borrows the public

money entrusted to him but is prevented from repaying it by political enemies and unscrupulous merchants who hurry foreclosure on his estate after
he has left for Europe. While Mrs. Norman serves as the scapegoat for domestic offenses, Phelps invokes another scapegoat to carry the burden of the
politician's guilt. Israel Mordecai, a stock figure resonant with anti-Semitic
New York fiction, is alternately described in the novel as villainous and
greedy—he is "ever ready to give assistance to the needy, (of course requir-
ing, as is prudent, proper security)" (*IN*, 283). The unjust foreclosure is the
first event in a sequence that leads Mr. Norman down the path of debauch-
ery. His character destroyed by the subsequent embezzlement allegation,
Mr. Norman begins drinking excessively and seeking amusements in the gay
European court. There, under the influence of aristocratic French ways, he
meets and begins his adulterous affair with Adele de Villette, a betrayal that
breaks his wife's vain heart and leads to her early death. Unfazed, Mr. Norman forges ahead until Adele deserts him, leaving him alone, in a state of
self-loathing that only his incredible transformation into the Hermit of
Valambrosa can alleviate.

The Hermit of Valambrosa is an inelegant plot device to say the least.
Still, it allows Phelps to play out, once again, ideas about conversion and
written self-expression. Mr. Norman's act of inscribing a confession is
shown to have a redemptive effect on his identity: at the point he chooses to
announce his religious conversion, he agrees to "lay aside the third person"
and tell the story "without that interposing screen" (*IN*, 248). His conversion
depends on his recognition that virtue is all, that knowledge, political
power, and status are meaningless without it. His autobiography complete,
Mr. Norman hands it over to William Landon, who passes it along to Mr.
Norman's son, Louis. Thus, like Ida's communication to the students at Science Hall, her father's exemplary narrative catalyzes a personal transformation and renews a vital relationship with kin and community.

Phelps's Troy lectures turn on the idea that original composition reveals
and fixes identity, and in so doing takes a measure of the woman or man behind the prose. By the time she writes *Ida Norman*, Phelps appears to recognize that writing is not so simple as this. In the novel, the conversion narrative, a special kind of original composition, highlights the malleability of
identity: bad people can reform by writing themselves anew. Yet what makes
conversion narratives plausible also makes crimes in writing possible—pla-

giarism, forgery, and literary hoaxes all involve the assumption of false identities for unvirtuous purposes. For this reason Phelps demonstrates that
conversions fixed in writing must be made public, where their veracity can
be tested and their implicit contractual promises policed. As a result of their
public, written conversion letters, Ida must play the part of a virtuous normal student, and Mr. Norman must act as an honest patriarch. Those
around them guarantee that their resolutions stick, that they remain the better characters they proclaim themselves to be. The critical skills Mrs. Newton imparts—and more important, the virtue that she represents and in-
stills—thus enable both the recognition of false identity and the legitimate
conversion of character. Teachers such as Mrs. Newton thereby safeguard
the virtue that early national literature deemed central to the project of
building a democratic republic.

Schooling a "Democratic Mix"

> Of all methods to render boys fitted for future success in life, in a republican country
> where men mingle together, with no acknowledged, hereditary distinctions, an ex-
> clusive education is one of the worst.
> —Almira Hart Lincoln Phelps, Ida Norman

By now it should be apparent that Phelps was convinced—and was dedicated to persuading others—that publicly supported schools staffed by single women with advanced schooling were the logical and best successors to
the forms of home instruction that had prevailed just after the Revolution.
But what happened to Phelps's conviction as more and better schooling became available to the young women about whom she cared so much? As The
Blue Ribbon Society (1869) demonstrates, Phelps never ceased fighting the
early national battle that pitted home against school. The Blue Ribbon Society, ostensibly a conversion narrative, advocates the kind of women's schooling outlined in Phelps's Troy lectures and Patapsco addresses and dramatized in Ida Norman. In doing so, it reinscribes Phelps's insistence that
female academies can provide a rhetorical education decidedly better than
any the most promising Republican Mother can deliver. But this time an-
tipathy toward maternal schooling is not balanced neatly with optimism
about democracy in the classroom. Phelps has grown, it seems, skeptical of
the democratic mix.

As we saw in Ida Norman, at mid-century Phelps promulgated the idea that ordinary men in the United States, no matter their origins, could fashion themselves into great and influential figures through hard work and proper education. This theme echoes the early national inflections of Phelps's 1833 Troy lectures: it is an "unfortunate state of things," she writes, "when one class, being led to feel that rank alone can give elevation, are thus deprived of an important stimulus to mental effort, and the other, depressed by the abjectness of their situation, can scarcely hope, by the greatest efforts, to rise above the sphere in which they find themselves placed!" (*LYL*, 96). Although in 1833 such words might have been spoken against the institution of slavery, here Phelps means to recall America's revolutionary break with monarchical government and landed aristocracy. Just as she does in her meditation on abuse in marriage, Phelps here brackets the internal turmoil brewing over slavery in the early republic. Another example: while in an 1859 address Phelps boasts that Cherokee students attend Patapsco (*HMP*, 34, 36), in her earlier Troy lectures she perpetuates the myth of the "vanishing Indian." The 1830s were, of course, a time of relocation and genocide for Native Americans, but Phelps's lectures give no hint of that abomination.[28]

Both her vanishing Indian discourse and her few references to slavery demonstrate how Phelps, like many other "magazinists" and educators of her day, largely avoided issues of race and sectional conflict in her writing. Although urban African American literary societies flourished at this time, Phelps's texts, like the other lectures and schooling fictions we take up, register no account of this. There is simply no Harmony-Grove for African American women, and racial identity in such institutions is for the most part erased. Thus it is not surprising that Ann Plato, an African American student in Hartford, Connecticut, in the 1840s, writes school compositions for publication that "seldom . . . deal with racial matters." In fact, what she does write shows her to be the perfect student of domestic economy. In her brief essay "Two School Girls," the model student is cast as one who "by constant economy . . . was able to secure every comfort, and to remember the poor. Her family was well regulated, and taught order, industry, and perseverance which she herself had learned." Effacing race in antebellum domestic discourse was not a universal strategy, of course. Catharine Beecher is a noteworthy exception, as evidenced by her 1837 *Essay on Slavery and Abolitionism, with Reference to the Duty of American Females* and the resulting written debate she engaged in with abolitionist Angelina Grimké.[29]

For Phelps the aversion to racially charged discourse might well have been rooted in her belief that agonistic debate on slavery could only lead to dissolution of the union. But Phelps was not averse to all controversy, as evidenced in her repeated return to the theme of white class struggle, often embedded in accounts of industrious children rising from humble origins: "It is the pride of this institution," she writes, that students from all circumstances "here meet on terms of equality, except as virtue and talents make a distinction. Our country is probably the only one in the world which exhibits such a scene" (*LYL*, 96).

Ideally, that is. In reality, Phelps recognizes that an impoverished childhood could limit a young woman's education or even foreclose the possibility of one altogether. For example, she admits that poor children are unlikely to get preparatory instruction in ancient and modern languages, yet she insists that students admitted to academies like hers should have such preparation. Of greater consequence, Phelps worries that poverty leaves children simply unable to learn. Education requires, she explains, a strong body and mind and a delicate balance between them. Poverty in infancy means an absence of nurture for the mental habits essential to learning later in life: "The children of persons in the lower classes of society usually live wholly for the body. Play and labor, eating and sleeping make up the history of their early days. Or if they go to school and learn to read and write, their intellectual exercises are of so low a nature, as to leave the balance greatly in favor of the body" (*LYL*, 52). Occasionally, Phelps notes, exceptional children may break free from wretched early training: "We sometimes see, even under such unfavorable circumstances, the workings of intellect, as if struggling to escape from the rubbish under which it lies;—we see spirits endued with great power and force burst opposing barriers and urge an onward course, mounting upwards like the eagle, impatient to gaze upon the fountains of intellectual light" (*LYL*, 52). However, such intellectual flights are uncommon: it is "rare for the children of very poor and debased parents to make such an escape from the chains in which mind is held by matter" (*LYL*, 52).

Despite the difficulties of the poor, Phelps maintains that the genius of the U.S. system resides in leadership that is largely self-made: "If we look to our state legislatures, our national congress, and the highest executive and judicial offices in the country, we do not find these places chiefly occupied by those who were born to wealth, or only taught the pride of aristocratic

distinctions. Most of the great men of our country have made their own fortunes" (*LYL*, 28–29). Doubtless these words are meant to inspire and not de-
ceive, however much they depart from reality. "Take courage," Phelps counsels, "and remember that to a certain degree, especially in our own country,
every one is, in a degree, the 'artificer of his own fortune,'" a story she will
tell again and again in the two-volume *Ida Norman* (*LYL*, 28).

By 1869, however, Phelps plots a different cultural narrative. *The Blue
Ribbon Society* suggests that children who inherit privilege necessarily have
better early educations than "purse proud" merchants, a class Phelps feels is
particularly resistant to conversion, both to Protestant Christianity and to
democratic education (*BRS*, 27 August, chapter 4). *The Blue Ribbon Society*
unfolds as a straightforward contrast between two young women and their
families. Alice Fenwick Apsley is the daughter of a judge. Her paternal ancestry includes the founder of Connecticut; her maternal ancestry is possibly
linked to British aristocracy. Alice's parents are well-educated and well-
respected in the community; they have wisely trained up their daughter to
be humble, empathetic, obedient, and faithful. Conversely, Eugenia Victoria
Maria Theresa, the daughter of the "purse proud" Patrick, has a lineage
whose "not very distinguished," "foreign" ancestry has been hidden by a
name change from the Irish McGoin to the Scottish Macgoin or Magoin
(*BRS*, 20 August, chapter 1). Although Patrick Magoin "pushed his way in
the world, going from one business to another . . . until he had become a
rich man," he married in his more humble days a beautiful but uneducated
woman (*BRS*, 20 August, chapter 1). Under the guidance of these parents,
Eugy, as she is called, grows to be an ignorant, spoiled, self-centered, and
faithless child. The brief novel chronicles Alice's and Eugy's time at Mount
Science Seminary, run by the venerable Mrs. Hamilton, and follows their
days together through to Eugy's conversion, after a careless accident leaves
her an invalid.

The Apsleys represent ideal parents. Although they love their daughter,
they recognize the need to send Alice away to be schooled. The judge counsels his daughter, "there is nothing in this life that does not change. . . . How
can we expect to be exempt from this general law? . . . Indeed, my child, you
have been too long brooded under the parental wing; your mind needs the
stimulus of trial and competition" (*BRS*, 20 August, chapter 2). Alice does
not want to leave home and briefly challenges her parents, arguing that she is

not a boy who needs to make his own way in the world, but a girl who can learn everything she needs at home. In reply, Alice's mother provides the familiar Phelps counterargument to Republican Motherhood: "No, Alice, I cannot teach you what experience alone can teach—that knowledge of human nature without which you can never be useful in society, nor even in the domestic circle. . . . Of course we love you, we advise you, but we are not good judges; we are blinded by our parental partiality" (*BRS*, 20 August, chapter 2). The dutiful Alice consults her Bible, resigns herself to the privations of boarding school, and puts on a stoical face for her parents' sake. Despite their resolve, the Apsleys are worried, and their anxiety over Alice's departure worsens when they learn that Eugy's parents, out of jealousy, have decided to send their daughter to Mount Science as well. "Though somewhat surprised and not much pleased," Judge Apsley sends Alice and Eugenia off together: "There seemed an opportunity presented of doing good, which his principles did not permit him to pass by, reluctant as he felt to send his child from home with such a companion,—but here was to begin her trial, and they must subject her to the ordeal" (*BRS*, 27 August, chapter 4).

Even in her Troy lectures, Phelps is not so idealistic as to say that all citizens of the new nation would be as satisfied as the Apsleys with the terms of equality in a national democracy. She recognizes that many would want to claim superior status, and that some young women would demand, as Ida and Eugy do, the privilege of being "parlor boarders," set apart from the "masses" of other young women. Phelps's response is to appeal to both patriotism and status: "We know," in the United States, "of no hereditary claims to respect, which can set aside the superior claims of merit; and if the attempt is made to render any school in our country of an *exclusive* character, it must, from the very genius of our government, and the nature of our institutions, prove as abortive as it is ridiculous" (*LYL*, 96). A family may pay for seemingly superior education, but it will not be a good bargain because knowledge in the new United States "cannot, like houses and lands, be purchased by money" (*LYL*, 94). Here is why: "Some may indeed, from a desire of this *exclusiveness*, pay such extravagant demands for the education of their daughters as cannot be afforded by persons of moderate fortunes; but the children thus educated will be obliged when they come forth into the world, to run the race of life by the side of those, who, having been inured to competition, are strengthened and prepared for the contest. When distanced in this race, and left to see their despised inferiors far before them, it will but add to their chagrin, that they had once been flattered with the idea of possessing peculiar advantages" (*LYL*, 96–97). In *The Blue Ribbon Society*, some four decades later, Phelps musters more sympathy for parents who resist democratic education. The Apsleys, the novella suggests, are right to worry about the likes of a Eugy Magoin and are right to wish that their daughter might remain in their contented home. Indeed, the narrator says, "In gazing upon her, one might have wished that she could always remain just sixteen, ignorant of the temptations and follies of the world. Were it not that she must be prepared to act her part in life, we could desire that she might not be sent even to the best boarding school, where must be exhibited, in miniature, the ambition, artifice and cold selfishness of the outside world" (*BRS*, 27 August, chapter 3).

Throughout her long career, Phelps maintains that young women of leisure as well as those compelled to labor would benefit from a balance of intellectual and physical work. She understands, however, that some parents—especially those who must pay tuition—would be suspicious of schooling that includes both a "democratic mix" of students and domestic labor as a subject of study. Such parents would, after all, expect some exclusivity for their money. And Phelps is willing to concede that, under adverse conditions, a school could be pulled down to the lowest common denominator. Still, Phelps emphasizes, parents should worry not about their children mixing with others of lower station, but instead fear their mixing with others of questionable moral character. The lowest common denominator, is, in other words, a moral one: "In a public school, where many young persons form a collective mass, there are dangers arising from their effects upon each other. 'As a little leaven leaveneth the whole lump,' so do pride, vanity, and disregard to moral and religious principles, spread from one and contaminate many" (*LYL*, 44). The fear of contagion takes Phelps back to her starting point: the need for schooled professional teachers. Mental and spiritual discipline in the person of a well-trained teacher would work to contain immorality by fostering "self-government" in her pupils (*LYL*, 46). Virtue, the foundation of democracy, would thereby be preserved.

Although not close to what we recognize as public education today, Phelps's conception of public schooling in her 1833 lectures and mid-century *Ida Norman* is decidedly liberal. She intends to diversify access to instruction and indeed insists that a democratic mix in the classroom—a pale mix, to be sure—is foundational to success in the industrious new nation. This may have been a particularly startling message for her Patapsco audience, which included many southern young women whom Phelps believed had been pampered by domestics. But *The Blue Ribbon Society* shows that after the Civil War Phelps had lost some of her enthusiasm for the project of democratic education. Phelps's representation of a juvenile (and antidemocratic) confederacy in the book could hardly have been found compelling by the many readers who had followed her career before the war. As it turns out, unity is more important than democracy in *The Blue Ribbon Society*, and Phelps only weakly veils her belief that the recent war was the result of childish folly. When Eugy joins the Order of the Blue Ribbon and marches around campus with her "band of confederates," Alice makes clear that their actions, their motives, and their words are merely the result of juvenile restlessness: "'Perhaps,' said Alice, smiling, 'they compare themselves rather to those worthies who have risen against oppression, and nobly dared to oppose the power that would have crushed them. But I am sure it would be difficult for any one to find aught to complain of in the mild government which is here administered'" (*BRS*, 3 September, chapter 6). Liberatory civic rhetoric, associated now both with those who favored abolition *and* with those who favored secession, remains one of Phelps's targets. By implication, their deeds, like those of the Blue Ribbon girls, are attributed to some "restless impulse" that "urges them forward to do something"—though nothing with defined moral purpose (*BRS*, 3 September, chapter 6). Given its scolding tone, it is no surprise that *The Blue Ribbon Society* made hardly a ripple when it appeared.[30] Phelps's glossing of a bloody civil war and her advancement of an early national model of education for young women make her work by 1869 decidedly anachronistic.

The Fruits of Democratic Teachers: Good Wives, Virtuous Politicians

It is difficult to discern from *The Blue Ribbon Society* just what Phelps believes are the wider consequences of women's education in postbellum America. Perhaps questioning the value of democratic schooling foreclosed speculation on what ends it might serve. But before the Civil War, Phelps was quite forthright in her appraisal of democratic schooling's broad social benefits. We have already surveyed the benefits for women described in

Phelps's lectures, addresses, and fiction. But it is clear—clearest of all in *Ida Norman*—that Phelps wants young men to be touched by the good work of democratic teachers as well. Consider, then, the influence Mrs. Newton has on Louis Norman and William Landon and, by extension, the sphere of political and legal power they come to occupy.

While the Normans do well to select Science Hall for Ida, they do less well for Louis, who attends the "highly aristocratic" Bourbon Hall, overseen by Mr. Delaplaine, a "foreigner" (*IN*, 78). That Louis's Bourbon Hall education is greatly at odds with democratic aims is a point Phelps makes sure her young readers will grasp. She interrupts the narrative to offer an impassioned essay on the importance of schooling that is not exclusive:

> Let American boys be taught to love their country, to revere its republican institutions, to understand the principles and genius of its government, and they will be, truly, patriotic. They will see in each member of society, an American sovereign; no matter how humble may be his occupation, how common his dress, how unpolished his address, he will be viewed as a constituent member of the body politic, filling his place in the political organism, and bearing his share of political accountability. With such views and feelings, how natural would be the desire to benefit the community at large, by improving common education; and by giving to those who possess so noble a birth-right, the intellectual and moral culture which would lead them to the knowledge and practice of their social and relative duties. (*IN*, 79)

As Phelps plots Louis's life in the wake of his family's financial reversal, the failings of Delaplaine and Bourbon Hall become apparent. Just as Mrs. Newton offers Ida the opportunity to teach at Science Hall, so Delaplaine offers Louis a position as a teacher at Bourbon Hall: "you might stay, and take care of the small boys, and be useful in a good many ways" (*IN*, 106). Plainly, Delaplaine means to exploit poor Louis, consistent with his running the school "rather as a business" than as an institution dedicated to the common good (*IN*, 106). Worse, readers learn, Delaplaine is dishonest. He pockets the 1,000 pounds that Mr. Norman sends him for tuition—half of which is to go to Mrs. Newton for Ida's education—and then suggests that Louis owes him a debt. Happily for Louis, his father, for all his faults, has made some good connections, one of which is with an honest lawyer, Mr. Ashburn, who emerges as a model of legal integrity and justice. Aware of the draft Mr. Norman had sent Delaplaine, Ashburn returns to Bourbon

Hall with Louis to square the account. While kindhearted Louis feels concil-
iatory toward Delaplaine, Mr. Ashburn is a harsh judge: "'And such a
scoundrel is allowed to educate youth; but he shall be unmasked, I owe it to
society to make his character known—a wolf set to guard lambs! Ah, Louis,
you treated him too well.'" (*IN*, 150). In addition to Ashburn's declaration,
Phelps uses her narrator's voice to make the point: "This man had gained
the confidence of the public, and parents entrusted their sons to his care. He
first became popular through the patronage of some influential persons,
who regarded his nobility, (and this might not have stood the test of
scrutiny,) his polished manners, and, above all, his Parisian accent, as enti-
tling him to the highest rank in his profession, of an educator of young gentleman" (*IN*, 148). Phelps is willing to concede that Delaplaine is a "man of
learning," and that Louis probably learned some subjects well under his
tutelage (namely, French and good manners) (*IN*, 148). Still, he does not attend to the more important studies that will lead a young man to be "a patriot, a useful citizen, a philanthropist, or a Christian" (*IN*, 149). Luckily,
Louis is blessed by the good fortune of Mrs. Newton's religious influence:
earlier in the novel, Mrs. Newton recognizes that Delaplaine does not attend to his students' moral needs and offers to take up this part of Louis's
schooling.

And yet, finally, it is not simply Mrs. Newton's vigilance that results in
Louis's success. Something deep within Louis is noble. Unlike Ida, he does
not "imbibe" his parents' immorality, nor is he "spoiled by the *bad education*
of his childhood" (*IN*, 79). Perhaps Phelps would have it that Louis's good
ethos is attributable to his gender, but whatever the reason, she creates a
character whose integrity is innate. Thus when Louis learns about his family's financial ruin from Mrs. Newton, he instantly determines to make himself "respected and useful" as a remedy, even though it means a premature
end to his formal education (*IN*, 92). Louis's burden is eased a bit because he
does not have to support Ida: Ida says, "Mrs. Newton has taught me that
women need not be helpless burdens upon their friends, nor useless beings
in society" (*IN*, 100). But mostly Louis depends on his own character for his
success. Because he has been far less pampered than his sister, he already
shows signs of self-reliance, evident primarily in a phenomenal work ethic.
"Depend on it," says one observer, "that young man will, one day, become
distinguished; he is born to lead others, and can never be kept down, in an

obscure position;—but he will rise, by the upward force of genius and merit, and not by management and intrigue" (*IN*, 105).

Louis does rise by his own hard work (and, though the narrator glosses over the fact, by his father's connections), moving from his clerkship in Ashburn's office to a position as a respected lawyer, whose skill we see in the trial scene that concludes the first volume of *Ida Norman*. In this scene, Louis is characterized by opposing counsel as a "young lawyer with nothing to lose, and every thing to gain" from the "power of his eloquence," a veritable David trying to "overcome a Goliath of the law" (*IN*, 282). But Phelps makes sure that readers understand the accusation is baseless. The narrative paints Louis as a gifted, eloquent lawyer who will use his verbal talents to undo the wrong committed against his father (Israel Mordecai's hasty foreclosure). Indeed, Phelps shows through contrast that it is Mordecai's lawyers who use rhetoric speciously: they portray their client as a philanthropist (which we know he is not) and James Livingston Norman as a despicable rake (perhaps, but as his autobiography attests, he had his reasons). Mordecai's lawyers thus construct an ad hominem defense, while Louis invests his case with calm, measured reasoning, supported by incontrovertible physical evidence. His manner is "cool and deliberate," "passionless," as if "moved by intellect alone" (*IN*, 286). He represents his father as simply a great man of "eloquence and genius" who had "erred" (*IN*, 287). Throughout his summation, Louis proceeds "calmly and without any perceptible agitation; stating the legal bearings of the case, which he scanned with clearness, and exhibited with force, without encumbering them with aught irrelevant, or of a nature to divide, or distract attention" (*IN*, 293). He produces documents showing that Mordecai and his associates planted the rumors that caused Mr. Norman's creditors to panic, from which the defendants profited greatly. Louis wins *Norman* v. *Mordecai* and the praise of his father who witnesses the feat: "'I was called eloquent,' thought he, 'but my speeches were made of fine words; this is the language of the soul!'" (*IN*, 293). In victory, the sins of the father are forgiven, and for that, democratic educational principles are to thank: hard work, virtue, and a love of the common good, all of which prepare Louis to participate in political life.

Yet political life, as Mr. Norman's story underscores, is a morally risky enterprise. At some time unspecified in the narrative, Louis, like his father, serves a term in political office. Unlike his father, though, he is drawn into service against his will and vacates the office at the earliest possibility; he does not seek nor fall victim to popularity. Louis accepts Mr. Ashburn's proposition that a man of "abilities which might enable him to be useful to his country" must seek office, but returns to the law because it is "too often degraded by the practices of men of mean and selfish minds" (*IN*, 146, 395). Louis thus becomes an exemplar of the responsible citizen who performs statesmanship as a public service but rejects it as a profession. It is William Landon, Ida Norman's future husband, who becomes the career politician, but not in the corruptible mold formed by Mr. Norman. William is dubbed one of "the rising men of our republic" who "support national honor, and promote national prosperity" (*IN*, 394). Like his sister, William has been multiply schooled—first by the hardships of poverty, later by a mother who could educate him in the classics and English literature, and finally by teachers connected to his sister and friends. When Laura makes Saturday visits, William takes the opportunity to learn Mrs. Newton's lessons secondhand, paying particular attention to the foreign languages Laura is learning. When Louis Norman visits, William joins his friend in the study of mathematics and the natural sciences. Finally, when William's employer, Mr. Selby, recognizes the boy's raw talent and gives him free time to improve his education, he jumps at the offer. His "recreation," as he explains it, "has consisted in study." He rejects the "theatre, or other places of amusement" for the "far more interesting employment, in books" (*IN*, 199–200). Mr. Selby, whose own son, the dilettante Frank, shows no initiative, recognizes the value of such a young man. "With your talents, energies and moral worth," he tells William, "you must rise in a country like ours, where there are no barriers of *caste*, nor *privileged orders*" (*IN*, 200). William Landon thus comes to represent the rare promise of self-education, devoting himself with equal enthusiasm to both higher studies and practical clerkship. This balance between intellect and know-how proves essential to his success. When William is tempted by the literature of German mystics to doubt his faith, his common sense, girded up by early religious training, pulls him back from the brink. In Phelps's moral scheme, then, there is no stopping an intelligent, sensible young man like William. Little wonder he becomes an "enlightened philanthropist," spending his money on the arts and charitable causes rather than amassing a fortune (*IN*, 394).

Phelps's novel ends, then, with the marriages of young men and women who have excellent schooling in self-governance and self-reliance. Although they have trained to be teachers, Laura and Ida become perfect wives for a new generation of statesmen who employ virtue and common sense to guard against the flattering, fawning world of politics. Mr. Norman's difficult wife has been replaced by the young graduates of Science Hall. Mr. Norman himself is replaced by young men who benefit indirectly from the same institution. Behind all of these relationships stands Amelia Newton, an activist for women's higher learning and independence, a woman who "objects" to such demeaning terms as "*authoress, poetess,* etc." ("we might as well say *Christianness*"), a woman who believes that anything "intellectual or spiritual, should not be distinguished by gender," yet who still schools all her students for their divinely destined "sphere of duty" (*IN*, 405). And behind Amelia Newton stands Phelps herself, whose lifetime of writing leaves little doubt as to the source of Mrs. Newton's optimism that Science Hall's graduates would see to it that America's democratic experiment would come out right.

7 Conclusion

Rhetorical Limits in the Schooling and Teaching Journals of Charlotte Forten

Tomorrow school commences, and although the pleasure I shall feel in again seeing my beloved teacher, and in resuming my studies will be much saddened by recent events, yet they shall be a fresh incentive to more earnest study, to aid me in fitting myself for laboring in a holy cause, for enabling me to do much towards changing the condition of my oppressed and suffering people. Would that those with whom I shall recite to-morrow could sympathize with me in this.

Charlotte Forten, *Journal* (1854)

⮑ *In the midst of the Civil War,* Almira Phelps threw considerable energy into editing a collection of essays she hoped would strengthen loyalty to the union while softening condemnation of "our erring brethren of the South." Her own contribution to *Our Country, in Its Relations to the Past, Present and Future: A National Book* (1864) is a blank verse poem that recites the history of the United States from colonial days through the War of Secession. Recurrent in its stanzas are images of sectional harmony, none so familiar as a return to her school at Patapsco, where Phelps asks readers to "view its inmates fair, who represent / The different parts of our republic vast— / For here assembled, in one common home, / Are daughters of the North and of the South." "Inmates fair," indeed. Fresh, charming, pleasing to the mind and eye, no doubt Phelps intends the phrase to signal these meanings. But it signifies more, of course. We can be reasonably sure that "fair" also describes the complexion of Patapsco's students, for how could the daughter of a free person of color chance attending school in Maryland, where slavery remained legal during Phelps's principalship? Thus when Phelps boasts that a Patapsco student from

"Southern Carolina loves full well / Her Massachusetts sister," we know that
the young women who reconcile the rebellious South and the abolitionist
North are, without question, white.[1]

Yet in an idealized Patapsco, as fictionalized in *Ida Norman*, we glimpse
wealth, privilege, and a desire to learn and teach that would not have been
unfamiliar to some African Americans living in the urban North. Their
story, however, is not to be found in the pages of a popular schooling novel,
nor is it documented in the writing guides, anthologies, compilations, or
domestic treatises that won wide acclaim in the antebellum period. Instead,
the best account of a free black woman's formal schooling in the antebellum
North can be found in the journals of Charlotte Forten, which she began
keeping while an advanced student at Higginson Grammar School in Salem,
Massachusetts, and continued through her subsequent training at Salem
Normal School, and teaching among the "contraband" slaves of South Carolina's Sea Islands.[2] Forten's diary enables us to imagine a bond between a
South Carolinian and her Massachusetts sister the likes of which Phelps
could never have committed to paper.

In late 1863, as Phelps compiled *Our Country*, she promised one contrib-
utor that she would "prefer not to ask contributions from those agitators
who have helped southern politicians to bring on the present crisis."[3] At the
same time Forten, whose journals reveal a young women enmeshed in such
agitation, returned to the Sea Island of St. Helena for a second stint as a
teacher of liberated slaves. There Forten commenced instruction of some
forty young people in a "comparatively comfortable room with a fire in it,"
possibly in the main house of a plantation she calls "the Perry Place."[4] How
much it resembled Patapsco's "mansion" of "massive . . . granite walls, and
pillars firm," and "Grecian portico" we cannot say,[5] but certainly Phelps's admiration for her students resonates with Forten's praise for hers, some of
whom she finds "quite advanced" after just a few years in school (509).
Forten's teaching assignment gives new meaning to Phelps's "pleasant
thought" that "in [her] Southern home there's room / For a fair Northern
sister."[6] On the Sea Islands, Forten finds a temporary southern home where
she can finally bring her talents as a teacher and writer to bear on "the condition of [her] oppressed and suffering people" (67).

Forten's preparation for her journey South arguably began with her father's decision to send her from Philadelphia to Salem, Massachusetts,

where she was enrolled in Higginson Grammar School for girls. A public institution, Higginson accepted both black and white students, unlike the racially segregated public schools of Philadelphia that Forten's father would not permit her attend. Tutorials at home readied her for the scholastic transition, although nothing could have prepared her to inhabit two communities with such seemingly different aims and discourses.[7] Simultaneously she found herself intimately acquainted with some of the most active abolitionist lecturers and writers of her day and immersed in Massachusetts's burgeoning experiment to formalize the training of teachers through a system of regional normal schools. The abolitionists around Forten at first appropriated civic liberatory rhetoric for their cause and then turned it on its head; the normal school promoted belletristic values of continuous self-improvement, as did the literary societies with which Forten would have been familiar from her youth in Philadelphia. Truly, then, Forten's schooling and early teaching journals, from mid-1854 through the onset of the Civil War, provide us with a narrative that illuminates the essential tension between two ends—rhetoric put toward civic needs or toward satisfying belletristic principles—and does so in ways that Phelps and an earlier generation of teacher-writers could not have contemplated.[8]

Forten begins her first journal with a modest paragraph entered on Wednesday, 24 May 1854. Remarkably, that entry and those from the next few days illustrate the clash of rhetorical principles that resound through the remainder of her journal writing. The first entry sets a simple, pastoral tone: "Rose at five. The sun was shining brightly through my window, and I felt vexed with myself that he should have risen before me; I shall not let him have that advantage again very soon. How bright and beautiful are these May mornings! The air is so pure and balmy, the trees are in full blossom, and the little birds sing sweetly" (59). Some sentences later, Forten tells us that after dinner she "took a pleasant walk by the water," where she "stood for some time admiring the waves as they rose and fell, sparkling in the sun" (59). Such celebratory language about nature and her use of it to characterize her own moods and experiences become commonplace in the days and months ahead. Yet no entry, not even her first, is an uninterrupted paean to the natural world. She reports that after passing by the water, she stops by a friend's house to read—apparently part of her routine—this time picking up Dickens's *Hard Times*. After recording a brief summary of the book's opening chapters, Forten shares that the day's social activity concludes with a visit from out-of-town guests, after which she spends time writing before going to bed. Thus Forten's first entry chronicles an ideal day in a schoolgirl's life: rising early, taking exercise out-of-doors, reading, surrounding herself with intellectually stimulating company, and evaluating her day's conduct in writing, thereby fixing it for posterity.

An entry made the next evening, 25 May, chronicles another life, one that calls for another kind of rhetoric. Forten is compelled to write by "something which must ever rouse in the mind of every true friend of liberty and humanity, feelings of the deepest indignation and sorrow" (60). That something is the arrest of Anthony Burns in Boston under provisions of the Fugitive Slave Law.[9] The capture and trial of Burns, an escaped slave from Virginia, were of enormous concern in the staunchly abolitionist Remond household, where Forten lived. Indeed, one hears the liberatory rhetoric of the Remonds' platform oratory registered in Forten's journals anytime she raises the subject of slavery, fugitive slaves, and the complicated politics of abolition. (Why the Remonds' oratory is not civic as well as liberatory is taken up in the next section.) But like her first journal entry, the second one is not the exemplar of a singular type. She shifts back to Romantic discourse and in so doing makes a rhetorical move highly suspect in female educational circles. She expresses melancholy—the "weather is gloomy and my feelings correspond with it"—the very sort of depressing sentiment that Tuthill and Phelps sought to discourage as inexcusably selfish (60).

Forten's journal entry on Friday, 26 May, introduces a third strand of rhetorical performance evident in her private writing. The Burns case still unresolved, Forten describes a troubling encounter with Miss Mary Shepard, her white teacher and dearest friend at Higginson Grammar School.[10] Although many future entries recount with affection time spent with Miss Shepard, their friendship is not without stress, as is apparent early on: "Had a conversation with Miss Mary Shepard about slavery; she is, as I thought, thoroughly opposed to it, but does not agree with me in thinking that the churches and ministers are generally supporters of the infamous system; I believe it firmly" (60–61). As the journal unfolds, this conflict between Christian institutions and abolitionist societies becomes more manifest, as does Forten's sense that her closest friends at school do not share her radical—that is, Garrisonian—antislavery beliefs. There is, then, a rhetorical self-fashioning that takes place on the pages of Forten's journal as she braids together the teacherly and political ethos that will enable her to survive her southern relief work. We look first at the origins of that self-fashioning in Forten's home schooling in Philadelphia and formal schooling in Salem. We then turn to the realm of oratory beyond home and school to discern the most powerful rhetorical influences on her as she matures from student into teacher. Finally, we conclude with an assessment of the cultural work that women like Charlotte Forten could do given the limits of rhetoric Forten herself discovers.

Rewriting Mrs. Graves: New Sketches of School and Schoolmates

In many ways, Forten's early accounts of her time in Salem resemble the most idyllic scenes of gentle learning portrayed in earlier schooling fictions. Forten records, for example, a thoughtful stroll through Harmony Grove, a woodsy Salem graveyard not unlike the secluded locale of Mrs. Williams's school in Foster's *The Boarding School.* Too, she documents a "composition afternoon" that Williams's students could have passed in the fictional Harmony Hall: "In the afternoon instead of attending to our usual exercises, we took our work to school and sewed while the compositions were read; I think 'composition afternoons' are very pleasant" (79). Although Forten is frequently homesick for Philadelphia, at the end of her first year, she reflects favorably on her experience at Salem's Higginson Grammar School: "The last day of the old year. I can scarcely realize that I have spent the whole of it away from home. Yet, although separated from many of my dearest friends, this year has been to me a very happy one. Happy, because the field of knowledge, for the first time has seemed widely open to me; because I have studied here, and, I trust, learned more than during any other year of my life. I have been taught how very little I really know, and, with the knowledge of my ignorance, I feel an earnest desire to become very much wiser" (119). Eager to learn, Forten begins her formal studies motivated to improve herself, to become, as we will see, the independent soul Phelps urged her students to be. But to achieve independence, Forten knows that she must depend on those wiser than herself, and she depends on no one more than her teacher, the talented and beloved Miss Mary Shepard. Her adoration for Miss Shepard recalls similar testimonials for teachers popularized in the boarding school fictions we have discussed in previous chapters, teachers such as Mrs. Williams (Foster's *The Boarding School*), Mrs. Norville (Graves's *Girlhood and Womanhood*), Mrs. MacOver (Tuthill's *The Boarding-School Girl*), and Mrs. Newton (Phelps's *Ida Norman*). Among other reasons, Forten admires her teacher for a quality she yearns to acquire herself: the "faculty of adapting herself to the society of all . . . making the time pass more pleasantly than any one else can" (102).

Forten's admiration for Shepard also often finds expression in highly romantic discourse. In the late summer of 1854, she writes: "This morning I took a delightful walk with her [Miss Shepard] in Harmony Grove. Never did it look so beautiful as on this very loveliest of summer mornings, so happy, so peaceful one almost felt like resting in that quiet spot, beneath the soft, green grass. My teacher talked to me of a beloved sister who is sleeping here. . . . Oh! how lovely it was this morning; all was so bright and beautiful, and yet so calm. Again, I parted with my dear teacher, feeling how much I should miss her society, in which I always find so much enjoyment" (94). Several months later, Forten's feelings intensify: "My beloved teacher and I walked home in the quiet starlight—star*shine* she said it might be called—and why not? we have sunshine and moonshine, and surely it is delightful—the light of those fair stars 'which are the poetry of heaven.' And more delightful it seemed to me with that dear friend, the remembrance of whose kind words and loving sympathy will remain, even after I have parted from her, one of the happiest of my life" (112). After passing her final examination in early 1855, Forten reflects on the inevitable loss of Shepard's loving sympathy after graduation: "I am extremely tired, but our dear teacher must be more so. I can scarcely bear to think how very soon I shall have to leave her. To me no one can ever supply her place" (128). Her teachers at Salem Normal School may not have taken Shepard's place, but Forten records her warmth of feeling for them and their school upon graduating a year and a half after leaving grammar school: "Our diplomas were awarded. I was lucky enough to get one. This evening we had a delightful meeting at the school house, our last. It was one of the pleasantest meetings we have had. And now I realize that my school days are indeed over. And many sad regrets I feel that it is indeed so. The days of my N[ew] England school life, though spent far from home and early friends, have still been among the happiest of my life. I have been fortunate enough to receive the instruction of the best and kindest teachers; and the few friends I have made are warm and true"

(160–61).[11] Appreciation for teachers, devotion to friends, and nostalgia for good times past: these are the conventional emotional responses we find scripted in the schooling fictions that circulated during Forten's youth. Whether Forten read Foster, Tuthill, Graves, or Phelps we do not know; their books would probably have been available to her. What is more certain is that the sentiments of popular schooling fictions were embraced by those around Forten, who believed that education for young women contributed to the general diffusion of knowledge needed to nourish democratic institutions and to secure a stable position in a social realm increasingly stratified by race, gender, national origin, and income.

But by the time she reached Salem, Forten had reason to doubt the power of education to secure stability, at least for African Americans. Catalyzing her doubts—and moving her pen—was turmoil surrounding stepped-up enforcement of the Fugitive Slave Law. As mentioned, very early in her grammar school career, Forten is engrossed and enraged by the capture, trial, and eventual return to Virginia of Anthony Burns.[12] Her journal entries on the Burns affair, far from employing the Romantic rhetoric of schooling fictions, draw heavily on the conventions of abolitionist oratory, conventions that harken back to—but do not fully reproduce—the civic liberatory rhetoric of the Revolutionary War. Reacting to the news that Burns would be sent South to "bondage worse, a thousand time worse than death" (65), she writes: "With what scorn must that government be regarded which cowardly assembles thousands of soldiers to satisfy the demands of slaveholders; to deprive of his freedom a man, created in God's own image, whose sole offense is the color of his skin! And if resistance is offered to this outrage, these soldiers are to shoot down American citizens without mercy; and this by express orders of a government which proudly boasts of being the freest in the world; this on the very soil where the Revolution of 1776 began; in sight of the battlefield, where thousands of brave men fought and died in opposing British tyranny, which was nothing compared with the American oppression of today" (65–66). But how should Forten respond to such oppression? In effect, she debates the matter over the course of several months' worth of entries. Sometimes she satisfies herself by contemplating how literature might work on the hearts of those divided on the question of slavery. Awaiting the Burns decision, she rereads Elizabeth Barrett Browning's "The Runaway Slave at Pilgrim's Point," after which she observes, "It seems as if no one could read this poem without having his sympathies roused to the utmost on behalf of the oppressed" (63). Other times, she imagines herself becoming an antislavery lecturer like Sarah Parker Remond, though she worries about the difficulty of public lecturing when she confesses—after performing for a visiting teacher at school—that "reading one's composition, before strangers is a trying task" (91). It takes time for Forten to overcome internal resistance to the proposition that teaching, her father's goal for her, may be the best way she can address the oppression of African Americans, both free and enslaved.

Most interesting in Forten's journals are the moments when the worlds of schooling fictions and antislavery activism collide. One such moment arises when Forten spots Miss Shepard at an antislavery meeting: "Miss Shepard was there, and she said that she was pleased with the lecture. I hope that she will be persuaded to attend the whole course. If she were better acquainted with the sentiments of the abolitionists, I do not think she could regard any of them as unchristian; but she would see them as they are— truly Christian, noble hearted, devoted to the Right" (106–7). The last lines are understated but telling: just four months before, Miss Shepard had told Forten that abolitionist thoughts threaten Christian spirit. Forten reports Miss Shepard's advice: "After school, had an hour's conversation with her [Miss Shepard] about slavery and prejudice. I fully appreciate her kindness, and sympathy with me; she wishes me to cultivate a Christian spirit in thinking of my enemies; I know it is right, and will endeavor to do so, but it does seem difficult" (67). Difficult, indeed. The issue of proper Christian conduct, particularly as it tempers hatred of slavery, becomes one that occupies page upon page in Forten's journal. The justification of hatred arises frequently in her conversations with abolitionist friends such as Charles Lenox Remond, her Salem host, and Remond's sister, Sarah Parker Remond: "Took a long walk with Miss Remond. . . . She thought that she was a very little inclined to misanthropy. I think so; and feel the importance of guarding against this feeling" (115). On occasion, she abstracts misanthropy from the context of abolitionist debates and considers it in the sort of literary-historical context sponsored by her schooling. Her reading of Hawthorne's *The House of Seven Gables,* for instance, prompts this disturbing observation: "hatred of oppression seems to me so blended with hatred of the oppressor I cannot separate them. I feel that no other injury could be so hard to bear, so very hard to forgive, as that inflicted by cruel oppression and prejudice. How *can* I be a Christian when so many in common with myself, for no crime suffer so cruelly, so unjustly?" (95). Repeated thought experiments like this lead Forten to moments of clarity but not to reconciliation of her double existence. Roughly a year later, now at normal school, Forten reiterates this clarity, and although she is further than ever from reconciling hatred of slavery with Christian morality, she is able to begin justifying her feelings and generalizing her experience: "I wonder that every colored person is not a misanthrope. Surely we have everything to make us hate mankind. I have met girls in the schoolroom—they have been thoroughly kind and cordial to me—perhaps the next day met them in the street—they feared to recognize me; these I can but regard now with scorn and contempt" (140). In this justification lie the seeds of discursive possibility: a quest to fashion a rhetoric that sanctions the articulation of strong emotions such as hatred, emotions that white rhetors considered distasteful in view of contemporary belletristic standards and illogical according to the conventions of neoclassical civic expression.

To understand why Forten's early journal entries document this search for a new rhetoric, it helps to go beyond the rhetorical resources on view in her journal to the broader realm of ideas about public expression evident in her schooling. One way to do this is to step back from her experience at Salem and examine the failed arguments that led her father to abandon hope of educating his daughter in Philadelphia and to identify Salem as an alternative venue. Not only do these arguments illuminate something of the Forten family's expectations for rhetorical education, they also illustrate the constraints on neoclassical civic rhetoric that limited its effectiveness for free African Americans writing and speaking in the North after 1800.

For the Fortens there were, first of all, arguments clustered around the matter of access to decent public schooling in Philadelphia. Although nothing in municipal or state law permitted it, the city's publicly supported schools had been essentially segregated from their advent at the turn of the nineteenth century. And while accommodations for white schoolchildren improved markedly over successive decades, accommodations for African American children did not. Buildings for black schools were few, small, and ill-equipped, and the Lancastrian system of monitorial pedagogy lingered in African American primary and grammar classrooms years after it had been banished from schools for whites. By 1840 perceived staffing and attendance problems at the grammar school nearest Forten's home prompted white school officials to propose its closure, a move that would have effectively ended public schooling for black Philadelphians at the third grade. James Forten, Charlotte's grandfather and an acknowledged leader in the African American community, led a successful campaign to keep the school open. His eloquence, honed as a speaker and writer for equal rights and the abolition of slavery, secured an institution that was prized, regardless of its inadequacy.

What remained was to push for adequacy, which to the generation of Forten's father meant integrated schools supported by whites and blacks alike. The task of arguing this case fell in part to Robert Purvis, Charlotte's uncle and, early on, neighbor. It turned out to be an argument so radical that Purvis could not make it and still live in Philadelphia proper. A target during a time of escalating antiblack violence, Purvis moved his family to suburban Byberry in the early 1840s, where some years later he mounted a campaign for school integration. In 1853 he announced that his "rights as a man and a parent have been grossly outraged" by the township's failure to support integrated schooling.[13] As a taxpayer, he expected nothing less than this support. But his argument—civic minded and logical—did not move school officials. In fact, the possibility of school integration was foreclosed when state law was changed in 1854 to permit racial segregation and to establish the term for African Americans' schooling at a mere four months. In hindsight, the narrowness of James Forten's victory and the subsequent frustration of his son-in-law's advocacy of integration are indicative of the broader erosion of African American rights that began to worsen with passage of the Fugitive Slave Law in 1793 and accelerated with black Pennsylvanians' disfranchisement in 1838, the year following Forten's birth.[14]

Hope for an integrated public sphere thus dimmed as Charlotte Forten reached school-age. Wisely, the Fortens, perhaps recognizing the hard limits of persuasion, redoubled their investment in a parallel culture of letters, separate but equal. Male and female mutual aid societies in Philadelphia provided the foundation for literary societies that supplied the cultural education denied as a public accommodation. Elizabeth McHenry notes that in 1837, James Forten asserted that African American literary societies held the power to defeat racism: "Thus we see that, whatever tends to disseminate the

principles of education, tends to raise us above the tide of popular prejudice; and whatever tends to raise us above the chilling influence of prejudice, must of reason tend to elevate our condition." Forten's words, coming
near the end of his life, are a departure from the sort of civic appeals that
characterized his earlier career: they center on the belletristic values that
would entice and yet vex his granddaughter several decades later.[15]

If civic rhetoric had lost efficacy in the fight for racial equality in Pennsylvania schools, the same could not be said of Massachusetts, at least in certain locales. In Salem the application of cold legal argumentation achieved
school desegregation in 1844 after many years of "agitation." Thus was created an integrated site for the study of belletristic values, very much apart
from the rhetoric of rights constitutive of that scene. The enabling legal argument was made by Richard Fletcher, Salem's city attorney, in an opinion
solicited by the school committee. In plain, unemotional language, Fletcher
sums up his position: "A colored man is a free citizen, with the same rights,
privileges, and duties, as any other man, so far as the constitution and laws
of this Commonwealth are concerned. He pays his share of the expenses,
and is entitled to vote and act as any other citizen. The children of colored
parents are, therefore, entitled to the benefit of the free schools, equally with
others. It may be said that the free school, provided exclusively for colored
children, is equally advantageous to them. I think it would be easy to show
that this is not the case. . . . Except in the case of taking property, for public
use, no man can be compelled to relinquish what belongs to him, for an
equivalent." So it was that the Salem school committee found the authority
to favor desegregation. Note, however, that the committee made its decision
on the authority of a white attorney, not directly at the behest of African
American citizens. And recall, too, that Forten, ten years later, reports that
she was the only African American student in her class. This gap between
rhetoric and reality was apparently not unusual in Salem's educational history. Progressive as it was, thirty-four years had passed between the town's
authorization of public schooling for girls and the opening of such a school
in 1827. Little surprise, then, that some of Forten's classmates found her
presence unusual.[16]

Still, it remains that advances in schooling for Salem's women and
African Americans came at the insistence of the same appeals to civic good
that left Philadelphia's white elite unmoved, and Forten's family could cer-

tainly appreciate this. So, with Charles Lenox Remond and his wife willing to take on Forten as a border in their Salem home, the stage was set for a young African American woman, extraordinarily gifted by any standard, to receive an education of superior quality at public expense. Just what Forten studied and how she studied it is not fully revealed in her journals. The Salem School Report of 1854 remarks that "The scholars are practised here more in the exercise of their reasoning powers, and drawing inferences or conclusions from the subject contained in their lessons, than in the mere recitation drill of committing to memory the words of the respective authors." And we know specifically that Shepard structured history and language lessons that informed one another, such that students would write compositions "relating to the early history of this country, and described in a very felicitous style the peculiar characteristics of [the nation's] pilgrim fathers."[17] A complex and engaging assignment, maybe, but imagine the problem for Forten, a woman who did not have and could not even invent "pilgrim" ancestry.

Instead, what she could point to was a patriot grandfather, among whose shining moments of civic participation was signing a petition in 1800 that questioned the legality of the first Fugitive Slave Law. She must have known that though the petition prompted debate in the House of Representatives, it was not accepted, primarily because—as would be the case for decades to come—the representatives feared the specter of disunion. But she also probably knew of the cutting remarks offered by Harrison Gray Otis, a Federalist representative from Massachusetts. Otis personalized his attack, reportedly saying that "he had never seen a petition presented under a more dangerous and unpleasant aspect." He complained that the petition "appeared to be subscribed by a number of individuals who were incapable of writing their names, or of reading the petition, and *a fortiori,* of digesting the principles of it." Worse, a "great part of the petition was improper, and the other part entirely unnecessary." He worried that congressional acceptance of the petition would "teach them the art of assembling together, debating, and the like, and would soon, if encouraged, extend from one end of the Union to the other."[18]

Otis and like-minded Americans had their way during Charlotte Forten's youth. But in having their way, they created the possibility of a resistance constructed from whatever discourses still seemed vital to persuasion, discourses of critique rather than celebration. For Forten, this means aligning her interest in things belletristic with her unwavering commitment to the abolitionist cause. The "Parting Hymn" she writes for her graduation from grammar school makes an attempt at this alignment. In the penultimate stanza, she tells her audience:

> May those, whose holy task it is,
> To guide impulsive youth,
> Fail not to cherish in their souls
> A reverence for truth;
> For teachings which the lips impart
> Must have their source within the heart.

But then she closes:

> May all who suffer share their love—
> The poor and the oppressed;
> So shall the blessing of our God
> Upon their labors rest.
> And may we meet again where all
> Are blest and freed from every thrall.[19]

The juxtaposition of the teacher's mission with that of the abolitionist's stops short of any synthesis, any resolution. How that resolution might come—if it is to come—is a question Forten takes up out of school, in the realm of the spoken word.

Taming Oratory: A Culture of Lectures

Forten's journal entries capture her fascination and frustration with oratory that emanates from two distinct sources: the abolitionist's platform and the lyceum stage. She comes of age at a moment when the platform is occupied by men and women whose words are taken (and generally intended) to be an assault on the U.S. Constitution and the immoral economy it sanctions. But also in that moment, a new community of American literary figures, some of whom Forten admires, is busy shoring up the very national identity that radical abolitionists are trying to tear down. Aware of the

irony—it is evident in the juxtaposed stanzas of her "Parting Hymn"—
Forten spends her hours out of school learning whether, how, and at what
cost she might bridge this profound rhetorical divide.

In one of her many reviews of oratorical spectacles in Salem, Forten
praises an antislavery speech made by Charles Remond, complimenting
particularly his ability to elicit the kind of deep concern for enslaved African
Americans that might actually provoke action, not just evoke pity. (Politically, Remond had grown radical in the 1850s with his advocacy of disunion.
Rhetorically, however, critics have noted stylistic conservatism in his sparing
use of metaphor, which set him apart from contemporaries such as Frederick Douglass.[20]) When Forten goes to hear Remond on a Sunday evening in
late 1856, he apparently speaks about the bloody invasion of the antislavery
stronghold of Lawrence, Kansas, by proslavery forces from Missouri. We get
a sense from Forten's approving remarks that Remond attempts to translate
"sympathy for the [white] sufferers" in Lawrence into sympathy for "the
poor slave, who for centuries has suffered tenfold worse miseries" (166).
Still, she sees the value in not diminishing the Kansans' situation: from a
strategic perspective, she feels glad "that *something* has roused the people of
the North at last" (166).

In a somewhat earlier review, Forten recognizes the value of female orators such as Abigail Kelley, who entreats women "to urge their husbands and
brothers to action, and also to give their aid on all occasions in our just and
holy cause" (64). Likewise, attending a lecture by Lucy Stone, Forten observes the female orator's ability to employ sentiment to good effect. Curiously, she makes no reference to Stone's speaking to a mixed assembly, nor
to her famously demonstrative character: "We found the hall so much
crowded that it was almost impossible to procure a seat. The lecture was
earnest and impressive, and some parts of it very beautiful. It was an appeal
to the noblest and warmest sympathies of our nature, in behalf of the oppressed. I saw many among her large and attentive audience, who had probably never attended an anti-slavery lecture before. I hope her touching appeal may not have been made in vain—that they may think rightly on this
subject. And from noble *thoughts* spring noble *words* and *deeds*" (116–17).
But Forten does not find nobility in the words of every antislavery orator
she hears. About a year after Stone's appearance, Forten records a critical response to a visiting speaker: "This evening listened to a tolerably good lec-

ture on slavery by Rev. Antoinette Brown. Her manner is too passive, and although she said some excellent things it was plain to be seen that she did not
know as much on this subject as on that of Woman's Rights" (146). Forten
must have known that the difference she implicitly marks between Stone's
and Brown's performances is attributable to a rift within the abolitionist
movement. Stone and Brown, close friends since their days together at
Oberlin College, disagreed but never broke over the fundamental question
of what Christians (and, explicitly, Congregationalists) should do about
slavery. While Stone was a committed Garrisonian, dissociating herself from
organized Protestantism because the various denominations refused to ex-
communicate slaveholders, Brown pursued abolitionist efforts within the
church, agitating for institutional reform that Garrisonians generally maintained would not come or would come too late.[21] Crucially, Forten's criticism of Brown's style translates into rhetorical terms her own struggle to
reconcile church politics and racial politics and to understand the implications of these politics in her relationship with Mary Shepard.

Conflicts in her personal life notwithstanding, Forten comes to expect in
antislavery oratory a rhetorical stance undiluted by appeals to a broader
range of human rights (including, naturally, the rights of women). She
sides, for example, with lecturers such as the Reverend James Applegate,
who denounces "all political action as being necessarily based on the Constitution, the very root of the evil" (116). Her "entire sympathy and approbation" for Applegate's position represents, in some sense, a repudiation of the
neoclassical rhetorical stance favored by her grandfather for most of his life
(116). In fact, one of James Forten's most memorable rhetorical performances had been a forceful argument—made entirely within a constitutional
framework—against an 1813 Pennsylvania Senate bill that aimed to block
the in-migration of free people of color.[22] But if four decades later Charlotte
Forten has decided that antislavery rhetoric ought to be positioned outside
of partisan politics, she has not yet decided where to situate herself with respect to organized religion.

Not until we encounter Forten's comments about a lecturer even more
radical than William Lloyd Garrison do we get an indication of how she
might square her religious and abolitionist convictions. In late 1856 she
writes: "Have just returned from Parker Pillsbury's lecture. One of the best
Anti-Slavery lectures I ever heard. While listening to him I could not help

thinking of Luther of old. Indeed as it has been said of Luther, I believe, 'his words were half battles.' Glorious indeed they were—those battles for suffering humanity. They excited me to such a degree of enthusiasm, that I could have risen and thanked and blessed him for them, then and there. . . . Such a lecture renews one's strength; make one feel equal to any labor, for the ennobling of mankind" (174). The comparison to Luther is slightly misleading, for Pillsbury had recently returned from a lengthy European tour during which he learned how to "balance perfectionism with practical strategizing, flattering his European audiences even as he advocated the most uncompromising and anticlerical positions." What Forten may have drawn from Pillsbury's oration, then, is permission to remain spiritual in a way unmediated by church involvement, to hate the ministers and congregants who refuse to acknowledge their complicity in upholding slavery while still loving the Christian God they together worship. Pillsbury would soon deny Garrison's order to moderate his attacks on clergy such as Henry Ward Beecher, who belatedly began speaking out in fulsome tones against slavery. Through the last mention of Pillsbury, in early 1858, Forten seems unaware of the tension growing between him and the Garrisonians, and seems, too, content with the idea, as Pillsbury put it, that she should "not be troubled, or lured from our noble purpose by the wiles of priests and political parties. . . . Our testimony is a diviner testimony, our mission a holier mission than theirs."[23]

As we have seen, upon arriving in Salem, Forten remains active in the abolitionist cause that was her family legacy, deepening her acquaintance with the commonplaces of antislavery rhetoric. Her journal entries also show that she capitalizes on her early education in *belles lettres* by plunging headlong into Salem's lyceum culture. She first attends the venerable Salem Lyceum during its twenty-sixth season, 1854–1855. Nineteen speakers appear over a five-month period, and Forten hears and comments on twelve of them. (In the three seasons to follow, she manages to attend about a third of the offerings.)[24]

Forten's forthright criticism of the twenty-sixth season's speakers gives us some sense of the form and content she expects a lyceum performance to deliver. For example, she thinks the Reverend Joseph P. Thompson a "fine lecturer," but would "have preferred hearing a lecture on some subject with which I was less familiar" (109). She calls Louis Agassiz's lecture "interesting and instructive," but is "somewhat disappointed, as I had heard him deliver a lecture nearly similar" (115). She does, however, make allowances for certain literary performances not new to her. Of James Russell Lowell's lecture, she writes, "I thought it very beautiful, and although I had previously read it, enjoyed it greatly," to which she adds, "his voice is rich and musical, but scarcely loud enough for a lecturer. But the great beauty of his thoughts and language causes the listener to forget any minor deficiency" (129). Weak performances are not always excused, though. John Pierpont, speaking on "The Effects of Physical Science upon the Moral World," apparently "lacked animation, and his lecture was extremely uninteresting to me. I was much disappointed in it" (124). If nothing else, a lecture had to be delivered well, as was the case with George W. Curtis ("a very fine orator, his voice rich and musical, and his manner polished and elegant") and R. C. Waterson ("a very interesting and eloquent lecture") (127, 129). What seems to appeal most to Forten—at least in the realm of literature and history—are lectures like that of Thomas Wentworth Higginson: delivered in a "very interesting and amusing" manner, he balanced speaking "sarcastically and severely" about the "customs of the old Puritans" with "a tribute of admiration and respect to their stern virtues and thorough consistency of action," an accomplishment Forten thought Mary Shepard, who missed the lecture, would have found instructive (112). (Recall here the "pilgrim fathers" essay she asks Forten to write.) The tenor of Forten's commentary indicates that she sought and enjoyed the "intellectual improvement" that the Salem Lyceum was incorporated to promote.[25]

Lengthy entries made late on several lyceum evenings suggest that Forten's expectations rise above self-improvement if the scheduled lecturer is an avowed abolitionist. She expects to hear what she would hear in the Remond household or at an antislavery meeting: persuasion aimed at provoking action. Sometimes Forten is disappointed. About Josiah Quincy, Jr., for example, she writes, "though evidently a man of somewhat liberal views [he] is widely different from his truly liberty-loving brother," the "noble-hearted author" Edmund Quincy—this because Josiah gives favorable mention to several founding fathers who are implicated in slaveholding (110, 112). Forten is kinder to Henry Ward Beecher, of whom she remarks, "I thought the lecture extremely interesting, and many parts of it very touching and beautiful. His manner is not at all polished or elegant, but he says so many excellent things with such forcible earnestness or irresistible humor, that we quite forget it. . . . In listening to Mr. Beecher one feels convinced of his sincerity; and we would always rather know that a person *means* what he says, even if we differ from him" (121–22). (At this point, some Garrisonians are not yet sure of Beecher's antislavery credentials.) Forten reserves warmth for the much-anticipated Theodore Parker, whose critical lecture on "The Anglo-Saxon Race" is "extremely interesting and instructive," so much so that she is able to summarize Parker's argument with a fullness she rarely invests in her lecture critiques (125). In this instance, the efficacy of abolitionist rhetoric and the eloquence of lyceum discourse merge to create a moment that Forten considers sublime.

As much as Forten appreciates Parker and his good words, her most substantial test of the lyceum's utility coincides with the last lecture of the season she attends. Before Ralph Waldo Emerson took the podium on the evening of Wednesday, 14 March 1855, Forten "had felt quite eager to hear the gifted men [*sic*], who . . . is thought in England to stand at the head of American literature" (130).[26] She finds the lecture on French culture to be "very interesting and entertaining," though she seems somewhat disappointed that it is not "flattering" to "the gay and fickle inhabitants of 'la belle France'" (130). And although Emerson is "a fine lecturer," he is, unfortunately, "a very peculiar-looking man" (130). This response—lukewarm compared to her rave for Parker—may say less than Forten was thinking, for at the time antislavery leaders hoped that Emerson would take a greater hand in persuading northern intellectuals to resist southern efforts to expand the slave economy. Tracing Forten's attitude toward Emerson forward in time lets us see how—indeed, whether—she manages to blend her angry politics of abolition into the belletristic aesthetic exemplified by the famed poet-scholar.

Forten's impression of Emerson is unchanged later in the year when she hears his Christmas Day lecture on beauty. She appreciates "his originality" but still finds that "his manner is not particularly interesting" (147). But a little over a year later, in early 1857, she writes upon hearing Emerson's "Works and Days" that it is "one of the most beautiful and eloquent lectures I ever heard" (191). She goes on at some length praising the lecture's (and the lecturer's) merits:

> The lecturer spoke particularly of the preciousness of time, the too often unappreciated worth of a *day*. We *must live* in the *Present* rather than in

the Past and Future, for the *present hour* alone is ours. *Now* we must *act—now* we must *enjoy*. Eternity is boundless,—yet the *present hour* is worth the whole of it. . . . Most beautifully did the poet philosopher speak of the earth and sky in many figures, the most beautiful of which was, I think, this—"The earth is a cup of which the sky is the cover, in which is contained the glorious bounty of Nature." Very many other eloquent and beautiful expressions I heard from those eloquent lips. . . . Never, never before have I so forcibly felt the *preciousness* of time. And oh, how deeply do the words and the presence of such a man as Emerson, make us feel the utter insignificance, the great inferiority of *ourselves*. 'Tis a sad lesson, but a most *salutary* one, for who, while earnestly feeling that *he is* nothing, *knows* nothing, comparatively, will not strive with all his might to *know* and to be something? (191–92)

In these plaudits for moving an audience to reject selfish materiality we have the sort of glowing notice Forten usually reserves for her favorite antislavery orators. And beyond noting the lecture's effect on others, she declares that she has learned a lesson herself: "Poets and philosophers! the great, the gifted of the earth. I thank you for teaching me this lesson—so sad, so humbling, yet so truly useful and ennobling!" (192). So highly does Forten esteem Emerson, this lecture becomes the standard against which all subsequent lyceum performances are measured. But the lyceum is never enough: she continues to seek and support radical antislavery oratory outside the lyceum circuit and, importantly, to demand that it too be humbling, useful, and—most of all—ennobling.

During this period, as Emerson "was becoming more adamant and determined in his opposition to the sin of slavery," he struggled to merge his surging abolitionist passions with his art. It was not easy for him; he certainly never gave himself over to poetry and prose committed exclusively to the abolitionist cause. Yet, as Len Gougeon points out, Emerson did by 1857 find ways to write antislavery poetry, a possibility he had rejected just four years before. Still, in his lectures, poetry, and essays, there is a rather bright line drawn between that which addresses the specifics of abolitionist politics and that which rejects politics altogether as distortive of just relations between self and other. The call to relevance is the call to the specific, but eloquence, what Emerson defines as the "best speech of the best soul," has an affinity for transcendental vision and is not so easily served up on demand.[27]

Forten faces a similar dilemma. In her "Glimpses of New England," printed in the *National Anti-Slavery Standard* in 1858, Forten experiments with the sort of meditation Emerson might have found attractive. She is then distressed to learn that Sarah Parker Remond "burst out most venomously upon my poor 'Glimpses'—accusing them of being pro-slavery and heaven knows what all. I *pity* her" (338). Whatever Remond's motives, Forten is reminded that to follow Emerson's example, to reserve some prose for purely belletristic expression, might be to raise the suspicions of those who believe no words can be spared until the institution of slavery is completely dismantled.[28]

The Search for Full Sympathy

A few months after Emerson visited Salem to deliver his lecture on beauty, the Reverend F. D. Huntington was scheduled to address lyceum ticket holders on "Common Sense." Precisely what Huntington said is not known, but his lecture may have touched on his notion of a "spiritual faculty," which, along with the other mental faculties theorized by the Scottish evangelicals, dictates that "by a law that cannot be broken, spiritual knowledge is not poured irresistibly into the mind." Rather, "we have to reach out for it, and work towards it, and strive after it, and little by little get the *feeling* of it, along with the *sight* of it." Forten probably missed the Harvard theologian's appearance—she does not comment on it in her journal—which is a shame, because her reaction might have illuminated how she thought oratorical and literary expression figured into the process of discerning the good that she, and those around her, should work toward, strive for, feel, and see. Still, if we return briefly to Emerson, we have a point of departure for tracing a path through Forten's journals that brings us fairly close to a conceptual understanding of rhetoric's root function in her world. Dorothy Broaddus notes that Emerson's definition of eloquence "echoes Quintilian's definition as the 'good man speaking well' and carries also Quintilian's insistence, reinforced by the philosophers and rhetoricians of the Scottish Enlightenment, that the 'good man' or 'best soul' was the most highly cultivated." What of this cultivation? As already discussed, we know that Forten was exposed to lessons in polite culture early on in Philadelphia and sustained herself in Salem with almost daily perusal of works by leading British and American authors. What this training enables in her she calls sympathy, and if it is one of her greatest possessions, it is also what is most lacking in her relationship with others. She tells us this again and again.[29]

While at school, within the sphere of white Protestant northern women, she hopes that they will commit as she has to the radical abolitionist cause. Yet the more progress Forten makes in her formal education—moving through the ranks as a normal student and as a beginning teacher—the more distant she feels from those around her. Her accounts oscillate between visions of delightful school days and experiences that are alienating and, ultimately, depressing. Even when representing groups of dear friends from whom she loathes separation, Forten repeatedly admits to missing something else: "More and more pleasant becomes my Normal School life. Yet I have made but very few acquaintances, and cannot but feel that among all of my school companions there is not a single one who gives me her full and entire sympathy" (133–34). Weeks later, she continues: "lonesome enough have I felt since school closed. I had no idea that I should miss the companions of my school hours so much. Had I but their entire sympathy I might truly be happy!" (137). And after an interval of four months, she writes: "Most happy am I to return to the companionship of my studies, ever my most valued friends. It is pleasant to meet the scholars again; most of them greeted me cordially, and were it not for the thought that *will* intrude, of the want [f]or *entire sympathy* even of those I know and like best, I should greatly enjoy their society" (139). Two years later, she reiterates these sentiments one more time: "I have so few to understand me—to give me their loving sympathy" (248).

Historians of rhetoric note that in the commonsense tradition there were several distinct definitions of sympathy, two of which, we argue, figure importantly in Forten's work. In Hugh Blair's *Lectures on Rhetoric and Belles Lettres* (1783), sympathy is fixed as a constituent of taste: "He whose heart is indelicate or hard, he who has no admiration of what is truly noble or praiseworthy, nor the proper sympathetic sense of what is soft and tender, must have a very imperfect relish of the highest beauties of eloquence and poetry."[30] Without this sympathetic sense, one is hard-pressed to appreciate eloquence. The idea that sympathy is a constituent of eloquence helps explain Forten's generally enthusiastic response to the literary lectures she encounters at the Salem Lyceum, as well as to the volumes of fiction and poetry—much of it Romantic and Victorian—she digests at an impressive rate. Her hunger for *belles lettres* and her desire to foster that appetite in others would seem to be an exercise (not unlike those laid out by Louisa Tuthill) aimed at nourishing a sense of taste refined enough to savor beauty beyond the realm of the material. But a fine appreciation of beauty is for Forten a potentially selfish act, consistent with the world of polite letters to which she aspires but offensive to one who recognizes that the material world beyond literature contains a multitude of sufferers in desperate need of sympathy—sympathy whose expression is not so much tasteful as it is a gift, an act of justice.

Although Blair never evolved such a "principle of sympathy," George Campbell did.[31] In his *Philosophy of Rhetoric* (1776) he writes, "Sympathy engages benevolence, and benevolence love. That benevolence, or the habit of wishing happiness to another, from whatever motive it hath originally sprung, will at length draw in love, might be proved from a thousand instances." To Forten, as we have seen, one instance matters more than any other: to borrow Don Burks's gloss on Campbell, Forten "insists there can be no persuasion without appeal to the passions because knowledge of a fact does not move us unless there is a feeling response to it." Paul Bator explains the implications. Appropriating from Hume, Campbell posits that "while it may be the business of logic to evince the truth, securing the conviction and consequent actions of the hearer fall under the provinces of eloquence associated with passion and understanding." Because sympathy is more substantial than mere passion, it "also provides a basis upon which any actions of the audience can be judged or evaluated." Thus sympathy takes its place in a "true system of ethics ... alongside taste, vivacity, and common sense" as "the basis for moral judgment or assent in rhetoric."[32]

We do not know, of course, to what extent Forten was familiar with Blair's and Campbell's rhetorical treatises, but whether she had such direct knowledge is really beside the point. Far more important is that we see Forten fashioning an eclectic "principle of sympathy" that resonates with both Blair's and Campbell's work on the subject. Neither integrated nor synthetic—definitions that would impose a coherence for which there is no supporting evidence—Forten's notion of sympathy appears consistent with one who experienced an immersion in literature, who watched the logic of neoclassical civic rhetoric fail African Americans with frustrating regularity, who saw the rising pitch of abolitionist discourse as inartistic but necessary, and who wished for but never realized (at least in Salem) a "full sympathy" that could sustain both art and action in the pursuit of a beauty and freedom.

Sympathy is an abstraction in much of Forten's writing, but her frustration in not finding it registers fairly concretely in one particular passage. In early 1857 Mary Shepard shows Forten, now a teacher at Epes Grammar School, two of George Stillman Hillard's new readers, texts that were reportedly adopted widely in Salem schools the next year. According to Madelyn Holmes, Hillard's readers may have been more secular than those they replaced, though no less invested in moral instruction, a fact that Forten might have appreciated, except for one thing: abolitionist sentiments are altogether absent from its pages.[33] She explains that the books: "contain excellent selections from the best writers; but with sorrow—with contempt for the author's cowardice, I noticed that he most carefully avoided the *mention* of slavery. Even in quoting from *Whittier,* the true poet of humanity, and in giving a beautiful sketch of him, not one word is said of his noble devotion to the cause of the slave,—not one line of the many glorious ones he has written for freedom, does Mr. H.[illard] *dare* to quote! Such moral pusillanimity is degrading, most pitiable" (183). This is a serious charge, but one phrased carefully enough that we can see it is motivated by more than anger at the exclusion of her friend John Greenleaf Whittier's antislavery verse. Such a reader could conceivably pull together the resources she needs to teach her students the sympathies her adult acquaintances lack. Yet Hillard's book does not, and she is confronted with material evidence that her balanced principle of sympathy may never be realized, even in something so mundane as a textbook.

Forten's health, always fragile, often worsens at times like this. She writes in her journal of feeling "utterly dispirited" and "most hopeless," emotional responses for which there seems to be no other outlet (165). She fights to quell her despair: "Tried to think cheerfully but, as usual, many sad thoughts *would* intrude,—thoughts of the unsatisfactory world, and of life, with its wearisome cares,—its constant *unrest.* But these thoughts must *not* gain ascendancy while the earnest and noble *labor* of life lies before me.—They shall not!" (171). She may hide these feelings from her friends and colleagues, but she cannot conceal her declining physical health, which causes her to take several leaves from teaching in Salem before quitting altogether

in 1860. Whether the emotional turmoil documented in her journal trig-
gered outward illness is a matter of some speculation; most recent commen-
tators find such a connection plausible.[34] Regardless of cause, though,
Forten's periodic invalidism forced her into dependence on friends and
family that—despite the behavioral norms of domesticity discussed in previous chapters—she absolutely deplored.

It may be that Forten finally finds the full sympathy she seeks in an unlikely place: among the sufferers in the South. In 1862 she joins the "rehearsal
for reconstruction" ongoing in the Sea Islands of South Carolina, the so-
called Port Royal experiment.[35] Having volunteered to teach English there,
Forten describes in her journal an emotional connection with students and
colleagues that at least on occasion surpasses anything she felt in Salem.
What is more, she is able to translate that sympathy into her account, "Life
on the Sea Islands," suitable for the readership of *The Atlantic Monthly,*
which publishes her two-part essay in mid-1864. Forten writes eloquently of
the landscape, its natural splendor contrasting with the refuse of war. But
Forten does not stop there. She writes with care about her students and
what they represent to her:

> It is wonderful how a people who have been so long crushed to the earth,
> so imbruted as these have been,—and they are said to be among the most
> degraded negroes of the South,—can have so great a desire for knowl-
> edge, and such a capability for attaining it. One cannot believe that the
> haughty Anglo-Saxon race, after centuries of such an experience as these
> people have had, would be very much superior to them. And one's indig-
> nation increases against those who, North as well as South, taunt the col-
> ored race with inferiority while they themselves use every means in their
> power to crush and degrade them, denying them every right and privi-
> lege, closing against them every avenue of elevation and improvement.
> Were they, under such circumstances, intellectual and refined, they would
> certainly be vastly superior to any other race that every existed.

It is as a teacher and *published* writer during the Civil War that the elements
of full sympathy come together for Forten—if only momentarily. And we
must remember, as Forten could not forget, that this moment arrives for her
not because of rhetoric's success, but because of its monumental failure. The
failure is not Forten's fault, of course, but it is something to be reckoned
with, not only by her, but by all women who struggle to invent, arrange, and

deliver arguments "promoting a higher, holier, and happier life" for themselves and those subject to the power of their sympathy.[36]

Coda

As she does upon graduating from Higginson Grammar School, Charlotte Forten pens a poetic meditation to mark her cohort's departure from
Salem Normal School. The poem is reportedly read aloud at commencement, though not by Forten. In the third stanza, she speaks to the romance
of pedagogy:

> But, with hope of aiding others,
>   Gladly we perform our part;
> Nor forget, the mind, while storing,
>   We must educate the heart.

Then in the next stanza she turns to curriculum:

> Teach it hatred of oppression,
>   Truest love of God and man;
> Thus our high and holy calling
>   May accomplish His great plan.[37]

Teach the heart hatred of oppression: a transparent gesture to her Romantic
and abolitionist values, sensibly arranged in verse but difficult for Forten to
arrange in life. We can imagine how Forten might have revised these lines
for delivery at Salem Normal School's quarter-centennial celebration in
1879, but imagine is all we can do because Forten most likely did not attend
the event. Many others did, including Miss Rebecca Gray, class of February
1860, who read a verse tribute to her alma mater. She asks what has changed
in the years since her graduation, and she answers:

> No war had twice ten years ago
>   Its many thousands slain;
> No Martyr's death had made to throb
>   Columbia's heart with pain.[38]

Forten would beg to differ. No doubt she would have been saddened by
Gray's erasure of the pain—Forten's and that of many thousands more—
pain felt so profoundly and for so many years before the Civil War. Does

that mean that Forten and teachers and writers like her failed to make an impression with their teaching and writing? Was their rhetoric empty? Aren't these the questions, or some variation of them, that haunt all of the teachers and writers we have taken up in this book?

If we assert that Forten—along with Foster, Murray, Graves, Tuthill, and Phelps—exerted the rhetorical power needed to right the wrongs of gender and race in their worlds, we would grossly overstate their influence. And if we assert that they wrote, spoke, and taught to resist fully the confines of a domesticity that was both gendered and raced, that would obviously be untrue, too. The problem, as Cathy Davidson rightly argues, is that in such matters "it is often hard to mark precisely where power ends and resistance begins." In the schooling fictions we examined, we discovered, as Lora Romero puts it, that an author's "progressive stance in one arena does not entail a progressive view in all other arenas." Thus, as Romero counsels, we should "temper our disappointment when we realize that authors have not done the impossible, that is, discovered the one key for the liberation of all humankind."[39] Indeed, Foster, Murray, Graves, Tuthill, Phelps, and Forten discovered neither a key, nor even a pedagogy, that would emancipate all women, but these writers did display remarkable inventiveness in applying the rhetorical resources at hand to efforts *they* considered to be progressive. And they did so in a surprising array of publishing venues: women's magazines, fiction, textbooks, and conduct guides, to name a few. Some of their students and readers doubtless used these resources as instructed and felt themselves and their worlds changed for the better; evidence from memoirs published later in the century confirms this sentiment. Others, as we know—Elizabeth Cady Stanton, for example—looked past the resources, taking from institutions such as the Troy Female Seminary the inventiveness and liberation they glimpsed there. Awareness of both possibilities has been our constant challenge while composing this narrative of a novel rhetorical tradition best not forgotten.

Appendix I Chronologies

Judith Sargent Murray

1751   Judith Sargent born on 1 May in Gloucester, Massachusetts. Educated in her parents' home, except for three months at a writing school.

1769   Marries John Stevens, merchant seaman.

1786   John Stevens dies in St. Eustatius, West Indies.

1788   Marries Rev. John Murray, Universalist preacher.

1789   Son, George Murray, born on 5 August (stillborn).

1790   Publishes "On the Equality of the Sexes."

1791   Daughter, Julia Maria Murray, born on 22 August.

1792–94   Publishes "Gleaner" and "Repository" essays in *The Massachusetts Magazine*.

1798   Publishes *The Gleaner* in three volumes.

1815   Rev. John Murray dies.

1818   Moves to Natchez, Mississippi, to live with daughter and son-in-law.

1820   Judith Sargent Murray dies on 6 July in Natchez.

Hannah Webster Foster

1758   Hannah Webster born on 10 September in Salisbury, Massachusetts. Attended boarding school sometime after her mother's death in 1762.

1785   Marries Rev. John Foster, pastor of First Parish Church of Brighton, Massachusetts. Six children born during marriage.

1797   Publishes *The Coquette*.

1798   Publishes *The Boarding School*.

1829   Rev. John Foster dies. Moves to Montreal, Canada.

1840   Hannah Webster Foster dies on 17 April in Montreal.

Mrs. A. J. Graves

Birth date and location unknown.

1841   Publishes *Woman in America*.

1844   Publishes *Girlhood and Womanhood.*

Death date and location unknown.'

Louisa Caroline Huggins Tuthill

1798   Louisa Caroline Huggins born 6 July in New Haven, Connecticut.

1815?   Possibly attends and graduates from Litchfield Female Academy, Litchfield, Connecticut.

1817   Marries Cornelius Tuthill, who attended law school in Litchfield in 1815.

1818   Son, Charles Henry Tuthill, born.

1820   Daughter, Cornelia Louisa Tuthill, born; Cornelius edits *The Microscope,* to which Louisa contributes anonymously.

1822   Daughter, Mary Esther Tuthill, born.

1824   Daughter, Sarah Schoonmaker Tuthill, born (would attend Patapsco Female Institute).

1825   Cornelius Tuthill dies.

1830   Publishes *Ancient Architecture.*

1838   Moves to Hartford, Connecticut.

1839   Publishes *The Young Lady's Home* and *The Young Lady's Reader.*

1842   Moves to Roxbury, Massachusetts.

1844   Cornelia Louisa Tuthill publishes *The Belle, the Blue and the Bigot.*

1846   Moves to Philadelphia, Pennsylvania.

1848   Publishes *History of Architecture from the Earliest Times.* Moves to Princeton, New Jersey.

1850   Charles Henry Tuthill dies. Publishes *Success in Life: The Lawyer;* three more titles appear in the series.

1859   Publishes *Edith, the Backwoods Girl.*

1870   Cornelia Louisa Tuthill dies.

1879   Louisa Caroline Huggins Tuthill dies on 3 June in Princeton, New Jersey.

Almira Hart Lincoln Phelps

1793   Almira Hart born on 15 July in Berlin, Connecticut, youngest of seventeen children in a blended family.

1804   Attends district school where sister, Emma Hart (Willard), is summer instructor.

1809   Teaches summer session in a district school near Hartford, Connecticut.

1810   Lives with sister, Emma, and brother-in-law in Middlebury, Vermont; pursues studies under sister's guidance.

1812	Attends cousin's academy (Nancy Hinsdale's Pittsfield Academy), among the first such academies to be chartered in Massachusetts.
1813	Returns to Berlin, Connecticut, to teach in the district school and, subsequently, to act as principal of the Berlin Academy.
1814	Establishes a boarding school in mother's house.
1815	Takes charge of an academy in Sandy Hill, New York.
1817	Marries Simeon Lincoln, a Federalist editor. Resigns position at Sandy Hill and relocates to Hartford, Connecticut.
1820	Son, James Hart Lincoln, born.
1821	James Hart Lincoln dies. Daughter, Jane Porter Lincoln, born.
1822	Daughter, Emma Willard Lincoln, born.
1823	Simeon Lincoln dies.
1824	Takes children to Troy, New York, where she teaches lower classes at sister's female academy and pursues advanced studies.
1829	Publishes *Familiar Lectures on Botany* (twenty-eight editions through 1872).
1830	Serves as acting principal at Troy Female Seminary.
1831	Marries the Honorable John Phelps, a Vermont state legislator. Moves to Guilford, Vermont.
1833	Son, Charles Edward Phelps, born. Publishes *Lectures to Young Ladies, Botany for Beginners* (sixteen editions through 1854), and *Caroline Westerley; or, The Young Traveller from Ohio.*
1834	Publishes *Chemistry for Beginners* (twelve editions through 1867).
1836	Daughter, Almira Lincoln Phelps, born. Publishes *The Female Student; or, Lectures to Young Ladies on Female Education* (retitled version of *Lectures*).
1837	Publishes *Familiar Lectures on Natural Philosophy* (six editions through 1866).
1838	Publishes *Familiar Lectures on Chemistry* and *Natural Philosophy for Beginners* (five editions through 1848). Becomes principal of West Chester Young Ladies' Seminary in West Chester, Pennsylvania.
1839	Becomes principal of Rahway Female Institute in Rahway, New Jersey.
1841	Becomes principal of Patapsco Female Institute, Ellicott's Mills, Maryland.
1848	Publishes first volume of *Ida Norman; or, Trials and Their Uses.*
1849	John Phelps dies.
1854	Publishes first and second volumes of *Ida Norman; or, Trials and Their Uses* together. Travels to Europe.

1855   Jane Porter Lincoln dies in train accident. Announces retirement from Patapsco.

1859   Publishes *Hours with My Pupils; or, Educational Addresses, Etc.*

1868   Publishes *The Educator; or, Hours with My Pupils* (retitled version of *Hours*).

1869   Publishes *The Blue Ribbon Society* serially in *The Star and Sentinel,* Gettysburg, Pennsylvania.

1879   Publishes *The Blue Ribbon Society; or, The School-Girls' Rebellion* as a novel.

1884   Almira Hart Lincoln Phelps dies on 15 July in Baltimore, Maryland.

Charlotte Forten Grimké

1837   Charlotte Forten born on 17 August in Philadelphia, Pennsylvania.

1853   Moves to Salem, Massachusetts. Attends Higginson Grammar School, where Mary Shepard is principal.

1855   Graduates from the Higginson Grammar School. Enrolls in Salem Normal School.

1856   Graduates from Salem Normal School. Teaches at Epes Grammar School, Salem.

1858   Resigns position at Epes Grammar School due to poor health. Soon returns to Philadelphia to live; teaches at a private school in suburban Byberry. Publishes poems in the *Christian Recorder* and *Anglo-African Magazine,* and essay in the *National Anti-Slavery Standard.*

1859   Returns to Salem to teach at the Higginson Grammar School. Publishes poems in the *National Anti-Slavery Standard* and the *Liberator.*

1860   Resigns position at Higginson Grammar School due to poor health. Returns to teaching, then resigns again for health reasons and returns to Philadelphia. Publishes poem in the *National Anti-Slavery Standard.*

1862   Teaches summer courses at Higginson Grammar School in Salem. In October, leaves for Port Royal, South Carolina, under auspices of the Port Royal Relief Association, eventually to teach on St. Helena Island.

1862–63   Publishes various essays on work in South Carolina in the *Liberator.*

1864   Resigns position as teacher on St. Helena Island and returns to Philadelphia. "Life on the Sea Islands" appears in *The Atlantic Monthly.*

1865   Moves to Boston; becomes secretary of the Teachers Committee of the New England Branch of the Freedman's Union Commission.

1869   Publishes translation of French novel, *Madame Thérèse.*

1871–72   Teaches in Charleston, South Carolina.

1872–73   Teaches in Washington, D.C.

1878   Marries Rev. Francis Grimké, Presbyterian minister in Washington, D.C.

1880   Daughter, Theodora Grimké, born on New Year's Day; dies six months later.

1885–89   Lives in Jacksonville, Florida, where Francis Grimké serves as minister.

1893   Publishes "Personal Recollections of Whittier" in the *New England Magazine.*

1914   Charlotte Forten Grimké dies on 22 July in Washington, D.C.

Appendix 2 From Hannah Webster Foster's
The Boarding School (1798)

Tuesday, A.M.

Writing and Arithmetic.

The young ladies being seated, this morning, their Preceptress addressed them as follows.

"Writing is productive both of pleasure and improvement. It is a source of entertainment which enlarges the mental powers more, perhaps, than any other. The mind is obliged to exertion for materials to supply the pen. Hence it collects new stores of knowledge, and is enriched by its own labours. It imperceptibly treasures up the ideas, which the hand impresses. An opportunity is furnished of reviewing our sentiments before they are exposed; and we have the privilege of correcting and expunging such as are erroneous. For this purpose, you will find it a good method to collect and write your thoughts upon any subject that occurs; for by repeatedly arranging and revising your expressions and opinions, you may daily improve them, and learn to think and reason properly on every occasion. By this mean you may likewise provide yourselves with a fund of matter for future use, which, without this assistance, the memory would not retain. It will be of great service to note down in your common-place book such particulars as you may judge worth remembering, with your own observations upon them. This will be a kind of amusement which will exercise your thinking powers at the time, and, by recurring to it afterwards, it may afford you many useful hints.

"The frequent use of the pen is calculated to refine and enlarge your understandings. Have you any talent at composition? it will be increased by cultivation.

"Neglect no opportunity, therefore, which your leisure affords, of delighting your friends, and accomplishing yourselves by the exercise of your genius in this way.

"Thrice blessed are we, the happy daughters of this land of liberty, where the female mind is unshackled by the restraints of tyrannical custom, which in many other regions confines the exertions of genius to the usurped powers of lordly man! Here virtue, merit, and abilities are properly estimated under whatever form they appear. Here the widely extended fields of literature court attention; and the American fair are invited to cull the flowers, and cultivate the expanding laurel.

"But the species of writing, which is open to every capacity, and ornamental to every station, is the epistolary. This, between particular friends, is highly agreeable and interesting. It is a method of interchanging sentiments, and of enjoying intercourse with those from whom you are far removed, which is a happy substitute for personal conversation. In a correspondence of this sort, all affectation, formality, and bombast should be laid aside.

"Ease, frankness, simplicity, and sincerity should be its leading traits. Yet let not your letters be composed of mere sounding terms, and verbose egotism; but intermix sentiment with expression, in such a manner as may be improving as well as pleasing. Letters of friendship should conduce no less to the advantage than entertainment of the person addressed; and mere cursory letters, of general acquaintance, must, at least, be written with propriety and accuracy. The formation of the characters, the spelling, the punctuation, as well as the style and sense, must be attended to.

"Never omit noticing the receipt of letters, unless you mean to affront the writers. Not to answer a letter, without being able to assign some special reason for the neglect, is equally unpardonable as to keep silence when conversation is addressed to you in person.

"By habituating yourselves to writing, what may, at first, appear a task, will become extremely pleasant. Refuse not, then, to improve this part of your education, especially by your frequent and dutifully affectionate epistles to your parents, when absent from them. Express your gratitude for their care, and convince them it has not been lost upon you.

"Always employ your pens upon something useful and refined. Let no light or loose compositions occupy your time and thoughts; but remember that what you utter in this way is in some measure the picture of your hearts. Virtue forbid, that this favourite employment should be disgraced by impurity, indelicacy, or the communication of vicious and ignoble sentiments!

"One of the sages of antiquity being asked why he was so long in writing his opinion, replied, 'I am writing your futurity.'

"Your characters during life, and even when you shall sleep in the dust, may rest on the efforts of your pens. Beware then how you employ them. Let not the merit of your attainments in this noble art be degraded by improper subjects for its exercise. Suffer not the expectation of secrecy to induce you to indulge your pens upon subjects, which you would blush to have exposed. In this way your characters may be injured, and your happiness destroyed.

"Celia and Cecilia were companions at a boarding school. When separated, they commenced an epistolary correspondence, on which each valued herself. Their former intimacy, which they termed friendship, prompted them to write with unlimited confidence; and, without the least reserve, to reveal every dictate of levity and thoughtless folly. They imagined themselves perfectly secure from the censure of the critic. Their education had not taught them, that a virtuous mind should shrink even from ideal indelicacy. Celia was courted by Silvander, a young man of whom she was passionately fond; but she had art and resolution enough to conceal her letters from his inspection, though he often solicited a communication of her correspondence. At length he became impatient for a perusal of letters which appeared so pleasing and interesting to the parties, and suspicious that some particular cause directed their privacy. Influenced by these motives, Silvander bribed a market-boy, who came from the village where Cecilia lived, and always conveyed the letters to and from her, to give them first into his hand. How astonished was he to find the lightness of mind exemplified in them! Purity of sentiment, delicacy of thought, and refinement of taste were entirely laid aside; and illiberal wit, frothy jests, double en-tendres, and ridiculous love-tales were substituted in their place. His name was used with so much freedom, and every circumstance relative to his intercourse, and pro-posed connexion with Celia, was bandied with such familiarity, that he was morti-fied, disgusted, and chagrinned, in the extreme. He had the policy, however, to con-ceal the discovery till he had copied a considerable number of Celia's letters, leaving out whatever had reference to his own affairs. He then revenged himself by disclos-ing his knowledge to her, avowing his indignation at her weakness, duplicity and folly, and taking an immediate and final leave. Not content with this, he even circu-lated her letters among his acquaintance. This fixed the stamp of ignominy on the correspondents; and their names and characters were rendered as ridiculous as scan-dal and malicious wit could desire.

"Celia was almost distracted at the loss of her lover; but when she found the method he had taken to punish her indiscretion, and that her reputation was thus materially injured, she secluded herself, in a great measure, from society. Her sensi-bility received a wound which could never be healed; and she lived and died in melancholy, regret, and obscurity.

"However censurable the unjust and ungenerous conduct of Silvander may be deemed, yet no adequate excuse can be offered for the young ladies, who dishonored their pens and their talents by a most improper and unbecoming use of both."

Appendix 3 From Judith Sargent Murray's
The Gleaner (1798)

<hr/>

No. LVII.

Perhaps he never saw the kindred line——

I pity, from my soul, every candidate for literary fame! If they are warm in the pursuit, and engaged with ardour in the profession of their election—if they are industrious in their application, and unoffending in their subjects, diligently labouring to endow them with every valuable property, of which they are susceptible—if the precepts they inculcate are enforced by the example of their own lives—if they do and are all this, they certainly have *much merit,* and are entitled to no stinted share of that applause, for which they are probably solicitous. But alas! how are their steps environed with peril! their family, their education, their persons, their characters—these all become standing subjects of conversation! while their matter, and their manner, are regarded as free plunder, and the invidious critic is deaf to the voice of candour!

What author but trembles at the critic's lash! and how many are deterred from the eventful path, by the apprehension of the lion in the way! And was *real merit* soothed and encouraged, were faults detected and pointed out with mildness, was strict *impartiality observed, and justice always the aim,* I, for my part, should bid the lion roar on, wishing, very sincerely, that his terrors might become properly influential.

It is the opinion of some persons of sound judgment and great abilities, that nothing more is left for a modern writer, than to give a *new dress to old ideas;* but great men are not infallible, and possibly this conclusion may be rather hastily drawn. Solomon said *"there was nothing new under the sun;"* but since the days of Solomon, what profound discoveries have been made; how momentous, how honorary, and how useful! How have the arts and sciences improved, and how has knowledge increased in the world. The use of the loadstone—printing, that capital vehicle of information—the art of war, *meliorated* by the composition and use of gun-powder, &c. &c. while hardly a day passes, on the which novelty peeps not out.

It is, perhaps, true, that the heaviest charge preferred against literary adventures, is that of plagiarism: After an original thought, a hue and cry is raised—it is traced from author to author—the cheek of innocence is tinged with the indignant blush, excited by suspicions of fraud; and a group of respectable characters are supposed to stand convicted of the high crime of *knowingly* and *wittingly purloining their neighbours' goods.*

To condemn, upon presumptive evidence, is both treacherous and cruel, and it is a procedure which finds no place in the decisions of equity. I do not contend that plagiarism is never practiced—far from it; I believe it constitutes the essence of many a volume, and that it is a kind of depredation, which is too often the *dernier resort* of the scribbler; but I *insist,* and I can produce proof positive of my assertion, that the charge of plagiarism is frequently *unfounded,* and consequently *unjust.* Originality is undoubtedly rare, and it is probable it will become still more so. A writer finds many subjects touched, and retouched, if not wholly exhausted; and, should his abilities embrace a new object, or even a novel arrangement, he is condemned, ere he can establish his hypothesis, however self evident it may be, to combat the giant prejudice, to wage war with a host of cavillers, to oppose himself to the burnished shafts of criticism, and to withstand the secret machinations of envy. But, every discouragement notwithstanding, I humbly conceive there is much more originality in the world, at this present time, than is commonly imagined.

What, I would ask, constitutes originality? or, in other words, cannot an original thought be twice conceived? Let not the critic sneer, before he permits me to explain myself. An idea is expressed in conversation, and a stander-by declares—"*I had this moment the same thought, Sir.*" Query: In whose bosom was the idea original? Suppose, that in the days of Homer, there had arisen, in the wilds of America, or in any other remote part of the globe, a genius, who had delineated every idea of that immortal bard, who had painted the charms of another Helen, arming monarchs and heroes in the licentious cause of a perfidious woman! whose fertile brain had teemed with other Hectors, skilfully opposing them to that Achillean arm, which was nerved for their destruction; suppose his sentiments, his similes and expressions had been nearly similar; and, (since nature, liberal in her operations, might have produced a *second prodigy,* the suggestion cannot be justly said to wear the features of *impossibility*) suppose proof irrefragable had been furnished, that not the smallest intercourse had subsisted between these children of indulgent munificence, and that they had not even a knowledge of each other's existence; should we not, in such an arrangement, have characterized both bards, as possessing original excellence?

For my own part, I am so far from regarding it as wonderful, that a *similarity of talents should exhibit a similarity of ideas, and even of expressions, that I am really astonished such similarity is not more frequently demonstrable.* Let us reflect for a moment—Two beings, endowed with strong understandings and clear perceptions, are educated in different and far distant parts of our world; but their language, their government, and particularly their religion is the same; from the same decalogue their precepts are drawn; virtue is the goal to which they are pointed, and from one source every excitement to virtue is educed. Maturity is at length attained; and, setting down to contemplate a given subject, ought they to be accused of plagiarism, although their productions receive a kindred stamp?

The good divine, whose mind hath been early imbued from that identical fount at which his cotemporaries have quaffed, receives a like education, and like academical honours; and with religious sentiments exactly corresponding with his brethren, he mounts the pulpit, and opens the sacred book, ordained at once a standard of his testimony, and the origin from whence he is to deduce those momentous truths, on which he is to expatiate. His text cannot vary, and he may be a stranger to the *flagitious crime of stealing*, although the branches growing upon one root, should resemble each other.

A writer may, *without being a just subject of reprehension*, enrich his page with the most brilliant thoughts of another; *he may himself be deceived;* from extensive and miscellaneous reading, scattered ideas, sentiments, and sometimes sentences, are collected. The volume of memory containeth may pages; and from childhood to ripening and declining years, what multifarious images are inscribed thereon. From this reservatory we naturally draw, and, it *may sometimes happen,* that ideas deduced from thence, *may be mistaken for original productions of the mind.*

, I once had a friend—were I at liberty to name him, every individual, acquainted with his *uncommon worth,* would bow to his superior merit: Ah! how have his fine qualities and gigantic talents been obscured by a train of adverse circumstances, all pointed and brought home to his bosom, by a natural propensity to melancholy. Unfortunate son of genius! I drop a tear over thy present misfortunes, while I recollect, with unabating admiration, the radiant commencement of they career. I know it, dear Sir, this apostrophe is nothing to the present purpose; and I sit corrected.

This poet (for a genuine poet he verily was) possessed a strong understanding, with a correct judgment, and a glowing fancy; and, what is not commonly an appendage to these advantages, his memory, also, was astonishingly retentive; and he was as far removed from the *practice* as he was from the *necessity* of plagiarism. Our bard, thus highly qualified, employed himself one morning in penning a poetical epistle to a friend, whose abilities were respectable. The epistle finished, forwarded and received, was perused with much surprize; for, strange to tell, it contained a number of lines that were found verbatim in a favourite author, with whose productions the person addressed had recently furnished his library! And *said lines bore on their margin no question marks!* It is the part of a *sincere friend* to point out a fault, and our poet was questioned on the subject; he detested plagiarism, and positively asserted his entire property in the problematic essay; but, *to the law and to the testimony*—the book was produced, and the poet eagerly seizing it, cast his eyes on the title page, which he no sooner traced, than instantly recognizing, he clasped it to his bosom with all that strong enthusiasm and *fine frenzy* which ever marked his character. The volume proved an *old acquaintance, which had been the delight of his boyish days, and of which he had long been in pursuit;* and it appeared, that writing in a similar manner, and on the same topic, he had drawn those lines from the store-house of memory, where they had been many years safely lodged, unconscious that the well adapted fugitives were not the *true born offspring of his own brain.* Now this, gentle reader, is a kind of plagiarism, if such it can be called, which cannot come under the description of fraud; and whatever may be the *effect* of its *operation,* it is indisputably *guiltless* in its source.

But, while *I pledge my veracity* for the *authenticity* of the foregoing anecdote, I readily grant that circumstances seldom concur to produce events of this complexion; and, conceding thus far, I expect that every person accustomed to reflection, will unhesitatingly acknowledge the propriety of what I have advanced, (viz.) *that similarity of ideas and expressions, when the subject is the same,* may often originate in different minds, evidently obtaining in those bosoms, where inborn integrity and conscious propriety had implanted *so strong a sense of right and wrong,* as to create a just

and spontaneous abhorrence to whatever could, *in the remotest degree, be denomi-
nated plagiarism.* I had lately an opportunity of conversing on this subject, with a female, to whom I am *naturally attached*—she has for many years been a scribbler, and
she feelingly lamented that she had repeatedly seen ideas, and complete sentences, issue from the press, which had long been contained in her manuscripts, and which
she had flattered herself with the privilege of presenting, as *original thoughts!* This,
however, happened more frequent in her prosaic, than in her poetical productions;
yet, even in the last, she adduced some instances of considerable similarity; from
which, by way of illustration, and for the amusement of the reader, I take the liberty
to select two. On the 28th of January, 1794, this penwoman wrote some lines on a
particularly interesting occasion, which lines contain the following simile:

> As the fond matron, while the flame ascends,
> Which her whole int'rest in one ruin blends,
> Wildly exclaims—Give me my infant train;
> Possess'd of them, the strokes of fate were vain:
> 'Scap'd from the wreck, she sees her girls and boys,
> And one short moment perfect peace enjoys.

Early in the year 1784, copies of the whole of this poem were put into the hands of
several gentlemen, who may perhaps recollect it; but still it is *only a manuscript;* and
it is not until within a few months, that she has met with that beautiful production,
entitled, the Botanic Garden, the offspring of an elegant European pen, *first published in the year* 1793; in which she observed, in the following highly finished lines,
the same thought.

> "Th' illumin'd mother seeks with footsteps fleet,
> "Where hangs the safe balcony o'er the street;
> "Wrapt in her sheet, her youngest hope suspends,
> "And panting, lowers it to her tip-toe friends:
> "Again she hurries on affliction's wings,
> "And now a third, and now a fourth she brings;
> "Safe all her babes, she smooths her horrent brow,
> "And burst thro' bickering flames, unscorch'd, below."

Now it is *demonstrably certain,* that neither of these writers *borrowed,* or, more
plainly speaking, *purloined* from each other. Producing, therefore, the foregoing lines
as proof in point, I proceed to the second instance. Previous to her perusal of the
Botanic Garden, she had been requested to write an ode on a very affecting occasion:
This ode was to be publickly chaunted, for the benefit of a worthy young man; and it
was an address to the benevolence of the audience. It is not my design to give the ode
entire; I only transcribe the part which is necessary to introduce the lines that she
imagined similar—thus they are expressed:

> Ye spirits bland, from heav'n descend,
> Around this hallow'd temple bend,

With aspect all benign:
Philanthropy, first-born of truth,
Of paradise the fairest growth,
　　Replete with powers divine.

Hov'ring around, we feel you press,
This consecrated sane to bless,
　　Its pious rites to guard:
Benevolence, religion twines
With blest munificence designs,
　　And its own reward.

Benevolence, whose genial sway
Commission'd hath the new-born day,
　　And burst the pris'ner's chains—
Its progress can arrest despair,
Can smooth the furrow'd brow of care,
　　While mild compassion reigns.

Thus, when enwrapt in Howard's guise,
To mortals lent from yonder skies,
　　And borne on mercy's wing;
The depth of human woe he fought,
With lenient balm assuaging fraught,
　　Returning light to bring.—&c. &c.

The ode was published; and the writer was some time afterwards attracted by a resemblance in the following energetic lines, found also in the Botanic Garden:

"The spirits of the good, who bend from high
"Wide o'er these earthly scenes their partial eye,
"When first array'd in virtue's purest robe,
"They saw her Howard traversing the globe;
"Saw on his brow her sun-like glory blaze,
"In arrowy circles of unwearied rays."

Many are the instances, which, from my own individual experience, I could record; and my volumes of manuscripts, that I was positive were enriched with many original thoughts, from my delay to publish, have now, alas! been generally forestalled. My plans, my ideas, my metaphors, *ah, well-a-day!* in almost every thing I have been anticipated; and whenever my lucubrations are presented, *innocent as I am,* the probability is, that I shall find myself indicted in the high court of literature for the debasing crime of plagiarism! Yet these Essays, although the offspring of many a careful hour, deducing very possibly their highest charm from novelty, have now lost, even in my own estimation, much of their power to interest and to please; and I do not, I am free to own, very deeply lament their fate.

But a recent discovery having stripped of originality this my youngest born, *my pet,* that I have cherished with such unremitted tenderness, culling for it the fairest flowers, *gleaning* every sweet, and adorning it up to my best abilities; and now to find, that after all, I have been rearing the bantling of another! It is really almost too much for my philosophy to bear; nor can my utmost equanimity prevent the hag vexation from adding another score to those furrows, which time and disappointment have already so deeply indented!!!

No, I can never part with it—still it is the child of my adoption, and I must ever remain its protecting father. Sympathizing reader, I will tell thee the story. Thou knowest how much I have prided myself upon the *title* of these numbers: It was ample enough for my purpose; it was unassuming; yea, as humble as the smallest particles which fall from the granary of the opulent dealer; and yet by the wonderful force of its elastic power, it could extend itself over the vast fields of science, wandering upon the superficies of the grounds, and snatching those gems which are sometimes the reward of industrious mediocrity.

It was, I have a thousand times said, a complete shield *from every accusation of literary theft.* It was—in short, it was abundantly commensurate with my most sanguine wishes; and what, in my estimation, inexpressibly enhanced its value, was, that I imaged it had *never before been thus appropriated.* Judge then, what were my sensations, when, two days since, turning over a volume written by Voltaire, I observed, among his account of literary publications, the following paragraph, which, by way of exciting thy commiseration, I shall transcribe, verbatim.

"*Miserable pamphlets!—the Gleaner!*—the Fault finder, &c.—*Wretched productions! inspired by hunger, and dictated by stupidity and a disposition to lying! &c. &c.*"

To find my *boasted title* thus unexpectedly flashed in my face; and to meet it, too, *coupled with infamy!!!*—But my feelings may be better *imagined* than *described;* and the candid reader, while he acquits me of an instance of *plagiarism,* so *impolitic,* and so *absurd,* will not fail to sympathize with, and to vindicate.

The mortified GLEANER.

Appendix 4 From Louisa Caroline Tuthill's
The Young Lady's Home (1839)

Chapter IX.
COMPOSITION.

> *"Books, paper, pencil, pen, and slate,*
>
> *And column'd scrolls of ancient date,*
>
> *Before her lie, on which she looks*
>
> *With searching glance, and gladly brooks*
>
> *An irksome task."*
>
> — Joanna Baillie.

A labored defense of woman's rights might do for the meridian of Constantinople. All the rights which she ought to claim, are allowed in this blessed country. The only danger now is, that she may overstep the bounds which modesty and delicacy prescribe, and come forward upon that arena of strife which ought to belong exclusively to man. All such encroachments should be frowned upon by an enlightened community, for "they foster that masculine boldness or restless independence, which alarms by its sallies or wounds by its inconsistencies." The bold and fearless spirit with which men enter public discussion and controversy, well becomes them, but should excite our admiration without provoking to emulation. The paths that are open to us are many, but they lie along "the cool sequestered vale." Such are the vicissitudes of life, that we need all the resources which can be accumulated. Few of you, my friends, probably either expect or wish to become authoresses; but you all wish to enjoy the pleasures of literature, and will not deny the utility of being able to write a perspicuous and pleasing style. Were it only for the sake of those "winged messengers of love" despatched to absent friends, you need an agreeable vehicle of thought. Letters should never be carelessly written; the style may be easy and graceful, and at the same time show that care and attention which is a mark of respect to the person addressed. Even the folding and superscription of a letter tells something of the character of the writer, and the deference she deems due to her correspondents. In early life we are not aware what insight these trifles give to the character and feelings, to those who have knowledge and experience. Far be it from you to cultivate the exterior graces alone; the respect and regard should be felt, of course, and a careful expression of it should be exhibited. A letter ought to be written in legible, neat, and if possible, elegant, handwriting; not that delicate cobweb scribble, which costs more to read than it is generally worth. When a letter is franked, or sent by a private conveyance, it should be folded in an envelope, as neatly as possible. Fashion regulates the mode of sealing; sometimes a single wafer is deemed almost an insult; the fastidious Chesterfield thought it so; at other times it is preferred, by those who are tired of the sickly sentimentality of mottos. Sufficient attention should be paid, even to this seeming trifle, to know what is the custom of the day, and to follow it.

Many fine examples of epistolary style are to be found in the English language. Miss More could lay aside her elaborate style, and all the pomp of diction which she could use on occasion, for the simple playful language of confiding friendship. Some of her letters are delightful, and many of her learned correspondents have given fine specimens of easy, sprightly, and graceful letters. Charles Lamb's letters, for vivacity, warmth, and colloquial simplicity, are unrivaled. Sir Walter Scott's letters to Miss Baillie, and many others, are charming, though they deal less than we could wish in the domestic details which he could render so amusing. Cowper, and his friend the Rev. John Newton's letters have been universally admired. There is in Washington's epistolary writing, not only the dignified simplicity that we should of course expect, but a pleasing, easy style. The letters of Franklin are so characteristic of the man as to be very amusing. They are written in the concise and spirited style of his other writings, and ornamented with occasional flashes of wit and humor. Modern memoirs furnish many excellent examples of this kind of composition; so many, indeed, that it would be impossible here to name them. None of them should be imitated, however, as models; a letter, to be agreeable, should be individual; that is, it should show exactly the author.

In some seminaries for young ladies, it is customary to insist upon their writing *poetry* for a school exercise. Oh, the intolerable burden of counting out lines upon the fingers, and making them match to words from the rhyming dictionary! Doubtless, facility in versification may be thus acquired by long practice, where there is no natural ear for the harmony of numbers. The altar is built, the wood is laid, but where is the fire, and where the burnt-offering? Sentimental scribblers, puffed up with self-conceit, they are in danger of becoming; and it is difficult to conceive of any advantage to be derived from forcing, or, endeavoring to create, a talent which has not been bestowed by the Almighty Author of our being.

But should young ladies never write poetry? If they are *poeta nascitur, non fit,* they will write "by stealth and blush to find it fame,"—not because it is wrong,—but true genius, and true sensibility, are ever accompanied by modesty and a high standard of excellence. There is little danger to be apprehended from repressing the early exhibition of poetical talent; if it really exist it will in time manifest itself; let education be judiciously conducted and the mind well disciplined, and it will not extinguish the fire of genius, but (to use a homely comparison) find it fuel to act upon.

Exercises in prose composition, that are often much disliked at school, are of acknowledged utility, and should not now be discontinued. Bacon says, "he seeth how they (his thoughts) look, when turned into words." We seldom know whether we have thoughts on any particular subject or not, until we endeavor to express them, and if we have, the expression gives to them more clearness and precision. Often when some idea seems beautiful as it floats vaguely in the mind, it is painful to find how all the beauty vanishes when it is "formed into words;" as the lovely vision of the painter's fancy, often resists all his attempts to fix it upon canvass. The conception was imperfect, and this could be demonstrated as the most frequent cause of failure in composition.

Coleridge somewhere says, or it may be in one of his translations from Schiller,

"There exist
Few fit to rule themselves, but few that use
Their intellects intelligently."

Many, perhaps, who feel that they are made for something better than mere ephemera, nevertheless suppress the noble aspirings of their nature, and strive to be like the fluttering myriads around them. Unworthy effort! you may for a time tame down your mind to dull mediocrity; but have you thus gained the good will of those for whom you sacrifice so much? No; they, even they, would despise you for trampling under foot the glorious riches of genius. You may be unfavorably situated for the cultivation of mind, for it is "not possible for the best minds to attain their full development but amid an atmosphere highly charged with the electricity of thought," yet, to the Giver, you are accountable for *all* his gifts, and your means are proportioned to your responsibilities.

But although every one is thus bound to use the talents that God has given, none need covet the possession of genius; well might the sainted Hemans exclaim,

"A mournful gift is mine O friends!
"A mournful gift is mine."

Something might here be said of the importance of the study of grammar and philology. They fill so conspicuous a place in the modern system of school education, that it may be deemed unnecessary to recommend them for farther attention. The philosophy of language is seldom understood by the young, and you would doubtless derive much advantage from a thorough examination of this subject. Horne Tooke's Diversions of Purley afford amusement and profound knowledge on this subject; Campbell's Rhetoric, is not generally employed as a class book, and should by all means be attentively read, as should also Alison on Taste, and Burke on the Sublime and the Beautiful.

Appendix 5   From Almira Hart Lincoln Phelps's
Lectures to Young Ladies (1833)

Lecture XX.

Rhetoric, Criticism, Composition.

The studies of Rhetoric and Criticism, are more especially designed for the cultivation of those faculties of mind, called *taste* and *imagination.* Taste has by many writers been termed a simple independent power or sense; but by Dr. Brown it is considered as a complex state of mind, which may be analyzed into *judgment* and an *emotion.* The human mind is formed with a susceptibility of certain emotions, as beauty, sublimity and ludicrousness; these emotions are those on which taste chiefly depends, or which, in conjunction with judgment, constitute taste. Thus a painter, having experienced the emotion of beauty, exercises his judgment in forming such combinations as may produce in others the same emotion. A poet must have experienced emotions, before he can by an effort of art produce them in others; and he exercises his judgment no less in the selection and combination of his images, than the chemist, who puts together substances in order to produce a certain result. That is, both the poet and chemist judge of the fitness of ideas and of objects to produce their determinate effects.

For a clear and interesting explanation of the elements of taste, and of its three most essential qualities, refinement, delicacy and correctness, I would refer you to the interesting and useful system of Rhetoric, now adopted as a class book in this Institution.* The author of this work has taken up the subject in a philosophical and practical manner. He at once informs the student that the art of writing well, is not to be obtained by a set of rules, but that "the store-house of the mind must be well filled; and he must have that command of his treasures which will enable him to bring forward, whenever the occasion may require, what has been accumulated, for future use." He dwells particularly upon the necessity of mental discipline, especially the previous cultivation of the reasoning powers; and observes that "the student who, in the course of his education is called to search for truth in the labyrinth of metaphysical and moral reasonings, and to toil in the wearisome study of the long and intricate solutions of mathematical principles, is acquiring that discipline of the mind, which fits him to distinguish himself as an able writer.["]

You will perceive that the different branches of knowledge we have already considered, are all conducive to one great end, that of enabling a person to compose with elegance and facility. And is this an object of little importance, even to our sex?

* Newman's Rhetoric.

We are permitted to use the pen as our tastes, genius, or mental acquirements may direct. Even the composition of a simple note of ceremony, attests the fact of mental cultivation, or the want of it; and a letter on the most common subject, plainly indicates the nature of the writer's education. Higher efforts of mind, such as stories for children, religious tracts, and works in the various departments connected with education, are all now considered as offering proper employment for the exertion of female talents. But it must be remembered that those talents should be cultivated with the most assiduous care—that the various fields of knowledge should be explored, as far as possible, in order to become a successful candidate for literary distinction. The time has gone by, when a publication meets with indulgence, because its author is a *woman;* we must now expect to be judged by our real merits, and our titles to approbation.

Grammar and rhetoric bear to each other an intimate relation; the former teaches the method of speaking and writing with accuracy, the latter of arranging our thoughts with propriety and elegance. The science of rhetoric is founded upon observations made by philosophers, of the nature and operations of the human mind, and by a critical analysis of the style, and an examination of the methods of arrangement of those authors whose works have been most generally approved. The chapter on Literary Taste in Newman's Rhetoric is well written, and calculated to give just ideas of the peculiar merits of different authors; it also happily illustrates the proper use of rhetorical figures. The chapter on style, is an interesting exposition of the qualities of a good style, and the modes of writing which characterize different individuals. This little work leads the pupil to a knowledge of the rules and principles of rhetoric, in an easy and simple manner, and has the merit of more originality than many school books, which profess to be improvements.

Blair's Lectures on Rhetoric have been deservedly popular: they are writ[t]en in a pure and concise style; but the larger work is too voluminous for beginners, and the abridgement, as is usually the case, is a mere skeleton, without suitable illustrations.

In pursuing the study of rhetoric, you should make it your constant aim to render your knowledge practical: you should examine authors, with a view of discovering their peculiar beauties or defects, and notice their use of the various figures of speech; each of which you should accustom yourself to distinguish, wherever you meet them. This might be rendered interesting as an amusement. When several young ladies are passing leisure hours together, one might ask others to point out, in a certain page or chapter of a book, all the comparisons, metaphors, antitheses, &c. which could be found. The suggestion and proper uses of figures, must be the result of much practice in composition, as well as the fruit of learning. The study of rhetoric will not at once give you the power of writing with ease and elegance: this requires a knowledge of nature and of the human heart, a habit of deep and serious reflection, and a taste at once delicate and refined.

Criticism is ranked in this institution as a higher study than the elementary works on rhetoric; it is indeed a department of rhetoric, but so extensive, that it has been treated separately by some distinguished writers. The best works on this subject which are now before the public are those of Kames, Alison, and Campbell. Kames' Criticism contains much valuable philosophy; the author appears to have studied the human heart with considerable success: his style is agreeable and he carries his reader along with him in an easy companionship. The study of this work is an excellent preparation for mental philosophy; indeed it was, by the author, designed to hold a middle rank between moral speculations and the study of the natural and mathematical sciences. Without attempting a theory and classification of the passions, Lord Kames gives a variety of practical illustrations of their operations and moving principles; and such as are calculated to be of great use to a young person on entering into life. The greatest objection to his work on criticism is the occasional obsoleteness of the style, (the third edition was published as far back as 1761) and a want of system in his arrangements. These faults may be remedied by the remarks of teachers, and care on their part to make a better arrangement. The practical part of criticism will not probably be acquired in a very great degree by the study of Kames, or any other author, but a new stock of ideas may be gained, and he power of making for yourself critical distinctions.

Alison is a writer of peculiar beauty and sweetness; the fault in his work, as a textbook on criticism, is that he confines himself to the subjects of beauty and sublimity, a sphere too circumscribed for so extensive a science. The politeness and respect with which Alison speaks of the "profound remarks of Lord Kames," furnish a pleasant contrast to the illiberality with which writers often speak of those who have preceded them in any particular department of literature. The whole work of Alison is replete with beautiful passages, calculated to inspire the reader with noble and just sentiments. In his essays upon the beauty and sublimity of the material world, he leads the mind to the delightful contemplation of nature and the Author of nature. After expatiating on the moral effect of the study of nature upon the mind, he finely and piously observes "there is yet, however, a greater expression which the appearances of the material world are fitted to convey, and a more important influence which, in the design of nature, they are destined to produce upon us: their influence, I mean, in leading us directly to *religious* sentiment. Had organic enjoyment been the only object of our formation, it would have been sufficient to establish senses for the reception of these enjoyments. But if the promises of our nature are greater—if it is destined to be a nobler conclusion—if it is enabled to look to the Author of Being himself, and to feel its proud relation to Him; then nature, in all its aspects around us, ought only to be felt as signs of his providence, and as conducting us, by the universal language of these signs, to the throne of the DEITY."

After remarking upon the effect of natural scenery upon elevated minds, he adds: "Even the thoughtless and the dissipated yield unconsciously to this beneficent instinct; and in the pursuit of pleasure, return, without knowing it, to the first and the noblest sentiments of their nature. They leave the society of cities, and all the artificial pleasures, which they feel to have occupied, without satiating their imagination. They hasten into those solitary, and those uncultivated scenes, where they seem to breathe a purer air, and to experience more profound delight. They leave behind them all the arts, and all the labors of man, to meet nature in her primeval magnificence and beauty. Amid the slumber of their usual thoughts, they love to feel themselves awakened to those deep and majestic emotions which give a new and nobler expansion to their hearts, and amid the tumult and astonishment of their imagination,

> To behold the present God
> On the rocks by man untrod,
> On the hill-tops wild and rude,
> On the cliff's deep solitude,
> Where the roaring waters move,
> In the darkness of the grove."

It is particularly on account of its moral effect that it is of so much consequence to encourage their instinctive taste for the beauty and sublimity of nature. While it opens to the mind of childhood, or youth, a source of pure and of permanent enjoyment, it has consequences on the character and happiness of future life, which they are enabled to foresee. It is to provide them, amid all the agitations and trials of society, with one gentle and unreproaching friend, whose voice is ever in alliance with goodness and virtue, and which, when once understood, is able both to soothe misfortune, and to reclaim from folly. It is to identify them with the happiness of that nature to which they belong; to give them an interest in every species of being which surrounds them; and, amid the hours of curiosity and delight, to awaken those latent feelings of benevolence and of sympathy, from which all the moral or intellectual greatness of man finally arises. It is to lay the foundation of an early and of a manly piety: amid the magnificent system of material signs in which they reside, to give them the mighty key which can interpret them; and to make them look upon the universe which they inhabit, not as the abode of human cares, or human joys only, but as the temple of the LIVING GOD, in which praise is due, and where service is to be performed.

Composition.

The study of Belles Lettres, or of rhetoric and criticism is introduced into education, principally for the purpose of improving the young in the art of composition. It is indeed pleasant to be able to judge of the performances of others, to know the causes of our approbation or disapprobation of literary works, to enter into the secret of the mind, and explore its mysterious laws, to compare the productions of genius with those rules which nature suggests, and to observe the uniformity of her operations in all well organized minds: all this is agreeable; but it is still more desirable, still more delightful to be able of ourselves to *execute,* to be able to catch the ideal train, as they glide through our minds, and paint them in all their freshness and originality for our own future examination, or for the inspection of others.

Of all the enjoyments granted to mortals, this is probably the most exquisite and the most elevated; to behold before us the image of our own minds, the glowing transcripts of our own thoughts, as delineated by ourselves; it seems to assimilate us in some degree with the great Creator of mind, when we are able to render its operations visible. Many who are conscious of elevated thoughts are destitute of a power of expression suited to these; many in whom the fire of genius is smothered by ignorance or prejudice, feeling within themselves the workings of a latent intellect, sigh for education as the greatest of human blessings, the means of elevating the mind and rendering its operations sources of the highest enjoyment. Under the greatest disadvantages, the light of genius has occasionally burst forth, discovering upon the shoemaker's bench a tuneful and sentimental Bloomfield, or at the plough a noble and high-souled Burns. But instances are rare in which unaided genius acquires the confidence to come forth, and try her pinions: education is required by most minds in order to give the courage and skill necessary for effort in the regions of composition. And besides, we must acknowledge that genius is not a common gift; I mean that fire which, unless it can have vent, consumes the soul. And in this we see the goodness of our Creator; for genius is of too fine, too exquisite a nature to bear the rude contact of worldly things; it droops and folds its wings when calamities assail; even the imaginary sufferings of a flower transplanted from its own home, a rose plucked from its parent stem, or the agonies of a poor worm or insect, are sufficient to call forth its tender and plaintive wailings,—how then can it look upon human sufferings, poverty, oppression, injustice, treachery, pain and death? Indeed we often see that mind which exhibits unequivocal marks of genius, early fading away, as if the atmosphere of the world were too cold for its sensitive nature; thus have Henry Kirk White and Lucretia Davidson,* and many others gradually sunk to an untimely grave, apparently through an excess of sensibility.

But is there no remedy for this? Must the fairest and best of human blossoms be given up to be chilled by the frosts, and blighted by the mildews of an ungenial world? Let a suitable and proper direction be given to sensibility, and it may be disciplined and chastened. Let education be properly conducted, and then will *reason* and *judgment* be brought to sustain and guide the trembling, aspiring etherial spirit, which is ever shrinking from real evils and refusing to look with steady eye upon the obstacles in the pathway of life. But, supported by reason and judgment, *sensibility* may learn to encounter evils and to overcome difficulties; especially does she need the aid of *religion* to reconcile her to earthly sufferings, in view of a happier future. I have spoken of sensibility, because I believe it always belongs to true genius, and to be the cause of those frequent failures in life which are observable among those who are highly gifted; but a proper mode of education may do much towards chastening, and giving it a right direction.

Lucretia Davidson, the lovely girl whose precocious powers have been the admiration of many, probably fell a victim to an extreme and morbid sensibility: many of you are aware that several years since, she was a member of this institution; some of you may remember her personally. She had, in her childhood, been indulged in her fondness for seclusion and solitary musings. Her education, owing to peculiar circumstances, had not been systematically and thoroughly pursued. On her entering the Seminary, she at once surprised us by the brilliancy and pathos of her compositions,—she evinced a most exquisite sense of the beautiful in the productions of her pencil; always giving to whatever she attempted to copy, certain peculiar and original touches which marked the liveliness of her conceptions, and the power of her genius to embody those conceptions. But from studies which required calm and steady in-

* Miss Davidson died at about the age of seventeen; a volume of her posthumous works, entitled "Amir Kahn, and other Poems," has received much praise from critics. The British Reviewers spoke of it as an extraordinary production, comparing her to their favorite and lamented White.

vestigation, efforts of memory, judgment and consecutive thinking, her mind seemed to shrink. She had no confidence in herself, and appeared to regard with dismay any requisitions of this nature. Even in geography, which was one of her studies, she found a difficulty in preparing herself for recitations. At the approach of an examination, she was agonized with the fear of disgracing her class by her appearance; and in order to calm her apprehensions, I had promised to ask her very few questions. When it came her turn to recite, instead of taking the subject next in order, which would have been an explanation of the "geological structure of the globe," and which the poor trembling girl had never felt an interest in knowing, I asked her to give some account of the peculiarities of the torrid zone. Miss Davidson's countenance brightened: she begun with the sweetest tones of voice to describe the vegetable wonders of those regions, the spreading bananas, the lofty bamboo trees, forests rendered impenetrable by the luxuriancy of vegetation, and blooming with perennial verdure and beauty. She spoke of the mighty elephant, the hippopotamus, rolling his enormous bulk along the rivers of Africa, the fierce lions and tigers, poisonous reptiles and ensnaring crocodiles, the great anaconda, winding his huge coils around his helpless victim; nor did she fail to describe that dreadful vampyre, which seeks the traveller in his hour of sleep and gluts itself with his blood. She then, with a new and kindling emotion, spoke of the brilliant fire-flies which illuminate those regions in the night as with a mass of liquid light, of the bounding antelope, and of the beautiful gazelle, whose brilliant and fascinating eyes are the admiration of the beholder.

So vivid in my mind is the recollection of her animated and enthusiastic manner at that time, the bright flashing of her dark eye, and the glow of her brilliant complexion, that the conception appears like reality, and it seems as if she now stood before me, the living image of youthful genius and sensibility. But the grave has for many years shrouded her form, once so interesting. We may not imagine the process which is going on in that dreadful laboratory, where the elements which compose the human body are separated and set free to enter into other combinations; we will rather say with the poet,

> "Not to the grave my soul,
> Not to the grave descend to contemplate
> The form that once was dear!"

it is better to think of the spirit as disencumbered of its load of clay, and an inhabitant of a purer world.

I have introduced the character of this young lady to show you the great importance of early mental discipline, for, lovely as genius and sensibility may be, in order to be useful, in order to be fitted for life, they must be sustained by the other mental powers. We see the evils of suffering any one department of mind to usurp unlimited power over the other. If one could not be a fine writer, without becoming unfit for the duties of life; if talents were necessarily connected with eccentricities, I would at once warn all my sex from attempting to acquire these dangerous gifts, but I trust it is unnecessary for me to point out the many ladies who at this time hold an important standing in the literary world, and are yet among the most active supporters of social and religious institutions, who are equally distinguished for domestic virtues as for high mental endowments.

But we are yet to go back to the first attempts of the pupil in the art of composition; this it is necessary to do for the benefit of the younger members of the institution, and of some others to whom the idea of writing compositions is new and appalling.

Those who are studying languages, will derive great assistance in composition from the habit of translating. It appears to me that this advantage has not been sufficiently estimated: were it indeed the only one, I should think it a sufficient compensation for the labor which is necessary in acquiring a language. If you take a fine passage of a Latin or French author, and attempt to translate it, the mind, gradually seizing upon the ideas, seems to adopt them as its own; and feeling itself elevated by this new acquisition, becomes capable of greater efforts.

In translating, particular attention should be paid to the exact import of words; thus, the word *sentiment* which in English is applied to opinions, is in French restricted to the feelings of the heart, it being derived from the verb *sentir,* to feel. The French would not then speak of *political sentiments,* but political *opinions;* they would speak of a sentiment of gratitude or love: when you reflect on the origin of the word sentiment, you will perceive that there is a propriety in making this distinction between this word and *opinion,* which is derived from a Latin verb signifying to believe. To those of you whose understanding and observation have not furnished you with a stock of ideas for composition, translation may be recommended as a substitute, until you have acquired the confidence and ability to compose.

I am aware, that of all your exercises, many of you find original composition the most difficult; indeed it is not strange you do so; when you write, you can only express by written characters the thoughts which you gained by reflection and observation. If you have reflected or observed but little, your stock of intellectual wealth must be small; and who can impart to others that which they do not possess? It may be said, then, why should we be required to write compositions before we are capable of writing well? I answer, that if you have but a small capital to begin with, your stores will increase by use; but permit me to caution you as to a choice of subjects; for beginners in composition, often choose such as would require a philosopher to investigate.

For example, let us suppose a young Miss, unaccustomed to confine her thoughts, for any length of time, to any given subject, writing a composition on *Gratitude.* She has a vague idea that *gratitude* is something praise-worthy, and begins by saying, "that it is a virtue that all should possess." When she has proceeded so far, she does not well know what more to say; but the composition must be written; and so she proceeds to say that every one ought to be grateful, and when they see people in distress, they ought to relieve their wants:—thus she goes from gratitude to *benevolence,* and, confounding the two virtues, destroys all distinctions of terms and ideas.

It is very important that in your attempts at writing you confine yourselves to subjects with which you are in some degree familiar. No matter how common, or trivial may be the theme; the object is to acquire a habit of expressing your ideas in writing, with clearness and simplicity. For example, give a description of your own dwelling house, state its length, width, and mode of construction, the materials of which it is composed; and a little reflection, with some previous learning, would suggest to you the improvements which have been made in the building of houses and other kinds of architecture. You might describe your own room, with its furniture, &c.; or, looking out upon the prospect before you, delineate in words the various objects before you. Any production of nature or art, might furnish you with ideas. For instance, suppose you should write about an apple—you may think this is a very insignificant subject—but nothing that God has made is insignificant; nor is the power of describing the most common object to be despised. Well, now begin to think what you could find to say about an apple: you all know to which of the kingdoms of nature it belongs; you know that it is a fruit originating from a flower of a certain kind—the kind of flower might be described, the usual height of the tree on which it grows, the climate most favorable to the growth of this tree, the various culinary uses of the apple, the evil purposes to which the ingenuity of man has perverted it, &c. I have yet touched upon few of the subjects which your theme might suggest, and yet much might be said upon each one of the abovementioned heads. A fly, a bee, or a butterfly, might afford subjects for your pen. I do not mean that you are in your descriptions of an apple or an insect, to write as a botanist or geologist would do, but that you express in simple language your own observations upon these, or any other objects. I have said your own *observations,* you will please to notice this, for without observation you cannot write on any subject, except it be merely to repeat like the parrot, what you hear from others. But by attempting to describe common objects you will see the need of observation and attention with respect to common things, and that learning is not confined to the knowledge which is contained in books.

By using your knowledge, however small the stock at first may be, you will continue to add to your intellectual stores; the idea of wanting to know something that you may communicate in your composition, will induce you to pay attention to objects around you, to hear the remarks of wiser people, and to recollect what you read in books. But do not allow yourselves to borrow from others. On reading a very spirited or profound composition from a young lady of limited talents and opportunities, a teacher immediately believes that it is borrowed, even should it chance that she has not before seen the same thing. This is not only stealing, but defrauding yourselves. If you begin with compositions, above your own capacities, you must continue them, or the deception will at once appear to your companions, as well as teachers. But I should very unwillingly believe that any pupil can be so lost to honorable sentiments as to wish to gain reputation for talents she does not possess, or so unjust to herself as to prevent her own improvement in the attempt to seem to be, what she is not.

You have heard some things that may be said upon an apple. Look around you, and you see innumerable objects in the productions of nature and art; all of these have peculiarities of their own, which may be described even with no other knowledge of them, than you may gain by your sight, hearing, taste, touch and smell,—innumerable comparisons between these objects will also naturally suggest themselves to your minds; as you acquire more knowledge, you will think of many relations existing between them which you now do not observe. The subject of geology, on which you all have the advantage of hearing lectures, will serve to lead even the youngest of you to reflect on the many things which may be said even of stones. You have perhaps thought that all were alike, but you now find that there is diversity of character among rocks, as well as people. The rocks are not morally or intellectually different from each other, since they are destitute of intelligence, and even of life, which plants possess—but rocks and stones are physically different, that is, their external appearance is various, and their chemical composition different.

When you walk or ride out, you can always meet with something animate or inanimate that may serve for the subject of a composition. When you see a person in affliction, or behold some one debased by intoxication, or taking the name of God in vain, emotions of various kinds will be awakened, and under the influence of these you might be led to write with facility. When you see a good person relieving distress, you will sympathize with the feelings of those who receive this kindness, and thus you may from your own observation and reflection, comprehend the nature and obligations of gratitude. Yet still you may not be able to investigate this emotion; for in order to do this, you would need to be acquainted with the operations of the mind, and to explore the recesses of the human heart, and the relations of cause and effect.

Although in some of the foregoing remarks I have more particularly addressed myself to the younger pupils, and those to whom the exercise of writing composition is new, I would say to all, be careful of going out of your own depth; study to understand the nature of your own minds, and occupy yourselves with subjects which you most readily and fully comprehend—write as if you had something to say, not as if you attempted to say something because you must write. If your minds are properly disciplined to habits of reflection, you must, with all that you are now studying, hearing and seeing, have something to say respecting your own observations, reflections, sentiments and opinions. It is well for advanced pupils, to write frequently on the subjects which they are engaged in studying.

A pupil in astronomy having beheld the heavens, traced the path of the constellations, contemplated the planets and the fixed stars, as they are arranged in their beautiful order, may surely find enough to say of such observations—she might, as genius or inclination prompted, state in precise and scientific language the various celestial phenomena, or with an imagination kindling as such scenes rise to a style of sublimity. Or if a Christian, and impressed with the thoughts of the Divine Power which created and upholds this wonderful universe, she would naturally be led to pour forth the devout expressions of a pious heart. Mechanical philosophy, optics, botany, chemistry, and all physical subjects, should lead the mind of the student to the observation of nature, and such observations will furnish matter for composition.

History and geography are fruitful in subjects for the exercise of the pen. Rhetoric and criticism are intended chiefly to teach you to arrange your thoughts with clearness and elegance, and to avoid errors which might offend the ear of taste, and rules of composition. Moral philosophy, leading the mind to reflect upon the reciprocal duties of mankind, and their common obligations to their Maker, cannot fail to suggest new trains of thought.

And when the empire of the human mind is first unfolded, as it were, upon a map before you, and the many devious windings of thought traced to their mysterious sources; when you are first led to perceive that the mind possesses the power of looking inwardly upon its own operations, how many new and interesting ideas spring into existence! Copy these in their own native freshness and vividness of coloring, and the transcript cannot fail of being delightful to others.

The first impressions which the various branches of literature and science make upon the mind, have a character of originality and enthusiasm, which cannot afterwards be caught—these evanescent emotions should then be secured by copies made when they are fresh and new.

I have not recommended the attempt to write stories from the imagination; this may be well occasionally, but it has the bad effect of bringing the mind too much under the dominion of fancy. It is better for young ladies to occupy themselves with realities, than to stray too much into the dangerous regions of imagination. Besides, the practice of writing tales has a tendency to form a tinselled kind of style, not to be compared in dignity or propriety with a simple and plain manner of telling truth. Indeed it is to be hoped that as the various departments of human knowledge become more filled with facts, and these facts are arranged according to the rules of science, ample scope will be found for the exercise of the human faculties;—and although we desire not to see the province of fiction deserted, yet we would see a higher rank awarded to those who search for and discover truth, who assist and perfect nature, than to the fabricators of those gossamer tales which receive all their coloring from the varying and illusive hue of fancy, and which have no higher aim than the amusement of hours, which are already too short and too few for the great objects of human existence.

Poetry is a species of composition which none should attempt except those who are strongly prompted by genius. True poetical talent is rare, and can never be forced into existence: when it is possessed, it should be regarded as a precious gift from the Creator of mind, and enlisted in the service of virtue and piety.

Notes

Preface

1. Eldred and Mortensen, "Reading Literacy Narratives"; Bizzell, "Opportunities for Feminist Research in the History of Rhetoric."

2. See, for example, Baym, *American Women Writers and the Work of History, 1790–1860; Feminism and American Literary History;* and *Woman's Fiction: A Guide to Novels by and about Women in America, 1820–70.*

1. Introduction

1. Clark and Halloran, introduction to *Oratorical Culture in Nineteenth-Century America,* 6–7.

2. Historians of rhetoric have begun to address the specific problems raised in composing narratives of women's schooling in rhetoric and composition. See Bizzell, "Opportunities for Feminist Research in the History of Rhetoric"; Gere, *Intimate Practices;* Gere, "Kitchen Tables and Rented Rooms"; Gold, "The Grimké Sisters and the Emergence of the Woman's Rights Movement"; Heath, "Toward an Ethnohistory of Writing in American Education"; Hobbs, introduction to *Nineteenth-Century Women Learn to Write;* Horner and Barton, "The Eighteenth Century"; Kolodny, "Inventing a Feminist Discourse"; Rouse, "Margaret Fuller"; Schultz, "Elaborating Our History"; and Tonkovich, "Rhetorical Power in the Victorian Parlor."

3. Mason, "The Salutatory Oration of Miss Priscilla Mason to the Young Ladies Academy at Philadelphia, May 15, 1793," 103; Friedman, *America's First Woman Lawyer,* 11–33; O'Neill, ed., *The Women's Book of World Records and Achievements,* 67. As we know, only recently have women been appointed to the Supreme Court. But the federal judiciary did see, as early as 1884, the appointment of women as part-time commissioners. Florence Allen was, however, the first woman appointed to a full-time post (Cook, "Women Judges," 85–86).

4. Clark and Halloran, introduction to *Oratorical Culture in Nineteenth-Century America,* 6–7, 8. See also Berlin, "The Demise of the Classical Tradition," chapter 2 in *Writing Instruction in Nineteenth-Century American Colleges.*

5. Broaddus, *Genteel Rhetoric,* 12. On a related issue, Charles Paine convincingly argues against histories (in particular, against James Berlin's work) that chronicle a villainous shift to belletrism; see *The Resistant Writer.* See also Johnson, *Nineteenth-Century Rhetoric in North America;* and Crowley, *Composition in the University.*

6. Ferguson, *Law and Letters in American Culture,* 5.

7. Brook Thomas argues that these legal influences continue to operate on literature well into the nineteenth century; see *Cross-examinations of Law and Literature.*

8. For discussions of the influence of language politics on literature before and after the American Renaissance, see Gustafson, *Representative Words;* Kramer, *Imagining Language in America;* and Warner, *The Letters of the Republic.*

9. See Korobkin, *Criminal Conversations.*

10. Hoff, *Law, Gender, and Injustice,* quotes the Adams's correspondence on p. 60. U.S. history provides numerous examples of liberatory rhetoric translating into conservative practice. Consider, for instance, the textbooks used in Freedman's Bureau schools during Reconstruction, or the primers designed to help "Americanize" European immigrants in the early twentieth century (Anderson, *The Education of Blacks in the South,* 30; Cremin, *The Transformation of the School,* 66–75). Such texts presented readers with models of standard American English while simultaneously instilling in them the consensus values ostensibly essential to maintaining a singular national identity. Similar values also informed the texts and instruction at federally sponsored boarding schools for Native Americans dating back to the early nineteenth century (Coleman, *American Indian Children at School;* U.S. Department of Health, Education, and Welfare, *A Brief History of the Federal Responsibility to the American Indian*). Schooling at many boarding schools presumptuously offered Native American students the great gifts of civilization, but often at considerable physical and psychic expense. What all of these examples have in common is the notion that personal freedom is best secured by becoming assimilated to a common culture governed by a common set of laws.

11. Hoff, *Law, Gender, and Injustice,* 55.

12. Occasionally one can hear this argument repeated, as in the claim that neoclassical civic rhetoric holds some appeal for feminist jurisprudence. See, for example, Sherry, "Civic Virtue and the Feminine Voice in Constitutional Adjudication."

13. Baym, *Woman's Fiction,* xxxii.

14. For more on women's domestic and sentimental fiction, see Baym, *Woman's Fiction;* Davidson, *Revolution and the Word;* Kelley, *Private Woman, Public Stage;* Tompkins, *Sensational Designs;* Samuels, *Romances of the Republic;* Samuels, ed., *The Culture of Sentiment.*

15. For a critique of the separate spheres metaphor, see Kerber, "Separate Spheres, Female Worlds, Woman's Place"; and a special issue of *American Literature,* edited by Cathy Davidson (especially her "Preface: No More Separate Spheres!").

16. See Connors, "Frances Wright"; Gold, "The Grimké Sisters and the Emergence of the Women's Rights Movement"; and Logan, *"We Are Coming."*

17. Science Hill Female Academy Papers, file 43. Used with permission of the Filson Club Historical Society, Louisville, Kentucky.

18. Baym advances this argument in "Writing New American Literary History," part 2 of *Feminism and American Literary History.*

19. Murray, *The Gleaner,* 718–19. Hereafter, page citations to *The Gleaner* (Union College Press edition) appear in the text.

20. This concept was most recently reintroduced into public debate about education with the 1983 issue of *A Nation at Risk: The Imperative for Educational Reform* by then-President Reagan's National Commission on Excellence in Education (U.S. Department of Education). The commission's call for reform is based on its understanding that for at least the past twenty years faulty literacy instruction has produced many functionally illiterate high school graduates. According to the commission, this decline in literate ability

among young people threatens the very integrity of the union. Numerous scholars have disputed the commission's findings, noting that narratives of educational decline have been popular in America since the late nineteenth century. During this same time, they report, various empirical measures show sustained—sometimes surprising—growth in generational literacy (Kaestle et al., *Literacy in the United States*, 76; see also Berliner and Biddle, *The Manufactured Crisis*).

But clearly the notion that poor or absent education harms democracy antedates the rise of industrial capitalism; this concern is voiced again and again in documents dating back to the Revolution. See Hobbs, introduction to *Nineteenth-Century Women Learn to Write*. In the tradition we discuss, Beecher is probably the most outspoken on this issue.

21. For a reconsideration of sophistic rhetoric, especially as it relates to gender, see Jarratt, *Rereading the Sophists*. See also Poulakos, *Sophistical Rhetoric in Classical Greece*.

22. On language and nation, see Baron, *Grammar and Good Taste*; Davidson, *Revolution and Word*; Gustafson, *Eloquence Is Power*; Gustafson, *Representative Words*; Jordan, *Second Stories*; Kramer, *Imagining Language in America*; and Simpson, *The Politics of American English*.

23. For a discussion of "rhetoric as immunity" in mid- to late-nineteenth-century men's education, see Paine, *The Resistant Writer*.

24. For discussions linking the eighteenth-century preoccupation with seduction to republican political theory and rational education, see Fliegelman, *Prodigals and Pilgrims*; Jasinski, "The Feminization of Liberty, Domesticated Virtue, and the Reconstitution of Power and Authority in Early American Political Discourse"; and Smith-Rosenberg, "Domesticating 'Virtue.'"

25. Bingham, *The American Preceptor*, 49 (the paragraph numbers and emphasis appear in the "Oration upon Female Education"; eighteenth-century typographical conventions have been updated). Hereafter, page references to *The American Preceptor* appear in the text. On Bingham's books and career, see Davidson, *Revolution and the Word*, 66; Nietz, *Old Textbooks*, 65–66.

26. Beecher, *Educational Reminiscences and Suggestions*, 238–66.

27. Norton, *Liberty's Daughters*, 228.

28. Rush, "Thoughts upon Female Education," 170.

29. Kerber, "'History Can Do It No Justice,'" 29.

30. For more on women's legal status in the early republic, see Crane, "Dealing with Dependence"; Hoff, *Law, Gender, and Injustice*; Hoffman and Albert, eds., *Women in the Age of the American Revolution*; and Lebsock, *The Free Women of Petersburg*.

31. Hoff, *Law, Gender, and Injustice*, 49.

32. Kerber, *Women of the Republic*, 12.

33. Rush, "Thoughts upon Female Education," 170, 172; Willard, *An Address to the Public* (see also Scott, "The Ever Widening Circle").

34. Mason, "The Salutatory Oration," 102.

35. See Gilmore, *Reading Becomes a Necessity of Life*; Graff, *The Legacies of Literacy*; Lockridge, *Literacy in Colonial New England*; Monaghan, "Family Literacy in Early Eighteenth Century Boston"; and Monaghan, "Literacy Instruction and Gender in Colonial New England." Perlmann and Shirley further remind us that studies of advanced and basic literacies need to be more carefully distinguished for this period. Specifically, they contend that the "ideal of republican motherhood" would have given basic literacy for

women "only a minor boost" and that "the expansion of schooling after 1790 would be less important for basic literacy than historians have thought" ("When Did New England Women Acquire Literacy?" 66). Although we have considered the conditions of basic literacy during this period, our focus is on rhetorical instruction more broadly defined, or, for lack of a more precise label, "advanced" literacy.

36. Monaghan, "Literacy Instruction and Gender in Colonial New England," 56, 60, 66.

37. Ibid., 67.

38. Monaghan, "Family Literacy in Early Eighteenth Century Boston," 348.

39. Monaghan, "Literacy Instruction and Gender in Colonial New England," 63.

40. Ibid., 68, 70.

41. See Ferguson, *Law and Letters in American Culture*, 3–84.

42. Brown, *Knowledge Is Power*, 163.

43. Kerber, *Women of the Republic*, 201–2; see also Norton, *Liberty's Daughters*, 256–57.

44. Schwager, "Educating Women in America," 163.

45. Before the rise of female academies in the last decades of the century, there were a few exceptional schools: in 1754 Anthony Benezet established a school in Philadelphia, and still earlier, in 1742, the Moravian Young Ladies Seminary had been established in Bethlehem, Pennsylvania; both offered a serious academic curriculum (Norton, *Liberty's Daughters*, 260, 283).

46. Norton, *Liberty's Daughters*, 259. See also Woody, *A History of Women's Education in the United States*, 1:217–34.

47. Graves, *Girlhood and Womanhood*, 15; Graves, *Woman in America*, xiii–xx.

48. Schultz, *The Young Composers*, 16.

49. Baym, *Feminism and American Literary History*, 125–27, 247 n. 10.

50. Kaestle, *Pillars of the Republic*, 70.

51. Graves, *Girlhood and Womanhood*, 31–32, 176.

52. Ibid., 116; Schwager, "Educating Women in America," 163.

53. Norton, *Liberty's Daughters*, 275.

54. See Kerber, *Women of the Republic*, 198–99; Norton, *Liberty's Daughters*, 264–66.

55. Nienkamp and Collins, introduction to *Female Quixotism*, xvii.

56. Schwager, "Educating Women in America," 157.

57. Norton, *Liberty's Daughters*, 273.

58. See Kolodny, "Letting Go Our Grand Obsessions"; Morrison, *Playing in the Dark;* Nelson, *The Word in Black and White.*

59. Kerber, "Separate Spheres, Female Worlds, Woman's Place," 18.

60. See Nietz, *Old Textbooks*, 115.

61. Davidson, *Revolution and the Word*, 14. Davidson discusses such groups in the context of the 1814 novel by Sarah Savage, *The Factory Girl*, in which the heroine organizes a study group of her fellow workers (12). We hasten to add, though, that actual reading and writing groups seem to have emerged slowly in the nineteenth century. See also Wexler, "Tender Violence," who argues for the restrictive nature of the literacy promoted by domestic fiction later in the nineteenth century.

62. Carson, "Imperfections of Female Education." Used with permission of the Filson Club Historical Society, Louisville, Kentucky.

2. Schooling Fictions

1. Fraser, *The Mental Flower Garden*, 5. Rush's endorsement appears with other recommendations following Fraser's preface. For more on Rush's thinking on language and social change, see Williams, "Religion, Science and Rhetoric in Revolutionary America." Williams does not take up Rush's forays into female education, but instead focuses on his relationship to religious and scientific debates of the time. Burgett visits some of Rush's ideas about gender in chapter 4 of *Sentimental Bodies*.

Hereafter, quotations from Fraser's major works are referenced in the chapter using the following abbreviations:

CM: The Columbian Monitor.

MF-G: The Mental Flower-Garden (1st ed., 1800).

MFG: The Mental Flower Garden (2d ed., 1807).

YGLA: Young Gentleman and Lady's Assistant.

Where they appear, eighteenth-century typographical conventions have been updated.

2. Kaestle, *The Evolution of an Urban School System*, 60.

3. For a discussion of this issue see Connors, "The Rise and Fall of the Modes of Discourse"; Gere, "Kitchen Tables and Rented Rooms"; Heath, "Toward an Ethnohistory of Writing in American Education"; Miller, "The Feminization of Composition"; North, *The Making of Knowledge in Composition*; and Varnum, "The History of Composition."

4. See Street, *Literacy in Theory and Practice*, 19–43; and Torgovnick, *Gone Primitive*, 3–41.

5. See among others Baym, *Novels, Readers, and Reviewers*; Burgett, *Sentimental Bodies*; Davidson, *Revolution and the Word*; Newton, "Wise and Foolish Virgins"; and Warner, *The Letters of the Republic*.

6. Baym, *Feminism and American Literary History*, 107, 110, 122.

7. Cremin notes that François Fénelon's 1687 essay on female education influenced Benjamin Rush's writing on the subject a century later (*American Education*, 120).

8. Brickley advances this hypothesis in her excellent study "Sarah Pierce's Litchfield Female Academy, 1792–1833."

9. Foster, *The Boarding School*, [3]. Hereafter, quotations from this book are cited in the text using the abbreviation *BS*; eighteenth-century typographical conventions have been updated. A chronology of Foster's life appears in appendix 1 and an excerpt from *The Boarding School* appears in appendix 2.

In addition to his involvement with Foster, Bingham authored a number of his own schoolbooks, among them *The American Preceptor, The Columbian Orator*, and *The Young Lady's Accidence* (Woody, *A History of Women's Education in the United States*, 1:339–40).

10. Newton, "Wise and Foolish Virgins," 140, 148.

11. For a definition and description of literacy narratives, see Eldred and Mortensen, "Reading Literacy Narratives."

12. Davidson, *Revolution and the Word*, 43.

13. See Haswell and Lu, *Comp Tales*; and Trimmer, ed., *Narration as Knowledge*.

14. Newton, "Wise and Foolish Virgins," 146.

15. Ibid., 147.

16. *The Complete Letter-Writer*, 4, 9, 11, 26, 30, 42, 125, 126.

17. Ibid., 61.

18. Mrs. Chapone, *Letters on the Improvement of the Mind*, 236–37, 238.

19. Ibid., 192, 193.

20. *The Complete Letter-Writer*, 17, 36, 53, 59.

21. Royster, *Traces of a Stream*, 83. Royster also cautions that it is necessary "to acknowledge the limits of knowledge and to be particularly careful about 'claims' to truth, by clarifying the contexts and conditions of our interpretations and by making sure that we do not overreach the bounds of either reason or possibility" (84). For further debates over feminist historical methodology in rhetoric and composition studies, see Bizzell, "Feminist Methods of Research in the History of Rhetoric"; Enos, "Recovering the Lost Art of Researching the History of Rhetoric"; Gale, "Historical Studies and Postmodernism"; Glenn, "Comment"; and Jarratt, "Comment."

22. Tonkovich remarks, "The texts these women wrote, although they claim to be nonfictional and transparent, are as carefully crafted and as deserving of close textual scrutiny as are their fictions" (*Domesticity with a Difference*, xvi).

23. Faulkner, *Absalom, Absalom!* 348 (italics in original); Giroux, "Liberal Arts Education and the Struggle for Public Life," 116.

3. A Commonplace Rhetoric: Judith Sargent Murray's Margaretta Narrative

1. Skemp, *Judith Sargent Murray*, 17.

2. For background on *The Massachusetts Magazine*, see Granger, "The Massachusetts Magazine." On Murray's plays, see Kritzer, "Playing with Republican Motherhood"; Richards, "How to Write an American Play"; Schofield, "The Happy Revolution"; and Schofield, "'Quitting the Loom and Distaff.'"

3. Murray was not the first woman to produce serial essays in English for publication in a magazine. In 1744–46 Eliza Haywood published her essays in the *Female Spectator*, "the first periodical for women actually written by a woman" (Spacks, *Selections from "The Female Spectator*," xii). *The Massachusetts Magazine*, in which Murray published, had both men and women in its audience.

4. Murray, *The Gleaner*, 55. Hereafter, page references are cited in the chapter. For readers' convenience, references are to the Union College Press edition of *The Gleaner*, which is based on the three-volume first edition (see Judith Sargent Murray [Constantia, pseud.], *The Gleaner*). A chronology of Murray's life appears in appendix 1, and an excerpt from *The Gleaner* appears in appendix 3.

5. Skemp, *Judith Sargent Murray*, 12.

6. For background on Murray's Universalist beliefs, including her marriage to John Murray, founder of Universalism in the United States, see Harris, introduction to *Selected Writings of Judith Sargent Murray*; Baym, introduction to *The Gleaner*; and Skemp, *Judith Sargent Murray*, 19–31.

7. Murray's own letters from this period, copied over into letter books some years later, can be found in her papers, on deposit at the Mississippi Department of Archives and History and available on microfilm.

8. For other discussions of Murray's narrative gender bending in *The Gleaner*, see Field, *Constantia*; Jacoba, "Prose Writings and Dramas of Judith Sargent Murray"; and Wilcox, "The Scribblings of a Plain Man and the Temerity of a Woman."

9. Newton, "Wise and Foolish Virgins," 153.

10. Smith-Rosenberg, "Domesticating 'Virtue,'" 160.

11. Brown, "Richardson and Sterne in the *Massachusetts Magazine*," 71.

12. In his 1952 book, *Plagiarism and Originality*, Alexander Lindey defines plagiarism as "the false assumption of authorship: the wrongful act of taking the product of another person's mind, and presenting it as one's own" (2). He contrasts this to copyright infringement, defined as "the copying of all or a material or substantial part of copyrighted and copyrightable matter," emphasizing that they are not the same, but rather overlapping legal concerns. In Murray's time, only the pirating of whole texts was legally actionable (2).

13. Bettig, "Critical Perspectives on the History and Philosophy of Copyright," 144–45.

14. Rose, *Authors and Owners*, 4.

15. Rose, "The Author in Court," 211.

16. Bettig, "Critical Perspectives on the History and Philosophy of Copyright," 144–45.

17. Patterson, *Copyright in Historical Perspective*, 184–92; quotations from pp. 184, 188.

18. As with the Statute of Anne, however, the law of 1790 did not itself clarify the relationship of the statute to a perpetual claim to work under common law. That matter was resolved some years later in *Wheaton* v. *Peters* (1834). Authors and their assignees—publishers—maintained exclusive control of published work for a set period of time, after which the work passed into the public domain. Thereby a balance was struck between private and public interests in the intellectual fruits of the nation. At the same time, authors maintained the perpetual control of common law over work left unpublished (Bettig, "Critical Perspectives on the History and Philosophy of Copyright," 148–49; Bugbee, *Genesis of American Patent and Copyright Law*, 129–48, 156). Regarding the very idea of constitutional and statutory copyright and patent protections, Bettig notes that the "philosophy of intellectual property reifies economic rationalism as a natural human trait," such that it is made to seem that creative and inventive people will not engage in creative and inventive acts unless they know the value of their productions will accrue to them and them only (146).

19. "*Pope* [v. *Curll*] suggests how from the very beginning of the story of authors' rights in England, issues of 'propriety' in the moral sense became inextricably entwined with issues of 'property' in the sense of economic interest" (Rose, "The Author in Court," 212).

20. White, *Plagiarism and Imitation*, 5, 6–7; de Grazia, "Sanctioning Voice," 287–89. Also, Joel Weinsheimer notes in *Imitation* that according to Samuel Johnson there existed "a community of mind in classical quotation. The classic is a work, literary or otherwise, which has become a pattern of consciousness defining an intellectual community and predisposing it to view the world in a certain way. The classics of whatever kind are therefore the locus of prejudice, and for that reason objectivity is their nemesis" (9).

21. White, *Plagiarism and Imitation*, 8, 9, 11.

22. Cash suggests that Sterne might have arranged his entries thematically rather than by author, stressing the public domain of ideas over individual authorship (*Laurence Sterne*, 218). Mallon makes the point that much depends here on whether one is a fan or foe of Sterne. Critics friendly to Sterne have, over the years, jumped though many hoops to defend what others perceive as the baldest form of literary thievery (*Stolen Words*, 12–24).

23. Mallon, *Stolen Words*, 31.

24. See Rosenthal, "The Author as Ghost in the Eighteenth Century," 40, on Young's

Conjectures on Original Composition. See also Rosenthal, *Playwrights and Plagiarists in Early Modern England;* Hobby, *Virtue of Necessity.*

25. Woodmansee puts what we know about Murray in a broader context: "Our laws of intellectual property are rooted in the century-long reconceptualization of the creative process which culminated in high Romantic pronouncements like Wordsworth's to the effect that this process *ought* to be solitary, or individual, and introduce 'a new element into the intellectual universe'" ("On the Author Effect," 27).

26. Johnson, *Rambler* "No. 143," 394.

27. Ibid.

28. According to Johnson, "not every imitation ought to be stigmatized as plagiarism. The adoption of a noble sentiment, or the insertion of a borrowed ornament may sometimes display so much judgment as will almost compensate for invention; and an inferior genius may without any imputation of servility pursue the path of the antients, provided he declines to tread in their footsteps" (ibid., 401).

29. Chibka, "The Stranger within Young's *Conjectures,*" 541.

30. Young, *Conjectures,* 4.

31. See Weinsheimer, *Imitation,* 61.

32. Young, *Conjectures,* 20, 21.

33. Kinneavy, *A Theory of Discourse,* 409–18.

4. Sketching Rhetorical Change: Mrs. A. J. Graves on Girlhood and Womanhood

1. Baym, *Woman's Fiction,* 77.

2. For more on adult education, see Kett, *The Pursuit of Knowledge under Difficulties.*

3. Boydston, Kelley, and Margolis, *The Limits of Sisterhood,* 5. (McHenry notes a similar connection between benevolent societies and early African American literary societies ["Forgotten Readers," 155].) Boydston, Kelley, and Margolis go so far as to suggest that "domesticity," of the kind practiced by white middle-class proponents of domestic economy, "may well have functioned as a precondition for nineteenth-century feminism" (5). However, as the title of their book suggests, this is not the major premise on which they hang their argument.

4. For more on Beecher's pedagogy, including composition pedagogy, see Tonkovich, *Domesticity with a Difference,* 152–54.

5. Ibid., 162.

6. Sklar, *Catharine Beecher,* 81.

7. Watts, *The Republic Reborn,* xviii. Watts continues, "Instead . . . republican traditions served as a seedbed for the growth of liberal commitments. The eighteenth-century notion of 'independence,' for instance, at once maintained a significantly different social meaning from nineteenth-century 'self-interest' while also providing a conceptual foundation for the latter's growth. Moreover, impulses toward individual gain and status-seeking certainly existed in colonial America, but they circulated as nascent, half-formed conceptions lacking the intellectual and economic framework to provide true legitimacy. Only in the period of the early republic did they gain solidity and widespread approval and cohere into a social creed" (xviii).

8. Halloran, "From Rhetoric to Composition."

9. See also work in speech communication by Guthrie, "The Development of Rhetori-

cal Theory in America"; and Reid, "The Boylston Professorship of Rhetoric and Oratory." Relevant work in composition historiography includes Berlin, *Writing Instruction in Nineteenth-Century American Colleges;* Broaddus, *Genteel Rhetoric;* Clark and Halloran, introduction to *Oratorical Culture in Nineteenth-Century America;* Johnson, *Nineteenth-Century Rhetoric in North America;* Miller, *The Formation of College English;* and Paine, *The Resistant Writer.*

10. Crowley, *Composition in the University,* 36.

11. Tompkins, *Sensational Designs,* 155. Tompkins draws here on David Reynolds, who makes a similar case for pulpit oratory. She observes that "the entire practice of pulpit oratory in this period shifted from an expository and abstract mode of explicating religious doctrine, to a mode in which sensational narratives carried the burden of theological precept" (153).

12. Graves, *Girlhood and Womanhood,* 83. Subsequent references appear by page number in the chapter.

13. Graves, *Woman in America,* 66.

14. A review of Catharine Maria Sedgwick's *Means and Ends* makes clear that Sedgwick stood on a similar platform: "An enlightened attention has not yet been sufficiently directed to the proper principles on which the education of American women would be conducted, with reference to the great principles of public policy on which our whole system of institutions is founded, and to the entirely peculiar state of society naturally growing out of them. We hear a great deal of the importance of female education, in a general sense; but we very rarely hear just views expressed—and still more rarely witness their practical application—of the bearing which the democratic freedom of our institutions ought to have upon the proper training of the American wife and mother, as contradistinguished from the females of the foreign aristocracies, by the prevalent tone and practice of which we are too much accustomed to model our own habits of thinking and acting" ("American Women," 128–29).

15. Graves, *Woman in America,* xiv.

16. See Campbell, *Man Cannot Speak for Her,* vol. 2, for various speeches by Stanton.

17. Okker, *Our Sister Editors,* 41; see also Finley, *The Lady of Godey's.*

18. Okker, *Our Sister Editors,* 41, 51–54; [Hale], "The 'Conversazióne,'" 2.

19. Phelps, "Hints about Periodicals," 671.

20. Ibid., 667, 671–72. We know from Phelps's own writing career, detailed in chapter 6, that tenderness, affection, and humility were but rhetorical points of departure for her forays into scientific and philosophical inquiry meant to parallel, perhaps even rival, that of men.

21. Herndl, *Invalid Women,* 44, 46.

22. Verbrugge, *Able-Bodied Womanhood,* 33.

23. Quoted in ibid., 20. See also Ehrenreich and English, *For Her Own Good,* 91–126.

24. Verbrugge, *Able-Bodied Womanhood,* 12–13.

25. Okker, *Our Sister Editors,* 28. See also chapter 9 of Tonkovich, *Domesticity with a Difference,* for a discussion of Beecher's revisions of heterosexual marriage and family organization.

26. [Hale?], "The End and Aim of the Present System of Female Education," 75. Although the article is unsigned, Okker believes its author is "probably Hale" (*Our Sister Editors*, 67).

27. Tonkovich notes another linking of education with business in the four authors she studies (Catharine Beecher, Sarah Hale, Fanny Fern, and Margaret Fuller) "Advocates of women's education, they urged other women to become teachers, while they abandoned teaching for more lucrative pursuits" (*Domesticity with a Difference*, xii). The point made by all of these authors is clear: writing about teaching and administrating pays better than teaching or administrating, a refrain that runs through the biographic details and fiction of nineteenth-century women.

28. In his study of nineteenth-century rhetoric, Paine suggests another limitation of the metaphor of rhetorical inoculation as it continues to be practiced today—that education conducted with such a purpose teaches students that culture is something removed from self rather than lived material out of which one constructs language, arguments, and self.

29. Graves, *Woman in America*, 122.

30. [Sedgwick], "Education of Young Ladies," 381, 382.

31. Ibid., 382, 383.

32. Ibid., 385, 387.

33. See Baym, *Woman's Fiction*, 64; and Okker, *Our Sister Editors*, 43–44.

34. [Hale?], "Boarding Schools," 148, 151; the article is unsigned but, according to Okker, "in all likelihood [was] written by Hale" (*Our Sister Editors*, 49). [Sedgwick], "Education of Young Ladies," 385.

5. The Commonsense Romanticism of Louisa Caroline Tuthill

1. Hale, *Woman's Record*, 803–5.

2. Baym, *Woman's Fiction*, xvi–xvii.

3. Ibid., xvii.

4. Horner, *Nineteenth-Century Scottish Rhetoric*, 33.

5. Tuthill, *The Young Lady's Reader*, n.p.; comments from "Recommendations" printed on front endpapers. Hereafter, quotations from Tuthill's major works (including a misattributed title) are referenced in the chapter using the following abbreviations:

BBB: The Belle, the Blue and the Bigot.

BSG: The Boarding-School Girl.

EBG: Edith, the Backwoods Girl.

YLH: The Young Lady's Home.

YLR: The Young Lady's Reader.

A chronology of Tuthill's life appears in appendix 1, and an excerpt from *The Young Lady's Home* appears in appendix 4.

6. Tuthill (1798–1879) was born in New Haven, Connecticut, the daughter of a wealthy merchant. Schooled there, and possibly later at Sarah Pierce's Litchfield Academy, Tuthill at eighteen married Cornelius Tuthill, a graduate of Yale. (After graduation, Cornelius studied law briefly before returning to Yale to study theology. Illness prevented him from preaching, and after his marriage to Louisa, he taught school and edited several influential magazines. He died in 1825.) Widowed, Tuthill turned to writing as a source of income, as well as intellectual fulfillment and Christian duty. Five early books appeared

anonymously; her *Home* and *Reader* in 1839 were the first works to bear her name. Tuthill's course of life is resonant with that of other women writing in the nineteenth century. According to various biographical dictionary entries, as a child Tuthill was a prolific writer, but as she matured, she "imbibed a strong prejudice against literary women, and firmly resolved never to become one." After the death of her husband, she took up the pen as "a solace under affliction," thereby breaking her resolve and beginning a career that would last decades (Hart, *Female Prose Writers of America*, 112; Allaback, "The Writings of Louisa Tuthill," 41–53.).

7. Mellor, "On Romanticism and Feminism," 7, 8.

8. Ibid., 8.

9. See Koenigsberg, "Arbiter of Taste"; see also Allaback, "The Writings of Louisa Tuthill."

10. Campbell stipulated that "conviction and persuasion have different ends and therefore require different means" (Johnson, *Nineteenth-Century Rhetoric in North America*, 52).

11. See Strychacz, s.v. "Stewart, Dugald," *Dictionary of Literary Biography*. Although in philosophical circles long thought to be a popularizer of his colleague Thomas Reid's writing, Stewart more recently has been appreciated as a founding figure in the British and American academic fields of political economy. See also Miller, *The Formation of College English*, 264–65.

12. See Stewart, *Elements of the Philosophy of the Human Mind*, 1–61, for an overview of the author's theory of mind.

13. Ibid., 104.

14. Ibid., 448.

15. Ibid., 428.

16. See ibid., chapter 6, section 3, "Of the Improvement of Memory."

17. Ibid., 34, 35, 42. On Blair and Campbell, see Golden and Corbett, *The Rhetoric of Blair, Campbell, and Whately*, 23–25, 139–41. See also Brock, *Scotus Americanus*, for a discussion of the religious and philosophical figures whose work (and who themselves) made the journey from Scotland to the U.S. at the turn of the nineteenth century.

18. One reviewer "implicitly sets Baillie within a nationalistic Scottish milieu dominated before her entrance by James Beattie, whereas clearly the major poetic voice in England in the ten years between 1785 and 1795 was that of William Cowper" (Curran, "Romantic Poetry," 187).

19. Ross, s.v. "Baillie, Joanna," *Dictionary of Literary Biography*. See also Clarke, *Ambitious Heights*.

20. Curran, "Romantic Poetry," 185–86.

21. Ibid., 186.

22. Ross, s.v. "Baillie, Joanna," *Dictionary of Literary Biography*.

23. One of Louisa Tuthill's publishers, Crosby and Nichols of Boston, frequently listed *The Belle, the Blue and the Bigot* along with other books Tuthill is known to have written. Tuthill disclosed her daughter's authorship as early as 1850 in a letter to biographer John Neal, but there is no evidence that she agitated for public correction of the error (for the text of Tuthill's letter, see Allaback, "The Writings of Louisa Tuthill," 32). Various literary encyclopedias published late in the nineteenth century do not enumerate *The Belle, the Blue and the Bigot* among Louisa Tuthill's works (and a few *do* list it under Cornelia

Louisa Tuthill's name), but, crucially, Lyle Wright's influential *American Fiction, 1774–1850* does misattribute *The Belle, the Blue and the Bigot* to Louisa, as does the Library of Congress's *National Union Catalog Pre-1956 Imprints.*

24. Sedgwick, *The Power of Her Sympathy*, 52.

25. This passage recalls how a record of Hugh Blair's lectures survived him and came to be published.

26. This is perhaps no more evident than in the new rhetoricians' interest in the relationship between persuasion and conviction. Persuasion cannot be dispensed with; it must be used to convince people to let go the prejudice instilled in them by practice of skepticism or false religion (usually code for Roman Catholicism). Establishing a link between persuasion and conviction points to one way in which the new rhetoric transformed the old. If Aristotelian principles dictated that rhetoric should seek probable truth, the new rhetoric figured the attainment of a singular, transcendent truth—Christian faith—as its end. Testimony about faith was thus central to the act of persuasion. See Johnson on Whately, *Nineteenth-Century Rhetoric in North America*, 50–60.

27. Ibid., 49.

6. Independent Studies: Almira Hart Lincoln Phelps and the Composition of Democratic Teachers

1. For a representative selection of women's suffrage oratory, see Campbell, ed., *Man Cannot Speak For Her*, vol. 2.

2. The Troy Female Seminary traces its roots back to the innovative boarding school Emma Willard founded in Middlebury, Vermont—a school that benefited from its proximity to Middlebury College. It was at Willard's boarding school that young Almira began a course of advanced instruction in the subjects she would one day teach.

3. Bolzau, *Almira Hart Lincoln Phelps*, 68, 71–79.

4. Ibid., 378. Phelps has been figured variously in feminist historians' efforts to reclaim the work of antebellum women writers. While she advocated advanced education for women, she also opposed women's suffrage. This seeming contradiction has fueled scholarly debate on the question of whether Phelps can be claimed as an early feminist. Thomas Woody's influential *History of Women's Education in the United States* (1929) positions early-nineteenth-century campaigns for female seminaries as a precursor to the women's rights movement that evolved later in the century, and so Phelps earns feminist credentials by way of her affiliation with Willard's Troy Female Seminary (1:458–59). In 1974 Keith Melder challenged this claim in "Mask of Oppression: The Female Seminary Movement in the United States." Five years later Anne Firor Scott affirmed Woody's earlier observation, particularly with reference to Troy, noting that "it is only in retrospect that the school can be seen to have been an important source of feminism and the incubator of a new style of female personality," one with an "intellectual component" ("The Ever Widening Circle," 3, 12). Most recently, in 1995 Robert Hendrick, offered this rebuttal to Woody and Scott: although "Phelps was . . . one of the most important nineteenth-century American female intellectuals," she "used her success as a science popularizer and educational reformer to defend conservative ideological positions, especially with regard to women" ("Ever-Widening Circle or Mask of Oppression?" 294). In fact, Scott's and Hendrick's positions are not so far apart. Scott recognizes that Phelps held and advanced "feminist" values simultaneously with "traditional" ones (3). Hendrick notes that Phelps

defended the "dependent status of women even as she sought their educational advancement" (294). In short, Phelps, in the volumes of prose she leaves us, shows how it was possible to be both a tireless champion of advanced education for women and a tireless critic of women's suffrage, all the while maintaining high demand for her published work.

5. Phelps, *Lectures to Young Ladies*, 40. Hereafter, quotations from Phelps's major works are referenced in the chapter using the following abbreviations:

LYL: Lectures to Young Ladies.

HMP: Hours with My Pupils.

IN: Ida Norman.

BRS: The Blue Ribbon Society.

A chronology of Phelps's life appears in appendix 1, and an excerpt from *Lectures to Young Ladies* appears in appendix 5.

6. The text of the petition is quoted in Bolzau, *Almira Hart Lincoln Phelps*, 386–400.

7. Quoted in ibid., 382–83.

8. Willard's argument, printed in *A Plan for Improving Female Education*, catalyzed nineteenth-century efforts to improve women's education. Willard's address was reprinted in a second edition in 1819 and later as a pamphlet by the Emma Willard Society, at the expense of one of its members, and apparently distributed to graduates of Troy Seminary. Called the *"Magna Carta of the higher education of women in America*," it remains a central text in the history of U.S. higher education (3). Today Willard's seminary survives as a preparatory school for young women, with a website that evidences a keen awareness of the institution's legacy (http://www.emma.troy.ny.us/).

9. This is not to mention the possibility of mental cruelty in marriage: "Too often those who are conscious of rectitude in the weightier matters of the law, omit within the sanctuary of the domestic circle, what they regard as lesser duties. . . . How little do we know of the sorrows and cares which oppress many who seem placed in enviable circumstances! We heard not the unkind word, the taunting sarcasm, we saw not the cold or scornful glance, which have inflicted deep wounds in that heart, supposed by us to be happy in the midst of prosperity" (*HMP*, 162–63).

10. In subsequent versions of *Lectures to Young Ladies*, Phelps adds a fifth part entitled "Teaching and Teachers" that makes these ideas explicit (see *The Fireside Friend*, 282–310).

11. See Salvatori. *Pedagogy*, 59–72; and Schultz, *The Young Composers*, 38–52.

12. In her prospectus for West Chester Young Ladies' Seminary, Phelps would extend the same metaphor: "In regard to teaching . . . I cannot bring forward any one process, as a certain and infallible method in all cases. There is, at the present day, too much *quackery* in education;—and the teacher who affirms that he has a specific for all minds, is as absurd as the physician who pretends that one medicine will cure all diseases. The general laws both of the mind and the body are so modified in each individual, by peculiar circumstances, that, in application either to the one or to the other, regard must be had to these modifications. The skill of the educator, like that of the physician, consists in discovering the variations of treatment required in different cases" (quoted in Bolzau, *Almira Hart Lincoln Phelps*, 102).

13. On anxieties about women's treatment in marriage, see Keetley, "Victim and Victimizer."

14. Phelps might also have thought, as did her second husband, that abolitionists were challenging a constitutionally sanctioned practice, and thus were undermining the rule of

law. The Phelpses left Vermont in 1838 after John Phelps, a member of the state legislature, found himself on the minority side of the debate on slavery. He maintained that "however it [slavery] was to be deplored, [it] was guaranteed to the southern states by the Constitution under which the General government of the United States has been formed" (quoted in Bolzau, *Almira Hart Lincoln Phelps*, 65).

15. Indeed, events in Phelps's own life made her wary of promoting intellectual activities at the expense of the physical. In 1832 her stepdaughter Lucy observes, "Mother writes a great deal, so much that I am afraid that she will injure her health" (quoted in ibid., 55). Lucy was right to worry: between 1831 and 1838 Phelps published at least five full-length books, resulting in a serious erosion of her health. Still, Phelps did not join the ranks of those who believed that women's schooling ruins their health. She insists, however, on using one's mind to maintain "a controlling power to alter and to correct" physical habits gone awry (*LYL*, 54).

16. Bolzau, *Almira Hart Lincoln Phelps*, 265; and Siffrin, "A History of Patapsco Female Institute," 58.

17. Phelps, "Essay on Female Education," 176.

18. Bolzau, *Almira Hart Lincoln Phelps*, 71–79.

19. Ibid., 178–92; the quotation from the *Howard Gazette* appears on p. 189.

20. On American editions of Blair's text, see Connors, *Composition-Rhetoric*, 73–75; for a treatment of the ideological context that gave rise to Blair's text, see Miller, *The Formation of College English*, 227–52.

21. Siffrin, "A History of Patapsco Female Institute," 94–95.

22. Bolzau, *Almira Hart Lincoln Phelps*, 179, 187–88.

23. Quoted in ibid., 170–71.

24. Ibid., 173.

25. Such a range was also practiced by Phelps herself, as well as by her husband. Her diaries, which spanned seventy-five years, were burned upon her death (ibid., 469). Phelps's husband, John, completed his *Family Memoirs* shortly before his death in 1849; it was published in 1886, two years after his wife's death.

26. Kinneavy, *A Theory of Discourse*, 393–444.

27. As was the practice at Troy Female Seminary, several slots at the imaginary Science Hall were held for "lottery" students who received scholarships. On arrangements at Troy, see Baym, *Feminism and American Literary History*, 125–28.

28. In the course of discussing botany in *Lectures*, Phelps laments that the great "medical knowledge" possessed by Native Americans "perished with themselves" because they had "no system for the classification or description of plants, nor any written language by which such a system might have been conveyed to others" (*LYL*, 211). And, according to Phelps, this lack of written language means histories of Indian life in the new nation have not survived: "ignorant of the arts of printing or writing," as Native Americans supposedly were, they "left no records of what they or their country once were" (*LYL*, 133). Both accounts rest on the unstated premise that by 1833 Indian tribal life is an artifact of the past. She represents the "disappearance" of Indians as an academic *fact* to be taught in the course of lectures on botany and ancient geography.

29. Baym, *Novels, Readers, and Reviewers*, 220. McHenry, "Forgotten Readers"; Williams, introduction to *Essays*, xl; Plato, *Essays*, 41; Beecher, *An Essay on Slavery and Abolitionism, with Reference to the Duty of American Females*; Grimké, *Letters to Catherine E. Beecher*.

30. Bolzau's exhaustive study of Phelps's published work turned up only one review of *The Blue Ribbon Society*. It appears, without attribution, in a Phelps scrapbook (Bolzau, *Almira Hart Lincoln Phelps*, 365).

7. Conclusion

1. Phelps, *Our Country*, viii, 378, 379.

2. In 1878 Forten married Francis Grimké, a Presbyterian minister, and took his last name (Stevenson, introduction to *The Journals of Charlotte Forten Grimké*, 51). A chronology of Grimké's life appears in appendix 1.

3. Phelps's letter to John P. Kennedy is quoted in Bolzau, *Almira Hart Lincoln Phelps*, 433.

4. Grimké, *The Journals of Charlotte Forten Grimké*, 509. Subsequent references appear by page number in the chapter.

5. Phelps, *Our Country*, 378.

6. Ibid., 379.

7. Forten received her primary education at home under the supervision of Margaretta Forten, her aunt, who taught at Sarah Mapps Douglass's private school (Davis, ed., "Charlotte Forten Grimké," 277).

8. Jacqueline Jones Royster's *Traces of a Stream* provides an excellent account of Forten's literacy work in the Sea Islands (143–52). See also Billington, ed., *The Journal of Charlotte L. Forten*, 20–29; Braxton, *Black Women Writing Autobiography*, 91–94; Cobb-Moore, "When Meanings Meet," 150–54; Peterson, *"Doers of the Word,"* 189–95; Stevenson, introduction to *The Journals of Charlotte Forten Grimké*, 37–49.

9. Von Frank, *The Trials of Anthony Burns*, 1–7.

10. Shepard began teaching in Salem at age sixteen and so was on the leading edge of a major gender shift in staffing of the city's schools. She probably attended the West School for Girls and began her career at the West School for Boys in 1840. She became principal of Higginson Grammar School (formerly West, the school she had attended as a girl) at the end of 1851, when she was twenty-seven. The curriculum for boys and girls was the same, with the exception of sewing, which was added at Salem's girls' schools in 1848. Shepard remained at Higginson for seventeen years, retiring in 1869 (Holmes, "Teaching in Salem, Massachusetts, 1830s–1860s," 15–16).

11. For a history of the Salem Normal School, see Pitman, "The Salem Normal School."

12. Von Frank describes the public unrest provoked by Burns's arrest as a "pocket revolution," one that "American historians had never mentioned." Invoking Hannah Arendt, he argues that "a revolution occurs when governmental policies are identified not just as despotic, but as simultaneously despotic and unnecessary or revisable." "The Burns case," he continues, "was at the heart of a revolution that had its own particular Bastille and riot, that toppled a government in Massachusetts, destroyed certain political parties, and extemporized others" (xii–xiii).

13. Purvis is quoted in Silcox, "Delay and Neglect," 461.

14. The disfranchisement of Pennsylvania's free people of color coincided with a general decline in the economic prospects of small-scale merchants and tradesmen, regardless of race. Thus Forten's father felt the double burden of reduced economic circumstances and increased racial discrimination (Peterson, *"Doers of the Word,"* 176–77; see also Blumin, "Mobility and Change in Ante-bellum Philadelphia"). During this time, free African Americans in the North responded to white racism and economic oppression in a

host of unusually resourceful—and effective—ways (see Horton and Horton, *In Hope of Liberty*).

15. James Forten is quoted in McHenry, "'Dreaded Eloquence,'" 54. McHenry and Heath remind us that "the portrayal of African American culture as oral has become unrelenting and has pushed aside facts surrounding other language uses—especially those related to reading and writing throughout African American history" ("The Literate and the Literary," 421). They document flourishing literary societies in Philadelphia and other large cities during the 1830s and somewhat later (425). For McHenry, this activity is tied to "civic responsibility" of the sort that James Forten advocated and that his children and grandchildren found increasingly difficult to practice ("Forgotten Readers," 156).

16. Kaestle, *Pillars of the Republic*, 177; Fletcher, "Opinion of the Hon. Richard Fletcher," 328; Stevenson, introduction to *The Journals of Charlotte Forten Grimké*, 31; Holmes, "Teaching in Salem, Massachusetts, 1830s–1860s," 15.

17. The school report is quoted in Holmes, "Teaching in Salem, Massachusetts, 1830s–1860s," 17, 18.

18. *Annals of Congress*, 6th Cong., 1st sess., 231.

19. Forten's "Parting Hymn" is quoted in Billington, ed., *The Journal of Charlotte L. Forten*, 219.

20. Wheaton and Condit, "Charles Lenox Remond," 308.

21. Lasser and Merrill, eds., *Friends and Sisters*, 9–10.

22. See Forten, "A Late Bill before the Senate of Pennsylvania." Bacon discusses the special problems that faced African American orators like James Forten as they spoke about rights and freedom. The shift from "adaptory" to "advisory" rhetoric in the antebellum period marks a turn away from black speakers' willingness to invoke documents such as the Declaration of Independence as common ground with audiences. Instead, speakers increasingly chose to advise audiences of their complicity in using the rhetoric of freedom to cover gross social and economic inequality ("'Do You Understand Your Own Language?'" 55–56). But advisory rhetoric did not always move its audiences: according to Bacon, "Many abolitionists . . . began to endorse . . . violence as they perceived the limits of their rhetoric" (65). Further, Bacon and McClish detail the rhetorical activity sponsored by various community organizations in antebellum Philadelphia with which Forten would likely have been familiar ("Reinventing the Master's Tools"; see also Bacon, "Taking Liberty, Taking Literacy").

23. Robertson, *Parker Pillsbury*, 114. Pillsbury is quoted in Robertson, 115.

24. The relevant syllabi from the Salem Lyceum are reproduced in Cameron, ed., *The Massachusetts Lyceum during the American Renaissance*, 20–21.

25. Cameron, ed., *The Massachusetts Lyceum during the American Renaissance*, 24.

26. Emerson's position in the abolitionist movement has been reevaluated of late. As Von Frank summarizes, "There has been for some time a tendency in academic circles to discount or deplore the social, moral, and ideological implications of Transcendentalism, and to regard Emerson himself as uncommitted to reform or as dissuaded from action by unattractive, privately held racial views" (xiii). The power of such criticism diminishes when we recognize the "high estimation in which Emerson was held at the time by abolitionist leaders, and then look a little less at what Emerson said and a little more at the evidence of his influence on the culture of antislavery" (xvii).

27. Gougeon, *Virtue's Hero*, 189–90, 232, 235; Emerson is quoted in Broaddus, *Genteel Rhetoric*, 55.

28. Peterson notes that Remond and Forten may have been jealous of one another's success, hence the former's disdain for "Glimpses" (*"Doers of the Word,"* 186).

29. Huntington, *Christian Believing and Living*, 40, 54; Broaddus, *Genteel Rhetoric*, 55.

30. Blair, *Lectures on Rhetoric and Belles Lettres*, 1:23.

31. Bator, "The 'Principle of Sympathy' in Campbell's *Philosophy of Rhetoric*," 420. This is not to ignore the possibility of a "civic function" in Blair's formulation of taste (see Agnew, "The Civic Function of Taste"). It is simply to say that Forten's own understanding of sympathy in relation to literature resonates with readings of Blair that do not foreground a civic function.

32. Campbell, *Philosophy of Rhetoric*, 132; Burks, "The Most Significant Passage in George Campbell's *Philosophy of Rhetoric*," 16; Bator, "The 'Principle of Sympathy' in Campbell's *Philosophy of Rhetoric*," 422, 423, 424.

33. Holmes, "Teaching in Salem, Massachusetts, 1830s–1860s," 24; see also Neitz, *Old Textbooks*, 92–93.

34. See, for example, Braxton, *Black Women Writing Autobiography*, 95; Peterson, *"Doers of the Word,"* 185.

35. See Rose, *Rehearsal for Reconstruction*.

36. Forten, "Life on the Sea Islands," 591, 676.

37. Forten's poem is quoted in Billington, ed., *The Journal of Charlotte L. Forten*, 221.

38. *Proceedings at the Quarter-Centennial Celebration of the State Normal School*, 48.

39. Davidson, "Preface: No More Separate Spheres," 456; Romero, *Home Fronts*, 5.

Appendix 1

Sources: Harris, introduction to *Selected Writings of Judith Sargent Murray*, xv; Skemp, *Judith Sargent Murray*, 11–12, 191–93; Marchione, "Hannah Foster"; Pettengill, "Hannah Webster Foster (1758–1840)," 134; Allaback, "The Writings of Louisa Tuthill," 6, 44, 47; Bolzau, *Almira Hart Lincoln Phelps*, 2, 7, 24–25, 26, 28–29, 33, 34, 36, 37–38, 42–43, 47, 48–49, 50, 51, 53, 63, 86, 97, 110, 118–19, 197, 198, 365, 382, 445, 469, 499, 500, 501, 502; Stevenson, introduction to *The Journals of Charlotte Forten Grimké*, xxxiii–xl.

Appendix 2

Source: Foster, *The Boarding School*, 30–35. Most eighteenth-century typographical conventions have been updated.

Appendix 3

Source: Murray [Constantia, pseud.], *The Gleaner*, 2:230–39. Most eighteenth-century typographical conventions have been updated.

Appendix 4

Source: Tuthill, *The Young Lady's Home*, 72–77.

Appendix 5

Source: Phelps, *Lectures to Young Ladies*, 249–64.

Bibliography

Agnew, Lois. "The Civic Function of Taste: A Re-assessment of Hugh Blair's Rhetorical Theory." *Rhetoric Society Quarterly* 28, no. 2 (1998): 25–36.

Allaback, Sarah. "The Writings of Louisa Tuthill: Cultivating Architectural Taste in Nineteenth-Century America." Ph.D. diss., Massachusetts Institute of Technology, 1993.

"American Women." Review of *Means and Ends*, by Catharine Maria Sedgwick. *The United States Magazine and Democratic Review* 6, no. 20 (1839): 127–42.

Anderson, James D. *The Education of Blacks in the South, 1860–1935*. Chapel Hill, N.C.: University of North Carolina Press, 1988.

Annals of the Congress of the United States, 1789–1824. 42 vols. Washington, D.C., 1834–56.

Bacon, Jacqueline. "'Do You Understand Your Own Language?' Revolutionary *Topoi* in the Rhetoric of African-American Abolitionists." *Rhetoric Society Quarterly* 28, no. 2 (1998): 55–75.

———. "Taking Liberty, Taking Literacy: Signifying in the Rhetoric of African-American Abolitionists." *The Southern Communication Journal* 64 (1999): 271–87.

Bacon, Jacqueline, and Glen McClish. "Reinventing the Master's Tools: Nineteenth-Century African-American Literary Societies of Philadelphia and Rhetorical Education." *Rhetoric Society Quarterly* 30, no. 4 (2000): 19–47.

Baron, Dennis E. *Grammar and Good Taste: Reforming the American Language*. New Haven: Yale University Press, 1982.

Bator, Paul G. "The 'Principle of Sympathy' in Campbell's *Philosophy of Rhetoric*." *The Quarterly Journal of Speech* 68 (1982): 418–24.

Baym, Nina. *American Women Writers and the Work of History, 1790–1860*. New Brunswick, N.J.: Rutgers University Press, 1995.

———. *Feminism and American Literary History: Essays*. New Brunswick, N.J.: Rutgers University Press, 1992.

———. Introduction to *The Gleaner*, by Judith Sargent Murray. Schenectady, N.Y.: Union College Press, 1992.

———. *Novels, Readers, and Reviewers: Responses to Fiction in Antebellum America*. Ithaca, N.Y.: Cornell University Press, 1984.

———. *Woman's Fiction: A Guide to Novels by and about Women in America, 1820–70*. 2d ed. Urbana, Ill.: University of Illinois Press, 1993.

Beecher, Catharine E. *Educational Reminiscences and Suggestions*. New York: J. B. Ford, 1874.

———. *An Essay on Slavery and Abolitionism, with Reference to the Duty of American Females*. Philadelphia: Perkins, 1837.

Berlin, James A. *Writing Instruction in Nineteenth-Century American Colleges.* Carbondale, Ill.: Southern Illinois University Press, 1984.

Berliner, David C., and Bruce J. Biddle. *The Manufactured Crisis: Myths, Fraud, and the Attack on America's Public Schools.* Reading, Mass.: Addison-Wesley, 1995.

Bettig, Ronald V. "Critical Perspectives on the History and Philosophy of Copyright." *Critical Studies in Mass Communication* 9 (1992): 131–55.

Billington, Ray Allen, ed. *The Journal of Charlotte L. Forten.* New York: Dryden Press, 1953.

Bingham, Caleb. *The American Preceptor.* Boston: Manning and Loring, 1794.

Bizzell, Patricia. "Feminist Methods of Research in the History of Rhetoric: What Difference Do They Make?" *Rhetoric Society Quarterly* 30, no. 4 (2000): 5–17.

———. "Opportunities for Feminist Research in the History of Rhetoric." *Rhetoric Review* 11 (1992): 50–58.

Blair, Hugh. *Lectures on Rhetoric and Belles Lettres.* Edited by Harold F. Harding. 2 vols. Carbondale, Ill.: Southern Illinois University Press, 1965.

Blumin, Stuart. "Mobility and Change in Ante-bellum Philadelphia." In *Nineteenth-Century Cities: Essays in the New Urban History,* edited by Stephan Thernstrom and Richard Sennett, 165–208. New Haven: Yale University Press, 1969.

Bolzau, Emma Lydia. "Almira Hart Lincoln Phelps: Her Life and Work." Ph.D. diss., University of Pennsylvania, 1936.

Boydston, Jeanne, Mary Kelley, and Anne Margolis. *The Limits of Sisterhood: The Beecher Sisters on Women's Rights and Woman's Sphere.* Chapel Hill, N.C.: University of North Carolina Press, 1988.

Braxton, Joanne M. *Black Women Writing Autobiography: A Tradition within a Tradition.* Philadelphia: Temple University Press, 1989.

Brickley, Lynne Templeton. "Sarah Pierce's Litchfield Female Academy, 1792–1833." Ph.D. diss., Harvard University, 1985.

Broaddus, Dorothy C. *Genteel Rhetoric: Writing High Culture in Nineteenth-Century Boston.* Columbia, S.C.: University of South Carolina Press, 1999.

Brock, William R. *Scotus Americanus: A Survey of the Sources for Links between Scotland and America in the Eighteenth Century.* Edinburgh: Edinburgh University Press, 1982.

Brown, Herbert R. "Richardson and Sterne in the *Massachusetts Magazine.*" *The New England Quarterly* 5 (1932): 65–82.

Brown, Richard D. *Knowledge Is Power: The Diffusion of Information in Early America, 1700–1865.* New York: Oxford University Press, 1989.

Bugbee, Bruce W. *Genesis of American Patent and Copyright Law.* Washington, D.C.: Public Affairs Press, 1967.

Burgett, Bruce. *Sentimental Bodies: Sex, Gender, and Citizenship in the Early Republic.* Princeton: Princeton University Press, 1998.

Burks, Don M. "The Most Significant Passage in George Campbell's *Philosophy of Rhetoric.*" *Rhetoric Society Quarterly* 13 (1983): 15–17.

Cameron, Kenneth Walter, ed. *The Massachusetts Lyceum during the American Renaissance.* Hartford, Conn.: Transcendental Books, 1969.

Campbell, George. *The Philosophy of Rhetoric.* Edited by Lloyd F. Bitzer. Carbondale, Ill.: Southern Illinois University Press, 1963.

Campbell, Karlyn Kohrs, ed. *Man Cannot Speak for Her*. 2 vols. New York: Greenwood, 1989.

Carson, Albana. "Imperfections of Female Education." File 13, Science Hill Female Academy Papers. Filson Club Historical Society. Louisville, Ky.

Cash, Arthur H. *Laurence Sterne: The Early and Middle Years*. London: Methuen, 1975.

Chapone, Mrs. [Hester]. *Letters on the Improvement of the Mind*. 2 vols. 5th ed. Boston: Thomas, 1783.

Chibka, Robert L. "The Stranger within Young's *Conjectures*." *ELH* 53 (1986): 541–65.

Clark, Gregory, and S. Michael Halloran. Introduction to *Oratorical Culture in Nineteenth-Century America: Transformations in the Theory and Practice of Rhetoric*, edited by Gregory Clark and S. Michael Halloran. Carbondale, Ill.: Southern Illinois University Press, 1993.

Clarke, Norma. *Ambitious Heights: Writing, Friendship, Love—The Jewsbury Sisters, Felicia Hemans, and Jane Welsh Carlyle*. London: Routledge, 1990.

Cobb-Moore, Geneva. "When Meanings Meet: *The Journals of Charlotte Forten Grimké*." In *Inscribing the Daily: Critical Essays on Women's Diaries*, edited by Suzanne L. Bunkers and Cynthia A. Huff, 139–55. Amherst, Mass.: University of Massachusetts Press, 1996.

Coleman, Michael C. *American Indian Children at School, 1850–1930*. Jackson, Miss.: University Press of Mississippi, 1993.

The Complete Letter-Writer. 2d ed. New York: Folsom, 1790.

Connors, Robert J. *Composition-Rhetoric: Backgrounds, Theory, and Pedagogy*. Pittsburgh: University of Pittsburgh Press, 1997.

———. "Frances Wright: First Female Civic Rhetor in America." *College English* 62 (1999): 30–57.

———. "The Rise and Fall of the Modes of Discourse." *College Composition and Communication* 32 (1981): 444–55.

Cook, Beverly Blair. "Women Judges: The End of Tokenism." In *Women in the Courts*, edited by Winifred L. Hepperle and Laura Crites, 84–105. Williamsburg, Va.: National Center for State Courts, 1978.

Crane, Elaine F. "Dealing with Dependence: Paternalism and Tax Evasion in Eighteenth-Century Rhode Island." In *Women and the Law: A Social Historical Perspective*, edited by D. Kelly Weisberg, 27–44. Vol. 1, *Women and the Criminal Law*. Cambridge, Mass.: Schenkman, 1982.

Cremin, Lawrence A. *American Education: The National Experience, 1783–1876*. New York: Harper and Row, 1980.

———. *The Transformation of the School: Progressivism in American Education, 1876–1957*. New York: Knopf, 1961; New York: Vintage, 1964.

Crowley, Sharon. *Composition in the University: Historical and Polemical Essays*. Pittsburgh: University of Pittsburgh Press, 1998.

Curran, Stuart. "Romantic Poetry: The I Altered." In *Romanticism and Feminism*, edited by Anne K. Mellor, 185–207. Bloomington, Ind.: Indiana University Press, 1988.

Davidson, Cathy N. "Preface: No More Separate Spheres!" *American Literature* 70 (1998): 443–63.

————. *Revolution and the Word: The Rise of the Novel in America*. New York: Oxford University Press, 1986.

Davis, Marianna W., ed. "Charlotte Forten Grimké." In *Contributions of Black Women to America*, 277–79. Vol. 2, *Civil Rights, Politics and Government, Education, Medicine, Sciences*. Columbia, S.C.: Kenday Press, 1982.

De Grazia, Margreta. "Sanctioning Voice: Quotation Marks, the Abolition of Torture, and the Fifth Amendment." In *The Construction of Authorship: Textual Appropriation in Law and Literature*, edited by Martha Woodmansee and Peter Jaszi, 281–302. Durham, N.C.: Duke University Press, 1994.

Ehrenreich, Barbara, and Deirdre English. *For Her Own Good: One Hundred Fifty Years of the Experts' Advice to Women*. New York: Anchor, 1978.

Eldred, Janet Carey, and Peter Mortensen. "Gender and Writing Instruction in Early America: Lessons from Didactic Fiction." *Rhetoric Review* 12 (1993): 25–53.

————. "Monitoring Columbia's Daughters: Writing as Gendered Conduct." *Rhetoric Society Quarterly* 23, nos. 3-4 (1993): 46–69.

————. "'Persuasion Dwelt on Her Tongue': Female Civic Rhetoric in Early America." *College English* 60 (1998): 173–88.

————. "Reading Literacy Narratives." *College English* 54 (1992): 512–39.

Enos, Richard Leo. "Recovering the Lost Art of Researching the History of Rhetoric." *Rhetoric Society Quarterly* 29, no. 4 (1999): 7–20.

Faulkner, William. *Absalom, Absalom!* 1936. Reprint, New York: Vintage, 1972.

Ferguson, Robert A. *Law and Letters in American Culture*. Cambridge: Harvard University Press, 1984.

Field, Vena Bernadette. *Constantia: A Study of the Life and Works of Judith Sargent Murray, 1751–1820*. University of Maine Studies, 2d. ser., no. 17. Orono, Maine: University Press, 1931.

Finley, Ruth E. *The Lady of Godey's: Sarah Josepha Hale*. Philadelphia: Lippincott, 1931.

Fletcher, Richard. "Opinion of the Hon. Richard Fletcher, on the Rights of Colored Children in Common Schools." *The Common School Journal* 6 (1844): 326–28.

Fliegelman, Jay. *Prodigals and Pilgrims: The American Revolution against Patriarchal Authority, 1750–1800*. Cambridge: Cambridge University Press, 1982.

Forten, Charlotte. *The Journals of Charlotte Forten Grimké*. Edited by Brenda Stevenson. New York: Oxford University Press, 1988.

————. "Life on the Sea Islands." Parts 1 and 2. *Atlantic Monthly* 13 (1864): 587–96, 666–76.

Forten, James. "A Late Bill before the Senate of Pennsylvania." In *Negro Orators and Their Orations*, edited by Carter G. Woodson, 42–51. 1925. Reprint, New York: Russell and Russell, 1969.

[Foster, Hannah Webster]. *The Boarding School*. Boston: Thomas and Andrews, 1798.

Fraser, Donald. *The Columbian Monitor*. New York: Loudon and Brower, [1794].

————. *The Mental Flower-Garden*. Danbury, Conn.: Douglas and Nichols, 1800.

————. *The Mental Flower Garden*. 2d ed. New York: Southwick and Hardcastle, 1807.

————. *The Young Gentleman and Lady's Assistant*. New York: Greenleaf, 1791.

Friedman, Jane M. *America's First Woman Lawyer: The Biography of Myra Bradwell.* Buffalo: Prometheus Books, 1993.

Gale, Xin Liu. "Historical Studies and Postmodernism: Rereading Aspasia of Miletus." *College English* 62 (2000): 361–86.

Gere, Anne Ruggles. *Intimate Practices: Literacy and Cultural Work in U.S. Women's Clubs, 1880–1920.* Urbana, Ill.: University of Illinois Press, 1997.

———. "Kitchen Tables and Rented Rooms: The Extracurriculum of Composition." *College Composition and Communication* 45 (1994): 75–92.

Gilmore, William J. *Reading Becomes a Necessity of Life: Material and Cultural Life in Rural New England, 1780–1835.* Knoxville, Tenn.: University of Tennessee Press, 1989.

Giroux, Henry A. "Liberal Arts Education and the Struggle for Public Life: Dreaming about Democracy." *South Atlantic Quarterly* 89 (1990): 113–38.

Glenn, Cheryl. "Comment: Truth, Lies, and Method: Revisiting Feminist Historiography." *College English* 62 (2000): 387–89.

Gold, Ellen Reid. "The Grimké Sisters and the Emergence of the Woman's Rights Movement." *The Southern Speech Communication Journal* 46 (1981): 341–60.

Golden, James L., and Edward P. J. Corbett, eds. *The Rhetoric of Blair, Campbell, and Whately.* New York: Holt, Rinehart and Winston, 1968. Reprint, with updated bibliographies, Carbondale, Ill.: Southern Illinois University Press, 1990.

Gougeon, Len. *Virtue's Hero: Emerson, Antislavery, and Reform.* Athens, Ga.: University of Georgia Press, 1990.

Graff, Harvey J. *The Legacies of Literacy: Continuities and Contradictions in Western Culture and Society.* Bloomington, Ind.: Indiana University Press, 1987.

Granger, Bruce. "The Massachusetts Magazine." In *American Literary Magazines: The Eighteenth and Nineteenth Centuries,* edited by Edward E. Chielens, 244–50. New York: Greenwood Press, 1986.

Graves, Mrs. A. J. *Girlhood and Womanhood; or, Sketches of My Schoolmates.* Boston: Carter and Mussey, 1844.

———. *Woman in America; Being an Examination into the Moral and Intellectual Condition of American Female Society.* New York: Harper and Brothers, 1841.

Grimké, Angelina Emily. *Letters to Catherine Beecher.* 1838. Reprint, New York: Arno Press, 1969.

Grimké, Charlotte Forten. *The Journals of Charlotte Forten Grimké.* Edited by Brenda Stevenson. New York: Oxford University Press, 1988.

Gustafson, Sandra M. *Eloquence Is Power: Oratory and Performance in Early America.* Chapel Hill, N.C.: University of North Carolina Press, 2000.

Gustafson, Thomas. *Representative Words: Politics, Literature, and the American Language, 1776–1865.* Cambridge: Cambridge University Press, 1992.

Guthrie, Warren. "The Development of Rhetorical Theory in America." Parts 1–5. *Speech Monographs* 13, no. 1 (1946): 14–22; 14 (1947): 38–54; 15 (1948): 61–71; 16 (1949): 98–113; 18 (1951): 17–30.

Hale, Mrs. [Sarah Josepha]. *The Lecturess; or, Woman's Sphere.* Boston: Whipple and Damrell, 1839.

———. *Woman's Record; or, Sketches of All Distinguished Women, from the Creation to A.D. 1868.* 3d ed. New York: Harper and Brothers, 1870.

[Hale, Mrs. Sarah Josepha]. "The 'Conversazióne.'" *The Lady's Book* 14 (1837): 1–5.

[Hale, Mrs. Sarah Josepha?]. "Boarding Schools." *Ladies' Magazine* 4 (1831): 145–54.

————. "The End and Aim of the Present System of Female Education." *American Ladies' Magazine* 8 (1835): 61–78.

Halloran, S. Michael. "From Rhetoric to Composition: The Teaching of Writing in America to 1900." In *A Short History of Writing Instruction: From Ancient Greece to Twentieth-Century America*, edited by James J. Murphy, 151–82. Davis, Calif.: Hermagoras, 1990.

Harris, Sharon M. Introduction to *Selected Writings of Judith Sargent Murray*, edited by Sharon M. Harris. New York: Oxford University Press, 1995.

Hart, John S. *Female Prose Writers of America*. 3d ed. Philadelphia: E. H. Butler, 1857.

Haswell, Richard H., and Min-Zhan Lu, eds. *Comp Tales: An Introduction to College Composition through Its Stories*. New York: Longman, 2000.

Heath, Shirley Brice. "Toward an Ethnohistory of Writing in American Education." In *Variation in Writing: Functional and Linguistic-Cultural Differences*, edited by Marcia Farr Whiteman, 25–45. Vol. 1, *Writing: The Nature, Development, and Teaching of Written Communication*. Hillsdale, N.J.: Lawrence Erlbaum, 1981.

Hendrick, Robert. "Ever-Widening Circle or Mask of Oppression?: Almira Phelps's Role in Nineteenth-Century American Female Education." *History of Education* 24 (1995): 293–304.

Herndl, Diane Price. *Invalid Women: Figuring Feminine Illness in American Fiction and Culture, 1840–1940*. Chapel Hill, N.C.: University of North Carolina Press, 1993.

Hobbs, Catherine. Introduction to *Nineteenth-Century Women Learn to Write*, edited by Catherine Hobbs. Charlottesville, Va.: University Press of Virginia, 1995.

Hobby, Elaine. *Virtue of Necessity: English Women's Writing, 1649–88*. Ann Arbor, Mich.: University of Michigan Press, 1989.

Hoff, Joan. *Law, Gender, and Injustice: A Legal History of U.S. Women*. New York: New York University Press, 1991.

Hoffman, Ronald, and Peter J. Albert, eds. *Women in the Age of the American Revolution*. Charlottesville, Va.: University Press of Virginia, 1989.

Holmes, Madelyn. "Teaching in Salem, Massachusetts, 1830s–1860s: Mary Lakeman Shepard and Mary Jane Fitz." In *Lives of Women Public Schoolteachers: Scenes from American Educational History*, by Madelyn Holmes and Beverly J. Weiss, 13–30. New York: Garland, 1995.

Horner, Winifred Bryan. *Nineteenth-Century Scottish Rhetoric: The American Connection*. Carbondale, Ill.: Southern Illinois University Press, 1993.

Horner, Winifred Bryan, and Kerri Morris Barton. "The Eighteenth Century." In *The Present State of Scholarship in Historical and Contemporary Rhetoric*, edited by Winifred Bryan Horner, 114–50. Rev. ed. Columbia, Mo.: University of Missouri Press, 1990.

Horton, James Oliver, and Lois E. Horton. *In Hope of Liberty: Culture, Community, and Protest among Northern Free Blacks, 1700–1860*. New York: Oxford University Press, 1997.

Huntington, F. D. *Christian Believing and Living*. Boston: Crosby, Nichols, and Company, 1859.

Jacoba, Madelon. "Prose Writings and Dramas of Judith Sargent Murray: Nurturing at New Republic." Ph.D. diss., Purdue University, 1987.

Jarratt, Susan C. "Comment: Rhetoric and Feminism: Together Again." *College English* 62 (2000): 390–93.

———. *Rereading the Sophists: Classical Rhetoric Refigured.* Carbondale, Ill.: Southern Illinois University Press, 1991.

Jasinski, James. "The Feminization of Liberty, Domesticated Virtue, and the Reconstitution of Power and Authority in Early American Political Discourse." *The Quarterly Journal of Speech* 79 (1993): 146–64.

Johnson, Nan. *Nineteenth-Century Rhetoric in North America.* Carbondale, Ill.: Southern Illinois University Press, 1991.

Johnson, Samuel. "No. 143. Tuesday, 30 July 1751." *The Rambler,* edited by W. J. Bate and Albrecht B. Strauss, 393–401. Vol. 4, *The Yale Edition of the Works of Samuel Johnson.* New Haven: Yale University Press, 1969.

Jordan, Cynthia S. *Second Stories: The Politics of Language, Form, and Gender in Early American Fictions.* Chapel Hill, N.C.: University of North Carolina Press, 1989.

Kaestle, Carl F. *The Evolution of an Urban School System: New York City, 1750–1850.* Cambridge: Harvard University Press, 1973.

———. *Pillars of the Republic: Common Schools and American Society, 1780–1860.* New York: Hill and Wang, 1983.

Kaestle, Carl F., Helen Damon-Moore, Lawrence C. Stedman, Katherine Tinsley, and William Vance Trollinger, Jr. *Literacy in the United States: Readers and Reading since 1880.* New Haven: Yale University Press, 1991.

Keetley, Dawn. "Victim and Victimizer: Female Fiends and Unease over Marriage in Antebellum Sensational Fiction." *American Quarterly* 51 (1999): 344–84.

Kelley, Mary. *Private Woman, Public Stage: Literary Domesticity in Nineteenth-Century America.* New York: Oxford University Press, 1984.

Kerber, Linda K. "'History Can Do It No Justice': Women and the Reinterpretation of the American Revolution." In *Women in the Age of the American Revolution,* edited by Ronald Hoffman and Peter J. Albert, 3–42. Charlottesville, Va.: University Press of Virginia, 1989.

———. "Separate Spheres, Female Worlds, Woman's Place: The Rhetoric of Women's History." *Journal of American History* 75 (1988): 9–39.

———. *Women of the Republic: Intellect and Ideology in Revolutionary America.* Chapel Hill, N.C.: University of North Carolina Press, 1980.

Kett, Joseph F. *The Pursuit of Knowledge under Difficulties: From Self-Improvement to Adult Education in America, 1750–1990.* Stanford, Calif.: Stanford University Press, 1994.

Kinneavy, James L. *A Theory of Discourse: The Aims of Discourse.* Englewood Cliffs, N.J.: Prentice Hall, 1971; New York: Norton, 1980.

Koenigsberg, Lisa. "Arbiter of Taste: Mrs. L. C. Tuthill and a Tradition of American Women Writers on Architecture, 1848–1913." *Women's Studies* 14 (1988): 339–66.

Kolodny, Annette. "Inventing a Feminist Discourse: Rhetoric and Resistance in Margaret Fuller's *Woman in the Nineteenth Century.*" *New Literary History* 25 (1994): 355–82.

———. "Letting Go Our Grand Obsessions: Notes toward a New Literary History of the American Frontiers." *American Literature* 64 (1992): 1–18.

Korobkin, Laura Hanft. *Criminal Conversations: Sentimentality and Nineteenth-Century Legal Stories of Adultery.* New York: Columbia University Press, 1998.

Kramer, Michael P. *Imagining Language in America: From the Revolution to the Civil War.* Princeton: Princeton University Press, 1992.

Kritzer, Amelia Howe. "Playing with Republican Motherhood: Self-Representation in Plays by Susanna Haswell Rowson and Judith Sargent Murray." *Early American Literature* 31 (1996): 150–66.

Lasser, Carol, and Marlene Deahl Merrill, eds. *Friends and Sisters: Letters between Lucy Stone and Antoinette Brown Blackwell, 1846–93.* Urbana, Ill.: University of Illinois Press, 1987.

Lebsock, Suzanne. *The Free Women of Petersburg: Status and Culture in a Southern Town, 1784–1860.* New York: Norton, 1984.

Lindey, Alexander. *Plagiarism and Originality.* New York: Harper and Brothers, 1952.

Lockridge, Kenneth A. *Literacy in Colonial New England: An Enquiry into the Social Context of Literacy in the Early Modern West.* New York: Norton, 1974.

Logan, Shirley Wilson. *"We Are Coming": The Persuasive Discourse of Nineteenth-Century Black Women.* Carbondale, Ill.: Southern Illinois University Press, 1999.

Mallon, Thomas. *Stolen Words: Forays into the Origins and Ravages of Plagiarism.* New York: Ticknor and Fields, 1989.

Marchione, William. "Hannah Foster: Brighton's Pioneer Novelist." *Brighton Allston Historical Society,* <http://www.bahistory.org/bahfoster.html>, accessed 12 January 2001.

Mason, Priscilla. "The Salutatory Oration of Miss Priscilla Mason to the Young Ladies Academy at Philadelphia, May 15, 1793." In *Women in American Law,* edited by Marlene Stein Wortman, 102–3. Vol. 1. New York: Holmes and Meier, 1985.

McHenry, Elizabeth. "'Dreaded Eloquence': The Origins and Rise of African American Literary Societies and Libraries." *Harvard Library Bulletin,* n.s., 6, no. 2 (1995): 32–56.

———. "Forgotten Readers: African-American Literary Societies and the American Scene." In *Print Culture in a Diverse America,* edited by James P. Danky and Wayne A. Wiegand, 149–72. Urbana, Ill.: University of Illinois Press, 1998.

McHenry, Elizabeth, and Shirley Brice Heath. "The Literate and the Literary: African Americans as Writers and Readers, 1830–1940." *Written Communication* 11 (1994): 419–44.

Melder, Keith. "Mask of Oppression: The Female Seminary Movement in the United States." *New York History* 55 (1974): 261–79.

Mellor, Anne K. "On Romanticism and Feminism." In *Romanticism and Feminism,* edited by Anne K. Mellor, 3–9. Bloomington, Ind.: Indiana University Press, 1988.

Miller, Susan. "The Feminization of Composition." In *The Politics of Writing Instruction: Postsecondary,* edited by Richard Bullock and John Trimbur, 39–53. Portsmouth, N.H.: Heinemann, Boynton/Cook, 1991.

Miller, Thomas P. *The Formation of College English: Rhetoric and Belles Lettres in the British Cultural Provinces.* Pittsburgh: University of Pittsburgh Press, 1997.

Monaghan, E. Jennifer. "Family Literacy in Early Eighteenth-Century Boston: Cotton Mather and His Children." *Reading Research Quarterly* 26 (1991) 342–70.

———. "Literacy Instruction and Gender in Colonial New England." In *Reading in America: Literature and Social History,* edited by Cathy N. Davidson, 53–80. Baltimore: Johns Hopkins University Press, 1989.

Morrison, Toni. *Playing in the Dark: Whiteness and the Literary Imagination.* Cambridge: Harvard University Press, 1992.

Murray, Judith Sargent. *The Gleaner.* 1798. Reprint, Schenectady, N.Y.: Union College Press, 1992.

———. Papers. Mississippi Department of Archives and History. Jackson, Miss. Microfilm, University of Kentucky Library.

Murray, Judith Sargent [Constantia, pseud.]. *The Gleaner.* 3 vols. Boston: Thomas and Andrews, 1798.

Nelson, Dana D. *The Word in Black and White: Reading "Race" in American Literature, 1638–1867.* New York: Oxford University Press, 1992.

Newton, Sarah Emily. "Wise and Foolish Virgins: 'Usable Fiction' and the Early American Conduct Tradition." *Early American Literature* 25 (1990): 139–67.

Nienkamp, Jean, and Andrea Collins. Introduction to *Female Quixotism,* by Tabitha Gilman Tenney. New York: Oxford University Press, 1992.

Nietz, John A. *Old Textbooks.* Pittsburgh: University of Pittsburgh Press, 1961.

North, Stephen M. *The Making of Knowledge in Composition: Portrait of an Emerging Field.* Portsmouth, N.H.: Heinemann, Boynton/Cook, 1987.

Norton, Mary Beth. *Liberty's Daughters: The Revolutionary Experience of American Women, 1750–1800.* Boston: Little, Brown, 1980.

O'Neill, Lois Decker, ed. *The Women's Book of World Records and Achievements.* New York: Da Capo Press, 1979.

Okker, Patricia. *Our Sister Editors: Sarah J. Hale and the Tradition of Nineteenth-Century American Women Editors.* Athens, Ga.: University of Georgia Press, 1995.

Paine, Charles. *The Resistant Writer: Rhetoric as Immunity, 1850 to the Present.* Albany, N.Y.: State University of New York Press, 1999.

Patterson, Lyman Ray. *Copyright in Historical Perspective.* Nashville, Tenn.: Vanderbilt University Press, 1968.

Perlmann, Joel, and Dennis Shirley. "When Did New England Women Acquire Literacy?" *The William and Mary Quarterly,* 3d ser., 48 (1991): 50–67.

Peterson, Carla L. *"Doers of the Word": African-American Women Speakers and Writers in the North (1830–1880).* New York: Oxford University Press, 1995.

Pettengill, Claire C. "Hannah Webster Foster (1758–1840)." *Legacy* 12 (1995): 133–41.

Phelps, John. *Family Memoirs: Written at Patapsco, Maryland, about Two Years before His Death, in 1849.* Brattleboro, Vt.: Selleck and Davis, 1886.

Phelps, Mrs. [Almira Hart] Lincoln. *The Blue Ribbon Society: For Young Folks and Their Parents.* Parts 1–5. *The Star and Sentinel* (Gettysburg, Penn.): 20 August 1869; 27 August 1869; 3 September 1869; 10 September 1869; 17 September 1869.

———. "Essay on Female Education." In *Transactions of the Eighth Annual Meeting of the Western Literary Institute and College of Professional Teachers,* 174–79. Cincinnati: Allbach, 1839.

————. *The Fireside Friend, or Female Student*. Boston: Marsh, Capen, Lyon, and Webb, 1840.

————. "Hints about Periodicals," *American Ladies' Magazine* 9 (1836): 665–72.

————. *Hours with My Pupils: or, Educational Addresses, etc.* New York: Scribner, 1859.

————. *Ida Norman; or, Trials and Their Uses*. 2 vols. in 1. New York: Sheldon, Lamport and Blakeman, 1854.

————. *Lectures to Young Ladies*. Boston: Carter, Hendee, 1833.

Phelps, Mrs. [Almira Hart] Lincoln, ed. *Our Country, in Its Relations to the Past, Present and Future: A National Book*. Baltimore: Toy, 1864.

Pitman, J. Asbury. "The Salem Normal School: Past, Present, and Future." *The Elementary School Journal* 30 (1930): 416–30.

Plato, Ann. *Essays; Including Biographies and Miscellaneous Pieces, in Prose and Poetry*. New York: Oxford University Press, 1988.

Poulakos, John. *Sophistical Rhetoric in Classical Greece*. Columbia, S.C.: University of South Carolina Press, 1995.

Proceedings at the Quarter-Centennial Celebration of the State Normal School at Salem, Mass. Salem: Observer, 1880.

Reid, Ronald F. "The Boylston Professorship of Rhetoric and Oratory, 1806–1904: A Case Study in Changing Concepts of Rhetoric and Pedagogy." *The Quarterly Journal of Speech* 45 (1959): 239–57.

Richards, Jeffrey H. "How to Write an American Play: Murray's *Traveller Returned* and Its Sources." *Early American Literature* 33 (1998): 277–90.

Robertson, Stacey M. *Parker Pillsbury: Radical Abolitionist, Male Feminist*. Ithaca, N.Y.: Cornell University Press, 2000.

Romero, Lora. *Home Fronts: Domesticity and Its Critics in the Antebellum United States*. Durham, N.C.: Duke University Press, 1997.

Rose, Mark. "The Author in Court: *Pope v. Curll* (1741)." In *The Construction of Authorship: Textual Appropriation in Law and Literature*, edited by Martha Woodmansee and Peter Jaszi, 211–29. Durham, N.C.: Duke University Press, 1994.

————. *Authors and Owners: The Invention of Copyright*. Cambridge: Harvard University Press, 1993.

Rose, Willie Lee. *Rehearsal for Reconstruction: The Port Royal Experiment*. Indianapolis: Bobbs-Merrill, 1964.

Rosenthal, Laura J. "The Author as Ghost in the Eighteenth Century." In *1650–1850: Ideas, Aesthetics, and Inquiries in the Early Modern Era*, edited by Kevin L. Cope and Laura Morrow, 29–56. Vol. 3. New York: AMS Press, 1997.

————. *Playwrights and Plagiarists in Early Modern England: Gender, Authorship, Literary Property*. Ithaca, N.Y.: Cornell University Press, 1996.

Ross, Marlon B. *Dictionary of Literary Biography*, s.v. "Baillie, Joanna."

Rouse, P. Joy. "Margaret Fuller: A Rhetoric of Citizenship in Nineteenth-Century America." In *Oratorical Culture in Nineteenth-Century America: Transformations in the Theory and Practice of Rhetoric*, edited by Gregory Clark and S. Michael Halloran, 110–36. Carbondale, Ill.: Southern Illinois University Press, 1993.

Royster, Jacqueline Jones. *Traces of a Stream: Literacy and Social Change among African American Women*. Pittsburgh: University of Pittsburgh Press, 2000.

Rush, Benjamin. "Thoughts upon Female Education." In *Classics in the Education of Girls and Women,* edited by Shirley Nelson Kersey, 169–79. Metuchen, N.J.: Scarecrow Press, 1981. First published in *Essays, Literary, Moral and Philosophical,* 75–92. Philadelphia: Bradford, 1806.

Salvatori, Mariolina Rizzi, ed. *Pedagogy: Disturbing History, 1819–1929.* Pittsburgh: University of Pittsburgh Press, 1996.

Samuels, Shirley. *Romances of the Republic: Women, the Family, and Violence in the Early American Nation.* New York: Oxford University Press, 1996.

Samuels, Shirley, ed. *The Culture of Sentiment: Race, Gender, and Sentimentality in Nineteenth-Century America.* New York: Oxford University Press, 1992.

Schofield, Mary Anne. "The Happy Revolution: Colonial Women and the Eighteenth-Century Theater." In *Modern American Drama: The Female Canon,* edited by June Schlueter, 29–37. Rutherford, N.J.: Fairleigh Dickinson University Press, 1990.

———. "'Quitting the Loom and Distaff': Eighteenth-Century American Women Dramatists." In *Curtain Calls: British and American Women and the Theater, 1660–1820,* edited by Mary Anne Schofield and Cecilia Macheski, 260–73. Athens, Ohio: Ohio University Press, 1991.

Schultz, Lucille M. "Elaborating Our History: A Look at Mid-Nineteenth Century First Books of Composition." *College Composition and Communication* 45 (1994): 10–30.

———. *The Young Composers: Composition's Beginnings in Nineteenth-Century Schools.* Carbondale, Ill.: Southern Illinois University Press, 1999.

Schwager, Sally. "Educating Women in America." In *Reconstructing the Academy: Women's Education and Women's Studies,* edited by Elizabeth Minnich, Jean O'Barr, and Rachel Rosenfeld, 154–93. Chicago: University of Chicago Press, 1988.

Science Hill Female Academy. Papers. Filson Club Historical Society. Louisville, Ky.

Scott, Anne Firor. "The Ever Widening Circle: The Diffusion of Feminist Values from the Troy Female Seminary, 1822–1872." *History of Education Quarterly* 19 (1979): 3–25.

Sedgwick, Catharine Maria. *The Power of Her Sympathy: The Autobiography and Journal of Catharine Maria Sedgwick,* edited by Mary Kelley. Boston: Massachusetts Historical Society, 1993.

[Sedgwick, Susan Ridley]. "Education of Young Ladies." *The Knickerbocker* 6 (1835): 381–87.

Sherry, Suzanna. "Civic Virtue and the Feminine Voice in Constitutional Adjudication." *Virginia Law Review* 72 (1986): 543–616.

Siffrin, Susie Utz. "A History of Patapsco Female Institute." Master's thesis, George Washington University, 1937.

Silcox, Harry C. "Delay and Neglect: Negro Public Education in Antebellum Philadelphia, 1800–1860." *The Pennsylvania Magazine of History and Biography* 97 (1973): 444–64.

Simpson, David. *The Politics of American English, 1776–1850.* New York: Oxford University Press, 1986.

Skemp, Sheila L. *Judith Sargent Murray: A Brief Biography with Documents.* Boston: Bedford Books, 1998.

Sklar, Kathryn Kish. *Catharine Beecher: A Study in American Domesticity.* New Haven: Yale University Press, 1973.

Smith-Rosenberg, Caroll. "Domesticating 'Virtue': Coquettes and Revolutionaries in Young America." In *Literature and the Body: Essays on Populations and Persons,* edited by Elaine Scarry, 160–84. Baltimore: Johns Hopkins University Press, 1988.

Spacks, Patricia Meyer. Introduction to *Selections from The Female Spectator,* by Eliza Haywood. New York: Oxford University Press, 1999.

Stevenson, Brenda. Introduction to *The Journals of Charlotte Forten Grimké,* edited by Brenda Stevenson. New York: Oxford University Press, 1988.

Stewart, Dugald. *Elements of the Philosophy of the Human Mind.* 1792. Reprint, New York: Garland, 1971.

Stewart, Susan. *Crimes of Writing: Problems in the Containment of Representation.* New York: Oxford University Press, 1991.

Street, Brian V. *Literacy in Theory and Practice.* New York: Cambridge University Press, 1984.

Strychacz, Thomas F. *Dictionary of Literary Biography,* s.v. "Stewart, Dugald."

Thomas, Brook. *Cross-examinations of Law and Literature: Cooper, Hawthorne, Stowe, and Melville.* Cambridge: Cambridge University Press, 1987.

Tompkins, Jane. *Sensational Designs: The Cultural Work of American Fiction, 1790–1860.* New York: Oxford University Press, 1985.

Tonkovich, Nicole. *Domesticity with a Difference: The Nonfiction of Catharine Beecher, Sarah J. Hale, Fanny Fern, and Margaret Fuller.* Jackson, Miss.: University Press of Mississippi, 1997.

———. "Rhetorical Power in the Victorian Parlor: *Godey's Lady's Book* and the Gendering of Nineteenth-Century Rhetoric." In *Oratorical Culture in Nineteenth-Century America: Transformations in the Theory and Practice of Rhetoric,* edited by Gregory Clark and S. Michael Halloran, 158–83. Carbondale, Ill.: Southern Illinois University Press, 1993.

Torgovnick, Marianna. *Gone Primitive: Savage Intellects, Modern Lives.* Chicago: University of Chicago Press, 1990.

Trimmer, Joseph F., ed. *Narration as Knowledge: Tales of the Teaching Life.* Portsmouth, N.H.: Heinemann, Boynton/Cook, 1997.

[Tuthill, Cornelia Louisa]. *The Belle, the Blue and the Bigot.* Providence: Blodget, 1844.

Tuthill, Mrs. L[ouisa] C[aroline]. *The Boarding-School Girl.* 5th ed. Boston: Crosby and Nichols, 1852.

———. *Edith, the Backwoods Girl.* New York: Scribner, 1859.

———. *The Young Lady's Home.* New Haven: Babcock, 1839.

Tuthill, Mrs. L[ouisa] C[aroline], ed. *The Young Lady's Reader.* New Haven: Babcock, 1839.

U.S. Department of Education. National Commission on Excellence in Education. *A Nation at Risk: The Imperative for Educational Reform.* Washington, D.C.: GPO, 1983.

U.S. Department of Health, Education, and Welfare. *A Brief History of the Federal Responsibility to the American Indian: Based on the Report "Legislative Analysis of the*

Federal Role in Indian Education" by Vine Deloria, Jr. Washington, D.C.: GPO, 1979.

Varnum, Robin. "The History of Composition: Reclaiming Our Lost Generations." *Journal of Advanced Composition* 12 (1992): 39–55.

Verbrugge, Martha H. *Able-Bodied Womanhood: Personal Health and Social Change in Nineteenth-Century Boston.* New York: Oxford University Press, 1988.

Von Frank, Albert J. *The Trials of Anthony Burns: Freedom and Slavery in Emerson's Boston.* Cambridge: Harvard University Press, 1998.

Warner, Michael. *The Letters of the Republic: Publication and the Public Sphere in Eighteenth-Century America.* Cambridge: Harvard University Press, 1990.

Watts, Steven. *The Republic Reborn: War and the Making of Liberal America, 1790–1820.* Baltimore: Johns Hopkins University Press, 1987.

Weinsheimer, Joel. *Imitation.* London: Routledge and Kegan Paul, 1984.

Wexler, Laura. "Tender Violence: Literary Eavesdropping, Domestic Fiction, and Educational Reform." In *The Culture of Sentiment: Race, Gender, and Sentimentality in Nineteenth-Century America,* edited by Shirley Samuels, 9–38. New York: Oxford University Press, 1992.

Wheaton, Patrick G., and Celeste M. Condit. "Charles Lenox Remond (1810–1873), Abolitionist, Reform Activist." In *African-American Orators: A Bio-Critical Sourcebook,* edited by Richard W. Leeman, 302–10. Westport, Conn.: Greenwood Press, 1996.

White, Harold Ogden. *Plagiarism and Imitation during the English Renaissance: A Study in Critical Distinctions.* Cambridge: Harvard University Press, 1935.

Wilcox, Kirstin. "The Scribblings of a Plain Man and the Temerity of a Woman: Gender and Genre in Judith Sargent Murray's *The Gleaner." Early American Literature* 30 (1995): 121–44.

Willard, Emma [Hart]. *An Address to the Public; Particularly to the Members of the Legislature of New-York, Proposing a Plan for Improving Female Education.* 2d ed. Middlebury, Vt.: Copeland, 1819. Reprint, with explanatory note, n.p., n.d.

Williams, Kenny J. Introduction to *Essays; Including Biographies and Miscellaneous Pieces, in Prose and Poetry,* by Ann Plato. New York: Oxford University Press, 1988.

Williams, Wade. "Religion, Science and Rhetoric in Revolutionary America: The Case of Dr. Benjamin Rush." *Rhetoric Society Quarterly* 30, no. 3 (2000): 55–72.

Woodmansee, Martha. "On the Author Effect: Recovering Collectivity." In *The Construction of Authorship: Textual Appropriation in Law and Literature,* edited by Martha Woodmansee and Peter Jaszi, 15–28. Durham, N.C.: Duke University Press, 1994.

Woodmansee, Martha, and Peter Jaszi, eds. *The Construction of Authorship: Textual Appropriation in Law and Literature.* Durham, N.C.: Duke University Press, 1994.

Woody, Thomas. *A History of Women's Education in the United States.* 2 vols. New York: Science Press, 1929.

Wright, Lyle H. *American Fiction, 1774–1850: A Contribution toward a Bibliography.* San Marino, Calif.: Huntington Library, 1939.

Young, Edward. *Conjectures on Original Composition.* 1759. Reprint, Leeds, England: Scolar Press, 1966.

Index

abolitionist rhetoric, ix, 28, 200–204, 210–11;
  civic liberatory principles and, 34, 191, 195;
  Emerson and, 206–7; national unity threat-
  ened by, 165–66, 178–79, 189–90
Adams, Abigail Smith, 5, 11, 19
Adams, John, 5, 11
Adams, John Quincy, 3
adventure schools, 19–20, 52
aesthetics, 94–99
African Americans, 21–22, 26–27, 178, 197–99.
  See also abolitionist rhetoric; Fugitive Slave
  Law
Agassiz, Louis, 204
Agnesi, Maria Galtana, 124
Allen, Florence E., 2
American Instructor, The, 17
American Preceptor, The (Bingham), 12, 27–28
Anthony, Susan B., 6
Applegate, James, 203
authorship. *See* copyright and authorship

Baillie, Joanna, 120, 125–26
Bartlett, Elisha, 104
Bator, Paul, 210
Baym, Nina, viii, 6, 21, 45–46, 90, 113–14
Beecher, Catharine, ix, 6, 9, 13, 92–93, 104, 146,
  178
Beecher, Henry Ward, 204–6
belletristic rhetoric, 3–4, 94–107, 112, 149, 191,
  197
Bettig, Ronald V., 249n18
Bingham, Caleb, 12, 25–29, 48
Bizzell, Patricia, vii
Blair, Hugh, 3, 114, 118, 124–25, 140, 169, 209–10,
  254n25
boarding schools, 90–93, 107–12, 244n10
Bolzau, Emma, 172
Boydston, Jeanne, 92
Brace, J. P., 114
Bradstreet, Anne, 18
Bradwell, Myra, 2
Brickley, Lynne Templeton, 47
Broaddus, Dorothy, 3, 208
Brown, Antoinette, 203

Brown, Richard, 19
Burk, Don, 210
Burns, Anthony, 192, 195

Campbell, George, 114, 118, 124–25, 140, 169, 210
Carson, Albana, 32–33
Cash, Arthur H., 249n22
Catholics and Catholicism, 22, 124–25, 135–36
Chapone, Mrs. Hester, 57, 59, 62
Charlotte Temple (Rowson), 76
Child, Lydia Maria, 6
Christian principles, 16–18, 142–44, 192, 196–97,
  203–4. *See also* Protestantism
Clark, Gregory, 2, 3
classical languages, study of, 68–69, 122
Coleridge, Samuel Taylor, 81
commonplace books, 30, 54, 57, 122–24
commonplace rhetoric, 77, 85–88
common school movement, 21
commonsense philosophy, 93, 98–99, 112,
  115–16, 118–25, 209
Complete Letter-Writer, The, 56–58, 60, 63–64
conduct fiction, 8, 48
conduct guides, 17, 24, 55, 64, 99
Conjectures on Original Composition (Young),
  83–84
consensus, public, 2, 5, 7
conversation, 37, 44–45, 58, 61, 62
copyright and authorship, 77–80, 82, 249n12
coquetry and courtship, 39, 71
Crowley, Sharon, 94
"cultivation," metaphors of, 26–27, 55, 70–71,
  74
Curran, Stuart, 126
Curtis, George W., 205

dame schools, 18
Davidson, Cathy, viii, 6, 29, 51, 89, 214
Davis, Cornelius, 34
De Grazia, Margreta, 80
democratization of education, 20–23, 32, 93,
  177–83
DeQuincey, Thomas, 81
devotional writing, 18

275